The Effective Pastor

The Effective Pastor

by

Robert C. Anderson

MOODY PRESS

CHICAGO

Library of Congress Cataloging in Publication Data

Anderson, Robert C., 1933-
  The effective pastor.

  Bibliography: p.
  Includes index.
  1. Pastoral theology.   I. Title.
BV4011.A49   1985   253   85-3107
ISBN: 0-8024-6361-4

1 2 3 4 5 6 7 8 9 10

Printed in the United States of America

To
DR. WARREN FILKIN
Beloved Teacher, Counselor, and Friend

Contents

Part 4
The Pastor's Administrative Tasks

Acknowledgments

I would like to express my sincere gratitude to John Bush, graduate fellow at Western Conservative Baptist Seminary, who helped research many of the areas of this book, wrote the discussion questions, and compiled the lists of reference books that appear at the end of each chapter. Also, I would like to thank Martha Hillstrom, who critiqued both the contents and the grammar in the manuscript. Additional thanks are due to Western Conservative Baptist Seminary, whose administration was gracious enough to give me time off from some of my regular duties to engage in writing, and to the long-suffering congregation of the Glisan Street Baptist Church in Portland, Oregon, whose pastor is earnestly trying to carry out the principles found in this book.

Introduction

B efore a person aspires to enter any profession, it is fair to ask him whether he knows what will be expected of him. Law or medical students can answer the question easily, but a potential clergyman finds it much more difficult. When people ask whether he is aware of the expectations of this chosen career, if he is at all bright he probably will ask them, "Whose expectations?" In the past two decades no profession has seen greater diversification of expectation than the professional ministry.

It is not that no one can say what a clergyman should do; almost anyone can and does. Contrast that with other professions—medicine or law, for instance—where almost everyone is intimidated by the solemn pronouncements of those in the field, and few would question their judgment. Not many people would pretend that they knew those professions better than the practitioner. Yet almost everyone claims that he knows the ministry better than the pastor. Certainly the seminary professor thinks he does: after all, he is the one preparing men for the ministry. Surely the denominational representative does: he is the one who does the placing. Most assuredly, members of the congregation do: they are the ones paying the pastor. Of course, expectations of the pastor's ministry differ markedly depending on the person with whom one talks. It seems that everyone is adamant in his observations as to what constitutes the proper duties of a pastor, even though few have training and experience in pastoring. And last but not least are the differing expectations among the pastors themselves.

In light of all those differing and sometimes conflicting expectations, is it possible to prepare a person to become a pastor today? It certainly is. It is just a greater challenge than ever before. Pastors still are human beings with personal and family needs, but they are faced with a plethora of responsibilities and have to know how to set priorities. They will be called upon to preach, teach, counsel, conduct weddings and funerals, baptize, dedicate babies, serve Communion, visit the sick, win the lost, provide leadership, and give direction to the flock to which God has sent them. Who teaches a person to perform all of those and the other duties that will be expected of him? Seminaries and Bible colleges can warn him and give him brief exposure to what he will experience. But being told about something and actually doing it are two entirely different matters.

As well as being challenged by differing expectations, the pastor suffers under the limitations of internship programs that come nowhere near the extensive programs offered by other professions. It is difficult for a prospective pastor to learn under the supervision of an experienced pastor while he is performing some of the pastoral duties. Thus the new clergyman often finds himself required to perform functions that he has heard of but never executed himself. Far from the halls of pastoral theology classes, who tells him how to counsel a couple who have just lost a baby? Who tells him how to prepare for ordination, how to leave one church gracefully and candidate at a church somewhere else? Who tells him how to visit a hospital patient and how to choose hymns appropriate to a worship service? No one does.

For several years, I have thought that there ought to be a book that would tell the young (and even the not-so-young) pastor what to do when he encounters such situations, a manual that would help him formulate basic principles and would guide him in specific situations. There once was such a book, *The Pastor and His Work*, by Homer Kent, Sr. (Chicago: Moody, 1963). For years it served as a handy guide to help the pastor through almost every kind of situation he might encounter. But no book except the Bible lasts forever. Kent's book has lasted much longer than many and has become a classic in the field; however, the field is developing so fast that it now is seriously outdated. In a meeting with Philip Rawley of Moody Press some months ago I mentioned my frustration in not having a successor to Kent's book from which to teach. Mr. Rawley's answer was, "Why don't you write one?" I have attempted to do just that.

Even though I have tried to cover every major subject I believed was possible, I feel the same sense of frustration that Homer Kent felt in the early sixties. Like my predecessor, I have had to pick and choose subjects, hoping that I would be wise enough to concentrate on the highlights of the ministry. I have tried to write for the great majority of pastors, realizing that I could not begin to address the varieties of specialized ministries that are emerging today.

I have written out of a career that has included a great many facets of ministry. My own experience spans many years in the pastorate, including a current pastorate that I serve in addition to my full-time career at the seminary. I have served as a mediator for churches and pastors in trouble. While teaching at both the master's and doctoral levels, I have counseled, taught, and advised prospective pastors and seasoned professionals. Although I do not feel that I am very old, my experience has been broad; I offer my words of advice to my spiritual sons in the ministry much as Paul did to Timothy.

Throughout the book, you will notice that I have used the pronoun "he" at all times to describe the pastor. I have not done so in the generic sense but feel compelled, at least by my interpretation of Scripture, to conclude that the office of pastor is one to which God has called males. Throughout my years, I have operated under the philosophy that not only can I love and respect those who disagree with me, but also I can disagree with them without becoming disagreeable. I hope that they will offer the same courtesy to me; and I hope in turn that the women who decide I am wrong and feel strongly that God has called them into the pastoral ministry may gain from this book.

Part 1

The Pastoral Role

1

The Pastor's Character and Calling

A few months ago a young seminary graduate stood before an ordination council, defended his doctrinal statement, and was about to leave the room while the council decided his fate when from the back of the church auditorium the voice of an old man was heard to insist, "Just a minute, young man. I have one more question for you." The older pastor directed the younger to open his Bible to 1 Timothy 3 and read the passage concerning the character qualifications of an overseer. After the young man did so, the older man, now standing erect, looked intently at the candidate and said, "Young man, does this passage describe you?" Not wanting to sound conceited the young man hedged, trying not to answer the question directly.

"Young man," said the elderly saint, "does or does not this passage describe you?" "Well, I guess so," was the cautious reply. Once again the old man persisted, "Guessing is not good enough. Does this passage describe you or not?" Finally the reply rang out, "Yes, sir, this passage describes me." The old man's retort was immediate, "Mr. Moderator, I have no further questions. I am fully satisfied."

During the course of each school year dozens of inquiries come across my desk regarding men who are being considered by churches and mission boards. I am supposed to rate those individuals according to qualifications that are specified in the reference form. Without exception, each inquires as to the abilities of the person being considered, his personality traits, and the talents of his wife. Rarely does a questionnaire deal with character traits.

3

Despite the fact that we call ourselves "evangelicals" and claim to be biblical in our approach, we fall far short of the biblical standard in this matter. Although the Bible often states the kinds of things that elders, pastors, or overseers do, nowhere does it specify the talents we may expect in them. Nowhere does it state that they must be exceptional managers, visitors, pulpiteers, or teachers. Although they need those qualities to perform their duties, the Bible's major emphasis is in an entirely different direction; instead of insisting on how well a person is able to perform a certain function, it focuses instead on what kind of a person he is.

The Pastor's Character

Who is a pastor? He is an ordinary person who knows the Lord Jesus Christ as his personal Savior, has experienced the call of God in his life for full-time Christian service, and knows that he is fit for such service because he meets certain biblical character qualifications. Because the Bible makes this emphasis, I think that it is fitting for us to examine those qualifications prior to looking at the gifts that should be present in a person looking seriously at making the pastorate his lifelong ministry.

"ABOVE REPROACH" (1 TIM. 3:2; TITUS 1:6-7)

The person who will succeed in the pastorate is one who has no hidden agenda, no skeletons in his closet that eventually will come out and haunt him. In his classic *The Preacher and His Models*, James Stalker says:

> The great purpose for which a minister is settled in a parish is not to cultivate scholarship, or to visit the people during the week, or even to preach to them on Sunday, but it is to live among them as a good man, whose mere presence is a demonstration which cannot be gainsaid that there is a life possible on earth which is fed from no earthly source, and that the things spoken of in church on Sabbath are realities.

In speaking of a man whom he knew who met those qualifications, Stalker relates:

> We who laboured along with him in the ministry felt that his mere existence in the community was an irresistible demonstration of Christianity and a tower of strength to every good cause. Yet he had not gained this position of influence by brilliant talents or great achievements or the pursuing of ambition; for he was singularly modest, and would have been the last to credit himself with half the good he did. The

whole mystery lay in this, that he had lived in the town for forty years a blameless life, and was known by everybody to be a godly and prayerful man.

Stalker ends this appraisal by insisting that "the prime qualification for the ministry is goodness."[1]

Such goodness demonstrates itself in a number of ways that will be illustrated as we consider some of the rest of the biblical qualifications.

"THE HUSBAND OF ONE WIFE" (1 TIM. 3:2; TITUS 1:6)

For centuries it has been debated whether or not the biblical injunction that an elder or overseer be the "husband of one wife" means that a divorced person may never have any place within the professional ministry. Personally, I do not think that is what the passages mean. Having stated that, however, let me assert what I say elsewhere in this book, that "divorce" isn't even a Christian word. I believe in the sanctity of marriage and that true Christian marriage is "til death do us part." A pastor, as a model for his people, should work the hardest of all people to keep his marriage intact and flourishing. Few things bring greater discredit to the church of Jesus Christ than pastors who divorce or are divorced by their wives.

Except in the most rare of cases, if divorce becomes a fact, a pastor should step down from his pastoral position and, if he intends to continue in professional Christian service, should plan to serve in some area other than the pastorate. In most cases, as a matter of fact, he will have no alternative. That decision will be made for him by his congregation. If by that time he has not faced his situation realistically, when he attempts to secure another pastorate the facts of the case will dawn on him. Very few congregations, including many of those who consider themselves members of "liberal" denominations, will agree to calling a pastor who has divorce in his background. The single exception to this may be if the divorce has occurred prior to his conversion.

Therefore, if a man is intent on remaining in the pastoral ministry, he had better consider his marriage to be the most valuable asset he has and put as much effort into it as necessary to keep it alive and well. (Later, I will consider in greater detail the relationship a pastor should enjoy with his wife.)

There is, I feel, an even deeper, more important aspect of these verses than avoiding divorce. Many Bible scholars believe that the

1. James Stalker, *The Preacher and His Models* (Grand Rapids: Baker, 1967), p. 56.

passages often translated "husband of one wife" are more properly translated "a one-woman kind of man." That delves into the situation even more deeply.

In the past few years, the church has been rife with scandal concerning clergymen who are cheating on their wives. Many times they are individuals God has used mightily—men with charm, poise, talents, and ability. Because of their irregular schedules, the daily temptations they face, and a variety of other reasons, clergymen are in a position where temptations of that sort are abundant.

The best advice I can offer to any man in the ministry is that he should flee from those temptations. He should not allow himself even to be present in situations where they are present. He should never go unescorted to see a woman who is alone at home. When he visits a woman in the hospital, he should be absolutely discreet in his behavior, watching carefully where he touches her and then being careful not to hold on too long to what he touches. More than anything else, he should avoid those things that corrupt the mind and erode the conscience. He should be careful not to view films or television indiscriminately, and under no circumstances should he feed the prurient recesses of his mind with pornography. When the seamier aspects of life invade his mind no matter how careful he is to try to keep them out, he should go to the Lord immediately and ask Him to cleanse his mind and make it pure once again. When a woman makes obvious advances toward him, he should flee those advances and should also avoid that woman as much as possible, so that she does not confuse the care he shows for her with what she may view as assent to her advances.

The pastor should avoid all appearances of evil, and this is especially true in his dealings with women other than his wife. The slightest, most innocent gesture may be misinterpreted by a woman living out her fantasies in regard to the pastor. The pastor who encourages this in any way, especially in not-so-innocent gestures of flirtation, is placing himself in a position in which he is likely to experience great trouble.

The pastor must by all means establish and preserve his reputation as being a "one-woman kind of man." He does that by exerting great effort to become and remain extremely close to his wife. He enhances his good reputation by mentioning often in public how attached he is to his wife, how dependent he is on her, and what a marvelous wife she is. If she lacks many "marvelous" characteristics, perhaps he can dwell on the few she does have. If we look hard enough we are bound to find something for which we can praise a person.

"Temperate" (1 Tim. 3:2)

The Greek word here means to be strong in a thing and self controlled, especially in the area of appetites. The key thought here is moderation. We are to avoid excesses whether those excesses consist of observing inordinately long work hours or practicing gluttony in our eating habits. The pastor who greedily pushes his way to the head of the potluck line and loads his plate with unreasonable quantities of food is not going to be a suitable model for anyone, nor is such action likely to endear him to his people. Likewise, a pastor may have sources of income other than his salary, but if he lives in a pretentious manner, dresses excessively well, or continually drives the most expensive cars, he is not being temperate in his behavior. The person who intends on staying in the pastoral office should establish a moderate life-style for himself and his family and stick by it. That does not mean that the pastor has to live in the slums while his parishioners live in mansions. He may live well without being extravagant and without appearing ostentacious.

"Prudent" (1 Tim. 3:2; Titus 1:8)

The word *prudent* carries with it the connotation of sensibility. There are a number of things that may be permissible but not prudent. If a person does those things in certain settings, he is bound to offend or antagonize people. A prudent man is one who does not engage in behavior he knows will be offensive to others. He is not loud or rude or boisterous in places and situations where such behavior is not considered acceptable. He does not flaunt a "macho" image, attempting to convey exaggerated images of his manhood. He is not overly competitive in his activities. I have seen people exhibit imprudence even by playing Scrabble with a killer instinct. God does not need such dreadfully insecure individuals in His pastoral service.

"Respectable" (1 Tim. 3:2)

The King James translates this word "of good behaviour." Intrinsic to the meaning of the Greek word is the idea of orderliness of personality, modesty, and decorum. Recently I heard a lady say, "It is so nice to have a pastor who you know always will say the appropriate thing. He actually thinks before he speaks. We haven't always had pastors like that." God wants people who have a sense of dignity about them. I do not mean stuffy people. I mean people who know how to conduct themselves properly. It is sad when the people of a congregation are continually being embarrassed by the speech and actions of their pastor, who should be a model for them. Coarseness, vulgarity, off-color jokes, offensive actions, lack of table manners— none have their place in a person who is going to occupy the position of pastor. Many pastors who are morally pure and have hearts right before the Lord will engage in some inappropriate action that repels others from accepting any ministry they would have been able to render.

Respectability pertains not only to speech and actions but also to dress. The person who hopes to become and remain a pastor will be one who finds out what the standards of respectable dress are in his community and then observes those standards. Standards, of course, will differ with the community. In Hawaii it is often considered respectable for a pastor to conduct the morning worship service in a short-sleeved shirt, without tie or suit coat. In North America that would be considered inappropriate. There is a standard of dress considered respectable for any professional in each community. The pastor should observe that standard.

In the seminary in which I teach, as a part of a course in philosophy of ministry I regularly bring in our assistant librarian to teach a class in etiquette. Unfortunately it probably is one of the classes that is received the most poorly. I say unfortunately because it is the class that often is needed the most. Not many of our graduates fail in the ministry because they fall prey to doctrinal errors. Numbers, however, have made an improper impact on the ministry simply because they are "klutzes," are continually making themselves offensive to people—and they will not change. Simple things—such as practicing acceptable table manners, placing a mint in their mouths when dealing with people in close proximity, and refraining from picking the nose, ears, or teeth in public—would give those people substantial mileage in being more acceptable to others. If they learned a few social graces in addition and were able to remember to express gratitude to people for every kind action no matter how small, they would be making major progress toward becoming the type of respectable person the Bible demands for the position of pastor. The person who basks in his crudeness and considers it a necessary part of his "macho" image probably should seek another vocation besides the pastorate.

"HOSPITABLE" (1 TIM. 3:2; TITUS 1:8)

The Greek word here means to be a "lover of guests." The Bible indicates that the person aspiring to the ministry must be a hospitable person. That does not mean that a pastor and his wife do not need privacy. It does mean that they will agree that their home is, in part, a tool for ministry to others. If they are hospitable, they will have a rich ministry themselves, and they will establish an appropriate model for others.

Some years ago my wife and I moved into a new community and began attending a nearby church. Although the program of the church was acceptable, we were chagrined to observe that in the four months we attended there, no one made any effort to invite us to their home or even to suggest that we join them at a restaurant for a snack following an evening service. After we had ceased attending the church, someone gave us a plausible explanation for its lack of hospitality. The pastor and his wife very seldom entertained in their home, and when they went out for a snack, they always did so with the same, small group of people. Because the pastor and his wife were not hospitable, the church lacked a positive model of hospitality and became known as an inhospitable church. Christians are to be hospitable people, and unless a prospective pastoral couple intend to serve as models of hospitality, they probably should consider some other area of Christian service.

There is the other extreme of course, where the pastoral couple is so hospitable they seldom have a moment of privacy. People seem always to be with them, and the pastor and his wife wear themselves out. There is a point where a person in public ministry needs to get away from people and retreat to the quiet confines of his home. That should not be carried to an extreme, however, to the extent that the pastor and his family live in virtual seclusion. The key is moderation, and the goal is a happy medium between the extremes. (More will be said concerning hospitality in the chapter concerning pastors' wives.)

"ABLE TO TEACH" (1 TIM. 3:2; 2 TIM. 2:24)

Elsewhere in this book I will speak to the dangers of those who are caught up in what I call the "pastor-teacher syndrome." That occurs when a pastor barricades himself in his study, spends forty-plus hours a week wrestling with the text, and refuses to be out among the people or to carry on the many so-called perfunctory duties of the ministry. God has room for very few of those types today, and if a person going into the ministry views himself as carrying on a "specialized practice" he had better reorient himself. In most cases, the person entering the pastorate is going to find himself called upon to assume the role of "general practitioner."

However, regardless of how broad and diversified he finds his ministry, a major portion of that ministry must necessarily be centered upon teaching. He will be called upon as a teacher in several roles. First is his pulpit role. This is the most public expression of his teaching tasks, and he should place a great deal of effort into it making sure that his sermons are interesting, instructional, and well-delivered. A good clue as to whether or not a person will be a good preaching teacher can be found in whether or not he is an interesting person. Before a person aspires to the ministry, he should sit down with others who will rate him objectively in his communicative skills with people, his present pulpit abilities, and his pulpit potential.

Preaching, however, is not the sum total of his teaching responsibilities. He will be called upon to interact with parishioners in a number of small group settings where he will find other less didactic teaching methods more appropriate and effective.

Finally, a great deal of his teaching will be accomplished by modeling. If he aspires to be a teacher, he had better learn how to be a proper model. Sometimes teaching by this method—either negatively or positively—is the most powerful teaching of all. Again, it will require that he be an interesting person, someone who will be able to attract others to him for that type of discipleship training. In many instances, and especially in those areas in which we desire to see attitudinal changes in others, one-on-one discipleship training is potentially the most effective of all teaching methods. Not everyone can do it successfully, however, and a person should weigh carefully whether or not he has the ability before he aspires to the pastorate.

"NOT ADDICTED TO WINE" (1 TIM. 3:3; TITUS 1:7)

The text here no doubt is referring to those who are such habitual users of wine that they are physically addicted to it. I do not think that there are many alcoholics in the pastorate, although the danger is as viable in that occupation as in any other. However, it is my conviction that there are a number of pastors and wives who are addicted to wine in the sense that they feel that they must continually use it both privately and publicly in order to demonstrate what they believe is their freedom in Christ. Note that when the text to which I referred was written, the consumption of alcoholic beverages had already become a serious enough problem that Paul had to warn against overindulgence. The problem has not diminished, but rather it has reached such huge proportions in our generation that had Paul lived today and had seen the carnage and heartbreak caused by alcohol abuse, I am convinced that the apostle would have advised the servant of God that a good rule of thumb was to avoid the use of alcoholic beverages entirely.

If anyone is to avoid being a stumbling block to those who are weak, surely it should be the pastor. How sad it would be for a pastor who has given his life to help others to find out that someone had become an alcoholic through following an adverse example he set. In addition to physical addiction, I believe that addiction may include being addicted to an idea or to the carrying out of a practice. Surely those types of addiction should be avoided so that we who are in the pastoral role may present a wholesome and exemplary image for our Lord.

"Not Pugnacious" (1 Tim. 3:3; Titus 1:7)

The other day I was speaking with a Midwesterner concerning a pastor who was experiencing problems with the government over an issue involving the formation of a Christian school in his church building. Both of us had agreed that the pastor had received "poor press." Media had pictured him as an irrational, unreasonable, Bible-thumping fundamentalist living in the dark ages. My friend from the Midwest observed that he had been living close by when all of the action was going on. Unfortunately, the pastor in question had been so pugnacious in his actions that he had played right into the hands of reporters who wished to capitalize on the stereotype. It seems that the pastor enjoyed a good fight, was happy to engage in one as often as possible, and had brought on himself most of the adverse media coverage.

I have known many pastors who were continually bristling for a fight. They were ready to engage in such action almost anytime and in any place. There is a sense in which we who are Christian leaders always should be ready for a fight if we can identify clearly that our adversary the devil is the person we are fighting. However, I am firmly convinced that the devil sidetracks many Christians and diverts their efforts against him by convincing people that they are fighting him, when, in reality, they are really fighting other Christians. A feisty person with a perennial chip on his shoulder had better wait until he can gain better control of himself before attempting to pastor.

If we could get to the bottom of a majority of the church splits and incidents that resulted in pastors being asked to leave churches, we would probably find that the root cause was not a theological disagreement at all but was a case of people who just could not or who chose not to get along with each other. In many of those instances we could trace the difficulty to a pastor with a fiery spirit who did not control his temper but, instead, lashed out in anger at someone in the congregation.

People who have this problem and look forward to pastoral service would be wise to use whatever means necessary, including professional counseling, to overcome it before going into the pastorate. If a person already is in the pastorate and suffers from an easily-provoked temper, he should run, not walk, to a competent Christian counselor who can help him overcome his difficulty before disaster results. That does not mean, however, that the pastor should be a Casper Milquetoast who never stands up to anyone about anything. It does mean that before he agrees to engage in a fight he makes sure that he is fighting Satan and not some other Christian, and that he makes certain he is defending some biblical principle and not just his own ego or one of his pet methods.

"GENTLE" (1 TIM. 3:3; 2 TIM. 2:24)

How many unfortunate incidents in the church could be avoided if Christians could learn to be gentlemen and gentlewomen. I am reminded of the little girl who was heard to pray, "Lord, please make bad people good, and good people nice." Unfortunately some pastors have all the finesse of a steam roller, pushing their way through many obstacles, injuring the saints as they attempt to make changes in the church.

The world is hungry for someone who is genuinely kind and gentle. Such a person may find, at times, that people take unfair advantage of him, but that is their problem, not his. If they cannot understand what he has to offer, they are the unfortunate ones. Recently I heard a Christian lady say, "Not only does our pastor feed us well from the Scriptures, but he makes it plain in so many ways that he really loves us. When we make mistakes, he is so patient and understanding. Even when he has to correct us, he does so in such a gentle manner." The lady who said this was sure that her church had got an extraordinary pastor. However, if we look realistically at the criteria the Bible lays down, a spirit of courtesy should be the norm among pastors instead of the exception. Before some men enter the pastorate, they need to spend time with God, allowing Him to grind off some of the coarse, rough edges of their lives and asking Him to make them truly gentle and kind.

"UNCONTENTIOUS" (1 TIM. 3:3; 2 TIM. 2:24)

Even though some people could not be described as pugnacious, they certainly should be labeled contentious. These are the people who glory in a good argument. Since they often are bright and articulate, many times they will end up devastating their opponents with words. The story is told of a certain theologian who was called to debate an atheist on a college campus. His logic was impeccable and his rhetoric impressive. In the course of the debate, he figuratively destroyed his opponent. Despite the fact that he won the debate, he was booed off the stage.

My father used to say, "A man convinced against his will, is of the same opinion still." One of the serious mistakes some Christians still are making is trying to argue a person into the kingdom of God. Often by the time a person has gone through college and is into seminary, he has fine-tuned the art of arguing. By the time he finishes seminary he may have developed it into one of his greatest skills. Such individuals enjoy nothing better than a good argument. Yet the practice of habitually arguing has an adverse effect on unbelievers and a devastating effect on Christians. When asked to express his opinion on a subject, a pastor should express it in a clear, gentle, nonthreatening manner. He should avoid being drawn into an argument. Arguments are usually destructive, and if a person has tendencies toward being an arguer, he should work to curb those tendencies before he undertakes a pastorate.

"FREE FROM THE LOVE OF MONEY" (1 TIM. 3:3; TITUS 1:7)

In my many years in the pastorate I have never established a dollar amount as the basis for my coming to a church. When church leaders have asked what I thought I should receive, I have asked them to make a comparison between the salaries of other men in churches of similar size, take into consideration the cost of living in that particular community, and then compare the figure they have arrived at with the dollar amount the church believes it can raise. If I felt that I was genuinely called of God to that group of people, I knew that God would be faithful in meeting my needs. He never has let me down. Through the years, never have we lived lavishly, but God nevertheless has consistently supplied more than our needs.

I have used this personal illustration because I am becoming increasingly alarmed at the number of young men graduating from the seminary who have exaggerated ideas of their own worth to a church as a professional. Often these men state a minimum figure they believe is necessary for them to receive before they will agree to serve the church. Even though they are still an untested product, many demand a salary that exceeds by several thousands of dollars the salary received by many of their seminary professors. I am not opposed to God's servants living comfortably. What I am concerned about are those who make salary a major consideration and never seem happy no matter how much money comes their way. That, to me, is an unworthy motive to seek the pastorate.

MANAGING "HIS OWN HOUSEHOLD WELL" (1 TIM. 3:4)

It is not true that the "preacher's kids" should be expected to be brats. History proves that an inordinate amount of "P.K.'s" have turned out exceptionally well, even to the extent that a much higher percentage of them succeed in life than the children of people in almost any other profession. The words of the Scripture here read, "Keeping his children under control with all dignity." The statement presupposes an understanding relationship between the father and his children. It requires that he be consistent in his discipline and true to his word.

If the pastor is to do that, he will not be able to do it alone. The mother of his children will have to work in partnership with him. If the pastor is inconsistent in his discipline to the extent of ignoring the children when they need discipline in public, or if he continually flies off the handle at every little infringement of his rules, he has deep trouble on his hands.

Unless the pastoral family is willing to take steps to make theirs a model family, I do not believe that the father of the family should be in the pastorate. That does not mean that the children should be expected to be perfect in every way. Expecting perfection is an impossibly hard burden to place on any child. It does mean that the children, in general, should be kept under control, should not be allowed to be "rowdies," either in the neighborhood or in the church building, and, when they transgress, should be brought back into control promptly and in a dignified manner.

A pastor should be a model of loving discipline. He should love his children more than his job, be extravagant in his expressions of love for and praise to them, and should treat them as genuine human beings capable of profound thoughts that can contribute to this life if he will but listen to them. Treating children in a denigrating fashion certainly is not God's way. When they are treated with the dignity prescribed in the biblical account, they will have a far better chance of growing up as productive individuals.

A family with continuously uncontrollable children is not a suitable model for a congregation. Unless parents can manage the art of parenting, they should not engage in the pastoral ministry.

"NOT A NEW CONVERT" (1 TIM. 3:6)

In the Christian community we have emulated the culture around us in that often we are likely to create a religious "superstar" out of a new convert, especially if that person was a celebrity prior to his conversion. The people we treat in this way begin to speak with authority on many subjects before they have had any biblical training. On the other hand, sometimes we postpone inordinately the process of their entering into Christian leadership, by requiring them to graduate from Bible college or seminary before assuming a pastorate. Yet during the course of their formal training, they may somehow bypass substantial on-the-job training or experience in a local church. The scenario may thus look something like this: The person is saved and immediately his potential gifts are recognized. He is urged to go on to seminary, which he does immediately. During seminary, in addition to working on his studies he finds it necessary to take a job in order to support his family. With the cumulative demands of family, seminary, and employment, he has little time left to get involved meaningfully in a local church. He graduates from seminary and, naturally, seeks to become the pastor of a church. *After all*, he thinks, *this is what everyone said my training was to accomplish.* Nevertheless, as far as training in an actual church is concerned, he is still a relatively new convert, an untried product. Often, when a church does call him, disaster is a result.

My only surprise in all of this is that more of those people do not end up as disasters. The grace of God must be generous indeed! The solution for this? Every person who is relatively young in Christ and who has not had a great deal of experience working in a church should seek as his first job the position of assistant pastor under an experienced pastor who will counsel and train him. When the senior pastor believes the man is ready, he should recommend him for pastoral service. Since assistant pastor positions are not always readily available, it may be that a seminary graduate who is still a rather recent convert may have to pursue secular employment while he completes his training in this manner.

ENJOYING A "GOOD REPUTATION WITH THOSE OUTSIDE THE CHURCH" (1 TIM. 3:7)

It should be standard procedure that a church considering a person to be their pastor go into the community where the man is presently living and talk to the non-Christians with whom he has contact to see what kind of a reputation he has among them. What sort of a neighbor has he been? Has he exemplified the Lord Jesus Christ among those in his neighborhood? How has he reacted when a neighbor's child beat up his child? What about those people with whom he has carried on business? Was he always looking for a special "deal" because he was a clergyman? Did he pay his debts promptly? Was he honest and straightforward in his business dealings with members of the community?

If he was in a business other than pastoring, what kind of a business reputation did he enjoy? Did he treat people honestly and squarely? Did he back up the product he was representing with service to his customers? If he was employed, what did his boss and his fellow workers think of him? By now the reader is discovering on the basis of this list of characteristics that many people already in the pastorate should not be there. Conversely, at least on the basis of those characteristics, there may be many fine Christians who are missing out on the thrill of serving God in the pastorate because they are not aware that they already meet all the character requirements.

"Not Resentful" (2 Tim. 2:24)

The words of Scripture here read "patient when wronged." The world's culture is so paranoid that many Christian leaders fall into the trap of that paranoia and imagine that everyone is out to get them. When someone does wrong them, it just confirms their suspicions. As a result, they become bitter and resentful, not remembering that the person who wronged them may have done so inadvertently, may have mistaken the leaders' motivation in a certain action, or may have responded rashly out of a set of frustrations he had experienced that particular day. If the Christian leader goes about piling up statistics against people he suspects have wronged him, he is going to become a bitter, disillusioned man of questionable value to the kingdom of God. A rule that I have found helpful is to expect the best of everyone. If a person does not live up to that expectation, forgive him, because he is human. If he persists in offensive action toward you, take him out to dinner and see what is bothering him. If he still persists, stay out of his way. Concentrate your efforts on other people, but, at all cost, never speak disparagingly of him.

"Having Believing Children" (Titus 1:6)

The Scripture here further elaborates on the attitude of children, saying that they should not be "accused of dissipation or rebellion." The crowning success of every ministry is for the pastor's children to grow up to know, to love, and to live for the Lord Jesus. Yet salvation is by individual choice. No matter how we live our lives before our children, there is no guarantee that they will make that choice.

If a majority of a person's children live for Christ, then we may conclude that the one or perhaps two who do not are guilty of rebelling against God and their parents. If a majority of the children go wrong, then serious questions need to be asked as to the effectiveness of the parents' witness. Most of those who are just going into the pastorate do not know, of course, how their children will turn out. However, they are obligated to take every step possible to see that their children are exposed to the gospel and are encouraged to receive Christ as Savior and Lord.

When the children do rebel when they grow older, the parents must come to the point where they realize that their children are going to have to sink or swim according to the decisions that they themselves have made. The parents cannot bail them out forever. During that transition period between childhood and adulthood, however, it is the responsibility of a Christian parent to require that as long as the child lives in his parents' home or receives financial support from them, he live up to the expectations of their life-style. If he chooses not to do that, he must suffer the consequences of his choice. He should be required to find another place to live at once, or his financial support should be cut off. If a person intends to make what he believes are adult decisions, then he should experience the consequences of his decisions and the responsibilities of an adult. When a child's parents have done all they can for him, that child must be judged on the basis of his own decisions, not those of his parents.

"Not Self-Willed" (Titus 1:7)

What we are urged to avoid in this passage is being selfish and arrogant in the choices we make. Unfortunately, some pastors are so self-oriented that they believe the sun rises and sets on the things they accomplish. A person need only talk with them to find that their conversation is dominated by a recital of their activities and concerns. The pastor is called primarily to be a servant, to give of himself as did his Lord before him. The person who is continually concerned about his satisfaction, the accomplishment of his goals, the forwarding of his career is not a servant.

"Not Quick-Tempered" (Titus 1:7)

We talked some of the point made here in Titus when we considered the pugnacious person, the one looking for a good fight who continually walks around with a chip on his shoulder. There are other persons, however, who though not actually pugnacious by nature, go through life with their springs so tightly wound that any little problem sets them off. They have a hard time controlling their tempers. Generally they are sorry after the incident has passed, but by then the damage is irreparable. Jesus does not condemn anger per se. But he does call misdirected anger "sin." We are to be angry and "sin not."

Sometimes a person's temper fluctuates with his blood sugar. A person who can control himself quite well most of the time will find himself flying off the handle at other times. Often he can trace those unfortunate times to periods when he was excessively tired, hungry, or both. A person who is quick-tempered all of the time probably needs to see a counselor and stay out of the pastorate until he is able to resolve the problem. A person who is periodically quick-tempered should examine his life-style, his sleep pattern, and the kind and quantity of food he consumes. It may be advisable for him to schedule a short nap on the days he faces a stressful agenda. He may learn to carry nutritious snacks with him and use them to revive a low blood sugar level. (In a following chapter about the pastor's wife, there is a section dealing with how the wife may keep her husband on a more even keel and not provoke him.)

A LOVER OF "WHAT IS GOOD" (TITUS 1:8)

Earlier in this chapter I quoted James Stalker's remark that the principle role of a pastor in any community is to exemplify goodness. As a further elaboration of that remark, I would like to assert that not only is the pastor to practice goodness, he is to love that which is good. When we love something, we devote time and energy to it. Those who are to serve Jesus Christ in the pastoral ministry will be those people who already have proved themselves to be pursuers of the good. They choose to benefit from the companionship of other good people. They do not waste their time and energies pursuing things that are bad or that pollute the mind and body.

I have had students at the seminary tell me they have watched so-called adult movies in order to get a perspective on what the world faces. That same person would not wade through a garbage can to find his dinner. If he did, he would come up a mess, smelling from garbage. A good man fills his mind with what is good so that increasingly he can think more good things. It is better for a person to be considered naive in the eyes of the world as long as he is considered a good man by God.

"Just" (Titus 1:8)

This characteristic is close to the last. A pastor is to be just in the sense that he is to be innocent, holy, and righteous in his character and actions.

"Devout" (Titus 1:8)

The King James translates this word "holy." The pastoral servant of God is to be a pious man and one whose piety stretches to more than outward symbols. His devotion should spring from intense love for God. His attitude of devotion to God will be contagious among his people.

"Self-Controlled" (Titus 1:8)

I wonder why the Holy Spirit listed so many synonyms for this quality in the life of a pastor. Could it be that He knew where a great deal of the trouble might lie? Probably a majority of the characteristics we have considered could be lumped together under the one broad heading of self-control. The person who with the help of the Holy Spirit can control himself certainly will have no problem succeeding in any task that God had in mind for him to do.[2]

Thus far we have considered many of the biblical characteristics necessary for a person to succeed in the pastoral ministry. There are some practical considerations as well, and these will be dealt with in the next section of the chapter as we consider what constitutes a "call" to the ministry.

Call to the Ministry

The sixth chapter of Isaiah records a unique call to ministry, in which the prospective prophet is caught up in an ecstatic vision and the Lord commissions him for the work. It would be very helpful if God planned a similar experience for all who showed an interest in the ministry. The fact is that He does not.

On almost every ordination council on which I have ever sat, inevitably the question has arisen, "Will you share with us your call to the ministry?" On most occasions the candidate fumbles for a bit

2. W. Robert Cook, paper, "Biblical Concepts of the Discipline of Church Leaders." I am indebted to Dr. Cook for the list of biblical qualifications discussed in this chapter.

and then tells how during the ministry of Brother So-and-So at his home church, an invitation was extended and the candidate "felt" the call of God on his life for the pastoral ministry. Is a call like that good enough? Is a subjective "call" the way God leads men to the ministry today in lieu of experiences such as Isaiah went through?

SUBJECTIVE CRITERIA

There is indeed a subjective side to a call to the ministry. People do go into the pastorate because they feel what they consider to be God's claim in their lives toward pastoral ministry. I would not try to negate either the authenticity of their feelings or their claim that the feeling comes from God. Accompanying that feeling, however, is often another, slightly different feeling, one that is not praiseworthy. The person who has this feeling wants so badly to be a pastor, that he will sacrifice almost anything in order to accomplish his goal, including the comfort and welfare of his family. If God is really in the call, I have no doubt that He can supply his needs and bless his efforts. However, if the desire the man has is purely subjective, and he is living out an unrealistic fantasy, then disaster may be the result.

OBJECTIVE CRITERIA

Along with subjective criteria, a person also must consider in a calm, cool manner objective criteria that are sometimes distressing. First, he must ask himself if he is fit for the ministry. In order to determine that, he must examine himself in light of the characteristics listed earlier in this chapter. If he does not meet those criteria or cannot foresee his being able to mature to the point where he does, he should abandon plans for the ministry, at least until he is able to observe a great deal more maturity in his life than he yet possesses.

Second, if he truly can say yes to all of the biblical requirements, he must ask himself certain practical questions. Does he really like people enough to give himself in service to them unselfishly? Is he comfortable with people, or do they threaten him? Would he be able to relate meaningfully to people in all kinds of situations, including those that may not be considered especially pleasant? Is he able to confront people lovingly? Is he an organizer, a motivator who is able to inspire people to undertake even greater and more exciting tasks? Is he an interesting person himself, or do people yawn at the very thought of his arriving? Even if he has a high degree of piety, if he is not a "people person," or is incapable of becoming one, he probably is not called to the pastorate.

Third, he must ask himself if he is able to communicate well with people. Is he capable of organizing his thoughts in logical fashion and presenting a sermon or lesson in such a way that people will follow his thoughts and do something about what they hear? Is he fluent of speech? I have heard cases where God has taken stutterers, given them great fluency, and overcome the problem for His glory. However, it would be better for the stutterer and for the church if he received that marvelous deliverance before he entered the pastorate, instead of becoming a pastor first and subjecting his people to the problem while he waited on God for healing.

I have known persons with speech defects who were effective speakers. Yet in every case they also possessed extraordinary gifts such as a strong and engaging personality or the ability to make content so captivating that the listener soon forgot about the impediment. Unless a person is extraordinary in ways such as those, and that fact is confirmed by the church, he probably should look for another avenue besides the pastoral ministry to serve the Lord.

Does the person have good physical stamina? Will he be able to hold up under the long hours demanded of him in the pastorate? How does he perform under stress? He most certainly will experience that in the pastorate.

Does the prospective pastor have administrative and leadership abilities? He may not be aware that those areas will consume a great deal of his time and will tax his talents, but they will, and he should be prepared for it.

Is he an attractive person? I am not referring necessarily to his appearance, although he should do everything he can to enhance the way he looks. People are attracted to others for many other qualities than appearance. How does he interact with children? Is he comfortable with the aged? Does he have a nice way about him when he deals with people?

Is he a disciplined person? Will he be able to manage his time wisely so that he can accomplish the many tasks required of a pastor? A person who continually wastes time and procrastinates to the extent of avoiding unpleasant duties probably should procrastinate before responding to what he feels is a call.

Is he a realistic person who is cognizant of what life is all about, one who will neither have unrealistic expectations of people nor try to impose unrealistic demands on them?

Before accepting any call to the ministry, the prospective pastor is wise to ask himself two additional questions. First, has he experienced sufficient training to prepare him for this challenge? Second, if he is married, is his wife biblically qualified to take on the role of a pastor's wife, sympathetic with his role as pastor, and willing to enter into partnership with him in the ministry to which he has been called? These matters will be covered in greater detail in subsequent chapters, but they need to be mentioned in this chapter, because they are crucial to a decision a person makes about becoming a pastor.

The pastorate is a demanding job and has unique requirements as its prerequisites. Not everybody can be a pastor—only those who meet the biblical requirements, sense the call of God on their lives, and have the appropriate gifts needed to make the office a success. Those who lack any of those may find that the pastorate is distasteful and disastrous for them. However, those who heed a genuine call from God, examine their lives, and find that they meet the biblical, subjective, and objective criteria that I have listed may step forward boldly. When they do so they will find the pastorate the most rewarding and satisfying job they have ever tackled. There is no higher calling than the pastorate. No wonder that the prerequisites of the call are so specific and demanding.

Questions for Discussion

To determine whether or not you are really fit for the ministry, you may want to answer these questions for yourself:

1. Do you like people enough to give yourself in service to them unselfishly?

2. Are you comfortable with people, or are you easily threatened by them?

3. Are you able to confront people lovingly?

4. Are you an organizer, a motivator, a person who can inspire people to undertake ever greater and more exciting tasks?

5. Do you have the capability of being an interesting person, or do people yawn at the very thought of your appearance?

6. Are you able to communicate? Can you organize your thoughts in logical fashion and present them in such a way that you will provoke attention?

7. Do you have physical stamina? Will you be able to hold up under long hours and during times of stress?

8. Do you have administrative and leadership abilities?

9. Are you an attractive person? Are you comfortable with children? with the aged?

10. Are you a disciplined person? Are you able to manage your time wisely?

11. Are you able to project realistic expectations upon people and thus solicit their support and encouragement?

12. Are you sufficiently trained for the challenge of the pastorate?

13. If you are married, is your wife biblically qualified to take on the role of a pastor's wife? Is she sympathetic with your role as pastor? Is she willing to enter into a partnership with you in the ministry to which you have been called?

Helpful Resources

Anderson, Clifford. *Count on Me*. Wheaton, Ill.: Victor, 1980.

Butt, Howard. *The Velvet Covered Brick*. San Francisco: Harper & Row, 1978.

Griffin, Daniel. "The Pastor and His Humanity." *Leadership* 1, no. 3 (Summer 1980):28-32.

Hendricks, Howard, and Chuck Swindoll. *Survival for the Pastor*. Portland, Oreg.: Multnomah, 1984.

Jones, Curtis G. *The Naked Shepherd*. Waco, Tex.: Word, 1979.

Lavender, Lucille. *They Cry Too*. Wheaton, Ill.: Tyndale, 1976.

McBurney, Louis. *Every Pastor Needs a Pastor*. Waco, Tex.: Word, 1977.

Needham, David. *Birthright: Christian Do You Know Who You Are?* Portland, Oreg.: Multnomah, 1981.

2

The Pastor's Personal Life and Study Habits

A pastor's wife I once knew described her years in the parsonage as "life in the fishbowl." Of all the professions, the pastorate may be the least private of all. Not only is the pastor on call twenty-four hours a day, but many pastors are under such close surveillance by members of their congregation and by the community at large that they and their families often find it hard to make a move without many people knowing about it. Because the pastor is under such close observation, he, more than any other professional person, needs to work hard to assure that he has both a private family life and a private personal life. Later chapters will focus on the pastor's obligations to and relationships with his wife and children. Here, however, I would like to discuss his obligations to himself.

Personal Life

Despite the fact that the pastor is a public figure, he is, as well, an individual with his own physical, psychological, spiritual, and emotional needs. Because of the excessive demands that sometimes greet him in his professional life, often it is easy for him to become absorbed in his tasks and ignore those important personal needs. As a result, little by little he may lose the vitality and freshness with which he began his work, and eventually he may experience a classic case of burnout, even becoming a casualty to pastoral service.

Physically, it is important for the pastor to ascertain how much sleep he needs to function effectively and then to arrange his schedule to meet that need. In surveying books on the subject, I find that many authors suggest an "early to bed, early to rise" regimen. That is fine if the pastor is a morning person. Not everyone is, though. Some people can arise bright and cheerful early in the morning, see the world through rose-colored glasses, and say pleasantly, "Good morning, Lord." Then there are others of us who just begin to blossom after 9:00 P.M. Some of our most productive work may be accomplished after everyone else has gone to bed. When such a person is forced to rise early in the morning, he is likely to be grumpy, nonfunctioning, and incapable of any productive work. The world is gray and bleak to him.

Despite the pressures of the so-called Protestant work ethic, there is no special virtue in rising early in the morning, especially if a person is a night person. Whatever his orientation, though, the pastor is wise in avoiding extremes. He may have to adjust his time for sleeping to accommodate the schedules of his wife and children and the needs of his congregation. It may be admirable for a pastor to arise at 4:30 A.M. to pray. However, if he requires eight hours of sleep, and if the early prayer time forces him into bed by eight thirty each evening, thus making him miss Bible studies, board meetings, and pastoral calls that must be made at night, his 4:30 A.M. wake-up time is unrealistic.

Conversely, the night person may choose to work until 3:00 or 4:00 in the morning, but if that means that he does not show up at the office until noon, he can expect to receive a great deal of criticism. There are a number of responsibilities that normally should be accomplished well before noon. Generally a pastor is safe if he arrives at his office, ready to carry on his day's responsibilities, by 9:00 A.M. Exceptions, of course, will occur when he has had to make an emergency call the night before.

In addition to a proper amount of sleep, proper nutrition is important also. As a society we have become addicted to consuming large quantities of sugar and caffeine. In the long run, consumption of too much of either of those may have disastrous effects on our metabolism. The pastor is especially vulnerable to misuse of both substances. Because he often keeps a hectic schedule, he finds that sugar and caffeine provide a temporary pick-me-up. Also, he is constantly in situations where not only are both sugar and caffeine available to him, but he is almost forced to partake for the sake of social acceptability. If the pastor is going to transact business during the day with a layman, it is just natural that they will "get together for a cup of coffee." Likewise, when the pastor calls on a family, it is considered normal etiquette to offer him a cup of coffee, and his hosts will expect him to join them in that tribal ritual.

Some years ago when the pressures of the pastorate were considerable, I found myself addicted to coffee in order to keep going. When I decided to quit, I experienced actual withdrawal symptoms. They were enough to convince me that for me, at least, total abstinence from coffee was desirable. I found out later that when I restricted my intake of sugar, white flour products, white rice, and all foods containing a heavy amount of chemical additives I felt much better than I had before. The pastorate is rigorous work and the demands of the job dictate that the pastor be alert and even-tempered as much as possible. Proper rest and nutrition as well as a sensible vitamin consumption certainly will help.

Added to those is recreation. I like to define recreation as anything a person likes to do that is not a part of his job. Some pastors opt for rigorous athletic pursuits. Others choose more sedentary activities. Whatever a person chooses to do, he should do it on a regular basis and out of range of a telephone. He should consider it an important part of his weekly schedule. There are times when the pastor will include family or friends in his recreational plans. There are other times when he needs to be alone, free of pressures, allowing his chosen form of recreation to recreate him.

Every pastor should have at least one day a week off. This is a necessity, not a luxury, if he is to maintain any efficiency in the pastorate. The choice of day will vary with his habits and schedule, and it may differ from week to week depending on the demands of the week. Many pastor friends have told me it is necessary that they leave home during days off, because if they stay home they are barraged constantly by phone calls or visitors. May I suggest two solutions to such problems. First, if the pastor purchases a home, it is advisable that it be located a sufficient distance away from the church building so that it is inconvenient for people to go to his home when they cannot reach him at the church. Second, for a nominal price, the phone company will install an extra telephone line into the pastor's home. The extra telephone should have an unlisted number. The number should be given only to family members, the church secretary, and the chairman of the board. Those other than family members should be instructed to use the number only in case of dire emergency. Thus, when the pastor is enjoying his day off or a special time with his family, he merely unplugs the telephone whose number is listed in the directory. If an emergency occurs or if family members need to reach him, they may do so by means of the "hot line," the second, unlisted number.

In addition to weekly days off, the pastor needs an occasional weekend away from the church, out of the pulpit. When I have served as adviser to churches that are constructing new constitutions or are writing out the specifications of a pastoral call, I always suggest that the churches specify that their pastor be released from all his duties at least one weekend in eight. If the pastor receives a weekend off, however, he should not expect an additional day off the succeeding week. Instead he should report for duty Monday morning refreshed and ready for a full week's activities.

As I write this, I serve not only as the pastor of a church but also as a seminary professor. Because of the heavy responsibilities of both positions, my church has insisted that I take off every sixth weekend whenever possible. In the past I have allowed outside speaking engagements to consume the weekend off. That practice, of course, defeats the purpose of the weekend. I would advise the pastor with a weekend off to spend it away from home. On his Sunday off, he may want to attend church with a congregation of another denomination, so that he may do so anonymously.

In order to maintain his own emotional and mental health, the pastor should establish a close friendship with another man with whom he feels safe in confiding. If the pastor is part of a multiple staff, an associate with similar interests may be the logical confidant. In other cases, he may find an extremely mature, amiable layman whose personality and interests mesh with his. If the layman is a member of the same congregation, the pastor must exercise care lest it appear that an exclusive relationship is developing.

Despite the fact that the pastor has a good friend, he does not have to restrict all of his Sunday morning conversation to that friend to the exclusion of others who may want to speak with him. It may be better, in fact, for the pastor to select his confidant from outside his church. A pastor or a layman from a neighboring church may prove the suitable close friend the pastor needs.

In rare cases, especially when a pastor is getting settled in a new location, he will have to rely on a close out-of-town friend with whom he corresponds or whom he telephones. If distances are not excessive, he may want to use his weekends off to meet the friend at a location suitable to both families.

The most important aspect of a pastor's private life I have left until last—his relationship with the Lord. Many people would take the relationship for granted and would insist that it is unnecessary even to mention it in a book such as this. However, I have learned from painful experience that a close walk with the Lord does not come automatically. Strange as it may seem, a person engaged in the active ministry may find maintaining his fellowship with the Lord the hardest work of all and the part of his life that requires the greatest amount of personal discipline.

The reason for that should be obvious. Satan knows that often those serving the Lord in positions of leadership are the most vulnerable at the point of their ego. Those of us who have been engaged in the pastorate for any length of time know that we have certain abilities, and we assume that we can "wing it" through many of the responsibilities of our ministry. If Satan can convince us that we can do the whole job in our own strength, he knows that in time we will run out of resources and become debilitated and ineffective. Or, what is even more devastating, we may fall into immorality.

The pastor is exceptionally susceptible to Satan's tactics in the latter area, probably because he is criticized only occasionally but is often fed by the adulation and praise of his people. When he starts taking himself and his abilities seriously, begins believing all the nice things people say about him, and moves away from his reliance on the Lord, then he is headed for serious trouble in his ministry. His only salvation is that he discipline himself steadfastly to schedule a time alone with the Lord each day. That time may vary, as long as it occurs sometime in the day's schedule. In my own case, I found that it was possible for me to arrive at my office well ahead of the secretary, park my car where it was inconspicuous, lock myself in the office, and unplug the phone for as long a time as I felt I needed to be alone with the Lord. At present, I spend a great deal of time commuting. Often I find the time valuable for discussing various things with the Lord and seeking His direction.

In addition, there are other moments in the privacy of my study when I can shut the door and spend productive moments with Him. The time of day and location are inconsequential. Wherever and whenever we spend time with the Lord, we always will find the period the most valuable part of the day. Disciplining ourselves to take time to be with the Lord is not easy. All kinds of excuses and pressures will intervene. But it must be done. If it is not, no matter how much time we have spent in His service, soon it will become apparent that we really do not know God well. Shallowness of ministry will be the principle clue.

Study Life

Integral to any ministry that can be considered truly successful is pulpit exposition of superior quality, the feeding of the people on God's Word. In order to feed his people, a pastor must be full of

God's Word himself, and he must be studying continually, seeking ways to interpret and apply God's Word to the lives of his people. To know God's Word requires that a person spend time in the Word. That means that the pastor must spend large blocks of his time in the study. To apply God's Word requires that the pastor spend adequate time with his people, getting to know them and their needs, so that his application of the Word will "scratch them where they itch." Many pastors are not able to balance the two aspects of their ministry properly, and, as a result, problems arise in their ministry. Let me illustrate with three case studies.

PASTOR A

John Jacobsen retired recently after thirty-two years of ministry at Meadowdale Church. For most of the congregation, his retirement was an emotion-laden occasion. For many of the adult members, Jacobsen was the only pastor they had ever known. He had dedicated them as infants, baptized them as adolescents, performed their wedding ceremonies, buried their parents, and dedicated their children. Pastor Jacobsen, a fatherly type, was respected and loved throughout the entire community, and he would be hard to replace.

One of the reasons replacing him would be difficult was that Jacobsen was a jack-of-all-trades. Never did he consider any job beneath his dignity. If the church building needed cleaning, painting, or repairing, pastor was on the spot doing the job. Because he was a capable and safe driver, he served for years as chauffeur for every special event and routine function. Nobody would be able to drive the church bus as well as Jacobsen. Every child who ever rode the church bus knew kindly Pastor Jacobsen. Being a capable musician, he often directed the choir, played the piano or organ, and as needed provided inspiring vocal solos. He was a whiz at office work and managed the finances of the little church, kept excellent records, and typed and printed the weekly bulletin and the monthly newsletter. He visited faithfully and often in the homes of his congregation; attended every youth, women's, men's, and children's event; was heavily involved in service to the community; and was faithful in his attendance at all denominational events. There were few people like Pastor Jacobsen!

Unfortunately, Pastor had little time to study. As a result, his people grew little in the Lord during his years of ministry with them, and the church remained about the same size numerically. However, there was little need to grow. Since Pastor did most of the work anyway, what was left for his people to do except to attend faithfully? That they did, and in many cases their attendance was the sum total of their Christian service.

Pastor B

Rodney White accepted the call to a church that had an active and powerful board of elders. From the very beginning, it was Rod's understanding with the other elders that his was to be a shared ministry. As pastor, he would be free to concentrate on the areas he liked the most and in which he did the best. Since Rodney was a "people person" and an effective personal evangelist, he began immediately to explore the community for people with whom he could relate. Everyone agreed that he was one of the nicest and most friendly people they had ever met.

Though seminary-trained, Rod had one problem. He hated to spend time in his study. Fortunately he had spent time in a previous pastorate and could rely for a while on the sermons he was forced to produce there. However, even those sermons were the result of hasty preparation. Many times, the outlines were borrowed totally from books of sermons written by others, the illustrations were stock ones instead of unique to Rod's life, and the delivery was poor because he had not practiced enough.

Rodney continues to spend an hour or two in his office each week reworking an old message or borrowing a new one and including within his notes a joke or two to promote good humor among his congregation. Many people are being won to Christ because of his witness in the community. When those people become new members of the church, it absolutely dumfounds them to find that the more established members of the congregation are dissatisfied with the pastor and his ministry.

Pastor White involves himself heavily in the community, and members of his congregation keep complaining that they can never find the pastor in his office when they want him, despite the fact that they try to reach him during his office hours. Mature Christians are frustrated because his sermons lack depth, and although the church continues to welcome new members into its midst, the membership door is a revolving door, with spiritually mature members leaving in utter frustration.

Pastor C

Lindley Fife never was very good with people. He was introverted and shy, completely lost in a crowd. However, in seminary he found himself an excellent scholar of the Word. Moreover, he became articulate in delivery, and when First Church called him as their pastor, the members were pleased that so small a congregation had been able to attract such a fine pulpiteer.

During his years in seminary, Fife had become convinced that each church needed to initiate a program where there was a carefully planned division of labor. Moreover, his study of the fourth chapter of Ephesians in the original language had convinced him that the last two offices mentioned in verses eleven and twelve were, in reality, one, and that God had called him to an office called *pastor-teacher.*

Because the teaching of God's Word was thus of major importance, Lindley decided that he would spend thirty-two hours each week in his study, immersed in the Word. Other pressing tasks were not his responsibility. Somebody else would have to do them, or they would not be done. After all, thought Lindley, *The exposition of the Word really is all that counts. If people merely listen to the Word and obey what it says, all of their problems will be straightened out.* Armed with that philosophy, the shy and introverted Lindley could thus avoid exposure to people. He was too busy in the Word to counsel, to visit his members, or to attend social events. Often his wife attended the latter functions by herself, finding herself at a continued loss to make excuses for her husband. He was not interested in dealing constructively with the problems of the church. If he became annoyed enough, he would merely dig into the Word, formulate a stock answer, and, in thunderous tones, let the biblical indictment fall on the appropriate persons—who may or may not have been listening to the sermon that day.

Although the people are still impressed with Lindley's continued, scholarly use of the Greek and Hebrew and are appreciative of the fact that he "fully and rightly divides the Word," they are not sure that they understand what he is talking about all the time, nor are they convinced that he truly understands and loves them. Actually, his messages do not relate to their lives, and the people have never been able to get close to him as a person. It is rumored that sufficient unrest is developing to make it prudent for Lindley to consider looking for another church.

Each of these case studies represents a real-life situation in which the pastor in question practices extremes in his ministry. In each case there is a terrible imbalance. In case *A,* the pastor does too much for his people, performing too many menial, perfunctory tasks. He deprives his people of the rich ministry he could give them from the pulpit, if he were to spend more time in study and prayer.

In case *B*, there is an imbalance between evangelism and edification. The pastor is so busy establishing relationships in the community that he is not able to meet the edificational needs of his own people. No one would criticize his enthusiasm for friendship evangelism, but, in his case, his zeal for friendship evangelism is not balanced by the ability to feed his people spiritually. His people are given too little spiritual food to grow in Christ and share in the ministry of evangelism. The two hours a week the pastor spends in his study is not sufficient time to prepare an adequate meal for the saints.

In case *C*, the pastor finds the study a safe and convenient place in which to hide from reality. Because he does not spend enough time with his people, the deeper he goes into the Word the drier he becómes. Increasingly, his sermons, although profound, are unrelated to the real problems of his people except when the pastor focuses his attention on someone who annoys him. The pastor spends too much time in his study and not enough time out among his people.

What, then, is the proper amount of time a pastor should spend in his study? There is no one answer. The optimum amount of time will differ according to several variables: the number of messages the pastor is required to prepare for his congregation each week, his reading speed, his degree of imagination and creativity, and the extent to which he has human or computer assistance to uncover information.

Although this chapter is not intended to be the final word on sermon preparation, some suggestions on the subject may prove helpful. First, if he is to speak authoritatively on any portion of God's Word, the pastor needs to be aware of the whole scope of Scripture. Therefore, he ought to plan to read through the entire Bible every year. When divided properly into daily segments, such a task is not inordinately time-consuming. He ought to read rapidly to get the overall gist of what God is saying through the record.

Next, in any given week the pastor should spend considerable time studying the portion of Scripture he will be expounding in his sermon the next Sunday. Such study will be rewarded. The very fact that a great number of pastors are able to prepare and present many effective sermons in a year, whereas professional secular speakers are able to produce only a few, testifies that if a pastor is faithful in his study and preparation of the Word, and if he prepares the sermon with a keen knowledge of the needs of his people, the Holy Spirit will supply a miraculous "plus" factor that will make the presentation effective in the lives of the listeners. However, even miracles require preparation, and I am convinced that the Holy Spirit is able to be involved as vitally in the preparation process as in the actual presentation of the sermon.

Whether he is a novice or is experienced, the pastor working on a new sermon should expect to spend at least fifteen to twenty hours preparing it. An experienced pastor overhauling an old sermon should plan to spend at least ten hours making it current and palatable to a new congregation. Shortcuts will work occasionally. Once in a while when he is caught unawares, a pastor may have enough accumulated knowledge even to wing it, praying all the while for the grace of God. Over the long haul, however, winging it will not work. The pastor's sins of omission will find him out.

Because it is necessary to devote so much time to the preparation of a single sermon, it would be wise for the pastor to discuss with his board exactly what duties are expected of him and what his people consider a reasonable work week for him. If the pastor suggests a certain number of hours of work as being appropriate, he should bear in mind that many in his congregation are expected to invest not only a given number of hours at their employment but also to spend many hours in the service of the church. A reasonable expectation for the pastor, then, might be the same number of hours as his busiest parishioner spends in his combination of work hours and church hours.

Having then established what the board considers a reasonable number of work hours, the pastor should tell the board the number of hours he must spend in his study preparing each sermon. In reviewing other areas in which he is expected to be involved, he may find it beneficial to let the board and the congregation as a whole know the variety of tasks facing him, so that they can make helpful suggestions as to how he best can utilize his time. In some cases, the people may decide that the pastor should reduce his number of presentations each week, opting to use him more extensively in ministries other than the pulpit ministry. In placing a limit on his overall hours of ministry they can help see to it that he does not burn out as a pastor.

As to the actual scheduling of a pastor's study time, the best arrangement will vary from person to person. When I was pastoring full-time, I found it best to preach only one sermon a week. I began its preparation early on Monday morning while the events of Sunday were still fresh. Under the watchful eyes of a church secretary who screened all calls, I secluded myself in my office, working as long into the week as necessary until the sermon was completed. Although the secretary ran interference for me, I remained available to respond to all genuine needs of members or to handle the crisis experiences of drop-in visitors to the church office that could not be handled by the secretary or a deacon.

For years it has been my practice to submerge myself thoroughly in the text, both through translations and in the original languages to the extent I am still able. In addition, I use any other information I can find about the passage, whether the source be commentaries, lexicons, books of sermons, or books written about the passage. Because I am primarily an expository preacher and delight in choosing books of the Bible through which I can preach passage-by-passage, after I have accomplished my background study I look for natural divisions in the text I am preparing and construct an outline. Then I go back to the text, my study aids, and my illustrative material in order to flesh out the message.

I believe sincerely that each sermon should call for some type of decision on the part of the hearer, and that the sermon should build toward that decision. I am primarily a manuscript preacher and get the rough manuscript into the hands of the secretary as early in the week as possible. In turn, she considers the sermon a priority matter, returning it to me quickly. In the event that I do not have secretarial help in a particlar week, I type the information myself into a computer and print it out in large block letters. Whether it was produced by the secretary or by a computer, I then live with the manuscript for the rest of the week, referring to it often enough to become thoroughly familiar with it.

If I have sufficient time, I appreciate being able to type the sermon into the computer myself. By the end of the week I inevitably notice changes that should be made or become aware of information that should be added. The computer allows me to do that easily, and it prints out a new manuscript with little effort.

On Sunday morning I arise early and go through the sermon manuscript at least two more times. By the time it is necessary to deliver the sermon, I am so familiar with it that I am freed from slavishly sticking to the printed copy. I find myself departing frequently from the thoughts originally in the manuscript, adding new, pertinent material that has occurred to me during the time I have studied the manuscript.

The process I have described for the preparation and presentation of sermons should not be viewed as a norm. There are many ways to prepare sermons. No doubt some are much better than my method. The method I use, however, has worked successfully for me.

After trying a variety of options, I found that Friday is the best time for me to take a day off. By that time, much of the week's work is accomplished, and I can refresh myself, knowing that I do not have a huge backlog of work hanging over my head. Moreover, I find that resting on Friday allows me to step into the pulpit Sunday in a refreshed, instead of a worn-out, state. If it is necessary for me to engage in church business on Saturday, I try to restrict those activities to the more relaxed ones, such as social gatherings. I try not to participate in anything that lasts late on Saturday night. For example, I request that all weddings be held early enough in the day to leave Saturday night substantially free. If I attend a party on Saturday night, I excuse myself as early as possible so that I can get the rest I need to give my best to Sunday's activities. Everyone seems to understand when I ask to be excused early on Saturday evenings. Often someone will comment in jest, "Oh, we almost forgot. Sunday is the day you work, isn't it?"

The first part of this chapter has focused on the pastor's personal life. The reader already has noted that the chapter is almost devoid of references to the pastor's need for individuality. For too long, the need to assert personhood has revolved around aspects of a person's behavior or appearance. Sometimes I have seen pastors continue to engage in actions they knew were offensive to their people, all in the guise of being able to assert their personhood. In flaunting their individuality by their actions, inappropriate clothing, or lack of proper grooming, they have succeeded in so disturbing the sensitivities of the very people they came to serve, that they limited their ministries considerably.

A person who has to flaunt his person by unconventional appearance or his Christian freedom by practices his people find unacceptable is, in reality, an extremely immature person. A truly mature person recognizes that his own personal needs are much deeper than external signs. He becomes secure in the person he is and does not have to assert himself by childish displays. That does not mean that he lacks concern for himself. He recognizes that he is a human being—a person with genuine needs—and he is careful to attend to those needs carefully so that he will stay fresh, alive, and enthusiastic for the important tasks that are integral to the ministry he has chosen.

In the second part of this chapter we considered a pastor's study habits, noting that preparing for his pulpit ministry is an important part of the pastor's overall ministry. People who will not or cannot study should not be in the pastoral ministry. Even in the area of study, however, there can be too much of a good thing. An essential part of a pastor's sermon preparation is the time he spends with his people, getting to know them and ascertaining their needs. That aspect of sermon preparation is not possible if the pastor barricades himself in his study and studiously avoids contact or interaction with people. The solution is balance, something that requires a great deal of discipline to maintain. All of his professional life a conscientious pastor will struggle to attain and maintain such a balance. Sometimes he will succeed. At other times he will fail. Then he must pick himself up and try again. But when he tries conscientiously, God always will reward his effort.

Questions for Discussion

1. Discuss the importance of proper diet, adequate rest, and fulfilling recreation in the routine of a pastor's life.

2. How many hours should a pastor work? Discuss the tension between being unproductive or lazy and becoming a workaholic.

3. What value do you see in having a close friendship with someone who can serve as a confidant?

4. What program for personal devotional life do you have? What could the professional clergyman do to strengthen that aspect of his daily agenda?

5. What is your personal viewpoint on the pastor's study habits? How do you resolve the tension between time spent in the study and time spent with the people? How do you propose to accomplish the weekly task of sermon preparation in the midst of a myriad of other important tasks?

Helpful Resources

Barclay, William. *Daily Celebration.* Waco, Tex.: Word, 1971.

Chambers, Oswald. *My Utmost for His Highest.* New York: Dodd, Mead, 1935.

"On Getting Overcommitted." *Christian Leadership Letter.* Monrovia, Calif.: World Vision, August 1982.

"The Workoholic: A Product of His Culture." *Christian Leadership Letter.* Monrovia, Calif.: World Vision, November 1981.

Foster, Richard. *Celebration of Discipline.* New York: Harper & Row, 1978.

Lewis, C. S. *Mere Christianity.* Riverside, N.J.: Macmillan, 1964.

Martin, Enos D. "Depression in the Clergy." *Leadership* 3, no. 1 (Winter 1982):81-89.

Muck, Terry. "Ten Questions About the Devotional Life." *Leadership* 3, no. 1 (Winter 1982):30-39.

Myra, Harold L. "Insights to Deepen Your Ministry." *Leadership* 3, no. 1 (Winter 1982):47-58.

Nouwen, Henri. *The Wounded Healer.* New York: Doubleday, 1972.

Packer, J. I. *Knowing God.* Downers Grove, Ill.: InterVarsity, 1979.

Patterson, Ben. "The Central Work of Prayer." *Leadership* 3, no. 1 (Winter 1982):114-17.

Spurgeon, Charles H. *Morning and Evening.* Grand Rapids: Zondervan, 1980.

Tozer, A. W. *The Pursuit of God.* Old Tappan, N.J.: Revell, 1982.

3

The Pastor's Tools

Recently I was foolish enough to complain about the high cost of dentistry to my dentist brother-in-law. As a reward for my folly he gave me a thirty-minute tour of his office, during which he pointed out each piece of equipment and how much it had cost him. Even though I will continue to growl over my dental bill, at least now I have a little better idea of why it is so high. Dentistry, like all other trades and professions, requires tools. The pastorate, as well, requires tools, but, unlike dentistry, there is no way to increase the price of the services the pastor performs in order to compensate adequately for the money he must spend on the tools that are needed in his profession.

Books as Tools

For years the principal tools of the pastorate have been books. Early in my ministry the church that ordained me recognized that fact, and, at my ordination service, took up a love offering to be used as a book fund for me. I could hardly contain myself. Early the next morning I was camped on the doorstep of a nearby seminary bookstore. When it opened, I engaged in the luxury of spending my entire book fund in one day, purchasing the tempting volumes that had always attracted me, but which I never before could afford. These I added to my library, a library that already had in it volumes my parents had given me when I was a child, books I had saved from my college years, and books that I had been required to buy in seminary.

I am still grateful for that gift of books on the occasion of my ordination.

There is an important point to note here. Seldom will the pastor succumb to the temptation to purchase too few books. Almost always his tendencies are in the opposite direction. To this day, I am a "bookaholic." I have to steel myself to get out of a bookstore without making a purchase, and if a book is on sale, I find it nearly irresistible.

In the past few years we have seen an explosion of books of all kinds in the Christian market. A great many of those are substantive volumes that will probably be valuable as reference volumes for a long while. They should be part of a pastor's library. Others books are written for the popular market. They may contain a good point or illustration or two, but the wise pastor should not buy them. Instead he should copy out the helpful points of information or interesting anecdotes, file away those bits of information for future use, and either hand the books on to others or, if they contain substantial theological error, discard them. In that way, the books will have supplied information the pastor needs without cluttering up his already crowded shelves. Moreover, he does not have to pack them up and move them every time he changes ministries.

There is still a third category of book crowding the shelves of Christian bookstores these days. Books in this category are the sensational, experience-based variety written by persons who appear to be oblivious to the facts of Scripture. Although their authors do not state it crassly, their attitude often seems to be, "Don't confuse me with theology. I know what I have experienced, and that's all I need."

A busy pastor will rarely have time for such books. Occasionally he may want to borrow one and skim through it, either to apprise himself of the type of thinking to which his members are being exposed or to refute some error that such books have introduced to some of his people. Yet unless he decides to become a specialist in refuting certain brands of error, he probably will not want to retain such books as a permanent part of his library. Many times the best thing to do with such works is to discard them after use so that they will not lead others astray.

One more point should be made. The pastor does not have unlimited shelf space, time, or money. Therefore, he should select his books with extreme care.

What books should be included in a pastor's library? Because so many books are published today, it is no longer practical to list individual titles in a volume such as this. However, here are a few helpful guidelines.

If a person was a pastoral major in a superior Bible college or seminary, he probably already has an excellent start. In most cases his professors tried to require texts of lasting value. In addition, many professors, if asked, will supply lists of books in their particular area of expertise that they believe will be helpful to those in the pastoral ministry. Others who have been helpful to me personally have been seminary and Bible college librarians who were perceptive and knowledgable concerning books pertaining to the ministry. How they keep up with all of those is beyond my imagination.

Another valuable ally in the selection of worthwhile books is the manager of a Bible college or seminary bookstore. Those people do not seem overly impressed by a profit margin, they have a sense of pride in what they are doing, and often they are aware of the best as well as the newest books written on a particular subject. Sometimes bookstore managers in conjunction with professors will draw up lists of recommended books for the pastor, adding notations concerning their relative value to a pastor so that he knows what books to purchase initially, which to add later, and the sequence in which he should add them.

BIBLE TRANSLATIONS

Despite the heavy emphasis in biblical languages they experience in their training, few pastors actually become experts in Hebrew and Greek. Whereas it is excellent discipline for the pastor to use the biblical languages to study the passage on which he will preach, he must be humble concerning his actual ability to use those languages. At best, he is an amateur, a part-time language student, one with limited training and exposure to the language. In sharp contrast, the people translating the Scriptures for contemporary versions are experts, scholars who have immersed themselves in the relevant languages. That does not mean that the studying pastor should not examine critically the work of translators when their work is controversial. Certainly he should do so. It does mean that the work of the translators may be extremely helpful to the pastor when he is puzzling over the meaning of a particular passage.

In addition to having a variety of translations, I personally have found it helpful to have a special Bible from which I study. The particular Bible I use has a variety of study aids built in. A number of study Bibles are currently available for purchase. Many colleagues in the ministry have told me that they find interlinear versions to be advantageous when they study. For a number of years I have enjoyed a version of the New Testament that prints the Greek text side-by-side with a contemporary English translation. For a long time I have admired those who carry the Bible only in its original languages and read directly from them, translating extemporaneously. That does not happen to be one of my skills, and I suspect that there are many in the ministry like me who need the additional tools I have suggested.

BIBLE STUDY AIDS

Bible study aids include Greek and Hebrew lexicons, word-study books, Bible dictionaries, atlases, encyclopedias, and concordances. Currently, many authors are writing scholarly Bible study aids. Also, contemporary periodicals are a good source for discovering new works and for obtaining an evaluation of them as they are produced.

Those wishing to purchase commentaries should be aware of certain facts. Though the commentary may prove an effective tool to use after a person has studied both the original text and contemporary translations, commentaries have their limitations. One-volume commentaries, for instance, though serving as quick resources, cannot because of their size begin to explore subjects to any degree of depth. Although they usually are written by a single author and may be expected to be consistent throughout, they are, nevertheless, sketchy. A really serious student of the Bible will want more complete information than they contain.

The greatest temptation for the serious Bible student lies in those encyclopedic sets of commentaries that are bound so beautifully and look so elegant on the bookstore shelf. Yet although the volumes are uniform in appearance and probably will look equally elegant in the pastor's office, they are not uniform in content or in style because their component parts are written by a variety of authors. Therefore, no matter how good the contents of one volume may be, beware of buying the set.

For years it has been my practice to preach through the books of the Bible. When it comes time to preach through a particular book, I survey all of the commentaries pertinent to that book, read all the reviews I can find regarding those commentaries, and ask my friendly seminary bookstore manager for his advice is selecting the volumes that will be the best sources of information. Then I select two or three books for purchase. They become permanent, valuable additions to my library and are a great help in preparing sermons and Bible studies. My library does not contain a single set of commentaries and so may not be as attractive as it could be, but for me, it is functional and useful.

BACKGROUND INFORMATION

In order to observe a proper hermeneutic, it is necessary to know the historical and cultural backgrounds of the people to whom the particular Scripture portion was directed. Of value here are Bible survey books, Bible history books, books that give information concerning Bible times and customs, and secular books covering the same period of history. Atlases and other books pertaining to biblical geography also should be purchased.

THEOLOGICAL WORKS

By the time a person becomes a pastor, very likely he will have in his library at least one or two classic volumes of theology. It has been my observation that much of our contemporary church is made up of people who are, for all intents and purposes, theological illiterates. The pastor, therefore, may find that several sound volumes of theology will serve as valuable background tools for him as he attempts to correct the condition. In addition to those substantive volumes, an increasing number of theological volumes are being written specifically for the lay person. The pastor will find those books helpful when he teaches his people theological principles.

Besides the two types of theological books I have mentioned, the pastor needs to read books that speak to contemporary issues in theology. Solid Christian journals also will help him keep abreast of current theological trends.

BIOGRAPHIES AND DEVOTIONAL BOOKS

As well as providing an excellent source of sermon illustrations, biographies and devotional books often serve as a source of great comfort, encouragement, and incentive for the pastor. In improving his own walk with the Lord, he will find it helpful to know where and how the great saints of yesterday walked. Also, it is advantageous for him to read what they themselves have written concerning that walk.

CHURCH HISTORY

Church history is one of the most neglected areas in the church today. Christians do not know who they are because they have never discovered their roots. When they do, they begin to understand why they believe as they do. They discover as well that no heresy facing the church today is new. It has been dealt with before, perhaps many times before, in the long history of the church. In discovering their roots, Christians may come to see themselves more clearly as part of God's overall plan in partnership with Christians throughout the ages. The perspective he gains through such study may be an antidote to the terrible cult of individualism that often cripples the efforts of the church. The pastor who desires to equip his people properly should have the proper tools to equip them in the area of church history.

CHRISTIAN EDUCATION

Recently a friend of mine bemoaned the fact that the Sunday school staff in his church contained so few good teachers. When I suggested that he offer a teacher-training course, he looked at me with a quizzical expression and said, "I need to take such a course before I can teach one." Although he had been seminary trained, he admitted that he did not take seriously the two courses in Christian education required for seminary graduation. At any rate, those two courses had been theoretical courses containing information about the history and philosophy of Christian education rather than courses teaching the future pastor how to run a Sunday school and train teachers.

A good knowledge of how to conduct an effective program of Christian education is not a peripheral matter—it is survival information. Concise, practical books that discuss organization and teaching methodology may be the most valuable books a pastor possesses. Such books may entice the pastor himself into using newer and more effective methods of helping his people learn.

We teach as we have been taught. Sometimes that is fortunate, and at other times it is unfortunate. It all depends upon our models. Often when a person has completed four years of college and three or four years of seminary he will know little except the lecture method. Although it is possible to use that method effectively, it is not suitable for every purpose. The pastor who is knowledgeable about a variety of teaching methods and who is able to use several of them effectively will be an excellent model for other teachers in his church.

MISSIONS

Missions encompasses the sum total of the outreach ministry of the Church—locally as well as abroad—and is vital. Rare is the church that strikes a happy medium between evangelism and edification. Rarer still is the church that is biblically balanced enough to carry on an effective ministry in both local and world outreach. An increasing number of books speak to those issues and put them in the proper perspective. They also supply helpful suggestions as to methodology.

ADMINISTRATION

Few people studying for the ministry envision the vast amount of time they will spend in administrative tasks. Although the potential pastor never may envision himself as an administrator, it is good for him to know what must be done and how to do it.

A myriad of correspondence, reporting forms, and records face every pastor. They are important to the efficient operation of the church and must be done. A pastor should know how to organize his own life in order to accomplish his tasks, how to organize the program of the church, and how to enlist and motivate others to carry out their tasks. There are a number of practical books that share such information.

MUSIC

An entire chapter of this book is devoted to the music ministry of the church. At this point it needs to be said that probably no other gift of God has been so abused and misused within the church as music. The pastor needs to know how to use music properly in the various functions of the church. He may never have had time to take a course in music, but there are valuable books on the subject, especially those on hymnology, that may bail him out of many difficult situations.

PASTORING

I have alluded to the fact that pastoring involves a little bit of science and a great deal of art. Because the pastor deals with people, and people are seldom predictable, it is difficult to predict the outcome of many of his encounters. It is valuable for him, however, to explore the successes and the failures of other pastors, to analyze their techniques, and to discover some basic principles that can be applied to his own ministry. Many books are available today that give such information. Some of them have been written prematurely, however. A number of them, for instance, paint attractive pictures of various non-traditional ministries and use those as models to encourage other people to start similar works. Yet the ministries about which the books were written may have dissolved only a few years later. When non-traditional methods are used, it is important to wait and see if the theory lasts over a reasonable period of time, before applying it to another work.

It is vital, also, for the pastor to have as a part of his library several handbooks providing orders of service for such events as weddings, funerals, and infant dedications; and for occasions that are only celebrated occasionally, such as the laying of a cornerstone, or an ordination. When those occasions occur, it is important for the pastor to know where to go for help in planning a program appropriate for the occasion. Such manuals will contain a wealth of help.

WORSHIP

Liturgical churches and pentecostal churches seem to know how to worship. Everyone in between seems to have forgotten how. Stimulating books on the subject of worship will keep the pastor aware of the need for the church to worship and will suggest ways he can create genuine worship experiences for his people.

Tools Other Than Books

As good and as necessary as books are as tools of the ministry, they are still primitive tools. There are times, of course, when circumstances mandate the use of primitive tools. Several years ago, for instance, I was stationed at a remote military outpost in a rural section of South Korea. One day we were fortunate enough to have a traveling military dentist visit us and pull from his jeep the things that were required to take care of our dental needs. Using mainly hand tools, he picked and chipped away at my teeth for what seemed hours. His drill was a portable unit run by peddle power, the motor being the foot of the dentist. The job was accomplished but probably was one of the most grueling experiences of my life.

I could not help but contrast that dentist with my "high priced" brother-in-law. When I visit him, I recline on a comfortable couch, he is careful to anesthetize me, and his drill works at super-fast speeds, cooled by water to alleviate any discomfort the heat might cause. There are occasions when he still uses hand tools, but they are rare. Normally, he uses the best technology possible in order to accomplish the job as efficiently as possible. As a result, I am more comfortable and thus more satisfied, and he is much more productive.

For years the only tools available to the pastor were books. That is no longer true. Many other excellent tools are available for improving the pastor's ministry.

Before listing some of the products that can be used to enhance a pastoral ministry, I would like to express my opinion as to their acquisition. Few tradespeople or professionals I know of object to having to purchase the tools necessary to their trade or profession. For instance, when my son was working in construction, his contractor made it plain that Rob was expected to purchase his own hammers. The pastor, as well, should be expected to purchase the tools of his profession.

A strange philosophy seems to have arisen recently that says that the purchase of such tools is the responsibility of the church. But the church seems always to have a surplus of areas competing for its money. Because of budgetary limitations, items of equipment for the pastor are often low on the church's priority list. Thus the pastor plods along, grumbling as he goes. He blames the church for not supplying him the proper tools, never considering that it is his own responsibility to purchase them. In some cases, even though the particular tool will be used primarily to enhance the program of the church, the church may never have experienced its use and therefore does not know how desirable it would prove to the ministry. In such instances, the fact that the pastor purchases and uses the tool in the ministry of the church often will whet the appetite of the congregation to the extent that they understand the tool's value and are open to purchasing it in the future. The purchase price of a particular piece of equipment may be the cost the pastor must bear in order to be a model for his people.

PERSONAL COMPUTERS

One of the most remarkable discoveries of the last half of the twentieth century was the invention of the silicon chip that enabled inventors to design the micro-computer. Those tiny computers, which occupy only a small portion of a desk top, now are capable of more functions than many of their ponderous forefathers. Moreover, substantial reductions in price have made them available to a large number of people who find them indispensable in accomplishing tasks that previously were considered tedious and time-consuming.

After discovering the joys of word processing by computer, I became convinced that every seminary student should purchase a computer and printer for his use during seminary and throughout the rest of his ministry. Through the years I was plagued by poor typing ability. Erasers, correcting tape, and correction fluid were of my standard equipment. When I was a student pounding out assignments on a portable typewriter, I spent as much time correcting as typing. The resulting product always was unsightly. Then I purchased a computer. Just the luxury of typing out an entire page on a screen, making my corrections instantaneously, having the computer take care of the margins and placement of lines, and then printing out a perfect page was enough to convince me that the computer was a wise purchase. Yet the machine can do much more—and those additional functions make the machine almost indispensable to me.

For example, instead of keeping massive files of illustrations, anecdotes, and other material from books I have read, all that I need to do is to type that material into a computer under the appropriate heading, or have my secretary do so. Then the information is readily available for inclusion into anything I designate, whenever I want. Synopses of books may be classified under pertinent topic headings or under subject matter headings. When it comes time to speak or teach on that topic, I do not have to spend time hunting through the library and reading through volumes to refresh myself on the subject. The material I need is already in my computer.

Rather than place confidential matter from counseling sessions in a file folder that must go into a file drawer someone could force open, exposing sensitive data, I now file the information on a computer disk and program the disk so that only I have access to the material, even if someone breaks into the filing cabinet and steals the disk. Backup copies of the disk are stored elsewhere.

Composing sermons on a computer allows for changes anywhere along the preparation phase, even last-minute changes. Moreover, the pastor may call illustrative material from the memory of the computer and place it within a sermon manuscript without even retyping it. If the pastor's eyesight is no longer perfect, he may command the printer to use bold type and large block letters when it copies out his sermon notes or manuscript.

Under ordinary circumstances, the typing of correspondence, whether by the pastor or his secretary, is a time-consuming process. The computer simplifies the task, and, because of its capacity to merge the text of a letter with a mailing list, makes it easy to prepare personalized copies of a letter that must be sent to a number of persons.

The pastor can use a computer to set up and maintain an appointment calendar, to keep track of his personal family finances, and to catalog his books. He can buy a program that analyzes his expenses and reminds him of certain maintenance, repair and replacement needs, and programs that will check his spelling and grammar. An increasing number of Bible study aids now can be purchased in computerized form. New integrated church packages can take care of every conceivable need from attendance and financial records to the scheduling of rooms and the sending out of birthday cards.

Church budgets can now be set up on computers, changed as much as needed right up to the time they are to be distributed, and printed out in rapid fashion for use by the congregation. The computer can tell the Sunday school superintendant what material and how much of it he should order; and the music director the contents of the music library, the hymns appropriate to the pastor's sermon topic, and when they were used last. Hundreds of other functions—taking care not only of the pastor's personal needs but also of the needs of the congregation—are now available in on a relatively small micro-computer, saving hundreds of hours of tedious manpower. The number of computer applications can only be expected to increase in the future.

As with any important invention, alarmists try to raise hysteria concerning its use. I have heard Christians say, "The computer is the tool the Antichrist will use to rule the world." An analysis of history will reveal that similar comments were made regarding many important advances as they appeared on the scene. The Old Order Amish, of which my great-grandmother was one, still do not use electricity, telephone, or automobiles for similar religious reasons. In my boyhood, many people had the same type of fearful attitude toward television. The very people who expressed such intense alarm in that day, now are senior citizens who will not leave their television sets. The proliferation of hundreds of thousands of micro-computers, none of which are connected to each other in any way, should alone dispel the fear that the Antichrist will use micro-computers to take over. And, besides, if my theology is correct, I will not have to worry about it anyway, because I will be in the presence of my Lord.

All theological absurdities aside, the personal computer has become such an important and valuable tool to the pastor that presented with a choice between buying a new automobile or a computer—which now costs much less than the automobile—I would walk to work, smiling all the way because of the workload my computer was saving me.

VIDEO RECORDERS AND VIDEO DISK PLAYERS

In the middle of the twentieth century, an agreement between marketing companies standardized the size of the audio cassette and made them available by the millions at low cost. That advance, along with the development and marketing of low-cost audio cassette players, opened up the possibilities for tape ministries on a scale the church never could have imagined. At last the Scriptures were available to blind people at a price they could afford. The sermons of numerous preachers could be heard around the world. Valuable instructional material and high-quality Christian music became available in a way they had not been before. Orchestras could accompany soloists in churches by means of the humble cassette. Cassette stereo equipment was installed in millions of automobiles, enabling businessmen to listen to Scripture portions, instructional tapes, or Christian music on the way to and from work.

There is a problem with instructional cassettes, one that every user will confirm. Whereas blind people may find it possible to concentrate on tape material well enough to learn effectively by audio cassette, sighted people find that they cannot. Their minds tend to wander. Often it is extremely difficult for them to concentrate for any great length of time on what is being said. That difficulty, coupled with the fact that learning retention appears to be impaired significantly when only one of the senses is employed in the learning process, limits greatly the use of audio cassettes as an instructional tool.

With a substantial reduction in the price of video recorders, the standardization of format, and the introduction of low-cost video-disk players, the medium of video became viable as an entertainment source and an instructional tool. Because video combines both sight and sound, it offers exciting results as a teaching medium; and because it is versatile, it can utilize many other media. For example, it is easy for the camera to focus on maps, chalkboards, art models, and photographs—some of which are so small that people in a normal classroom could not see them unless they left their seats and came up close. Also, video can employ motion pictures, filmstrips, slides, and overhead transparencies as part of a presentation. While a lecturer talks about Israel the camera can be focused on pictures of the places the lecturer is describing. Because a videotape can be stopped and started at will, it can be used to impart information by means of a lecture or another means of presentation, and then to pause, allowing the viewer to think about, discuss, or write down their reactions to the material being presented. Even long lectures can be broken up in this manner catering to those who have a short attention span.

With the exception of the micro-computer, the video recorder is the most versatile and valuable tool a pastor can find. Through tapes and disks available for purchase or rental from Christian bookstores, the pastor may engage in a program of continuing education that includes as its resources some of the leading speakers, teachers, and pulpiteers in the world. A number of seminary courses are now available in this medium, so that the pastor can work at his own pace toward a seminary degree, or if he has a degree, can enhance the education he has already experienced.

The pastor can use similar material to train his people as he discovers tapes that are pertinent to their needs. For example, the seminary courses he is viewing as a part of his continuing education can be used to train people in the congregation who are elder material, but lack the necessary skills. Using video is a wonderful way to train Sunday school teachers, ushers, nursery attendants, home visitors, and future evangelists. The variety and scope of training available to the local church is now limited only by the human imagination.

If the video recorder is coupled with a camera, other exciting uses may result. Permanent records can be kept of significant family and church events. Also, when special preachers, teachers, or lecturers come to the church, their messages can be preserved—with their permission, of course—and used over and over again with various groups.

Teachers and budding preachers can see themselves in action so that they can note and correct their mistakes. The pastor's sermon can be recorded for shut-ins. Review of those tapes will give the pastor a first-hand critique of what actually took place in the pulpit the Sunday before. Missionaries on furlough can record presentations to be used in subsequent missions conferences. As young people engage in summer ministries, videotapes can be made and sent back to the congregation at home. When sister churches a great distance away are having a special anniversary or other celebration, a church can use a videotape to send them an appropriate greeting.

Even if a church has only a videotape recorder and not a video camera, it can tape important television programs to be used later to provoke class discussion. (Care should be observed, of course, to observe copyright laws scrupulously.) The potential uses of the video recorder as an instructional tool are nearly endless.

Videodisk players cannot record directly from television or by means of a camera. Their great advantages, however, are their portability and ease of use, the low costs of disks, and the little trouble it takes to store the disks in a small space. Excellent uses for the disk player include presenting Bible stories, sermons, choir cantatas, and all types of instructional material. The disk player is the natural successor to the filmstrip projector, because it is relatively inexpensive to produce material through its use and because it combines picture and sound on one disk.

Once again I am suggesting that it is advisable for a seminarian to invest in at least a videotape recorder before or while he is in seminary. The recorder may prove helpful to him during seminary as he begins to explore its uses, and most assuredly it will prove exceptionally helpful to him in the pastorate. Even if the church to which he is called has already purchased video equipment, the possibilities for his personal use alone make the expenditure a worthwhile one. If the church to which he is called does not have video equipment, he will have the joy of introducing the church to the world of instruction the medium offers.

OVERHEAD PROJECTORS

Someone has said that the average seminary professor would be totally incapacitated if he did not have an overhead projector upon which to scribble illegible notes and place unprofessional transparencies. I would hope that the situation is somewhat better than that, but most instructors have yet to use the overhead to best advantage.

In many cases, the overhead has become the successor to the blackboard. Easy to use and without the distracting squeak of chalk, the overhead projector offers the additional advantage that the instructor may face his audience when he uses it. In this visually-oriented world, many pastors find that points of a sermon are remembered much better by the congregation when he projects those points on a large screen. Sometimes the pastor can use the overhead projector as the means of including clever cartoons, illustrations, or other graphic presentations, thus giving fullness to the sermon and clarifying the points he is making. If the pastor finds himself uncomfortable in using the overhead while he preaches, he may ask someone who already knows the outline of the sermon to project the major points of the sermon as they are reached.

The overhead has many teaching applications. Besides projecting the major points of a lesson, it may be used to project pertinent newspaper or magazine clippings. (The articles must be transferred to a transparency first, however.) Also a number of curriculum companies offer a great variety of commercially-prepared transparencies that enhance lesson presentation. The overhead can be used to write down points raised in a discussion, or it can be employed in place of a flannelboard to tell stories. Transparencies of Bible characters can be made from Bible coloring books, for instance, and introduced as the story unfolds. In a business meeting, many items of interest to the congregation can be projected for the congregation to consider.

The most flagrant misuse of the overhead comes when people attempt to project material too small for the target audience to see. A rule of thumb is to test the transparency beforehand by viewing it from the last row of seats in the room to be used. If it cannot be read easily, it should not be used.

Although I cannot begin to mention all the ways an overhead may be used, suffice it to say that an overhead projector is an extremely valuable tool. However, despite its great popularity and usefulness, the pastor should not take for granted that the church calling him will have one. Or, if the church has purchased one or more, the pastor should not assume that there will be enough to go around when he needs one. Therefore, the pastor will find it a great help to buy one of his own. In large cities there are audio-visual supply houses that deal in used overhead projectors. Generally, the overheads they sell are ones turned in by school systems as they update their equipment, but many times the machines are in excellent shape and can be purchased for a reasonable price. Three things should be checked before the purchase is made: the lenses, the lamp, and the fan. If they are intact and operational, the machine should be usable. When he shops for a used overhead, a person should take along a transparency and ask the salesperson to let him try out the product before he makes his purchase.

SLIDE PROJECTOR

Thirty-five millimeter slides are marvelous tools for chronicling important events in the life of a congregation. When slides are taken in a professional manner and projected in the proper setting with the proper taste, few media are more impressive and entertaining.

Recently, at an anniversary celebration for our church, one of the members presented a series of slides that included pictures from every era in the church's history. Everyone strained to distinguish long-time members, who of course were much younger when the pictures were taken. Probably that was one of the warmest and most entertaining evenings we have spent together in a long time.

Slides can be used in many ways. They can document the lives of individual people or families. They can provide an extremely interesting historical record of the important events and people in the life of the church. A pastor who owns such equipment can document the history of his own family and that of the congregation.

Slides have a variety of uses in Christian education as well. There are commercially produced slides containing teacher-training material, extensive slides of the Holy Land that may be purchased or rented, and hymn slides to be used at special occasions such as Easter and Christmas.

Teachers often take slides of children posing in costumes enacting scenes from Bible stories. Later they record a narration to be played in conjunction with the slides to tell that particular story to the children's classmates. Children who participate in the learning process in this manner often increase their learning retention remarkably.

Still another practical use for slides is to take pictures of children in the congregation, record their voices in song, and combine the music and the pictures in a special musical presentation for their parents. Whatever the use of slides by a congregation, the medium is one in which a person can spend a great deal of money and receive poor results or can spend relatively little money and obtain excellent results. It all depends on the photographer.

Should the pastor buy his own equipment? Probably he should. Despite the presence of a number of shutterbugs in almost every congregation, seldom will the church itself own a thirty-five millimeter projector. If the pastor is not too insistent on having a projector with a great many gadgets, he can purchase a serviceable one for a very reasonable price.

FILMSTRIP PROJECTORS

Despite my desire to see filmstrip projectors replaced by other media, I do not think that will happen overnight. Unless a sophisticated and relatively expensive filmstrip projector is purchased that combines picture and sound, the operator generally has to set up and coordinate two pieces of equipment, making the medium cumbersome to use. However, filmstrips offer such a wide range of instructional material that they still are valuable instructional tool for the church. They are relatively inexpensive to purchase and still cheaper to rent. There are a number of rental sources, including seminary libraries, that allow churches to use filmstrips they do not wish to purchase.

If a pastor goes to a church that does not own a filmstrip projector and will not agree to purchase one, I believe the pastor himself would be wise to purchase a simple, low-cost projector, just to give the church an idea of the resources available through the medium.

By now, the reader probably is groaning, "This man wants to spend me broke." It is true that together all of the items I have mentioned represent a considerable outlay of money. However, for many of the items, the expenditure need be made only once. All of the machines I have mentioned are durable. By the time they wear out, it is likely the pastor will be in a church large enough either to have purchased such equipment already or to have a budget large enough to do so. Again, the question may be raised: "Does the pastor really need all of these things? Could he get along only using books?" Absolutely. But why should he when such a great many resources are available that would make his ministry so much more effective? Were my dentist brother-in-law to ignore technological developments in his field and restrict his work to the use of primitive hand tools, I would question his judgment—and seek another dentist. Just as we would expect a dentist, physician, carpenter, or plumber to purchase and use the best tools available to his trade, should we not expect the person practicing the most important profession on earth to do the same?

Questions for Discussion

1. Discuss what importance books have in the life and ministry of a pastor. What books have you read recently that have influenced you or have had relevance to your work as a pastor?

2. List at least five ways each of the following tools of the pastorate can be used effectively: micro-computer; video recorder; overhead projector; slide projector; filmstrip projector.

3. Suppose someone said, "The only thing I need is my Bible; that was good enough for the apostle Paul, and it's good enough for me!" How would you defend your use of modern tools of the trade in the light of such a statement?

Helpful Resources

Anderson, John W. *The IBMPCXT Integrated Management System for Local Churches.* Chicago: Computers for Churches, 1982.

Barber, Cyril J. *The Minister's Library.* Vol. 1. Rev. ed. Chicago: Moody, 1985.

———. *The Minister's Library.* Vol. 2, Grand Rapids: Baker, 1983.

Bedell, Kenneth B. *Using Personal Computers in the Church.* Valley Forge, Pa.: Judson, 1982.

Branson, Mark Lau. *The Reader's Guide to the Best Evangelical Books.* San Francisco: Harper & Row, 1982.

Davis, Mike. *Computers and the Church.* Champaign, Ill.: Stipes Publishing, 1982.

Getz, Gene A. *Audio-Visual Media in Christian Education.* Chicago: Moody, 1972.

Merchant, Harish D., ed. *Encounter with Books: A Guide to Christian Reading.* Downers Grove, Ill.: InterVarsity Press, 1970.

4

Ordination

Currently there is a healthy recognition among many people that the age-old division of clergy and laity is an artificial one generated and perpetuated by man and not by God. As a result, the pastoral office, which for centuries remained on a pedestal, once again has been brought down to a more realistic place of leadership and servanthood among the people.

Unfortunately, however, human beings have the tendency to counter an extreme not by taking a moderate, middle-of-the-road position but by swinging to a position at the other end of the spectrum. Such a reaction occurred with regard to the pastorate. In order to correct the perceived abuses in the old, divided clergy-laity model, many modern pastors and churches went so far to the other extreme that they made the position of pastor almost indistinguishable from other ones.

In matters of dress, for example, many pastors discarded the business suit for the more casual look of some of their parishioners. They failed to remember that their position in the community is regarded as a profession and that people in general expect professionals to act and dress with a certain degree of decorum and dignity. I would not choose to be represented in court by an attorney who wore blue jeans and a sweatshirt there. In such attire, he would have difficulty getting a favorable hearing for me, either from a judge or a jury. They would not take him seriously. Likewise, I would not want to be led by a pastor who, in trying to construct a common bond

between himself and his people, adopted dress and demeanor designed to convince people how ordinary he was. Such a practice
would erode my confidence in him as a professional, and it would
limit the service I would allow him to perform for me. If I were in
the hospital, for instance, I would not want to be embarrassed by the
appearance or demeanor of a pastor who was trying to prove his
commonality.

A Rationale for Ordination

One of the attempts at commonality observed in many pastors
recently has been the unwillingness of some of them to be ordained.
Such men believe that the ceremony places a pastor in a class of
persons separate from the laity and for that reason should be abandoned by the church. By refusing to be ordained, they neglect a
number of compelling facts. First, the Bible indicates clearly that in
the early church there was a specific process whereby leaders were
chosen and set aside for service. Titus 1:5 is only one of many
references pointing to the idea of the ordaining process. Although it
is unclear today exactly what ordination in those days involved, it is
fairly certain that when the church recognized that a particular individual had certain necessary qualifications, some type of public ceremony was held to acknowledge the special role in the church that
individual would be taking. The ceremony that took place probably
involved the laying on of hands. The people who were thus set aside
were recognized as being qualified to engage in a specialized ministry in behalf of the church. If servants of God capable of such specialized ministries were so delineated in that culture, is it not in
order for us to engage in a similar process appropriate to our culture?
The biblical examples in themselves would seem to say so.

Second, the fact that an examination by a person's peers precedes
the actual act of ordination is of great value to the ordaining church
and to the ordinand. While not negating the authority of the local
church to ordain, the ordination council of peers demonstrates the
need of the local church for interdependence with sister churches.
Thus, the ordained is not being set aside for special service simply
because he is charming or has charismatic ability to sway his own
people. Instead, he is examined as objectively as possible by selected
individuals who have educational backgrounds similar to his.

When a person passes such an examination, it signifies that his
peers agree with the ordaining church. As a result, his ministry gains
a credibility on a wider basis than the local church. That credibility
may in turn result in an even greater admiration for his ministry by

the church he serves. If their pastor can conduct himself in an exemplary fashion before others in the pastoral ministry, he must be competent and knowledgeable indeed.

Without ordination, it is merely the pastor's opinion or the opinion of the pastor and his congregation that he is fit for an equipping ministry in the church. What would happen if his congregation were to change its mind about him? At that point credibility would be hard to obtain. With ordination, the wider Christian community adds its voice. The pastor does not have to depend on the whims of a single congregation. He is recognized by other churches, also.

Third, just as the secular community expects a lawyer to pass a bar exam and a physician a medical exam, so it expects that persons engaged in professional ministerial services pass some type of qualifying exam. In some states a person must be ordained in order to perform marriages. In other places, funeral directors will not call upon a person to conduct a funeral unless he is an ordained minister. In many towns, those who are ordained have greater access to hospitals than those who are not ordained. Last, but not least, certain tax benefits accrue to those who are ordained. It is as inappropriate for a pastor to refuse ordination as it is for a graduate of medical school to refuse to take his medical exams and obtain a license.

Fourth, although a pastor always needs to remember that as a person he is no different from anyone else in his congregation, the office he holds is unique and important, and it needs to be set apart. Therefore, whether he likes it or not, by virtue of the fact that he occupies the pastoral office, he is due certain honor, according to the Scriptures (1 Tim. 5:17). Thus it is appropriate to distinguish the office, if nothing else, through such a procedure as ordination.

Once the choice for ordination has been made, what are the mechanics of the process? For much of the material presented here on the subject, I am indebted to Pastor Ross Laidlaw, who has spent much time on ordination councils and in helping to establish procedures for such councils.

Licensing

As a means of considering ordination, it will be helpful to look at an intermediate procedure called *licensing*. Licensing usually is the action of a single congregation and does not require the rigorous examination that is part of ordination, nor does it require a special ceremony. In licensing, the church recognizes that a person has specific ministerial capabilities, and, in effect, it gives formal approval of that person's carrying out certain specified ministerial functions.

Often licensing is used when a person is called to a pastorate while he is still engaged in his theological training. Though he is capable of carrying on many of the functions of the pastorate, he may not be ready yet to face the rigors of an extensive theological examination by other pastors. In other instances, staff members may be called to a church for specific ministries, though perhaps their training has been limited. Because the laws of many states require that a person be either licensed or ordained to perform marriages, licensure may be a desirable procedure for the staff member and for the church he serves. There are other benefits to licensing, such as tax relief.

Although licensing does not hold the same status as ordination, it may be a helpful stop-gap measure. It gives the person who has been licensed a degree of stature in his ministry, for it represents his church's public recognition of his abilities. May I stress, however, that licensing is not a proper substitute for ordination. If the licensed person continues on in an equipping ministry in the church, he should seek ordination as soon as it is practical.

Prerequisites for Ordination

Generally, the person seeking ordination should have completed theological education appropriate to the ministry to which he is called. For some equipping ministries, it will be necessary for him to have completed both college and seminary. For others, he will need a Bible college degree. For still others, he will not need training in a Bible college or seminary. All that will be necessary of him will be to be a person of mature Christian stature who has a rich background in the Word and who has demonstrated his proficiency in pastoral skills.

A businessman may choose to retire early in order to serve the church. For many years he has been a keen Bible scholar and thus is well-versed in the Word. Through the years, pastors have discipled him in the essential skills of the ministry. There is a church-planting opportunity, and, because he invested wisely when he was employed, he and his wife could get along on minimum additional support. In view of his age, his background, and his vocational goals, it would be unrealistic to expect him to complete seminary. Instead he might be expected to pursue a limited program offered through videotape by a nearby seminary. He would take courses that would round out his training and expose him to areas in which he previously considered himself weak. If at the conclusion of that limited, specialized, training he believes he is ready to face the tasks of an equipping ministry, he should come before an ordination council to be examined in preparation for his being set apart in a special way for the ministry to which God has called him. Even though he may not have completed Bible college or seminary, the combination of a godly walk, diligence in the Word, discipling by his pastors, and specialized training may make him a knowledgeable and well-prepared candidate for ordination.

In addition to a person's having completed an educational program appropriate to his calling, he should have, in most cases, at least a year or two of experience in some form of active ministry. Such experience will help him ascertain whether or not the ministry is something for which he is really fit, something to which he feels he can devote many years of service.

An initial period of ministry will be allowed his congregation to determine whether or not they feel he is suitable for the ministry on a long-term basis. Having viewed his performance for at least a year, they will probably be able to decide fairly objectively if they should ordain him at once, ask him to wait a while longer, or suggest to him that he is not suited for the ministry and should explore some other vocation.

The person seeking ordination may find that the period of service prior to ordination helps him sort out his own thoughts in regard to his ability to sustain a long and successful ministry. Also it will give him the opportunity to observe how well his wife fares in a ministerial setting. Sometimes people have fantasies concerning what the ministry is like, carry those fantasies throughout college and seminary, and then engage in the active ministry only to find that the pastoral ministry is nothing like they imagined. As they look objectively at the tasks in which they are engaged in the actual ministry, they find that they cannot see any observable fruit, nor can they say that they have enjoyed what they have been doing. It is far better for them to find that out before the rigors of ordination, when they can more gracefully withdraw from the ministry, then afterwards, when they are more firmly committed.

In addition to the prerequisites I have noted, the overwhelmingly important requirements are those character requisites specified for Christian leaders in the epistles to Timothy and Titus. Before even considering ordination, a person should examine those scriptural mandates carefully. If the verses do not describe him, he should not seek ordination.

Preparing for Ordination

INDIVIDUAL PREPARATION

For at least a month before an ordination council is held the candidate should immerse himself in study of the Bible, theology, and church polity. He will be required to write a comprehensive paper to be shared with members of the ordination council. The paper should include a thorough statement of his theological views and should articulate clearly his own philosophy of ministry. Even though the paper is to reflect accurately the position of its author, it is wise for him to steer away from religious hobby horses, potential red flag areas, or statements that are included for shock value. Although the ordinand should be aware that everyone on his council may not agree with him in every point of his theological statement, he should avoid deliberately antagonizing such people with nuances of doctrine that they may consider bizarre or avant-garde.

Each ordination examination will differ markedly. However, the person being examined will be wise to prepare himself to answer questions in these areas:

A. Church History
   1. Pentecost and the beginnings of the church
   2. Major councils—Trent, Nicea, and so on
   3. The Reformation
   4. The formation of major denominations
   5. Recent historical developments
B. Denominational History
   1. Where did the particular group or denomination he is a part of originate?
   2. What has characterized its development?
   3. In what ways is it distinctive?
   4. What is its history and position in regard to missions?
C. Bible
   1. Inspiration and revelation
   2. Books of the Bible
   3. Structure of the Bible
   4. Bible writers
   5. Canonicity
   6. Biblical use; the candidate should be able to locate references that outline
     a. The plan of salvation
     b. Answers to controversial theological issues
     c. Answers to practical problems faced today by the church and by individuals
D. God
   1. Nature
   2. Image
   3. Predestination—election

   4. Creation
   5. Trinity; the candidate should be ready to identify the charac-
      teristics and mission of each Person
E. Satan and angels
   1. Origin of sin
   2. Powers and principalities
F. Man
   1. Original creation
   2. Fall
   3. Depravity
   4. Transmission of sin
   5. Conscious punishment
   6. Conscious bliss
G. Redemption
   1. Substitutionary atonement
   2. Effect of the blood of Jesus
   3. Terms: justification, propitiation, regeneration, and so on
H. Sanctification
I. Glorification
J. Eschatology
K. The Church
   1. Nature
   2. Government
   3. Leaders
   4. Congregational authority
   5. Ordinances
L. Procedural Matters
   1. How and whom to baptize and why
   2. Grounds for receiving members
   3. Whom to marry
   4. How to evangelize
   5. Devotional life
   6. Ethics
   7. Deportment toward the opposite sex
   8. How to work with church leaders
M. Personal Matters
   1. When has the candidate last shared the gospel?
   2. Is his wife supportive?
   3. How easily does he lose his temper?
   4. What will he do if the council votes not to ordain him?

   In addition to book preparation, the ordinand should take steps
that will allow him to be rested, confident, and poised when the

examination takes place. The suggestions that follow are from Pastor Ross Laidlaw. Laidlaw says that a candidate for ordination should

1. Have someone knowledgeable quiz him a few days before the council so that he gets the feel of being under the gun for the two or three hours the ordination examination will take.

2. Get proper rest for several days before the council meets.

3. Eat properly the day before and on the day of the council. He should stay away from sugar.

4. Come before the council in humility and avoid a smart-aleck attitude.

5. Be sure he understands the questions put to him. He should ask for further clarification if a question is not clear. It is possible, even, that in the act of rephrasing the question, the interrogator may actually give him the answer.

6. Answer only what he is asked. If one word is sufficient, he should give it.

7. Be prepared, especially in the first sections of his paper. Generally the heaviest questioning will occur there.

8. Use his Bible frequently.

9. Keep cool, rather than becoming angry or rattled.

10. Stay away from novel interpretations or positions.

11. Opt for practical and simple answers rather than detailed philosophical or technical answers, unless the latter are called for.

12. Be aware that all members of the council may not agree with his position but will want to assure themselves that he is able to defend it.

13. Admit when he does not know the answer. A simple "I don't know" is appropriate and acceptable. There may be persons on the council itself who would have to answer the question in the same way.

PREPARATIONS TO BE MADE BY THE ORDAINING CHURCH

Many candidates for ordination will discover that an ordination has not been held in their church for many years, and that, as a result, the leadership of the church will look to them for instruction in how an ordination should be conducted. If the ordaining church is a member of a fellowship of churches, the fellowship may have a standing committee that advises candidates and churches in such matters. It is advisable for the candidate to meet first with the chairman of the committee and follow his instructions. His advice will be helpful for the church in its preparations. Also, often it will give the candidate valuable insight into the quirks peculiar to his denomination and into ways he can avoid pitfalls when he faces the council. Whether or not there is a denominational advisory committee, the pastor who is helping the church make preparations for his ordination will find it necessary to do the following:

1. Obtain the approval of the church leadership and of the congregation to call an ordination council.
2. Set dates for the meeting of the ordination council, and for the ordination itself, in the event the council approves the candidate.
3. Issue invitations to prospective participants from sister churches. Usually each of those churches is invited to send its pastor and two other representatives. If the church is a member of a fellowship of churches, officials of that fellowship should be invited also. In addition, if there is a Bible college or seminary nearby, especially one affiliated with the same denomination as the ordaining church, often the school is invited to send a representative.
4. Coordinate arrangements with the appropriate committee of the host church for setting up a room where the examination may take place, providing meals and refreshments for council members and guests, and arranging for overnight housing for out-of-town guests, if that is needed.
5. Settle upon an appropriate method of questioning. One method I find very successful is for the ordaining church to select three or more interrogators, each representing a major area such as systematic theology, Bible knowledge, or pastoral theology. Each interrogator is given a specified period of time to examine the candidate publicly. After he has done so, questions from the floor are in order. However, they must be addressed to the candidate through the interrogator. The question must be pertinent to the particular area of questioning the interrogator has been pursuing. If the interrogator feels the question is unfair or irrelevant, he may disallow it. Interrogators used for this purpose can be experienced pastors or college or seminary professors. Upon the recommendation of the candidate, the church leadership should arrange for the services of those people, if it is decided that this is the procedure the church will follow in the ordination examination.
6. Arrange to have hosts present when the delegates arrive to greet them, to equip them with name tags, and to give them writing materials and extra copies of the candidate's doctrinal statement. Tasty refreshments also are welcome to weary travelers, and usually will pick up their spirits and improve their mood. It will create an open and objective atmosphere for the questioning that will take place.

Suggested Order of Procedure for an Ordination Council

At the scheduled time, the prospective council members, the guests, and the candidate and his family should assemble in the appointed room. The elements of the procedure are listed below.

1. Call to order by the temporary moderator, usually the chairman of the denominational ordination committee or a senior pastor from a nearby church
2. Prayer
3. Roll call of churches
4. Recognition of any guests present
5. Reading of official action of the church
6. Motion to form council
7. Election of moderator
8. Election of clerk
9. Introduction of candidate
10. Prayer for candidate
11. Sermon by the candidate; or highlights of his doctrinal statement
12. Examination of the candidate
13. Motion to close the question period
14. Dismissal of the candidate and all guests
15. Decision of the council
16. Decision of the council presented to the candidate
17. Motion to dissolve the council
18. Prayer of dismissal

Instructions for the Clerk of an Ordination Council

Because ordination is an extremely important step, it is vital to keep accurate records of the decisions made by an ordination council. Probably the most important person present at such an event, next to the candidate himself, is the person chosen as clerk. The person elected clerk should

1. Keep a record of all the proceedings of the council.
2. Attach the list of delegates from the sign-up sheet.
3. Attach a copy of the official action of the church. (If a written copy is not available, he should write out the paragraph that is read by the moderator.)
4. Prepare a typed copy of his final minutes. It will not be necessary for the clerk to note the questions and answers in the minutes.

Only the flow of activities and the motions need be included. He should make four copies of those minutes and any relevant attachments. (See items 1-3 immediately above.)

5. Mail one copy of the formal record to the candidate, one copy to the ordaining church, and additional copies to denominational offices as appropriate.

6. Keep one copy of the formal record in his own file.

Examination for Ordination

The most important segment of the occasion will be the examination of the candidate. Usually the procedure is similar to the following:

1. The candidate gives a personal testimony that includes an account of his conversion and his walk with the Lord.

2. The candidate relates to the council what he believes constitutes a "call" to the ministry and why he feels he is called.

3. The candidate is questioned concerning his doctrinal position, his philosophy of ministry, and any other theological or practical questions the council feels are important. If major interrogators are not utilized, the moderator of the council has the privilege of disallowing questions he considers inappropriate or not pertinent.

Following the adjournment of the council, depending on the time of day and the distance the council members must travel, it is appropriate for the church to provide refreshments or an entire meal for delegates and guests. Because the church has invited the guests to perform a service in its behalf, meals and overnight accommodations are provided free of charge. If the candidate has been successful, the leadership of the host church should announce the time for the ordination service itself and should extend to the council members an invitation to attend.

The ordination service should be planned at a time convenient to the greatest number of people in the host congregation. In addition, consideration should be given to selecting a time that is convenient for guest participants. The service should be a joyous, festive occasion of celebration for the ordaining church, the ordinand, and his family. It is the time to make use of the finest musical resources of the congregation, to sing stirring congregational hymns, and to make the ordinand and his family feel like very important people. It is the ordinand's day, and he, not the participating guests, should be kept in the spotlight.

Elements Contained in a Typical Service of Ordination

Besides the use of music, to which I already have alluded, the
ordination service often will contain the following elements:

Report of the ordination council
Scripture
Ordination sermon
Charge to the church
Charge to the candidate
Ordination prayer
Welcome to the ministry
Presentation of certificate
Benediction by the newly-ordained minister

Typically the candidate for ordination selects the preacher for the
ordination sermon.

All ordained ministers present and the officers of the ordaining
church lay hands on the candidate as he kneels for the ordination
prayer.

Following the benediction it is appropriate for the chief lay leader
of the church to escort the newly-ordained minister and his family to
a gala reception in the social hall. This is the proper time for lace
tablecloths and silver service, even if they have to be rented. The
menu should include fancy sandwiches and extravagant goodies, ca-
tered, if necessary. The occasion is one that demands elegance. After
all, it happens only once in a person's life.

At this point, I believe that it is proper to add a personal note. In
the chapter concerning the pastor's tools, I referred to the fact that
the church that ordained me was thoughtful and generous enough to
give a substantial offering so that I could add a significant number of
volumes to my library. Even though I did not pastor that church but
instead went on from there to military service, I shall never forget
their generosity, nor shall I ever cease to have a warm spot in my
heart for that congregation. Somehow, a gesture such as that seems
right for this special occasion. Perhaps the newly-ordained minister
has enough books but may need one of the other valuable tools of
the ministry named in that chapter. How does the ordained make
that need known? First, when he is considering ordination and the
chairman of his church asks him how an ordination takes place, the
pastor gives him a copy of this book. By the time the chairman reads
this far, he will know that it is appropriate and heartwarming for the
church to give its pastor a special gift on the occasion of his ordina-

tion. Now all that is left is for the chairman—who has already read this chapter—to ask the pastor what he needs!

Questions for Discussion

1. What importance do you see in having an ordained clergy? Develop a theological stance concerning the ordination of clergy, supporting your view from the Scriptures.

2. In what sense does ordination give credibility to a pastor's ministry?

3. Does ordination provide the Christian community with an opportunity to scrutinize candidates for ministry so as to eliminate candidates who are truly unqualified? What improvements would you suggest in the arrangement followed in your community or denomination?

4. What is licensing? What value does it have? How is it different from ordination?

5. What do you believe should be the minimum requirements for ordination into Christian ministry? Do you think that exceptions should be made to this minimum standard? What importance does Bible college or seminary training have in equipping the candidate for ordination and ministry?

6. What preparations should a candidate for ordination make just prior to his ordination council?

7. How may the local church assist in making the ordination council a successful one?

Helpful Resources

Lewis, Gordon R. *Decide for Yourself: A Theological Workbook.* Downers Grove, Ill.: InterVarsity, 1977.

Osborn, Ronald E. "Ordination: Appointment to Public Ministry." In *In Christ's Place: Christian Ministry in Today's World.* St. Louis, Mo.: Bethany, 1967.

5

The Pastor's Wife

Enshrouded in the mists of time is the legend of Mrs. Cranmer, wife of the first Archbishop of Canturbury. Henry the Eighth had succeeded in breaking the iron rule of Rome, and the Church of England, at last, was an entity in itself. The Archbishop set a brave precedent in marrying. However, the populace was not yet ready for such scandalous behavior. As a result, Mrs. Cranmer spent most of her married life in hiding. It is said that when the Archbishop desired that his wife travel with him, she was forced to journey in a wooden box with ventilating holes in it. In light of such a precedent, the modern, harried pastor's wife would agree that pastor's wives have indeed come a long way.

The Role of the Pastor's Wife

EXPECTATIONS DIFFER

Just what is the expected role of the pastor's wife? To answer the question, we must ask an additional question: "Whose expectations are we considering?" Surely the expectations differ from congregation to congregation, and within each church. Moreover, expectations differ markedly even among the women bearing the honored title. There are those who take the position seriously, feeling that they, as much as their husbands, are hired to do a job. To them, the expression *pastor's wife* is the title of their position, and they have a clear idea of the requirements and details of the position. One of these "wonder women" stands out prominently in my memory. This dear saint served as the church secretary, handling all of the pastor's correspondence and typing his sermons. In addition, she was the church janitor, the pianist, and the organist. She held Sunday school in her home, and she supervised the church nursery. Because her husband had exaggerated ideas of what her image should be, her home was continually spotless, her children were quiet and well mannered, and, regardless of the circumstances, she was always neatly attired in a dress, lest anyone making a surprise visit to the pastor's home think poorly of her. At the time I knew her, she was bearing up magnificently. I have heard since, however, that her son became a drug addict, and that she and her husband ran away from the pastoral ministry and joined a cultic commune in Florida where neither of them has any ministerial responsibilities.

Contrast that with another picture. Fresh out of seminary, a gifted friend of mine married a "sweet young thing" many years his junior. Although she had a modest educational background, this pastor's wife was convinced that she was a wise and liberated woman who would make her mark on the world. It was agreeable to her that her husband should become a pastor, but members of the congregation were to know in no uncertain terms that she was her own person: the church had hired only her husband, not her. My friend was called to a church in a staunch conservative town on the Canadian prairies. Our heroine was consistent with her threats and made her position known loudly and clearly. Moreover, she encouraged her husband also to "shake up the saints." The saints were properly shaken one day when their new pastor arrived at a funeral he was to conduct wearing blue denim jeans and a red flannel shirt, strumming his guitar, and singing a contemporary song.

Probably the wife's strongest display of individuality, came when she sunbathed on the front lawn of the parsonage, which was located on a busy street. Usually she wore nothing but a brief bikini. To be sure, her show of individuality became the talk of the town. Undoubtedly she had other assets besides her physical charms, but the congregation had a hard time discovering those because she rarely attended services, refused any job within the church, and chose her circle of friends from outside its membership.

Despite her husband's considerable gifts and abilities, his tenure at the church was extremely short. After he and his wife left the area, the two of them continued to exhibit marks of immaturity. Soon they could not get along with each other, and eventually they were divorced. An exceedingly gifted young man became a casualty to the ministry, never again utilizing in the church the combination of gifts and training God had provided for him.

In the first example, the woman viewed herself in an official position: pastor's wife. In the second, our svelte young thing saw herself merely as the wife of a man who just happened to choose the pastorate for his vocation. In the first case, there were elaborate role expectations. In the second, there were none. The pastor's wife viewed herself no differently than she would have had she married a plumber, a factory worker, or a businessman.

Surely there must be a happy medium between these two extremes. Certainly God does not expect any of his children to be doormats, especially one who marries a pastor. The pastor's wife who feels she is in danger of becoming a doormat needs to take action to make sure she does not become one. On the other hand, although God expects each of his children to be his or her own person, a pastor's wife who flaunts self-constructed idiosyncracies is not asserting her personhood. She is merely dramatizing her immaturity.

THE BIBLE STRESSES CHARACTER

What is a proper biblical role for a pastor's wife? The evidence is sketchy and focuses primarily upon the character of the person rather than her actions. In 1 Timothy 3:11, for instance, the wife of a deacon is expected to be "dignified," not a malicious gossip, but "temperate, faithful in all things." Undoubtedly those attributes should apply to the wife of an overseer as well. In addition, because 1 Timothy 3:4 instructs an overseer to manage his household well, and because his wife is part of that household, it is logical to conclude that she should be manageable. Moreover, because Titus 1:8 indicates that an overseer should be hospitable, it is logical as well, to expect that his wife should be willing to join him in extending hospitality. In addition, she should exhibit the other attributes the Bible requires of every godly Christian woman and wife, including the scriptural demand that both she and her husband be submissive to one another, each in his uique way, as is outlined in God's Word.

When we add to this list the fact that the desired behavior of all the saints—both male and female—is "for the work of service" (or ministry), according to Ephesians 4:12, it is clear that a pastor's wife cannot view her role in the church as that of a passive bystander. Moreover, whether she likes it or not, she and her children are required to be models of what a Christian family should be. Surely if a pastor is enjoined to keep "his children under control with all dignity" (1 Tim. 3:4), his wife should be expected to join him in that effort.

What can we conclude from the scriptural evidence? I believe that the picture the Scripture paints of a pastor's wife is of a mature, godly, Christian woman who performs a distinctive ministry in the church and who does her best to act as a model Christian wife and mother. They should be women of godliness, maturity, and wisdom that others in a congregation will want to emulate. Is it then not reasonable and scriptural to conclude that if a man has a wife who does not meet those qualifications, he should remain out of the pastoral ministry until she does? I think that such an assumption is valid and scriptural.

PRACTICAL CONCERNS

Besides the biblical considerations we have explored, there are some practical concerns also. Because the pastorate is so demanding, a pastor's wife must be in sympathy with her husband's selection of the ministry as his life career. If he is to perform his ministry with any degree of assurance, he needs to know that he has her full support. Should there be a significant degree of hesitancy on her part, it might be wise for him not to accept a pastoral call. The issue is one the couple should settle before he goes to seminary, if at all possible. If they cannot agree, he should consider delaying his seminary entrance until they do. If they marry while he is in seminary, they should discuss the matter carefully before the wedding to ascertain that they are of one mind. If they are not, and he is convinced that God has called him to the pastoral ministry, they should seek counsel and, if necessary, delay their wedding plans until their differences have been worked out.

If those differences persist, it may be advisable for the couple to abandon their plans for marriage, and each seek another partner with whom he can agree. For a couple to live in a continuous state of tension over the pastorate, or worse yet, to enter constantly into verbal battles concerning their views, will be devastating to their relationship and debilitating to the pastor's ministry. A pastor who consumes his energy in that way cannot invest himself wholeheartedly in the work of the ministry.

Whether we like to admit it or not, when a church calls a pastor, it does not merely hire one person. It calls a team. Even if the wife works far in the background and is not especially visible in the kind ministry she performs, her sound and firm backing of the pastoral office is necessary if the pastorate of her husband is to flourish.

Churches that are considering the calling of a person to their pastorate are wise to become well acquainted with his wife. They should spend a good deal of time questioning her kindly but intensely as to how favorably she views her husband's ministry. There are rare cases where a man can be successful in the pastorate without his wife's encouragement and support. Those cases however, are the exception rather than the rule.

In addition to being sympathetic to her husband's role, the pastor's wife should be committed to serving the Lord in and through the church. That does not mean, however, that she needs to consider herself a "Jill of all trades" or a public personality. If she has platform abilities, it is important for her to exercise those abilities in a way that complements her husband's ministry rather than upstages him. She may be a quiet person whose gifts are not public ones. Rather than seeking a role in the spotlight, she may elect to teach the toddlers or work in the nursery. Such ministries may in the long run prove more valuable to the kingdom of God than the more public ones. The most important thing is that she attempt to discover and develop the gifts God has given to her as a Christian woman and to blossom and flower within those areas. It is the obligation of her husband to help her do so.

I happen to be blessed with a multi-talented wife. Through the years of our pastorates, I have done my best to help her bloom in whatever area she was concentrating upon at that particular time. As she has exercised and developed her teaching, speaking, musical, and administrative gifts, we have discovered a pattern that has worked well for us. Although she has served in a variety of appointed ministries, she has tried to steer clear of any elective office, leaving room for the other women of the church to serve as officers of church organizations and members of church boards.

Regardless of her choices of ministry, the pastor's wife should remind herself that her effort is part of an overall church program and that she is working as part of a team, not only with her husband but also with the total membership of the congregation. There may be times when it is difficult for her to sit on the sidelines and let another woman take the spotlight, especially if the pastor's wife is more competent. But such an experience will not be entirely negative. It will develop her character, and it will assure others of her generous spirit. As she encourages competent people in the congregation to develop their gifts and serve in the more visible church ministries she may miss out on some of the acclaim she might otherwise have had, but she will be the recipient of the undying gratitude of those whom she encourages to minister.

There may be times when there are jobs to do that she does not find particularly appealing. If no one else is willing to do them, the pastor's wife may choose to serve as a model to others by demonstrating her willingness to take on the jobs. She can encourage others to join with her in accomplishing a needed if not especially glamorous service. She does not need to feel forever compelled to do that job, however. After she has served for a reasonable period of time in the position, if her efforts are needed elsewhere, she should feel free to back out of the unappealing job graciously, leaving the position vacant if necessary. She will have demonstrated her willingness to serve where no one else would serve, and she will have made whatever point was needed by the members of the congregation.

Although it is reasonable for a pastor's wife to expect to take on an undesirable task from time to time, she should not feel constrained to engage in a public ministry for which she is not equipped. As a pastor-husband gains a certain degree of prestige, for instance, many people expect that his wife will naturally be able to rise to the role of an engaging public speaker. In reality, she may be very shy and may consider public speaking the last thing she would ever desire to do. When pressure is put upon her to be what she is not or to minister where she is not gifted, she should learn to decline as graciously as possible. When pressures persist, she will need to learn to say in a gracious but firm tone, "I'm sorry but I must say no to that opportunity." Because she will have explained her position already on taking such appointments, there will be no need for further comment or apology.

A MODEL FOR OTHERS

So far we have looked at the easier tasks of a pastor's wife. The real challenge comes at home as she seeks to be a helpful, supportive wife to her husband and a godly model for her children. In this chapter I will not begin to list the number of Scripture passages that apply to this phase of her life. Every biblical norm that describes the godly woman, wife, and mother applies here. Moreover, because the pastor's wife finds herself in a position that often demands much public visibility, she should be challenged to strive for consistency in godly actions, because whether she likes it or not she will be called upon constantly to serve as a positive model for others. That modeling will include her faithfulness in attending church services. She must make it an item of high priority to attend Sunday morning and evening functions, the midweek service, if there is one, and, as much as possible, all important women's events and major social occasions.

Such expectations are not unrealistic, because many other women of the congregation will be expected to be equally faithful in attending the events. Of course, there will be times when the pastor's wife is ill or worn out and needs the rest she can get only by staying at home. Most people in the congregation will understand that and will expect her occasional absence from church events. The important thing is that her absence should be the exception and not the rule. Occasionally the pastor's wife will have to miss a number of church events because one of her children is ill. During such an illness, it would be appropriate for the pastor to rearrange his schedule so that he can stay with the sick child, releasing his wife from her role as a nurse and allowing her to attend functions that are meaningful to her.

A WIFE AND HELPER TO HER HUSBAND

Probably the most important role of the pastor's wife is that of wife and helper to her husband. Her participation in that role may take many forms. If she or her husband finds it desirable or necessary for her to be employed outside the home, for instance, her support role in behalf of her husband may vary markedly from that of the wife who spends her hours maintaining a household and caring for children at home. The pastor whose wife is employed outside the home should expect to make it a priority to schedule regular periods each week when he assists his wife in household chores and takes his turn doing the marketing. If there are a number of preschool children at home, whether or not his wife is employed, the pastor should schedule regular periods each week when he takes over babysitting responsibilities, thus freeing time for his wife to spend in ways she finds fulfilling. A smart pastor's wife will insist on his doing so, not only for the sake of her own continued sanity but also for the benefit of her husband, who needs to learn lessons about the ways of children that can be gained only through intense personal involvement with them.

Her Relationship to Her Husband

KEEPING HERSELF ATTRACTIVE AND DESIRABLE

The special relationship of the pastor's wife to her husband is an exceedingly important one. There are few positions placing as many demands on and as much pressure upon the professional as the pastorate. Moreover, there are few vocations presenting so many opportunities for marital infidelity as the pastorate. Often the pastor is not on a fixed schedule. He does not punch a time clock, nor is he responsible to anyone but himself for most of his schedule. Women often call upon him for counsel. Sometimes they do so in an attempt to gain attention they feel is lacking from their husbands. Because a pastor is an important figure, at times women fantasize about having a more intimate relationship with this person who is so kind, understanding, and approachable. Throughout the history of the pastorate, the professional road has been strewn with women who looked at the pastor as a viable and desirable conquest. In turn, many pastors who have felt sorry for themselves because of their demanding schedules, the pressures of home, and the temptations afforded by their office, have succumbed to sexual temptations. Sometimes those pastors have been men who were exceedingly strong in every other aspect of the ministry. Frequently they have been extremely gifted men. Yet they have allowed themselves, their ministries, and their families to be destroyed through their immoral behavior. Through that means, Satan has been effective in forcing out of the ministry men who otherwise would have been considered immovable.

There are several ways in which a pastor's wife can make sure that that does not happen to her husband. First, she has an obligation not only to her husband but to herself as well to keep herself as attractive in appearance as possible. She may not have the native good looks of a beauty queen, but through good grooming, diet control, appropriate choice of clothing, proper hair care, and the judicious use of makeup, she can make homecoming something to which the pastor looks forward. Twenty minutes of effort often is all that is necessary. She owes it to herself, to her husband, and to their marriage to do so.

Second, she needs to do everything possible to keep herself attractive inwardly. Even though she may not have the time or the inclination to read extensively, fine instructional radio programs, cassette tapes, magazines, and newspapers are rich sources for spiritual and intellectual stimulation. Scripture tapes especially may prove beneficial in helping her grow as a model Christian woman. People who are as well educated and are as widely exposed to current events as are pastors need wives who are able to converse on subjects other than baby sniffles and neighborhood gossip.

Third, she needs to cultivate the art of becoming the best lover her husband could ever want. As she becomes sensitive to his emotional needs and, if necessary, teaches him how to be responsive to hers, he will find no need ever to stray unless he has serious psychological problems for which he should seek counsel.

Fourth, the wise pastor's wife is one who is too smart to unload on her husband the frustrations that have been a part of her busy day. She learns to present to her husband solutions to problems where she can, employing them on her own whenever possible, and asking her husband's help in working out others only when such help is needed. That does not mean that she cannot give vent to her frustrations, seek her husband's emotional support, or draw from his experience in finding answers to problems. It does mean that she learns enough self-control to greet him in a calm and loving manner at the end of the day, feed him a tasty and nourishing dinner, seek his aid in putting the children to bed, and, then, in a quiet and rational way ask him for his help in handling the problems she faces that are too big for her to deal with alone. Of course she cannot always be consistent in this. There may be times when problems mount in partnership with hormones, producing sufficient pressure so that she may not be able or may not even care to control her emotions. Even mature wives can be expected to experience those occasional exceptions to the rule, but they should strive to make such periods less frequent.

A good rule of thumb to follow is that when a wife must approach her husband with problems, she should never do so until he has eaten and is refreshed. The more that rule is followed, the less serious conflict the pastor and his wife are likely to experience in their marriage.

There is still one more area in which the pastor's wife may assist her husband's ministry significantly. Often gossips and malcontents within the church will not have the courage to share their juicy tidbits with the pastor himself but will unload them on the pastor's wife, hoping she will pass them along to the pastor. A judicious pastor's wife will learn to respond properly to the conveyers of such messages, sift through the information for anything of real value, share with her husband what she feels is important, and spare him from the trivia that is mere gossip and undeserved complaints. Rather than enlarging every message and dropping it on her husband for shock value, she will realize that probably he has already almost all that he can bear. In love for him and in deference to his ministry, it is wise for her to shelter him from such banter.

RAISING GODLY CHILDREN

In another chapter we discussed the biblical obligations of the pastor as a father to manage his own household well. Such management of children will not be possible unless husband and wife work out a mutually agreed upon philosophy of child rearing that is scriptural and then work together to achieve it. Although no one should expect a pastor's children to be perfect, they should expect that his children will be raised in a climate of love and discipline. The pastor's family ought to be a model family.

Often it is easy for a mother to mete out love but leave disciplinary matters to the father. It is better if both partners share in providing love and discipline for the children. To be able to do that requires great wisdom; and such wisdom, in turn, is built upon careful observations bathed in prayer.

Sometimes it is difficult to find the fine line between excessive permissiveness and the domineering stifling of personality. Proverbs 22:6 gives the overall advice: "Train up a child in the way he should go, even when he is old he will not depart from it." The problem is that seldom are we able to stop long enough to analyze that particular child in his uniqueness in order to determine the way that *he* should go. Instead we attempt to impose upon the child the way *we* want him to go. We must do our best with each child to assert the importance of his personhood and help him, with the aid of the Holy Spirit, to reach the highest potentials God has in mind for him. Asserting and respecting his personhood includes avoiding embarrassing him in public or before his peers.

When we consider the complex job of raising children, we are aware that it is the task in life for which we are least prepared. To do the job at all, we must study the task and the child and then work at the job with the greatest diligence possible. No human job demands more teamwork, and the team must be composed of the husband and wife, the Holy Spirit, and the child himself—all working together in harmony.

Mistakes will be made. Members of a congregation will understand that. But the most significant lessons concerning the rearing of children the congregation will learn from the pastor and his wife will come from the way the couple handles their mistakes. Do they strive for some justice and a great deal of mercy when they deal with their children? That is how God deals with us. Do they discipline fairly and consistently? Are they extravagant in their love of and praise for the child as a person? Do they affirm the good qualities and the wise choices he makes? Are they willing to apologize to their children when they have wronged them, either inadvertently or in an emotionally tense setting?

Much is at stake in the way the pastor and his wife raise their children. If they continually fail in their efforts, they will not be credible sources of help for others who need advice concerning their parenting responsibilities. Moreover, no matter how well a pastor and his wife relate to the children and young people of their congregation, if they fail to relate properly to their own children, their success with the children of others will pale into insignificance in the eyes of those who observe them. Charity—as well as godliness, courtesy, and wisdom—begins at home.

One more word of biblical wisdom. A wise parent works hard toward developing a child who will more and more take over responsibility for his life, who will make his own decisions as an individual. As a child grows older he must be given the latitude to make some choices of his own, even if those choices result in mistakes. Protecting a child from the mistakes of life does not prepare him for the realities of life. Sooner or later he will have to face life and make his own decisions. If he has had a chance to ease into the process, he will do far better than if the responsibility is placed on him all at once.

Whether or not a child makes mistakes, and whether those mistakes are small or large, there will come a time in the life of each parent when he must let go completely, assuring himself that although his effort was imperfect, with the help of God and his marriage partner, he did the best he could. If indeed he has done his best, others will recognize that. At that particular juncture, the child who has matured into an adult must assume responsibility for his own actions and must be evaluated no longer on his parents' performance but on the basis of the wisdom and maturity he himself exhibits in the choices he makes.

We are still in the midst of a period when wayward, grownup children want to blame their problems on their parents. Undoubtedly many parents were unwise, selfish, or denigrating in their dealings with their children when they were growing up. In other cases, however, wise, godly parents acted well in behalf of their children. Nevertheless, one or more went astray, and the parents received the blame. Satan would like to burden Christian parents under a weight of guilt. The pastor and wife who have lived as godly examples before their children and have raised their children using biblical principles must not succumb to that type of intimidation.

Despite the heartbreak caused by children who go astray, a merciful God can use even that tragedy for His glory. We never truly empathize with a person until we have gone through what he has gone through. If the pastor and his wife have never experienced that sorrow themselves, it would be easy for them to look with consternation at another couple who has straying children. On the other hand, when the tragedy occurs in the pastor's home and people in the congregation observe faithfulness and consistency in their pastor and his wife, then the lay people can be assured, "I have a pastor and wife who truly understand, because they have been through what I have been through."

As tragic as the circumstances may be, the crisis may build depth and understanding into the pastoral couple that might not have been possible before. Moreover, when people in the congregation observe the pastor and his wife living victoriously in spite of the problems they are having with their children, they will realize that the couple is a fitting model to emulate under similar circumstances.

Her Obligations to Herself

Still one more area of relationship must be explored: the obligations a pastor's wife has to herself. She must learn to be herself—but before doing that she may need to discover exactly who she is. Since birth, many of us have tried with varying degrees of success to measure up to role expectations imposed on us by others. Parents, school teachers, Sunday school instructors, church officers, youth sponsors, peers, employers, college instructors, and neighbors are just a few of the many people who try to tell us who we are and how we should act. With such a proliferation of voices, is there any doubt that confusion would result?

SHE IS SPECIAL

The pastor's wife is not immune to such pressures. She needs to remember that she is a unique human being. She is like no other human ever created, and the combination of talents, abilities, and gifts she has is different from anyone else's. Because of who she is, there are things she can do and others things she cannot do. Her response to situations will be unlike that of any other human being and will reflect where, when, and how she was raised. As one-of-a-kind, she needs to recognize her uniqueness, develop those qualities that are her strengths, and stress the areas in which she is specially equipped. Whether it takes the understanding guidance of a loving friend, a wise husband, or a professional counselor, the pastor's wife needs to come to the place where she accepts—and indeed is satisfied, if not happy—with who she is. Not until she becomes secure as a person is she going to realize her full potential as a wife, mother, and Christian worker.

When she can accept and look objectively at herself, then powerful things may happen. She may be able to make her strengths stronger and her weakness less weak. She may come to the point where she accepts the idea that there are areas in which it is impossible for her to function, and turns those areas over to the Lord, joyfully, and without guilt.

MATURITY TEMPERS HER INDIVIDUALITY

Although it is important for a pastor's wife to recognize her uniqueness and become comfortable with who she is, it is important that she understands that asserting who one is is not synonymous with dressing in bizarre clothing or engaging in activity others may consider strange. Earlier in this chapter we cited the example of a young pastor's wife who asserted herself by flaunting her idiosyncracies. Her behavior, we suggested, was merely an expression of immaturity. Instead of asserting her personhood, she was only keeping them from knowing the excellent qualities she had. Of course the pastor's wife must be herself, but she should learn to assert her uniqueness in ways that will not repel and offend people. Naturally there will be picky people who glory in being offended. I am not referring to such persons. I am suggesting that the dress and actions of the pastor's wife should conform to what is considered acceptable behavior in the particular culture in which she has been placed to minister.

HER HOME REFLECTS DISCIPLINE AND GENEROSITY

Being one's self should not be equated with appearing unkempt in public or with leaving one's home in a constant state of disarray. No matter the amount of money she has for clothing or the demands made on her time, every pastor's wife ought to practice regular habits of personal hygiene and to attire her body in a tidy and presentable manner. Not every pastor's wife is a potential recipient for the good housekeeping award, nor should she feel compelled to be. However, she can keep the dishes washed and put away even if she has little ones underfoot. She can train her children to keep their toys in specific places, so that at least one room in the house is presentable at all times to those who may drop in unexpectedly.

All pastors' wives do not need to be gourmet cooks, nor would their food budgets permit them to assume the role very often, even if they wanted to. However, simple, wholesome, nutritious meals are a reasonable expectation, for a family's vitality and health depend on such. In addition, it does not hurt for the pastor's wife to prepare a little extra for someone who may be in need. As Christians, for example, we have a special obligation to feed the hungry. From my earliest remembrance as a pastor's child, I remember my mother's asserting that she would never turn away anyone from our door who was hungry. Often, because of the person's physical condition, she would not invite him inside the house. However, every hungry person who ever knocked on our door received a simple, nutritional ministry from my mother. I feel that her action should be the Christian norm.

SHE DEVELOPS SUPPORTIVE FRIENDSHIPS

In ministering to herself, a pastor's wife should have a good friend besides her husband. Many books insist that a pastor's wife cannot have a close friend in the church her husband serves. I disagree. There is not a more natural place to look for a friend than in the body. However, the need of a pastor's wife for a close friend in whom she can confide does not mean that the pastor's wife and her friend should form an exclusive little clique, or that they should spend all of their time together. If people are secure in a friendship, the relationship does not have to exclude other people. There are many times and places where friends can develop and maintain their friendship. During other occasions they need to treat others in a friendly and caring manner.

Although a friend is a person who likes us and supports us in good times and bad, a good friend is not necessarily the person upon whom we dump everything that bothers us. Just because we love someone is sufficient reason for us to spare him from some things that may cause pain or hinder his Christian growth. Consequently, a good friend is not necessarily the one on whom a pastor's wife should unload any bitterness or animosity toward the church she may feel. A suitable recipient for that unburdening would be, perhaps, a more mature pastor's wife in another church or even a professional Christian counselor. Real friends are those who attempt to build up rather than tear down each other.

HER HUSBAND IS HER BEST FRIEND

A wife's best friend, of course, should be her husband. We have referred already to what he may expect of her. There are many things she should ask of him, in turn. Because the children are equally theirs, she should expect him to arrange for a time each week when she is released from her mothering responsibilities so that she and her husband can do something enjoyable together that has nothing to do with church duties. If the wife does not take the initiative on this matter, the husband will often lose himself in his work and their relationship will deteriorate.

Happy times together do not need to be expensive. Simple relaxation—such as walks, bicycle riding, easy sports, and window shopping—is available, along with the more expensive activities. Although it is wondeful to be able to engage in the more expensive outings, many times the simple low-cost events end up being the most fun and are the ones people remember for the rest of their lives. The pastor's wife should encourage (not nag) her husband until he establishes the habit of taking her out on at least one "date" a week in which children are left at home and church business is left behind.

She Keeps in Touch with Family

In deference to herself and to her needs, it is important for the pastor's wife to maintain close relationships with her parental family, especially if it is supportive. If her own parental family is in a state of disorder, sometimes her husband's family can be a great source of strength and encouragement for her. Money invested in letters and telephone calls to family members is a wise and worthwhile investment. Periodic vacation visits to parental homes may provide a valuable source of psychological and emotional renewal.

She Maintains Her Relationship to God

Most important, a pastor's wife needs to establish and maintain her relationship with God. Despite, or should I say because of, her demanding schedule, she needs to set a definite time each day to be alone with the Lord and in His Word. Nothing will defeat her sooner than a lack of spiritual resources. Yet when the pressures of life invade us, spiritual renewal is often the area we neglect first. How foolish we are not to recognize that such a lapse is precisely what Satan desires.

Advice from a Pastor's Wife

Any chapter about the pastor's wife would be incomplete without words of advice from a pastor's wife herself. That advice, along with much of the information in this chapter, comes from the best pastor's wife I have ever known, Rosella Anderson, a woman who has always been a better pastor's wife than her husband has been a pastor. Her advice follows.

1. A wife should never criticize her husband's messages. When asked, she should point out the good points first and then share her ideas on how her husband may improve.
2. The pastor's wife should never attempt to pry information out her husband following one of his counseling sessions. If he feels that

the information is pertinent, he will share it with her.

3. A pastor's wife should keep her home a welcome one. Not only should she invite people in when they knock at her door, and not keep them standing outside on the doorstep, she should be sensitive to why they have come. Are they in need, or are they simply making a friendly visit?

4. On Sundays in the church building, the pastor's wife should be friendly to everyone, not just to her special friends.

5. A pastor's wife should be a good listener, and she should be slow to give advice.

6. The pastor's wife should speak cautiously. Many times it is better to leave things unsaid. If in doubt, don't say it!

7. An informed pastor's wife should be familiar with her husband's library. Often she will be asked questions on vital issues such as marriage, death, and prayer. It is nice to know where she can find some of the answers.

8. How busy a wife wants to be in the church should depend not only on her own abilities, but how busy her husband wants her to be.

9. If a wife is employed, no matter how enamored she may be with her position, her husband's ministry necessarily demands the highest priority.

By now the reader has discovered that this chapter is in sharp contrast to much of the material written about the pastor's wife today. Today, the prevailing philosophy seems to be that almost anyone can be a pastor's wife because, after all, she is free to live her own life. She does not need to involve herself in her husband's ministry. In this chapter I have attempted to dispel that myth, and I have taken sharp exception to the philosophy behind it. I have insisted that there are clear biblical directives as to how Christian women should live and serve, and even more stringent requirements placed on those who are married to leaders. Because I believe that the pastorate is the highest position of all in the Christian church, I contend that it is reasonable to expect pastors' wives to conform to unusually high standards. If the wife of a pastor is absolutely unwilling or unable to do so, her husband should question seriously the notion that God actually wants him to be in the pastoral ministry.

Only an exceptional man can succeed in the pastorate without the support of a sympathetic and understanding wife. Even the exceptional men are faced with extraordinary pressures and temptations. No matter how strong they think they are, their ministry often ends in disastrous ruin if they do not have the wholehearted support of a faithful and understanding wife.

My position may be unpopular in our culture, but I believe that it is valid and should be considered carefully. God requires that pastors be men of extraordinary dedication and commitment. He requires no less of their wives. God does not necessarily call "wonder women" to become pastors' wives. He does call women with exceptional attitudes: those who are committed to being a member of a pastoral team with their husbands, those who are intent on serving God in the unique position of pastoral ministry. If there is no higher calling on earth than the pastorate, surely the calling God gives to the person who works alongside the pastor to sustain him, to encourage him, and to prompt him toward growth is of high importance. Here is a rare servant of God indeed!

After I had brought an earlier draft of this chapter to a close, a veteran pastor's wife, whom my wife and I consider a valued friend, read this chapter and shared with me a pertinent insight. She said, "When I was a young pastor's wife I found myself becoming very bitter because of the demands placed upon my husband and me. It would have been easy for me to feel sorry for myself and claim that life in the parsonage wasn't fair. Just at the right time, however, a wonderful book came into my hands explaining that, as a pastor's wife, I should not look at the things I was giving up but at all I was gaining from the valuable experiences of life through which I was going. Nowhere else could I have the opportunities for growth and service I was gaining as a pastor's wife. As a result of that book, my entire attitude toward the pastorate changed. I am convinced that when our attitudes toward our calling are correct, then all of the circumstances we face will eventually work out all right."

I am certain that she is right. The pastor's wife needs to work in partnership with the Lord to cultivate a proper attitude toward the task that God has given to her in partnership with her husband. That is a first requisite. If she is able to take such a step, and thereby keep herself from becoming embittered and self indulgent, all of the other qualities we have talked about in this chapter will be realized ever so much easier.

Questions for Discussion

1. Describe the tension between being hired along with the pastor and being completely independent of his ministry. How would you suggest that the tension be resolved?

2. What do the Scriptures indicate is the proper role for the pastor's wife?

3. Why is it important that someone contemplating Christian

ministry spend considerable time discussing the ministry with his wife or future wife?

4. How may a pastor's wife aid him in ministry? How can she be supportive and yet still maintain her own personhood, responsibilities, and duties as a wife and mother?

5. What particular advice would you give to a woman as she and her husband begin their first pastoral experience?

6. What obligations does the pastor's wife have to herself? What opportunities does she have that are not available to other wives?

Helpful Resources

MacDonald, Gail. *High Call, High Privilege.* Wheaton, Ill.: Tyndale, 1981.

Mace, David R., and Vera Mace. *What's Happening to Clergy Marriages?* Nashville: Abingdon, 1980.

Nordland, Frances. *The Unprivate Life of the Pastor's Wife.* Chicago: Moody, 1972.

Nyberg, Kathleen Neill. *The Care and Feeding of Ministers.* Nashville: Abingdon, 1961.

Oswald, Roy M. *Married to The Minister.* Washington, D.C.: Alban Institute, 1980.

Senter, Ruth. *So You're the Pastor's Wife.* Grand Rapids: Zondervan, 1979.

Sinclair, Donna. *The Pastor's Wife Today.* Nashville: Abingdon, 1981.

Taylor, Alice. *How to Be a Minister's Wife and Love It.* Grand Rapids: Zondervan, 1968.

Truman, Ruth. *Underground Manual for Ministers' Wives.* Nashville: Abingdon, 1974.

Part 2
The Pastor's Relationships

6

Living in Harmony with His Family

As early as 1928, when Nolan Harmon wrote his classic work *Ministerial Ethics and Etiquette*, he warned both experienced and prospective pastors that "foremost among the duties of a minister are those he owes to his home and family. This is universally conceded, but too often the minister's home is immolated upon the altar of his work. The pastor has a hard task, but the pastor's family often has a harder one."[1]

Pressures on the Pastor

From the Culture to Succeed

If that warning was appropriate to Harmon's day, how much more relevant it is to our day. In the years since Harmon wrote, our society has experienced changes greater than those in all the centuries prior to that time. Life has become exceedingly complex. The work ethic seems to have been replaced by a corporate success syndrome that measures a person's worth in terms of prestige, promotion, wealth, and appearance. Small wonder that many North American men identify the core of their lives with their job instead of with their family life and measure their worth, not by the kind of husband and father

1. Nolan B. Harmon, *Ministerial Ethics and Etiquette* (Nashville: Abingdon, 1928), p. 46.

they are, but by how well they do at work.

Although they may come home and complain about their jobs, many men act as if they consider home life a mere interlude between working hours. As a result, for many men who are trying desperately to succeed, the hours at work become longer and longer and the hours at home become consistently shorter.

The pastor is not immune from that cultural syndrome. He, too, has been bit by the bug of success, and the forces that influence him often intensify the pressures brought on by the success syndrome.

When the graduate leaves seminary, his professors let him know in subtle ways that, because he was such a successful student, they expect him to be a successful pastor. The alumni director and seminary administrators are also much in favor of his succeeding. If he does so and his church grows large, they hope he will remember his theological roots and use his influence to see that his alma mater is included in the budget of his church. Such action on his part will alleviate the stringent financial conditions the seminary faces and will make life a little more tolerable for those long-suffering administrators. Denominational officials as well hope the new pastor will succeed. If he does, their programs will be supported in better fashion, and there will be fewer trouble spots for them to worry about. Last, the members of his own congregation hope that he will succeed—but here may lie his most nagging problem. For in any given congregation there are probably many different ideas as to what constitutes pastoral success and how to achieve it.

Thus, the pastor hears a cacophany of voices all requiring differing expectations of him but all convinced they are right. Because he is likely to be success-oriented to begin with since he is likely to be more than a little insecure, for he knows that he cannot measure up to all of the expectations people have placed upon him, he may try harder and harder to succeed, exerting more and more effort, and utilizing an ever-increasing number of work hours to do his best to be "all things to all men."

FROM THE FAMILY FOR RELATIONSHIP

When, on top of all the other demands, he experiences pressure from home because his family members have the audacity to express the idea that they too have needs, their requests may be the last straw. By then the demands of his job may have consumed nearly all of his energies, and he may have lost sight of the fact that he has a number of roles to fulfill.

Reconciling Relationships

SOMETIMES WORK, SOMETIMES FAMILY

Though he does not realize it, his is not a case where one role should supersede all others at all times. Such thinking is neither logical nor biblical even though the philosophy has appeared frequently in books on the pastorate. For example, though some writers insist that the pastor's responsibility to his family should always take precedence over other responsibilities, a more realistic picture of the pastor's competing roles is to say that, depending on the particular circumstances involved at a certain time, the demands of any specific role may take precedence over the demands of the others. To this point, Harmon writes helpfully.

> There are times when an emergency at home demands every thought of the father or husband; there are times when an emergency in the church becomes so imperative that it takes precedence over all home duties. This will be admitted. What is not so easily remembered, however, is that a minister's relationship to his family is as high and as sacred as that to his church.[2]

RESPONSIBILITIES INTERLOCK

What Harmon calls for is a "most beautiful interlocking of work and duties. The better the father, the better the pastor; the better the guide for the children of others, the better the guide for one's own children."[3] That is the balance toward which every pastor should strive.

Many exemplify such a model. Unfortunately, many others do not. They fall prey to extremes. Some gravitate to the extreme exemplified best in a statement made to my wife recently by another pastor's wife. She said, "Everyone in our church has an excellent pastor except the kids and me. We don't feel as if we have any pastor at all."

Others dote on their families so much that they are constantly involved in family matters and have little time to give energy and direction to the church. (Frankly, I believe that many pastors in the latter category are lazy or timid and enjoy loafing around the house most of the day if they can get away with it. There may be more of this type in the ministry than one would care to admit.)

Still others are plagued by "little girl" wives who continually

2. Ibid., pp. 46-47.
3. Ibid., p. 47.

whine at their husbands until they give them the attention they want. Often such a wife is so possessive of her husband that she forces him to spend most of his time at home instead of at work. Unfortunately, he may do as she bids just to keep peace in the family.

Needless to say, the pastor who spends too much time doting on his wife and family is not the person with which we are principally concerned in this chapter. He will be forced into accepting pastorates in progressively smaller churches as each new church catches on to his attitude. Soon he will run out of possibilities entirely, and then he will not be in a position to cause damage any more. However, rather than the lazy or self-indulgent type, it is the highly motivated, success-oriented pastor for whom I have the greatest concern. He probably has the best chance of making the greatest impact for God. Yet if he does not do his "homework" carefully, he may eventually lose his wife, his children may become wayward, and, because of one or both of those problems, he may become a casualty to the ministry.

Obligations to His Family

PROVIDE FOR THEIR PHYSICAL NEEDS

What may be considered the proper biblical standard for a pastor in establishing and maintaining his relationships with his wife and children? First, he should provide for their needs, including their financial needs. The Bible says that a man who does not provide for his family "has denied the faith, and is worse than an unbeliever" (1 Tim. 5:8). The pastor's obligation to provide for his family does not mean that his wife and children should expect to live a life of luxury. It means that they have a right to expect that their breadwinner will provide enough for them to have a life-style at least commensurate with the standard of living enjoyed by the majority of the people in their congregation and by the people living in the surrounding community.

It is inexcusable for a pastor's family to live at a poverty level while those in their church or community have a much higher standard of living. When members of the pastor's family are constantly ashamed because their clothes are poor, their house is dilapidated, and their food is scarce, the father of the household is derelict in his duties. If the church believes it is absolutely impossible to pay him properly, the pastor should declare that he intends to take a part-time job. If the church does not allow him to do that, he should resign, take a secular job, and wait until God provides him with a pastorate in a church that can meet the physical needs of his family.

I cannot imagine how many instances of tension in a pastor's home arise solely from monetary limitations. In the strongest terms I know, I want to declare that God does not expect a pastor's family to undergo such privation except in rare cases when a majority of members of a congregation are in similar straits. In most instances, God expects that the financial needs of a pastor's family will be met, and He considers it scandalous when that does not happen.

SPEND QUALITY TIME WITH THEM

The pastor's wife and children have not only physical needs but emotional needs as well. Those can be met only as the pastor sets aside blocks of quality time to spend with his wife and children. In the chapter on the pastor's wife, I spoke about the necessity for the wife to take definite steps to meet her husband's needs and to make sure that he understands how he can meet her needs. Even though that chapter is addressed to the wife, the husband should read it carefully so that he himself may be aware of his responsibilities. If a marriage is to be truly successful, it will be so only as husband and wife sensitively "fine tune" themselves to the emotional, physical, and psychological needs of the other.

In the pastor's household, the real danger, as I see it, is that the pastor often becomes so busy helping other people who have horrendous problems that he does not take the time to thoroughly understand the problems of his own household, nor does he consider them serious problems, if he even recognizes that they exist. It is possible that compared to the problems other people in his church are facing, the problems of his wife and children seem insignificant. However, they are not insignificant to the persons experiencing them. The pastor needs to remind himself constantly that his own family should have an understanding listener and counselor as much as others in his congregation who have troubles.

Although the pastor needs to spend quality time with his wife and children, that time should not be quality time as he defines it. For instance, little closeness between husband and wife is enjoyed when the husband spends the majority of his night home glued to the television screen watching a football game while his wife sits across the room alternately reading her magazine or fuming. A child may not regard as quality time outings that are planned insensitively. A pastor I know of was faithful in keeping his Saturdays free for his children. He planned all kinds of excursions for them—and regardless of their wishes, the children had to follow Daddy's plans. He did not stop to consider that the outings caused his children to miss out on important activities they had planned with their peers. His son, for example, operated under a distinct disadvantage with the hockey team because he could never make Saturday practices. Eventually he lost his spot on the team. Although his father spent Saturdays with him, the boy was not exactly grateful. His father, however, could not understand why his son was sometimes sullen and rebellious.

Quality time with children is best defined by the children themselves. For one child quality time may consist of enjoying his father's full attention at the dinner table. What a luxury for the child to be able to babble on uninterrupted about his day's activities and other subjects that have captured his interest. How nice it is when an adult actually considers a child to be a person with valid opinions!

In many families, such conversations between parents and children are stifled because the adults are so insensitive and stupid they believe that children should be "seen but not heard." May I add, too, that the dinner table is not the best place to correct a child on his table manners. The dinner hour should be the most pleasant of all hours in the day and should not be made a training table. There are exceptions, of course, when a child's behavior becomes entirely intolerable. When that happens, however, the child should be directed to leave the table and go to his room. His problem can be dealt with afterwards when the situation is not as emotional.

Be There for Dinner

It is important that the father of a household make the dinner hour a priority item on his agenda and that he spend the hour devoted entirely to his family. When infrequent dinner meetings make it impossible for him to be with his family for dinner, he should do his best to make up for the lost time.

Two or three times a month—or even more, if his schedule and finances permit—it is good for the pastor to take his wife out for dinner. Before depositing his children in the arms of a baby sitter, he should take a few minutes to sit down with the children at the dinner table as they enjoy the dinner prepared for them.

He should plan special times for his children, too. A child is excited and gratified when his daddy sets aside an occasional evening just for him, asks his help in planning something special, and then devotes the entire evening to being with him.

Make Bedtime a Happy Time for the Child

Bedtime is an extremely important time for little children. It should be made a happy time. Whenever possible, Daddy should be there to share the experience. The reading of a story by Dad or Mom may be the highlight of a child's day, and the prayer time to follow may offer important, intimate moments where parents may share the love of Christ with their children.

Be Creative in Finding Time for Companionship

When children enter their teens and begin spending evenings away from home in school activities and in dating, it is often helpful to them if a parent is up when they arrive home. It is important that the parent not adopt the role of an inquisitor, thereby conveying to the child that he is not trusted. Instead, if the parent "just happens" to be up—perhaps finishing a project—and makes himself available to the adolescent child in a non-threatening manner, the parent may find those some of the finest and most rewarding hours he has ever spent with his child.

As my children grew older and progressively more independent, often their employment hours forced them to come home late at night. When they came home, they were too wound up to go right to bed. As often as I could, I stayed up with them. Some of the best hours I spent with my nearly grown children were those late-night and early-morning hours. Even though I was tired the morning after, I was convinced that the time spent the night before was well worth my weariness.

View Their Actions Realistically

One way a pastor can minister to his children is to view their actions realistically. After all, they are children, and they should be allowed to act as children. That does not mean that they should be allowed to terrorize the neighborhood or run throughout the church building wreaking havoc. They need to be disciplined children so that the pastor's family can serve as a proper example to other families in the congregation. But they should be allowed to make mistakes. Moreover, they should not be badgered or placed under undue stress if their school grades are not always perfect—even though the low grades may be threatening to their parents.

Maintain a Private and a Public Life for Them

Following the same line of thinking, the pastor owes it to his family to maintain a private life for them as well as a public life. The inability of many pastoral families to find a suitable private life is not a new problem. In speaking to this issue, Harmon writes:

The family of the minister should not be made to serve as slaves of the church, nor should their home be used as a public convenience for the entire membership. "Don't let ministerial life and domestic life get mixed," Lloyd C. Douglas wisely counseled in *The Minister's Everyday Life*. The minister's family, like any other in the congregation, ought to take an active part in the work of the church and its several departments. However, to force the wife into the position of assistant pastor and the children into becoming prodigies of childish ecclesiastical leadership is wrong. It is not fair to the family and it spoils the Church."[4]

As a postscript directed specifically to the pastor in his relationship with his wife, Harmon adds:

No matter what role the congregation expects her to play, the minister very properly sees his wife as HIS wife, to love and to cherish, to protect and support. He must not forget that she married him, not a whole congregation—at least that is what she thought she was doing.[5]

The Marriage Transcends Children

One more consideration is extremely important. I believe it is absolutely urgent that the pastor always consider his wife his best friend and his children his next best friends. As friends, their feelings and opinions are important. Both the wife and the children should be respected and their attitudes taken into consideration when major decisions are made that will have dramatic effects on them. Children view life from a limited perspective. Nevertheless, their perceptions are real to them and should be viewed as important by their parents. Good friends are worthy of respect and should be given that respect.

In conveying that idea to his children, it is important for the pastor to make plain that their mother is his best friend, the most important person in his life, and deserves the most respect of all. Marriage is for life, and children are only loaned to parents for an indefinite period. When the parents cease carrying on the everyday functions of parenthood, they will still be husband and wife and must continue to relate to each other.

It is important, therefore, that as husband and wife the parents keep in touch with one another and not let the overwhelming responsibilities of parenthood make them forget the need they have for one another. If, when the children enter adolescence, they attempt to pit father against mother, attempt to break up the sense of solidarity so

4. Ibid., p. 48.
5. Ibid., p. 49.

necessary to a communicating married couple, or attempt to play one parent against the other for their own selfish ends, the pastor and his wife should recognize the tactic for what it is. More than any other time in their life together, they should unite in their efforts and let that child know that the marriage partner, not that child, receives first priority. If disciplinary problems with the child become desperate enough so that someone is forced to leave the home, the child should be the one who leaves and not the marriage partner. Although the child may not want to hear information of that sort at the moment, in a long run such a stand by the parents will build into his life an order and stability he would not realize if his selfish wishes were honored.

The High Importance of the Family

Although the church is the most important institution on earth, the family runs a close second. If his family is destroyed or it fails, a pastor's ministry in the church may be brought to a calamitous end. Therefore, there are times when the needs of his family should take clear precedence over those of the church members or the demands of his job. There may come a time when he will need to remove himself from the ministry for a short period so that he can more properly meet the needs of his family. Then when he returns to the pastorate, he will do so with a firm family base upon which to build the new ministry. Next to his relationship with God, there are no more important relationships than those of a husband and wife and a father and his children. Those relationships must be preserved and enhanced at all cost.

Questions for Discussion

1. What tensions do you see existing between a pastor's work at the church and his duties as a husband and father? How do you respond to the statement "The minister's relationship to his family is as high and as sacred as that to his church?"
2. What do you believe are the proper biblical standards for a pastor as far as his relationship with his wife and children are concerned?
3. Does a pastor's life-style necessarily have to include financial deprivation? When is it appropriate for a pastor to ask for a raise in light of a family financial need?
4. How may a pastor insure that he is giving adequate time and emotional support to his own family? How may a pastor insure that

the ministerial life and the domestic life do not get mixed?

5. List several examples of times in a pastor's life when the needs of his family take precedence over those of his church. List several examples of times when the needs of the church will take precedence over those of the pastor's family.

Helpful Resources

Alexander, Olive J. *Developing Spiritually Sensitive Children.* Minneapolis: Bethany, 1980.

Baley, Robert W. *Coping with Stress in the Minister's Home.* Nashville: Broadman, 1979.

Dahl, Gerald L. *Why Christian Marriages Are Breaking Up.* Nashville: Thomas Nelson, 1979.

Dunker, Marilee Pierce. *Man of Vision, Woman of Prayer.* Nashville: Thomas Nelson, 1980.

Garsee, Jarell W. *What You Always Wanted to Know About Your Pastor Husband.* Kansas City, Mo.: Beacon Hill, 1978.

Issue on the Pastor's Family. *Leadership* 2, no. 4 (Fall 1981).

Switzer, David K. *Pastor, Preacher, Person.* Nashville: Abingdon, 1979.

Wilt, Joy. *Raising Your Children Toward Emotional and Spiritual Maturity.* Waco, Tex.: Word, 1977.

7

Shepherding and Leading His People

Of all the relationships on earth, the relationship a pastor enjoys with his people is unique, and, apart from that he has with his family, probably is the most rewarding. The pastor is leader and shepherd. Although he leads his people, he is still accountable to them. There is a dynamic balance required in the relationship. When that balance is maintained, a pastorate generally progresses well. The trouble is, many pastors seem never to get the knack of reaching, no less maintaining, that balance. They swing from one extreme to the other. Elsewhere in this book we have spoken of those extremes and have related some examples. In this chapter I would like to speak of the philosophy that I believe should be the foundation for a pastor's actions. In later chapters I will focus on the specific kinds of relationships the pastor should enjoy with his people.

A pastor friend remarked to me recently, "When your graduates get out of seminary, some of them think that all they have to do is preach well in order to succeed in the ministry. You need to tell them that their people will have different entry points. Not everyone starts out at the same stage. There are some who will only be reached as the church extends its relational hand to them, and some Christians who will grow, not on the basis of listening to sermons primarily, but through a deep, lasting, meaningful relationship with their pastor." I assured him that although much of this book is relational in approach I would devote a chapter specifically to the relational aspect of a pastor's ministry.

The Members of the Church Are Due Respect

THE AUTHORITY RESIDENT IN THE LOCAL CHURCH

In my examination of the Scriptures I find no higher authority on earth than the church of Jesus Christ, meeting and acting as a composite body. In the Great Commission found in Matthew 28:18-20, Jesus makes plain that He does not share His authority with anyone, even the elders of the church. He says, "All authority has been given to Me in heaven and on earth" (Matt. 28:18). On the basis of that authority He gave His followers certain commands.

Because the church universal is Christ's present manifestation on earth, and the local church the physical embodiment of that church, it may be concluded that the authority of Jesus Christ is resident in the local church. Although others may argue otherwise, I see no biblical precedent for any ecclesiastical organization to exercise authority over the local church. Neither do I see any biblical justification for officials of a local church exercising authority over the larger body except for the authority specifically designated to those local officials by the body as a whole.

Therefore, just because a man is called to be the pastor of a church, does not mean that he has unlimited authority to dictate to that body. In reality, since the composite body itself is the final possessor of authority, he, as pastor, has only as much authority as is delegated to him by the church. Now, in turn, when a local congregation designates that specific authority to a pastor, then individual members of the body have the obligation to submit to him in those areas in which he has been given authority. However, in all other areas, the pastor has the obligation and duty to submit to the composite membership.

BELIEVERS ARE PRIESTS, SAINTS, AND MINISTERS

There is a practical, cogent reason for his submitting to the membership, and that is this: church members are not merely sheep, even though there is a sense in which all believers, pastors included, are sheep. They are also believer-priests, saints, and ministers of the gospel, as the Bible makes clear. Leaders are given to the church for only one purpose: to enhance the ministry of those ministers. Therefore, though many in a given church may experience their priesthood only in an embryonic form, still they have received the title from God and are due the respect appropriate to priests, saints, and ministers.

Believers Need to Know Their Heritage

A major premise of the book *Birthright*, by David Needham, is that many Christians really do not know who they are. When they are finally convinced of the fact that they are priests and ministers, they will begin to act the part. The principal problem, however, is that often they do not get much help from their church leaders in realizing the potential of their identity. For instance, I have seen repeated instances of seminary students' moving aggressively into their first pastorates with behavior that betrayed how little respect they had for the people they had to come to serve. Thus, they did little to convince the people of their identity as priests and ministers. Often a new pastor is so enamored with change and so convinced that change is the only desirable posture for a church to take, that he goes into a pastorate determined to do things in a new way even before he has taken time to survey whether or not what is already going on is effective. When people resist his arbitrary demands, he denigrates them, telling his peers that he is having trouble with "retrogressive" people who are failing to submit themselves to his authority. When the church rejects the methods he has tried to impose, he labels the body ignorant.

May I suggest that the body is not ignorant at all. The pastor is probably the ignorant one. The congregation may be resisting his ideas because they have not observed a sufficient degree of maturity in him to warrant their placing trust in him. Or they may have been turned off to the man because of his cavalier attitude towards them.

There Is Wisdom in the Composite Body

Although all of us have observed exceptions to the rule, it is true, nevertheless, that there is great wisdom in the composite body. Such wisdom and discretion seldom will be present in the leadership alone or even in the sum total of the individual parts acting independently. If a pastor is wise, he will recognize and respect the wisdom that rests in the congregation as its members act together, and will demonstrate his respect by taking the decisions of the assembly to be wise counsel. He should continually treat the individual members of the assembly with the respect due to them as priests and ministers, because God, not he, has designated them as such.

The Members of the Church Should Be Treated with Love

A few years ago a good friend of mine left a loving and prospering ministry to assume the pastorate of a large city church that had just experienced a split under a strong-minded pastor. Many of us advised my friend against going into the situation, but, finally, when it was clear that our advice was of no avail, we asked him, "How in the world are you going to tackle that situation?"

"That's easy," was his reply, "I'm going to love the people lavishly and preach the Word faithfully."

He did not go to his new charge with the idea that he was ministering to a bunch of troublemakers, but, instead, he approached the people with respect, realizing that they had potential but needed first to be healed. Today the church is flourishing under his ministry. It has grown far bigger than anyone expected it would, and it has a ministry of outreach to the neighborhood that is the envy of many nearby churches.

Elsewhere in this book we have discussed the need for the pastor to preach the Word faithfully. There is also a need for him to love the people lavishly. Love has to come from God to be genuine. A person cannot fake it. If he tries, eventually he will be found out. Underlying the proper actions of a pastor for his people in all the circumstances of his ministry—in the pulpit, at funerals, during hospital visitation, and in counseling sessions—must be a firm foundation of love and respect that arises from a pastor's relationship with God.

DEVELOP PERSONAL RELATIONSHIPS

Some people are easy to love. Although the pastor will want to uphold those people regularly in prayer, he will not have to pray as hard about his relationship with them as he will about his relationship with those who are not easy to love. As he prays through and agonizes with God over the relationships that are the hardest, he may find that God works the greatest miracles of all in the lives of those "unlovely" people. They may well become the greatest trophies of his ministry. He may find it necessary to spend much time with the people he finds the most difficult to love, especially if they are church officers. Educators tell us that preaching is of little effect in getting people who are mature in years to change their attitudes. More direct methods of teaching that involve the learner tangibly in the learning process may work best. One of those ways is to develop a one-to-one relationship with the person we desire to change.

BECOME INTERESTED IN OTHERS

One of the greatest instructors I have had in learning how to relate to people is my wife. She seldom begins a conversation by speaking about herself or even about her ministry. Over the years, she has developed the art of asking people key questions about themselves. As a result she has becomes genuinely interested in them. They in turn become aware that she is interested in them and cares for them. The pastor who endears himself to his people will talk with them and will get them to talk about themselves. In expressing his interest in people, he should interact with people of all ages, including children. Often a pastor will win the hearts of parents because he shows a genuine concern for their children in listening attentively to those little people.

Some months ago I spoke to friends concerning an intense young pastor who had just come to their church. I asked them how he was doing, and they replied, "He is just great in the pulpit but poor in personal relationships. When he visits in our home, he seldom shows any interest in us or what we are doing. Instead, he is all business, church business. He talks at great length about what is and should be going on in the church, but we feel that he is too interested in reaching church goals. We have never gained the impression that he loves us."

Months later I had the privilege of having that young pastor in a doctoral class in which we talked over some of the essentials for changing people, including the necessity for establishing meaningful relationships with them. The young man was bright and perceptive, and he paid attention to what was said; the Holy Spirit worked in his life to use that teaching to bring about a definite improvement in his ministry. When the course in which I had discussed those concepts was over, I spoke once again with my friends in his church. I asked them how things were going. This time their faces lighted up. "There has been a dramatic change in our pastor. He is not so much concerned about programs and methods anymore, but it is becoming apparent that he is concerned about us as people."

They went on to relate how the pastor had taken a special interest in things that were important to them as a couple. They became enthusiastic about his ministry not because he was such a great preacher or because the church was growing, though both of those were true. They were excited because he had become a true pastor to them instead of merely an organizer and pulpiteer. He had found practical ways of demonstrating love for his people. Today his ministry is a success, whereas before it was a horrible example. Love the people lavishly, then preach the Word faithfully. Probably there is no better prescription for a successful ministry.

Candidating

No chapter concerning a pastor's relationship with his people would be complete without commenting on the process by which the prospective pastor is introduced to his people, that complex tribal ritual unique to churches with a congregational form of government: candidating. Many times I have thought how easy it would be if in our denomination pastors were assigned to particular churches by a district secretary or bishop. All the guess work would be eliminated, and the pastor could focus his attention upon impressing one man, the man who made the assignment. Yet pastors who serve in denominations that are episcopal in government tell me that even in their churches, there is increasingly a move toward local autonomy. Thus, the bishop who is wise and discreet consults with the local church before he assigns a particular pastor to it. Otherwise, he is likely to find himself in trouble.

PROTOCOL FOR INITIAL CONTACTS

In the standard candidating process to which a majority of the readers of this book will be exposed, there is an established procedure by which men who wish to pastor churches are put in contact with churches needing pastors. The candidate makes known in a discreet way that he is available by composing a résumé and sending it to appropriate sources, such as the placement department of his alma mater, the district secretary of his denomination, and the national placement agency of his denomination. Those sources then send copies of the résumé to churches that have solicited placement help. In each case, the placement director tries to ascertain which of the applicants would be appropriate for that particular church.

In addition to sending his résumé to the appropriate denominational officers, the prospective pastor may pursue other avenues. But again, he should do so discreetly. For instance, if he hears about a church that needs a pastor and he is interested, tribal ritual in most cases dictates that he not contact the church directly. Instead, it is better for him to send his résumé to a person he knows has some contact with the church, such as a seminary professor. That person can put his name before the church. In the past few years, many pastors have placed ads in Christian publications informing readers of their availability. In most church circles, however, such a tactic is frowned upon and is likely to create a bad impression of the person who does it.

THE SCREENING OF CANDIDATES

After a church receives a number of résumés and adds to those the names its members have submitted, the pulpit committee establishes the order in which potential candidates will be contacted. Actions by the pulpit committee should be kept entirely confidential. After the priority list is drawn up, the secretary of the committee begins contacting candidates in the order of the committee's preference. Often, many of the candidates suggested by members of the congregation are relatives of theirs or are pastors of churches more prominent than the seeking church. Usually, the pulpit committee will quickly eliminate relatives and will need only a short phone call to pastors of larger churches to eliminate them as well from the list of potential candidates.

THE TELEPHONE INTERVIEW

At last the pulpit committee decides on a person who it believes is the best available under the circumstances. Because it is impossible to know if he is compatible with the church merely on the basis of a résumé, personal contact begins. Initially such contact may take the form of a conference call between the candidate and the pulpit committee, especially if the candidate and the committee are separated by long geographical distance. If the church is small or if finances are tight, ordinarily the pulpit committee will give stronger preference to candidates who do not live far away, so that the church may save moving expense.

THE CANDIDATING WEEK

If the committee is satisfied with its telephone interview, it may decide to pay the candidate's way to meet with them, may elect to travel to his location and see him in action, or may do both. During his meetings with them, although the candidate should be cordial, he should act as naturally as possible, so that the committee can get an accurate idea of whether or not he is the kind of man they are seeking. The candidate should ask penetrating questions as to the type of ministry the church is expecting and the circumstances under which he would be asked to come as pastor. Even as he meets with the committee, he should consider that he is ministering to it. If it turns out that the church the committee represents is not the right spot for him, he will have asked questions and planted ideas that will help the committee in its further decision-making.

A potential pastor should be fairly certain that he wants to be called by a particular church before he agrees to spend the church's money in coming for a candidacy period. When he agrees to candidate, he should insist that his wife accompany him, even if she has to do so at his expense. If possible, the candidating process should take at least a full week. Often a Monday through Sunday period works out well. Since the week is likely to be a rigorous one, it is best that the children be left at home.

During the candidating week, the prospective pastor should visit as many homes of the congregation as possible to get a cross-sampling of the people he and his wife will be serving. He should meet with as many groups of people as possible, and he should encourage them to ask questions of him just as he, in turn, will ask questions of them concerning what they expect from a pastor.

As the candidating week progresses, he should do his best to penetrate the power structure and learn where the real power of the church lies. Especially should he try to learn who the tribal leader—or leaders—are. When he does so he should then arrange to meet with that person or group of persons. Such meetings may have to be arranged discreetly, because many times the real leaders of the church do not occupy any official office. If the candidate feels comfortable working with the power bloc of the church he may want to pursue further meetings with the pulpit committee and the board of the church.

Regardless of whether or not the candidate feels that the candidating week is going well, while he is there his attitude should be one of ministry to the people. As a result, whether or not he receives or accepts an actual call, the people will have been enriched and blessed by his visit. He should make himself available to them on an intensive basis—there will be plenty of time to catch up on his sleep when he gets home.

Before he leaves the area he will be able to tell whether or not the pulpit committee still thinks he is a viable choice. At that point he should arrange to talk to the pulpit committee concerning the details of the pastoral call they are prepared to make. If he thinks the working conditions and the salary structure are acceptable, he should allow the process to move toward full term. If conditions are not what he thinks are acceptable, then he should express his concerns to the pulpit committee. They may want to terminate the relationship at that point.

THE VOTE OF THE CHURCH

If all signals still are positive, and he believes the candidating experience has been a success, he should return home to await the vote of the church. If the first vote is not 90 percent or higher, probably the candidate should refrain from accepting the call. Resistance to a person's ministry tends to increase rather than decrease during the course of a ministry. A pastor who starts out with more than 10 percent of his congregation opposing his call is likely to experience insuperable opposition in the days when his ministry grows more mature.

LEAVING THE OLD PASTORATE

If the church extends the call and the candidate accepts, he should move to that location as quickly as possible. If he is already pastoring a church, he should submit his resignation as soon as possible, with an appeal to the church to form a pulpit committee immediately so that the congregation will experience little time between pastors. In addition, he may suggest denominational officials upon whom the leaders of the church can call for the names of potential interim pastors.

In the time before he leaves the church for his new field of service he should be careful to see that his ministry is cordial, friendly, and positive. The closing days of his ministry in the church are not the time to whip the people for their past misdeeds. Rather, he should use the time to patch up misunderstandings and restore relationships with people with whom he has had difficulty. He should do his best to leave the church as a friend to everyone, and his sermons should be positive messages of encouragement and motivation to the people. It is important, also, that he avoid a lame duck mentality during the period. Because he works as a pastor in behalf of the kingdom of God as well as of a particular parish, he will be wise to work as hard as ever in his closing days at a pastorate, to work as though he were going to stay there forever.

During the week of his departure, it is proper for him to pay special visits to people with whom he has enjoyed a particularly meaningful relationship. If he leaves in a loving and gracious spirit with a positive attitude, it will be a sweet and honorable parting, and the people he leaves will have fond memories of him.

Questions for Discussion

1. What tensions do you see between the pastor's role as leader and shepherd? How may these tensions be relieved through relationship building skills?

2. List the appropriate steps to be taken in establishing an initial relationship with a congregation.

3. Why is it important that a pastor be discreet in the way he

makes his résumé available or in the way he makes known that he is seeking consideration as a pastoral candidate?

4. What suggestions would you make regarding the actual visit in a candidating situation? What preparations should the candidate make? Who among his family should go with him? What should his attitude be toward the pulpit committee and toward the members of the congregation?

5. Make a list of questions the pastoral candidate might ask. Likewise, make a list of questions that might be asked by the examining church.

6. Why is it important that if a congregation extends a call the vote be at least 90 percent or higher?

7. If the church extends a call, what should the pastor's attitude be toward the church he currently serves? How may he insure that he concludes his ministry there in a cordial and positive manner?

Helpful Resources

Brister, C. W., James L. Cooper, and J. David Fite. *Beginning Your Ministry.* Nashville: Abingdon, 1981.

Gillaspie, Gerald Whiteman. *The Restless Pastor.* Chicago: Moody, 1974.

Grider, Edgar M. *Can I Make It One More Year?* Atlanta: Knox, 1980.

Hahn, Celia A. *The Minister Is Leaving.* New York: Seabury, 1974.

Harris, John C. *The Minister Looks for a Job.* Washington, D.C.: Alban Institute, 1977.

Kemper, Robert G. *Beginning a New Pastorate.* Nashville: Abingdon, 1978.

Oswald, Roy M. *The Pastor as Newcomer.* Washington, D.C.: Alban Institute, 1977.

8

Working Effectively with Church Officers

The principle of leadership is written indelibly into the pages of the Bible at almost every juncture. Just as it is necessary for man to have some internal form of organization for his body to function, so the Body of Christ, being an organism, also must have an internal organization for it to function and survive. An organizational pattern, of course, revolves around some type of leadership. In a later chapter I will express my feelings concerning churches that have overorganized themselves to the extent that they have too many chiefs to get the job done. In this chapter, however, I would like to address the special type of relationship I believe should exist between the pastor and other leaders in the church.

The Principle of Mutual Submission

My examination of Scripture reveals two kinds of church officer: elders, who equip the saints for the ministry of the Gospel, and deacons, who supervise the service ministries. Despite the confusion many feel over the nature of the two offices and over which office should rule the other, and how, I believe a built-in biblical principle applies to all relationships that should hold between the persons who are elders or deacons in a church. That is the principle of mutual submission. All leaders in a church are to be accountable to each other and to the church. Intrinsic to the job description of an elder is that he be an equipper, a discipler. Discipling may take the form of

one-to-one discipling; one-to-few discipling, such is as carried on
through a Sunday school class; and one-to-many discipling, such as
takes place from the pulpit.

By virtue of the fact that he is an elder, the pastor has discipling
responsibilities. Yet many young elders, and some older ones, have
the misconception that they are on the top of the heap and thereby
have the right—even the obligation—to disciple everybody. Sometimes a man who is theologically trained imagines that he has all the
answers. He believes it is appropriate for him to impose those answers on everyone else in the congregation, and he goes about the
business of doing so with a grim determination. If he were more
realistic, he would realize that he is not the possessor of all wisdom.

God gave His church a plurality of wise leaders. A really wise
pastor will realize as he disciples some of the leadership that there
are those in the leadership who should be discipling him. If he is
bright, he will keep himself from clashing with the older leadership
of the church but will form a team with them. The older leaders will
counsel him on matters in which he may tend to be a bit impetuous,
and he, in turn, will share new ideas with the older leaders, asking
them to mull over the ideas and consider their wisdom. Then when
new ways of doing things are presented to the congregation they will
be backed by a united front.

Deal Astutely with a Tribal Leader

Foremost among those from whom he should seek counsel is the
Tribal Leader. Every church has one, and in most cases it is committing professional suicide for a pastor to cross him seriously. I know
of a church where pastor after pastor has followed each other in rapid
succession. Each of those pastors was young, and each has been
intent on bringing about radical change. In each case the pastor's
short tenure could be traced to his engaging in pointed, direct confrontation with the Tribal Leader. It seems that none of them had
learned the knack of winning him over, and, no doubt, he became
ever more difficult to win because of the increasing number of pastors with whom he had difficulty.

The tragedy of the matter was the leader and the pastors probably
had identical basic goals. All of them wanted to see people come to
know Christ as Savior, and all of them wanted to see their church
grow. The older man was wary of cooperating with the new pastor in
adopting new methods, because he had seen so many of them fail in
the years he had been in the church. As for the new pastors, each
began with youthful enthusiasm, feeling sure he knew what to do to

push the church off dead center and propel it ahead. Instead of digging in for a long stay and winning over the older membership of the church before attempting something new, the young pastors began imposing new methods almost immediately, attracting a certain number of people who became their adherents. Then when the major showdown came, inevitably a split resulted and the church was left with the same older leadership, including the Tribal Leader.

How much more effective those pastors would have been had they recognized that in that particular church the pastor was not the principal leader. If any of them had come to such an understanding, and if any of them had been able to submit himself to the authority of that older brother, progress for the church would have come. It would have been dramatically slower than the new pastors would have wanted but there would have been permanent beneficial results.

The Right to Be Heard

Recently a student of mine responded to an inquiry from a church in the Midwest. When the job description came, it was evident that the church was looking for a Sunday morning preacher and Bible teacher. The job description explicitly stated that the person who filled the position would not begin as an elder. Instead, after he had been with the church for some months, the people would evaluate him to determine whether or not he was elder material.

At the time, I was shocked at what the church proposed and advised my student to look elsewhere for employment, which he did. The more I have thought about it, however, the more I have come to the conclusion that the church had a valid point. Why should a young man fresh out of theological training be given automatically the exalted office of elder? And in turn, why should he think he has enough knowledge and experience to run everyone and everything?

To the young prospective pastor, especially, I feel it necessary to offer this advice: do not go into a pastoral ministry thinking that you have all the answers and that the older leaders of the church are necessarily ignorant or retrogressive. They may have far greater wisdom than you, especially in practical matters. Attach yourself to them. Ask them questions. Respect their judgment. In most cases you will prosper and mature greatly if you do. Moreover, the church and your ministry will remain intact. You may not be able to move ahead as fast as you want, but progress will come as you gain credibility and experience and as you begin to emulate more and more the gentleness of the Chief Shepherd, the Savior.

Developing Leaders

In sharp contrast to the situation that faces the newly arriving pastor when the leadership of a church is exceptionally strong is the situation that faces a new pastor when there is little or no leadership at all. In that case, whether he likes it or not, even the pastor fresh out of seminary will be forced to take on the major leadership role. He will be the person providing most of the guidance the church experiences. It is likely that he will try to get the Church going through the proliferation of programs. If he is multi-talented and has a wife who is energetic and equally talented, he and his wife may soon have a three ring circus of programs on their hands. Those participating in the programs may find them exciting, but soon the pastor will notice that he does not have quality time to spend in ministering to his people or in equipping the kind of leadership the church needs so desperately. Often pastor-wife teams in churches of this kind labor intensively for a number of years in one location and then experience such intensive burnout they are forced to leave the ministry.

It would have been more appropriate for the pastor and his wife to have concentrated on one program at a time, training leadership for the program well enough so that those persons could take over the program and equip others to do it as well. When one program was solidly established the pastor and his wife could begin a new program.

Meanwhile, as that training was going on, the pastor should have been identifying those in the church who had the potential for over-all leadership positions. He should have equipped those people for the positions in which they fit best. The pastor might have been able to equip only one or two persons at a time. In that case, if the constitution directed that the church have a certain number of church officers, the congregation might have elected to wait to fill those positions until leaders who fulfilled the biblical requirements were available.

What about the experienced pastor? What if he comes into a church where the leadership is inept? The obvious answer is that he is going to be forced to work with what he has until he can equip those people or train their replacements. Until he can train them or replace them, it is important for him to remember that, in the final analysis, it is God who chooses all leaders. Though he may have the tendency to become impatient with them because of their lack of training, ability, and effort, he should treat them with dignity and respect, trying his best to be submissive to them where possible, even as he expects them to submit to his leadership. Often God surprises us. The most profound thought may come from the lips of someone we had considered totally inept. If God is indeed the author of leadership and the chooser of leaders, then He is able to perform His work through the most unlikely candidates. If we doubt that, we who are a part of the active pastoral ministry should take a careful and penetrating look in the mirror.

Questions for Discussion

1. What is the principle of mutual submission? How may an attitude of submission guide a pastor toward effective leadership?
2. What is a Tribal Leader? What roles does that person play in the leadership team of the church?
3. What suggestions would you make to a young, newly arriving pastor as he contemplates making many changes in his church?
4. What may an experienced pastor do to move the church toward change and growth without causing injury to leadership that may be untrained or even inept?

Helpful Resources

Adams, Arthur M. *Effective Leadership for Today's Church.* Philadelphia: Westminster, 1978.
Bruce, A. B. *Training of the Twelve.* Grand Rapids: Kregel, 1979.
Cook, Jerry, and Stanley Baldwin. *Love, Acceptance and Forgiveness.* Glendale, Calif.: Gospel Light, Regal, 1979.
Green, Michael. *Called to Serve: Ministry and Ministers in the Church.* London: Hodder and Stoughton, 1964.
Greenleaf, Robert K. *Servant Leadership: A Journey into the Nature of Legitimate Power and Greatness.* Ramsey, N.J.: Paulist, 1977.
Hagstrom, Richard G. *Getting Along with Yourself and Others.* Wheaton, Ill.: Tyndale, 1981.
Stott, John R. W. *One People.* Downers Grove, Ill.: InterVarsity, 1968.
Trueblood, David Elton. *Your Other Vocation.* New York: Harper & Row, 1952.

9
Dealing Honorably
with All

In the past few chapters we have considered some of the people with whom it is necessary for the pastor to have meaningful and solid relationships. There are still more people who may not be quite as important to the pastor's success as those we have named, but who can enhance his ministry or detract from its effectiveness, depending on the way the pastor handles his relationships with them. Although the people discussed in this chapter are by no means an exhaustive list of the pastor's contacts, they are among the most significant.

Other Sheep

When Jesus talked about having other sheep not "of this fold," I do not think he was referring to the Baptists down the street. There is no positive gain to the kingdom of God when Christians move from one evangelical church to another. I believe firmly that pastors should observe scrupulous ethics in avoiding the stealing of sheep from another congregation. If there is clear indication that the losing congregation does not believe in the essential doctrines of the Christian faith and does not offer a biblical plan of salvation and Christian growth to its membership, then, in my opinion, it has ceased to be a church and its members are a fair target for any evangelical group. Even in dealing with such people, however, it is important to do so in a kindly, gentle manner, making sure that they are not being pressured to change churches and that the decision they make is clearly theirs. The reputation of the receiving church in the community may be at stake. Besides that, it may be that the leadership of the losing church, including the pastor, needs to receive Christ. If people are wooed away from the church in a crass and crude manner, all communication with the people in it may stop, leading to a halt in future evangelistic efforts directed toward them.

In dealing with people from other evangelical churches who express dissatisfaction with their church, it is important that the potential receiving pastor make no effort to persuade them to make a change. He has an obligation to inform the losing pastor that his members are attending another church and have expressed dissatisfaction with the church in which their membership resides. That pastor then may take whatever steps necessary to try to correct the problem causing the dissatisfaction. If he is unsuccessful in doing so, he may want to let the receiving pastor know what has taken place, especially if the people leaving his church were what he would consider troublemakers. Under no circumstances should a pastor deliberately try to steal another's sheep. The practice is unethical, and it will establish a horrible reputation for the pastor who tries it, one that will follow him for the rest of his ministry. In addition, often the sheep that are easy to woo away are no bargains to begin with. They may be the type of person who drifts from church to church, depending on which church can offer their family the most services at any particular time.

The pastor of the receiving church should be especially careful when he deals with people who have been dismissed from membership in other evangelical churches. The dismissing church may have been in serious error. It may have acted in an improper fashion. But careful investigation should be made to determine whether or not that is the case. Homer Kent, Sr., advises strongly that

> the pastor and the membership committee will do well to investigate disqualified members of another church carefully before they are admitted into membership. Otherwise the church may be inviting trouble similar to that which caused their withdrawal from the church that disqualified them. These applicants should demonstrate a proper Christian attitude before they are admitted. Only Christians who are right with the Lord should be admitted into church membership.[1]

Other Pastors

Relationships with other pastors should be fraternal, honest, and professional, whether or not the other pastor is a member of the

1. Homer A. Kent, Sr., *The Pastor and His Work* (Chicago: Moody Press, 1963), p. 62.

same denomination. Just as it is unethical to steal another pastor's sheep, it is equally unethical to try to destroy his reputation. How I wish it was unnecessary for me to write this section. The fact is that many pastors are the worst gossips around when it comes to passing on word concerning fellow pastors. Their gossiping no doubt arises out their own feelings of insecurity. Frequently, an insecure person tries to enhance his own reputation by tainting the reputations of others. Such conduct is always an indication of sin in the life of the person spreading the gossip. The one who gossips may be the greater sinner than the person who is supposed to have transgressed. The insidious thing is that often the gossip is clothed in spiritual terms. "I am sharing this with you as a matter for prayer," the tune goes. A similar melody may contain the words "We must preserve the church from sin and error at all cost. Therefore I feel compelled to share this with you so you may be aware of this person's actions."

It is probable that what the pastorate needs today more than anything else is men who will be loyal to one another and who will defend one another. Even when a brother is proved guilty of a specific sin, his fellow clergymen should let him know that they care for him, bleed for him, and, although they do not condone the sin, are aware that every man, no matter who he is, will find himself beset by overwhelming temptation at one time or another. An appropriate phrase at such a time is not one of condemnation for the brother. Instead, one should say, "There but for the grace of God go I."

Even worse than spreading malicious gossip based on a brother pastor's proved sin is the making up of gossip from innuendo or unsubstantiated reports. Most countries punish murderers, but, oh, that someone could invent a suitable punishment for the person who slays another by destroying his reputation. On second thought, I'm sure there is suitable punishment, but that is dealt out by God, not man. The offender himself may be the instrument of that punishment, for as he continues to spread stories about other pastors, his reputation as a gossip catches up with him, and his own ministry is destroyed.

Predecessors

A pastor enjoys a peculiar bond with those who precede him and those who succeed him in a church. Often when a new pastor comes into a situation it appears to him that everything the former pastor did was wrong. Because it is still his honeymoon period, the people may be praising him and criticizing his predecessor. It is easy to fall in with such talk rather than discourage it. It would be good for the new pastor to remember that one day he, too, may be in a similar spot. Homer Kent, Sr., gives sage advice.

> Every pastor should make it a strict policy to refrain from speaking disparagingly of his predecessor. Failure at this point is bound to react unfavorably on the present pastor sooner or later. No matter how adverse his opinion of the former pastor, the latter in all probability has some friends in the congregation. Why incur their enmity at the start when no possible good can result from uncomplimentary remarks? Individuals in the office of pastor may fail at times, but the office is one of honor, and to disparage the person of one who holds it or who had held it is likely to dishonor the office. Failure here gives evidence of lack of the fruit of the Spirit (Gal. 5:22). Criticism can easily degenerate into the evil of gossip from which the minister, of all persons, should be separate.[2]

Books giving advice to new pastors used to warn the pastor that under no circumstances should he discuss his new church with his predecessor lest it color his opinions and thus his actions toward the people whom he serves. Such advice may be in order if the new pastor is easily impressed and incapable of making up his own mind, but usually it is not. In the last two churches I served, before agreeing to become pastor I made it a point to sit down with my predecessor and try to get an objective view of the congregation. Rather than flavoring my view prejudicially, his comments gave me rich insights into the congregation. They enabled me to tread softly in certain areas and avoid making some of the mistakes my predecessors made. It also gave me a better picture of the power structure of the church so that I knew from the start who was really in charge. I was thus able to spare the time it would have taken me to learn the power bloc. I could begin to work immediately with those who determined what would or wouldn't move in that church.

In addition to getting to know my predecessor beforehand, I did my best to praise his accomplishments before the people and to hold him in honor. When significant anniversaries approached I invited back as many of my predecessors as possible to take part in the celebration. When families in the church invited a predecessor of mine to conduct a wedding or a funeral, I have tried to stay out of the way. Often I merely attended the event without taking an active part in it, preferring to allow my predecessor his place in the sun, rather than attempting to participate in the event because of my pastoral office. Unless the family and my predecessor especially wanted me to participate as a show of unity between the two of us, I have stayed far in the background.

2. Ibid., p. 53.

In turn, when I have been invited back to a former parish to conduct a special event, I have declined as graciously as I could, saying, "Look, I love you people and I would be delighted to come. I'm honored that you asked me, but you have another pastor now, and, in deference to him, I would appreciate it if you would ask him instead of me."

To this date I have never returned to preach in a former parish. That is not because I have not been invited to do so, nor is it because I believe that it is ethically wrong. It is simply because I have never left a ministry under unfortunate circumstances. It always wrenched me apart to leave—I always left in tears, and I am just too much of a "softy" to return to a former pulpit. Too many precious memories would confront me. A time may come when I can return and preach at a former parish without losing control of myself. At present, though, that time does not seem to be near.

Successors

The best advice I can give to a person regarding his successor is to advise him to stay out of his successor's way. If a successor asks, his predecessor may choose to inform him of vital information regarding the congregation. It is my policy, however, to withdraw from the scene as much as possible and let my successor enjoy the spotlight. When he establishes himself and becomes secure enough in his ministry to invite me back for some festive occasion, I will return gratefully, remembering, however, that I am only his guest. When members of his parish call me and suggest that there are problems with his ministry, I listen attentively in order to try to defuse the situation, try to make no prejudicial statements, and refer the caller back to his pastor or to the appropriate denominational official, if I sense that mediation is indicated. Under no circumstances will I interfere. When I meet my successor, if he wants to tell me his troubles, I will listen attentively and pray with him. But I will not enter the situation or deal with any of his people in his behalf. My ministry in that community is a thing of the past. I have friends and I have memories, and those will suffice.

Denominational Officials

It is extremely unethical for a pastor to accept the call to a church with the idea in mind of taking the church out of the denomination to which it belongs. If he cannot agree to work within the framework of the denomination, he should refuse the call to the church from the very start. It is another story, however, if the denomination involved makes what the pastor believes are detrimental major theological or methodological changes after he accepts the pastorate. Then it is up to him to call in the appropriate denominational official, have him explain the denomination's point of view to the church, present his own feelings to the church while the denominational representative is present, and allow the church to vote on the question of remaining in the denomination. During the period preceding the vote, there should be no lobbying by anyone. If the church votes to stay in the denomination and the pastor feels he can live with the decision, the matter is settled. If he feels he cannot, he should tender his resignation, arrange to move out of the community as quickly as possible, and seek a call to another church. Under no circumstances should he stay in the community, split the church, and become pastor of the dissenting faction. That would be extremely unethical.

Most churches are members of denominations, whether they are called that or not. As soon as a church enters into a cooperative effort with another church and establishes a mission board to carry on their joint missions responsibilities, it is part of a denomination. Denominations are simply a way to accomplish jointly what local churches cannot accomplish as well alone. They are designed to be a supporting agency that gives help to the local church.

During my many years of ministry I have been active in three different denominations. With each of them I have found the fellowship sweet and rewarding. I am the kind of person who needs other people and would not think of being part of any local work that was totally independent, if such even exists. At times the denominations I served made requests of me and of my church that I considered impossible or impractical for us to fulfill. In each case I responded that the request seemed to be inopportune for our church at that particular time. I always received a sympathetic and understanding note in reply, saying that the denomination was happy to abide by the decision of the local church. I never experienced any pressure to conform.

Whether we call them denominations, fellowships of churches, or associations, it is nice for a pastor to belong in a special way to someone else. In this day of fierce independence and individuality, it is appropriate to return to the biblical standard of interdependence. When the going gets rough, it is comforting for a pastor to know that there are fellow pastors who will come to his aid and support him in prayer. When a church is beset by problems or does not know where to look for a pastor, it is nice to know that there is a representative

from an association of churches who can help the church sort
through its problems or recommend a suitable group of men from
whom they may choose a man for their pastor. Both pastors and
churches are wise, I believe, to keep close to their sister churches.

That does not mean that a pastor or church should not engage in
constructive criticism when improvement clearly is indicated. Sometimes, for example, a denominational official will have stayed beyond his prime and have become a detriment to his fellowship of
churches. Such situations must be dealt with calmly and in love.
Scathing, biting criticism, offered in an unloving spirit clearly is not
Christian behavior. Harmon states:

> Criticism and disparaging remarks about one's own denomination are
> sometimes heard from the pulpit. Often this is done in the spirit of the
> family circle whose members feel that they have the right to criticize
> each other since they love each other. However, it is not wise nor will it
> always be understood when a member of a family or a church publicly
> criticizes his own. To say the least, it is in bad taste.[3]

One only needs to go through a period of extreme testing to find
out how helpful it is to have others of the same family at his side.
The experience will be proof enough for him that if his church is a
member of a fellowship of churches, he should stay as close as possible to other members of that fellowship for the strengthening of
their ministries as well as his own.

One's Country

A story is credited to Dwight L. Moody that may or may not be
apocryphal. It is said that a follower met Mr. Moody on the street
one day and asked the great evangelist where he was going. "Why, to
vote," was Mr. Moody's reply. With that the follower asked, "If your
citizenship is in heaven, why do you bother with such?" Mr. Moody
is reported to have said, "Even though my citizenship is in heaven, I
still own property in Chicago."

The Christian must always remember that he is a citizen of heaven
and of the country in which he holds his earthly citizenship. He has a
duty to both. As a citizen of his earthly country, he has an obligation
to vote, to pay taxes, and to obey the laws of the land to the extent
that his conscience is not violated by his doing so. If obeying a
certain law means doing what he believes is wrong, then a higher

3. Nolan B. Harmon, *Ministerial Ethics and Etiquette* (Nashville: Abingdon, 1928), p.
   121.

authority takes over. He must make any effort necessary to resist that law by peaceful means.

Earlier in my ministry I could not conceive that such a situation would arise in the country of my birth. As government seems to have taken over an increasing portion of a person's life, I see such action now as not only possible but probable. There are indications that churches, which formally enjoyed a control-free status with the government, are coming under increasing pressure to bow to governmental control. That pressure must be resisted. In my personal opinion, Christians need to stand their ground and, if necessary, suffer the consequences, which may include incarceration, for defending their faith.

It is important that the pastor as a religious leader does his best to prevent government from interfering with the rights of churches. In addition, he may feel God's calling to speak out against vice in his community that is permitted by the government. He and his people may decide to picket so-called adult entertainment establishments in their neighborhoods or to protest the sale of pornography from supermarket shelves.

The pastor should encourage his people to be active in politics and run for public office. Rarely will it be possible for the pastor to pursue the latter. One exception might be when a pastor is called to a church in a small town or city where participation in local government is not a full-time job. In such instances, the pastor may wish to run for the city planning council, the school board, or even the city council itself. The most important job of the church in regard to government is for church members to pray for governmental leaders. The pastor should lead his people in doing so by setting the example himself. People cannot pray intelligently for anything, however, unless they know what to pray for. The pastor and his people should fulfill the biblical responsibility of being informed citizens so that they may pray intelligently for those in positions of power.

The pastor may wish to take an even greater interest in the welfare of his country by serving as a chaplain in a National Guard or Reserve unit in his community. If it does not offend his conscience to do so, his participation may be a good way for him to exercise the responsibilities of his citizenship and to contact many young men and women in his community he ordinarily would not meet.

The Importance of Effective Relationships

In this chapter we have only begun to explore a few of the relationships in which a pastor is likely to find himself. Again, may I emphasize the importance of such relationships and repeat what I have written earlier. It is my conviction that most of the trouble experienced by a pastor in his ministry is not doctrinal but relational. If a pastor is able to form effective, meaningful relationships with the people with whom he comes in contact, in most cases, he will succeed in the pastorate. If he has severe relational deficiencies, he is likely to become a casualty to the ministry and end up in some other profession. It would be extremely helpful if young men anticipating the ministry were to take whatever tests are necessary to see if relational deficiencies exist in their lives. If they do exist, then the person should seek professional counseling to help him work out his difficulties, or he should abandon his plans for the pastorate.

Summary of Professional Guidelines

The past four chapters have dealt with the kinds of relationships in which a pastor may expect to engage. Recently, a group of pastors formed a committee to draw up succinct guidelines to govern such relations as we have mentioned. The document they produced is reproduced in part below. It is a fitting summary of those things we have been considering in the last four chapters.

Code of Ministerial Ethics

The following standards are set forth in an effort to create professional understanding and to preserve the dignity, maintain the discipline, and promote the integrity of our chosen profession—the ministry of Jesus Christ.

MY PERSON
- I will endeavor to pray daily; to read, study, and meditate upon God's Word; and to maintain extended times of contemplation.
- I will plan time to be with my family, realizing my special relationship to them and their position as important members of my congregation.
- I will seek to keep my body physically fit through proper eating habits and planned exercise, renewing myself through a weekly holiday and an annual vacation.
- I will try to keep myself emotionally fit, keeping in touch with my feelings and growing in healthy control of them.
- I will strive to grow through comprehensive reading and through participation in professional educational opportunities.

MY PROFESSION
- I will seek to conduct myself consistently with my calling and my commitment as a man of God.
- I will give full service to my congregation and will accept added re-

sponsibilities only if they do not interfere with the overall effectiveness of my ministry in the congregation.

- I will consider a confidential statement made to me as a sacred trust not to be divulged without consent of the person making it.
- I will responsibly exercise the freedom of the pulpit, speaking the truth of God's Word with conviction in love; and will acknowledge any extensive use of material prepared by someone else.

MY FINANCES

- I will advocate adequate compensation for my profession and will assist the congregation to understand that a minister should not expect or require fees for pastoral service to them.
- I will be honest in my stewardship of money, paying bills promptly, asking no personal favors or discounts on the basis of my professional status.
- I will give tithes and offerings as a good steward and example to the church.

MY CONGREGATION

- I will seek to regard all persons in the congregation with equal love and concern and undertake to minister impartially to their needs.
- I will seek to be friends with all members, yet retain the right to seek close friendships within the congregation.
- I will exercise confidence in the lay leadership, assisting them in their training and mobilizing their creativity.
- I will seek to lead the church in a positive direction to achieve the goals we have mutually agreed upon. I will remain open to constructive criticism and to suggestions intended to strengthen our common ministry.
- I will candidate at only one church at a time. I will respond promptly and definitely to a call, and I shall seek to deal fairly with the church I am presently serving.

MY COLLEAGUES

- I will not perform services in the area of responsibility of my colleague in the Christian ministry except upon his request and/or expression of concern.
- I will, upon my departure, recognize that all pastoral functions should henceforth rightfully be conducted by my successor. I will seek and honor comity arrangements made with fellow pastors.
- I will, upon retirement or withdrawal from the ministry, refrain from engaging in pastoral functions within the church fellowship unless approved by the pastor.

MY DENOMINATION

- I will cooperate with the personnel of my denomination on the district and the national levels and will offer responsible criticism in order that our common service in the kingdom of God might be more effective.

- I will not use my influence to alienate this church from its chosen denomination. I will resign immediately, should I cease to hold practices and principles commonly held by our denominational fellowship.
- I covenant in the sight of God with my colleagues in the ministry to strive to keep this code of ministerial ethics.[4]

Questions for Discussion

1. What obligation does the pastor have to inform other pastors when members of their congregation begin to attend his church?

2. What questions should be asked of those who come from other churches and express numerous complaints about their former church?

3. Is it ethical to receive into our membership Christians who have membership in another local evangelical church?

4. What attitude should a pastor have toward the clergy of other churches? What if they belong to "way out" groups?

5. What would you do if you learned that a brother minister had been found to be having an affair with his secretary?

6. Upon beginning a new pastorate, what attitude should you have toward the former pastor? How will you respond should members of the congregation be critical of his ministry? What can you do to honor him and his office?

7. What advantage is there in conferring with the former pastor prior to taking a call from a church? Are there any disadvantages?

8. Following your resignation, what relationship should you have with the church?

9. Of what value are denominations, fellowships of churches, and associations?

10. Should a pastor ever accept a pastorate with the intention in mind of seeing the church change denominations?

Helpful Resources

Coker, Sam, Frank Harrington, Earl Paulk, and Bill Self. "What to Do with Church Hoppers." *Leadership* 5, no. 1 (Winter 1984):125-36.
Schaller, Lyle E. "Helping Your Successor Succeed." *Leadership* 3, no. 3 (Summer 1982):93-97.

---

4. Taken from the Code of Ministerial Ethics, Columbia Baptist Conference.

10

Pastoral Visitation

Were we to look for a biblical precedent for pastoral visitation, we would have a difficult job indeed. We could point to the journey of Peter to Cornelius, and to Paul's visits with Priscilla and Aquila, and Timothy and his family. Nevertheless, there is not enough biblical evidence to prove conclusively that such visits were routinely pastoral in nature. Each of them seems to have been made with a special purpose in mind. Peter's visit to Cornelius was a unique evangelistic journey directed specifically by God. On that occasion, Peter assumed the role of evangelist. Paul's visits cast him in the role of church planter, missionary, and evangelist. Along with the examples of obedience set by those apostles, the Bible supplies examples of Christian families who extended hospitality to itinerant preachers.

Probably the clearest case for New Testament visitation can be made by referring to Acts 2, where a great deal of visitation seems to have taken place. However, rather than the visitation being the task of the apostles or elders, there is every reason to conclude that the activity was a people-movement, with visitation occurring joyfully and spontaneously, as Christians—who shared so many other things—were compelled by their love for each other to spend time together.

In the early church there was no clear demarcation of clergy from laity. Historians are not quite sure when that division occurred, but the two distinct classes of people seem to have been present in the church at least by the fourth century. The division did not occur as an instantaneous process but was the result of a gradual movement in that direction. Eventually, as the roles were differentiated, the tasks were delineated. The concept of every believer's being a priest deteriorated into a condition in which only a special class of people were called priests. To these people was given the total responsibility for the ministry.

How unfortunate was that shift in thinking concerning the priesthood. The very genius of the Christian faith is its insistence on the priesthood of every believer. When that view of the priesthood has been upheld, each Christian has felt a holy obligation to look after the welfare of other Christians. When there were glaring needs for which individual Christians could not find a solution, the church in that location banded together to find a mutually acceptable solution. Thus we see in Acts 6 the choosing of seven men "full of the Spirit and wisdom" to supervise the distribution of food to the needy widows, so that the apostles could be absorbed in other tasks that were more in keeping with their spiritual gifts.

Although there are many indications that the early church gave financial support to its leaders, I am not able to find scriptural support for the idea that those leaders were expected to carry on a systematic visitation program with every member of the church. There is historical evidence to indicate that people lived much closer to one another. Therefore, no doubt the leaders of the early church were very much a part of a closely woven community, were an integral part of the life of that community, and were readily available to the people in the community who had needs.

Home Visitation

THE PASTOR'S ROLE

One of the more controversial subjects we will cover in this book is home visitation. Opinions on this subject often range wider than theological differences among pastors. Some will insist that a pastor must know his people in order to minister appropriately to their needs. Adherents insist that it is impossible for a pastor even to preach meaningfully to his people unless he visits regularly in their homes and is aware of the particular problems they face.

Others would take a quite different position. They insist that the very division of labor begun in Acts 6 was initiated for the express purpose of relieving church leaders of such perfunctory responsibilities as visitation so that they might devote their time to study and prayer. Advocates insist that it is impossible for a pastor to spend the time he needs in the Word and still carry on a program of regular, routine, every-member visitation.

FREQUENCY OF VISITS

To this confusion of positions is added the differing expectations of members of a local congregation. Some look back to days when the congregation was small, and they could expect frequent pastoral visits. As far as they are concerned, the pastor is not doing his job if he does not visit them often. "Surely it is not too much to expect him to visit at least once a month," they say.

Still others are terribly lonely. Maybe the children have all left home. Perhaps the spouse has died, or the person has been divorced recently. They say, "Surely the pastor ought to be aware of my need and should visit me."

On the other end of the spectrum is the person who considers routine pastoral visitation an invasion of his privacy. His speech may sound something like this: "If I need him, I will call for him, but until then, I would prefer that he not bother me." Others on this side of the spectrum, but more moderate in approach, are not quite as hostile toward pastoral visitation and may regard it as an inconvenience. They ask, "Why does he always have to visit when I'm trying to get the kids into bed or am watching my favorite television program?"

In a more moderate position are those who would be delighted with an occasional visit by the pastor but feel guilty if he visits too often. They might voice their concern in this way: "He is such a busy man and has so many things to do. I hate to have him neglect his own family responsibilities just because he feels he has to visit me." Even though such a person enjoys a pastoral visit, it does not have to occur very often in order to keep him happy.

The first year of ministry will give the pastor the chance to assess the lay of the land as he learns who desires routine pastoral visitation and at what frequency. When he sifts out the information he uncovers, he will probably find that a few people desire visitation frequently, some do not desire it at all, and a great many will be satisfied if he visits their homes when they invite him. He will be left with a visitation schedule that is fairly moderate and easy to manage. Conditions change, however, and people's needs change, so it is not a bad idea to include a "wish slip" in the bulletin from time to time. One of the most prominent check boxes on that slip should be one indicating the person would like to receive a pastoral visit. Through this means the pastor will get some indication as to where and when there are visitation needs.

The New Pastor's Visitation Program

BEGINNING HOME VISITATION

Where does a pastor begin? What should be his strategy? Obviously, the very beginning of a person's ministry in a particular church is a good place to start. At that point the pastor is not bogged down in community activities, and he has not had time to launch the church projects he has in mind. If he is called to a small or medium-sized church, he can set as a primary goal the visitation of every home unit represented in his congregation. Making such visits is a higher priority at this point than any program he may wish to initiate.

In engaging in such visitation, he should first query the leadership of the church as to an appropriate time to visit particular homes. He should visit married couples at a time when both husband and wife are home. Their working hours may differ, so the pastor should call ahead and schedule his visit accordingly. Under no circumstances should he just "drop in" until he knows the people extremely well and is certain that spontaneous visits are appreciated. If the pastor arrives and finds only the wife at home, even though he made the appointment with both husband and wife, he should stay only momentarily, exchange pleasantries, and promise to call again for another appointment.

Sometimes when the pastor telephones for an appointment it will be obvious to him that the party he is calling does not desire a visit. It is wise not to press the issue but to thank the person for the time spent on the telephone and to move to the next appointment.

MAINTAINING A GOOD REPUTATION

For the sake of his reputation and in order to minister on a long-term basis in the community, never should the pastor visit in a home alone with a woman. A possible exception to this rule may be an elderly, grandmotherly type. However, these days, there are instances where even visits to those persons are not safe. I am not being cynical at this point, only practical. Nothing can damage a pastor's reputation as quickly and extensively as scandal. Whether that scandal arises from an actual encounter or is the figment of someone's overactive imagination, it can be equally destructive to a person's ministry. It will terminate the ministry the pastor has in the location where the scandal arises, and it may plague him for the rest of his life, perhaps serving to close all available doors to future ministries.

In addition to avoiding scandal, there is a second cogent reason for avoiding solo pastoral visits to women. No man, even if he is a pastor, should consider himself above temptation. It makes sense for the pastor to eliminate the opportunity to succumb to temptation. When he visits a woman the pastor would be wise to bring his wife with him, or, if she is unavailable, to have an elder or deacon accompany him.

On the occasions when it is necessary or desirable to make such a visit during the day and the persons who usually accompany the pastor are unavailable because they have household responsibilities or are at work, one of a reserve cadre of retired people who have agreed to make such visits should go with him. Often he will be able to equip the retired person well enough so that eventually he can assume the duties of visitation.

ENLISTING A CORPS OF HELPERS

The first year of ministry is a good time for the pastor to locate people in his church who have the qualities necessary to be good visitors and to equip them for this important ministry. Since different types of people have different types of needs, it is wise to choose people with a variety of backgrounds and personalities so that they may minister successfully to as many different kinds of people and problem situations as possible.

The challenge of the pastor or other staff members is to give the people he selects the training they need and then to assign them to specific kinds of ministries, such as to shut-ins, retirees, single family households, or various other persons in need. The larger the number of people recruited and trained for the task, the less time-consuming and burdensome the task will be to the people who perform it and the more people will be visited on a regular basis.

There are many lonely people who, though they would appreciate a pastoral visit from time to time, would be extremely happy with any visit on a regular basis from a caring, concerned Christian who would agree to become their friend. Techniques of visitation, interaction with people, and sensitivity to them are not difficult to learn of the learner is open, alert, teachable, and cares genuinely for people.

The pastor may want to conduct formal classes for his visitor trainees, instructing them in some basic do's and don'ts. However, most visitation skills are best learned through observation and participation. It is wise for the pastor and other skilled visitors to have trainees accompany them on some of their visits. Then, after the visits, they should participate in debriefing, so that the trainees can ask questions as to why a specific action was taken.

Although I do not find the term *deaconess* in the Bible, I like the concept, and I think that many European church bodies have a more biblical picture of the position than we do in North America. I see the position of deaconess as an appointed rather than a elected position. Older women of the church who have been freed of parenting responsibilities can be equipped to teach and minister to the younger women and to families in need. Properly trained, they can be a great source of comfort and strength to shut-ins. If they have nursing skills, those also may be employed to help people. Sometimes they will want to offer their services as substitute grandmothers, babysitting so that young mothers can get away from their children for a little while, even if it is only to go shopping.

If the women selected as deaconesses have financial needs, the church should consider paying them adequately so that their needs are met. If they are financially independent, the church still should give them a modest stipend. It will add prestige to the job and will help to hold them accountable.

What I have suggested as a ministry for older women may work equally well for some of the older, retired men of the congregation. They, too, can lend a hand in the visitation ministry. Often they can combine a visit with the use of a practical skill. Perhaps a young mother without a husband needs a faucet fixed or a stair repaired. Again, the kind of discretion I suggested the pastor practice should be exercised by the men in the congregation. No matter how old the man is, it is wise for him not to visit a woman alone. Discretion in this matter will make possible a long and sustained ministry.

Arranging for Social Events

During the initial year of extensive visitation, the pastor should concentrate on scheduling as many events as possible that will help him get to know the people of his church. Those events might include periodic get-togethers in his home for church leaders and their spouses. Or the pastor might meet for breakfast or lunch with one, two, or several of his leaders at a time and place convenient to them. At the conclusion of such meetings, the pastor should do his best to pick up the check, although in many cases someone else will have "outfumbled" him already. People like to treat their pastor to a meal, but they do not like a pastor who always expects a handout. They want him at least to express a willingness to pay.

The pastor and his wife should attend as wide a range of social events as possible, not only during the first year but for the duration of their ministry. Especially helpful to the pastoral duo are social events held in the homes of members. While attending such events, the pastor and his wife should circulate among the guests as much as possible. At the same time, they should be sensitive to individual needs. Many times a person who would not think of coming to the pastor's office for counsel will engage him in conversation at a party and pour out the needs of his heart.

Persons Needing Frequent Visits

If a person who is visited frequently still indicates that he is not visited enough, the pastor should double-check to see if the person has any glaring needs. If he does not, at the conclusion of the pastor's next visit he should urge that person to accompany him on subsequent visits that same evening. Often such a strategy will give a person who selfishly demands attention in this matter an idea of the size of the pastor's visitation task. He is likely to be much less demanding of the pastor in the future.

For others who are not content unless the pastor himself visits them personally on a regular basis, the pastor should employ the tactic of patient waiting. To maintain the peace and support of such people, the pastor should arrange his schedule so that he visits them as often as he can. As they mature in the Lord, get to know their pastor better, and begin to appreciate how heavy his schedule is, many of them will become far less demanding of the pastor's time.

In addition to the "squeaky wheels" who want the pastor's attention, the pastor should visit people with genuine needs as often as possible. Those include shut-ins, the bereaved, the aged, and all who are hospitalized. Hospital visitation will be discussed in greater detail later in this chapter.

Visitation of New Members

If at all possible, it is important for the pastor and his wife to visit on a social basis with each new member. In some churches, growth is slow, so that does not present much of a problem. The pastor and his wife may call on new members in their homes or they may invite the new members to their home for a time of fellowship and dessert. In churches where growth is fast and the pastor's income modest, the church might pick up part of the cost of the parties, or members of the church might supply the refreshments. Such occasions establish a more personal bond between the pastor and the new members than does the limited contact that takes place at the church door following the morning service. In addition, social events held in the pastor's home are usually much warmer and more successful than similar events held in a church parlor or fellowship hall. Despite the wear and tear on the furniture and rugs, they are valuable occasions, and the pastor who holds them is wise.

Visitation of Guests

Of great concern to a church that wants to grow is the visitation of guests. Ushers should be careful to have visitors sign the guest register and fill out visitors' cards. The church will thus have double insurance against missing the names of any visitors. It is important that each local guest be visited as soon as possible after he has attended church, preferably the same week. If the pastor is able to fit such visitation into his schedule, that is desirable. However, many times a staff member or a friendly, outgoing lay person also can do the job well.

The visitor from the church should give the person he visits an attractive brochure describing the church. Also, the visitor should be trained in communicating the gospel and be open to the opportunity if it arises. I do not believe the issue should be forced upon people in the very first visit. The person doing the visiting should, instead, be friendly and open, attempting to establish a relationship with the people he is visiting. After he has gained credibility with them and they have become a bit better acquainted with the church and its ministry, then he may want to press the issue.

Unless people are in desperate need of help and are willing to express that need, they are ordinarily reluctant to commit themselves to any cause unless they believe in the people who are inviting them to do so. High pressure, would-be evangelists have a tendency to press for a decision on any chance meeting. A person may be intimidated into taking whatever action is necessary to get the caller to leave him alone, but often there is a great question as to whether or not such a commitment to Christ is genuine.

Pastoral Visitation in a Large Parish

When a pastor is called to a large parish, he may find it impossible to visit all of his people. He should, however, make it a top priority to visit with all of the leadership, both in their homes and in his. It is also helpful for him to attend as many social events as he can and to visit with as many people as possible during those events. He should make it known that he loves it when people invite him to their homes, and he should make himself available for those occasions. Even in a large congregation, a good pastor will periodically visit the shut-ins, the aged, and the bereaved. A high-priority matter is the visitation of every member who is hospitalized. They know he is busy, will be delighted to see him, and will remember forever the fact that he took time out of his busy schedule to visit with them. The more detailed and frequent follow-up hospital visitation may be delegated to an associate, an elder, or a deacon.

The most important point to be emphasized in regard to routine pastoral visitation is that the pastor should do everything he can to get to know his people. He should let them know that he is a warm, caring human being to whom they are important.

Hospital Visitation

Of all the depersonalizing experiences in life, hospitalization has to be one of the worst. Once he has checked into a hospital, a person is stripped of his clothes, his dignity, and his individuality. He becomes a pawn of those who are treating him, but he has no assurance that they will even explain to him what is being done to a body that, until then, he had considered his own property.

Clad in a nondescript hospital gown that provides extensive ventilation in the rear, he is put into an oddly-constructed bed that is so high off the floor that he must use a footstool or a course in gymnastics to get in or out of it. His room is located on a noisy passageway through which people come and go all day and all night. On the rare occasion when he is able to sleep, someone invariably barges into his room, turns on the light, takes his temperature—which has not altered a degree since he entered the hospital—and gives him a pill so that he may sleep better.

He is deprived of everything personal and comfortable, is given an arm bracelet that identifies him by number, and is put through nearly every conceivable test science can devise so that the hospital may justify the purchase of the tons of equipment for which it has spent so many of his hard-earned dollars. He is disgruntled, discouraged, lonely, and more than a little scared. During such a time, a pastoral visit is of exceptional value to him.

LEARNING OF HOSPITALIZATIONS

Many churches have what is called a prayer chain. That is a calling tree designed to inform the entire congregation by telephone of specific urgent needs and to encourage people to pray for those needs. If the pastor makes sure that either he or his spouse is included in the prayer chain, he will usually be informed when a member of the congregation is hospitalized. The pastor should also establish other channels designed to inform him of hospitalizations, realizing that many members of the congregation who would not trouble him by phoning such news, strangely enough will expect him to know automatically about all hospitalizations. They will expect a visit from him soon after their entry. Members should be urged to call the pastor when they receive news of hospitalizations. The church secretary should establish effective channels of communication so that he or she can keep the pastor informed. The leadership of the church, likewise, should be trained to keep the pastor up-to-date.

VISITING THE HOSPITAL ROOM

When receiving news of a hospitalization, the pastor or church secretary should call the hospital to determine if the patient is indeed registered there, to find out the severity of the ailment, and to get an idea of the length of time the patient is expected to stay. Many people can no longer afford the luxury of long hospitalization. They are admitted briefly for surgical procedure and are dismissed that same day.

If the patient has been admitted that very day and it is anticipated that he or she will stay awhile, it is a good idea for the pastor to plan an evening visit. By then, most medical procedures should be finished and the visit may occur in a fairly uninterrupted fashion. Unless the patient has undergone extensive surgery, this is a good time for a prolonged visit. Cheerful conversation, the reading of the Scriptures, and a prayer will bring reassurance to the Christian. If the patient has misgivings and questions and there are not too many other people present, often he will use the opportunity to seek answers from the pastor. This is not a time for pat solutions but for sensitivity, calmness, and reassurance.

An excellent rule of thumb for the pastor to follow is this: If the door is closed or the curtain pulled around the patient's bed, always respect his privacy. Inquire of a nearby nurse, who, in turn, will check to see if the patient may have visitors. Such a procedure will save the patient and pastor embarrassment, and it has legal ramifications. In certain localities, I am told, if someone invades a patient's privacy, he may be sued.

When he visits a patient, it is advisable for the pastor not to sit on the patient's bed. Sitting on the bed may cause the patient discomfort, and it is always improper etiquette. Some pastors I know, and even some hospital chaplains, do that on a regular basis and get away with it. I have always considered it rude and insensitive, except in those rare cases where the patient himself has invited the pastor to do so.

The pastor should remember that the hospital room is the patient's present home. Certainly the rent is high enough! Therefore, the pastor should conduct himself as the patient's guest, being careful to be gracious and thoughtful. He should be cheerful but not boisterous. Laughter may prove painful to a person who has undergone surgery, and loud talk may disturb him and the other patients. The pastor should stand or sit where the patient does not have to strain to see him. That may require helping the patient adjust his bed, if he so desires.

The pastor should be encouraged to touch the patient, especially when he prays with him. Touch in itself can have a healing effect. Sometimes patients feel that hospitalization has singled them out as someone who is diseased and therefore unacceptable. The touch of another person reassures them that they are not outcasts. When touching a woman, the pastor always should be especially discreet. Holding her hand when praying with her is appropriate.

If it is evident that the patient is tiring or if a significant number of other guests arrive, it is wise for the pastor to excuse himself and leave. Before doing so, he may want to invite the other guests to join him in prayer for the patient. Flowers from the church are a tangible way of telling the patient that his brothers and sisters in Christ care for him. It is wise for the pastor to make sure that those responsible see that each member who is hospitalized receives that gesture of concern.

Visiting the Surgical Patient

When the patient is scheduled for surgery, it is wise for the pastor, an elder, or a deacon to visit with him immediately before the surgery and pray with him, even though the surgery may be scheduled for early in the morning. A short time of prayer, a Scripture verse, and a word of reassurance may calm many who face surgery with dread.

If close relatives of the patient intend to wait at the hospital during surgery, some representative of the church may want to wait out the ordeal with them until the surgery is over and the patient out of danger. Unless the immediate prognosis of the patient is extremely guarded, it is not advisable for the pastor to visit the patient until he has been brought back to his own room. At that time, a short, quiet visit with a brief prayer is in order. If the patient is asleep, he should not be awakened. The pastor may want to jot a short note on his business card and leave it for the patient when he awakens. The pastor should plan to visit the patient at least once more after the surgery, coordinating his efforts with other members of the church so that the patient is visited every day. If there is an extensive period of convalescence at home, the pastor should plan to visit there as well.

HOSPITAL VISITATION BY THE PASTOR OF A LARGE CHURCH

What I have been projecting here is an appropriate pattern of visitation for an average pastor. Pastors of extremely large churches will not be able to engage in such activity. But for the pastor of such a church, it is not too much to ask to expect him to make at least one visit to those of his congregation who are hospitalized.

HELPING THE FAMILY

When members or friends of the church are hospitalized, an efficient deacons' organization will spring into action, visiting the home and determining whether or not the needs of the family are being met. Needs may include the preparation of meals, the cleaning of the house, the paying of bills, babysitting, and transporting family members to and from the hospital. Where the illness is serious, out-of-town relatives may decide to encourage the family by a personal visit. The relatives may need transportation to and from the airport or bus station.

In some cases, the patient may not be fully insured and will need assistance from the congregation in paying his hospital bills. If it is the wife of the family who is convalescing after surgery, it may be appropriate for members of the church to continue supplying meals to the family along with babysitting services during the convalescent period. During the hours of the husband's employment, it may be helpful if a mature woman from the congregation stays with the convalescing wife, answers the phone, helps the children to get off to school, and keeps them occupied when they arrive home from school, so that the mother can continue to rest.

PRESENTING THE MESSAGE OF SALVATION

Hospital visitation can be a fruitful and appreciated ministry. People often are more receptive to the things of the Lord during hospital stays, though that does not give the pastor carte blanche to use pressure or scare tactics to evangelize them. The conversation between patient and pastor may turn to spiritual matters merely because the pastor is there and the patient is thinking through the really crucial issues in his life. When a conversation moves in this manner and a pastor is not sure of a person's spiritual condition, it is always proper for the pastor to inquire whether or not the patient has experienced salvation. If the person is unsaved, it is important for the pastor to ask him if he would like to be saved. If the answer is negative, the pastor should drop the subject. If the answer is affirmative, the pastor may have the glorious privilege of leading the patient to the Lord.

DEALING WITH THE COMATOSE PATIENT

If the patient is comatose and it appears that he is both unsaved and near death, it is important for the pastor to talk to him as if he is able to hear and understand everything that is said. In many cases, when such patients have returned to consciousness, they could tell people everything that was said to them while they were comatose. Because there is so much at stake here, the pastor should always present the plan of salvation as simply and effectively as he can and allow the patient to make a decision—one that only the patient and God will know about.

DEALING WITH THE TERMINALLY ILL PATIENT

I believe firmly that a person has the right to know if he is dying so that he may engage in whatever spiritual preparation he feels is necessary. But physicians often try to withhold that information from the patient in an attempt to keep him calm and prolong his life as long as possible. At such a time, the pastor may be able to discern the patient's overall needs better than the physician and, as a result, may be bound morally to disobey the physician's orders. There is no suggestion here that the pastor blurt out the fact of the patient's impending death. What is meant is that if the patient asks about his condition, the pastor should tell him the truth. If the patient does not bring up the matter, I believe that the pastor has the obligation to approach him. He can ask the patient, "Joe, are you aware that you are very seriously ill, and there's always a chance that you may not make it?" Then the pastor can talk with the patient about the spiritual preparations a person should make before he enters the presence of God.

I stress this point so strongly because I am convinced that there are occasions when the patient's rights actually are being violated because people are withholding vital information from him, even to the extent of lying to him. We who are Christians know that prolonging life on this earth under any condition, or at all cost, is not a suitable Christian goal. The state of a person's heart before God is a much more important consideration than trying to keep him alive for a few more hours in a disintegrating body.

VISITATION CONNECTED WITH CHILDBIRTH

Childbirth, usually a time of great joy and celebration, may be a time of great trauma. Nervous prospective fathers as well as mothers-to-be may find comfort in a pastoral visit, especially if complications are suspected. During a time of potential danger, it is good for some mature saint, if not the pastor himself, to stay close by the couple in case emotional support is needed. If a child is stillborn or born with a severe handicap, the couple will need pastoral support as soon as possible. The pastor may not be able to do much more than cry with the couple, pray with them, and give them some assurance from Scripture. At such a time, what he says is not as important as the fact that he is there.

The pastor should be careful in what he says, however. He should always avoid being judgmental, no matter how much bitterness may pour from the parents. Also, he should avoid mouthing pious platitudes or saying that he understands their sorrow, if he has never gone through such an experience himself. Above all, he should refrain from assuring them that there is plenty of time for them to have other children. All their present hopes, plans, and dreams are bound up in the child they lost.

When the delivery is routine and successful, the pastor may wish to visit the new mother and baby in the hospital at least once. The visit should be short and scheduled carefully. It should not occur during the hours the mothers are nursing their new babies. If the pastor does not feel well, he should not visit the maternity ward until he recuperates fully.

DEALING AS A PROFESSIONAL WITH HOSPITAL STAFF

The pastor who wishes to be effective in hospital visitation always establishes friendly relations with hospital personnel, including physicians. However, the pastor should not allow himself to be intimidated by such people. He should remember that he is every bit as well prepared in his profession as they are in theirs and that he is almost always able to minister much more wholistically to the patient than the physician, who frequently is concerned only with treating a person's body. I am not suggesting that the pastor give medical advice or interfere with medical treatment. I am insisting that the pastor has valuable input into a patient's life that many physicians do not even know about. There are times, therefore, when pastor and physician will conflict. One of those, as noted above, may be during the final illness of a terminally ill patient.

DEALING WITH INSENSITIVE AND NEGLECTFUL HOSPITAL STAFF

There is another reason the pastor should attempt to be objective, as well as friendly, in his relationship with the hospital staff. In my experience as a hospital chaplain, I became aware of incidents when hospital personnel were unnecessarily crude, rough, unsympathetic, and even negligent toward a patient. I have found physicians and nurses, for instance, who treated mature patients as if they were mentally retarded, refusing to explain to them what and why they were undergoing a specific procedure. Additionally, I have seen nurses who treated the patient and his family members as something subhuman and refused or neglected to respond to a patient's needs when the patient drew those needs to the nurse's attention. Such behavior is rare, but it should not be permitted to reoccur.

Poor examples of the medical profession should be reported to the proper authorities. Probably the first person to whom the report should go is the hospital chaplain, if there is one. The next person is the hospital administrator and then the board. If none of those persons takes satisfactory action, the local or regional hospital board or commission should be informed. Before taking such steps, however, it is advisable for the pastor or church representative to stay at the hospital long enough to observe personally at least one example of unsatisfactory conduct. If the pastor cannot document the conduct himself, he should pursue proper remedial efforts with the corroboration of family members who are willing to testify to the abusive behavior they have witnessed. It is necessary to obtain documentation and corroboration of such accusations. The word of the patient alone is not necessarily good enough, for sometimes actions that the patient perceives as being harmful are actually medical procedures necessary for his welfare.

COOPERATING WITH THE HOSPITAL

By and large, the pastor's deportment in a hospital should be one of support, encouragement, and cooperation with medical personnel.

Before he enters intensive care units, for instance, he should always inquire at the nursing station concerning the condition of the patient. At that time, he should ask permission to see the patient and should find out if there are any limitations regarding the length of his stay or any conditions governing his visit. Likewise, when he visits people in isolation units, he should follow hospital policy, including washing his hands, wearing a gown and mask, and respecting any other procedures specified by the nurses.

For Those Who Love It, a Rich Ministry

There are pastors who dislike hospital visitation immensely and try to avoid it at all cost. When a pastor dislikes something so intensely, he is likely not to do his best when performing that function. In this case, the pastor should identify and equip others to carry on the bulk of the ministry of hospital visitation, reserving for himself those visits he believes he is compelled to make. No doubt there are others within the congregation who do not see hospital visitation as being so odious and will perform the ministry exceedingly well. There may be still others in the church who love such a ministry and will pursue it as much as possible. If their results match their zeal, then they are the people who should specialize in this vital form of ministry.

One pastor I know loves hospital ministry so much and performs it so well that every day he visits both hospitals in his town. When he arrives, he sorts through the patient cards and selects those who have indicated a preference for his denomination. Before he visits them, he confers with the nursing staff and physicians, finding out how he may be of assistance to the patient and to the medical personnel. Through the years, the medical staff has learned to trust him and to rely on him. Often, nurses and physicians refer him to certain patients. His gentle, kindly, and warm manner automatically brightens a hospital room. As a result of his visits, many patients and their families have found him irresistible. A great number have committed their lives to Christ because of his ministry. His church has grown dramatically over the years. He attributes much of that growth to contacts he has made in visits to the community hospitals.

Visitation of the saints by the saints is biblical. Though often inconvenient and sometimes embarrassing for the person making the visit, visitation is not only important, it is a significant means of welding a congregation together. When we visit one another, we become aware of each other's needs and then are able to minister constructively to those needs.

The idea of pastoral visitation is not a biblical one, as far as I can determine, except as I see New Testament elders equipping others for the work of the ministry. As I observe their actions, I see many examples of equipping by modeling. The problem posed by many pastors today is that they either try to equip while refusing themselves to engage in the job they are teaching, or they do the work of the ministry without bothering to equip anyone else for it. The better approach is a combination of both, in which a ministering member of a congregation not only observes his pastor's example but receives proper instruction as to why the pastor does what he does. As a result he may then go forth not only to do the task for which the pastor has trained him but also to equip others to do that ministry, too.

Questions for Discussion

1. What do you see as the biblical precedent for the pastor's ministry of visitation?

2. What is your philosophy of pastoral visitation? Do you believe that it is solely the responsibility of the pastor, or do you feel that the responsibility should be shared with the leaders of the congregation?

3. When is the best time in a pastor's ministry to a particular church for him to attempt a program of every-member visitation?

4. Why is it not advisable for a pastor to visit in a home alone with a woman?

5. What strategies might a pastor employ to enlist the help of others in his congregation in a ministry of visitation?

6. Besides actually visiting a member's home, how may a pastor make contact with his people?

7. How would you prioritize your visitation list? Whom would you place at the top of the list? Why? In what order would you place others on your list?

8. Why is it important for a pastor's people to feel that he is a warm, caring human being?

9. What may a pastor do to reduce the trauma of a member's hospitalization? What are some pitfalls to avoid when visiting members in the hospital?

10. What should be the pastor's relationship to the personnel and physicians at the hospital?

11. Develop your own philosophy of pastoral visitation. List the possible opportunities that exist in your situation. How will you accomplish your goals without limiting yourself in other important areas?

Helpful Resources

Braden, Doyle W. *How to Set Up and Conduct a Weekly Visitation Program.* Nashville: Convention Press, 1982.

Folprecht, William. "Ideas That Work: How to Be a Blessing to Hospital Patients." *Leadership* 2, no. 3 (Summer 1981):94-95.

Gibble, Kenneth L. "Preparing Parishioners for a Pastoral Visit." *Leadership* 2, no. 4 (Fall 1981):55-58.

Sisemore, John T. *The Ministry of Visitation.* Nashville: Convention Press, 1954.

11

Pastoral Counseling

As a pastor becomes established in a community, he builds credibility with his own people and with the community at large. As a result, he often finds himself in demand as a counselor. Despite the substantial increase in the number of professionally-trained career counselors in recent years, a large amount of the counseling that takes place in many communities falls upon the shoulders of the local pastor.

Motivations for Seeking the Pastor's Counsel

There are several reasons for the counseling burden falling upon the pastor. Undoubtedly, one of those is that there still is a stigma attached to anything appearing to be mental illness. Because a "shrink" is associated with "crazy people" by much of the populace, and few want to admit that they are crazy, many people will seek all kinds of intermediate solutions before turning at last, in desperation, to a psychologist or psychiatrist for help. One of those intermediate sources is the local pastor. A visit to him may be made for any number of respectable reasons and need not indicate an admission of mental illness.

A second reason people look to the pastor for counseling help is because generally he is much more accessible than the professional counselor. Despite the fact that the clergyman's schedule may be fuller than the counselor's, the pastor has the reputation of being a soft touch whose compassion and sense of duty are so intense he is reluctant to turn down anyone for anything. Therefore, whereas a troubled person may find it necessary to make an appointment weeks ahead of time in order to see a psychiatrist or psychologist, his pastor probably will agree to see him on relatively short notice.

The third, and perhaps most important reason for the popularity of the pastor as a counselor is that usually his counseling does not involve a fee. That is a legitimate concern for people with modest incomes. For others, however, who merely want to play the counseling game, the lack of a fee merely makes easier an elaborate subterfuge. These people have no real intention of dealing with their problems, but they want to convince themselves and others that they are genuinely interested in doing so. By going to the pastor, they can take care of appearances without having to invest any money on a process they know will never succeed. Still another group of people go to a pastor for counseling because he does not charge a fee. These persons really want help and can afford to pay for it. Yet it is their pattern to try to get by every situation in life as cheaply as they can, the one possible exception being the pursuit of their own pleasure. Even though they would prefer to see a psychiatrist or psychologist, they are dissuaded from doing so by what they believe are the exorbitant fees charged by professional counselors. The pastor's services are free, they reason, and are too good a bargain to pass up.

There is a fourth reason people choose to receive counseling from their pastor rather than a psychologist or psychiatrist: they truly love and trust him. They are confident that he is a wise man of God and are certain that he will be able to help them. They trust him and value his judgment. They appreciate his wisdom and always come to him before seeking any other counsel. Because they see the pastor as a unique servant of God, they are convinced that he has God's answer to their problem. Such people seek the help of a professional counselor only in a dire emergency. Under no circumstances would they ever enlist the aid of a non-Christian counselor. To them, the wisdom of the most humble Christian exceeds the knowledge of the most highly trained unsaved counselor.

Equipping Lay Counselors

With the increasing complexity of life and the growing demands of people who think they need counseling, it is legitimate to ask, "How can the pastor cope with the constantly increasing demands on his schedule?" Unfortunately, for many pastors there is no satisfactory solution because they have forgotten one of the most important factors of their ministry, the work of equipping others for ministry. Thus, while continuing to minister, they neglect training others to carry out a part of the ministry. It is my conviction that perhaps 90 percent of the counseling needs faced by any congregation could be performed expertly and sensitively by concerned, dedicated Christians who love people enough to listen to them. In addition to an attentive ear, those people will need training that will teach them how to assist the counselee in identifying and constructively dealing with his problems.

In the past, lay counselors have been discouraged from such pursuits. Recently, however, an increasing number of professional counselors have come to recognize that they cannot do the job alone. They have begun to view themselves not only as therapists but as partners with the pastor in the equipping of the saints for the work of ministry. Periodic workshops now are being conducted in major cities where laypersons receive training in a few basic counseling techniques and are taught to recognize where specific cases are beyond their competency. They are taught to refer those cases to a professional. People trained in this manner are able to relieve the pastor of much of his counseling load and are able to aid people who ordinarily would have to wait long weeks for the services of a therapist. In addition, counselees seeking the help of such a layperson may find him more easy to relate to than the professional. Instead of a "shrink," here is a person much like the counselee, one who faces the normal problems of everyday life, a friend who can understand, accept and pray with him.

Whereas it may take a person several visits to establish a sense of rapport with the professional, his confidence in his fellow church member may have been established already. This is assuming that the particular church community has established within it a sense of warmth, acceptance, and trust. When such prevails, it is easier for Christians to follow the Bible's command to "bear one another's burdens."

It is unfortunate that Christians have to a large measure abdicated many of the "bearing" responsibilities, leaving them to professionals. There are many reasons for the abdication. Our society discourages people from being truly intimate with one another. An even more compelling reason is that the professionalism and specialization in our society conveys the idea to laypersons that only a professional can attempt a counseling ministry.

In the case of counseling, that attitude may have been conveyed by professionals who were insecure in their own field. However, even those people, in their more quiet moments, have to admit that both psychology and psychiatry are infant sciences with little empirical data on which to depend. In sharp contrast, people have been successful in counseling other people since the beginning of time and without the help of psychological theory. In the past few years such persons as Jay Adams and Gary Collins have done much to get laypeople involved in the counseling process once more. Collins and others have performed a further service by producing valuable resource materials that help the layperson to develop counseling skills.

As an equipping elder, the pastor ought to be training his people for the ministry of counseling. He will have to be careful in his choices, of course. Just as in any other ministry, there are people who are appropriate to the task, and there are those who are not because of their personalities.

If the pastor is not properly equipped in this area, he will need to seek such equipping for himself as well. Audio-visual, commercially-produced seminars now available provide valuable insights. In large metropolitan areas, hospitals, clinics, and other agencies offer training for counselors at negligible cost to the students. Additionally, in many places there is an increased recognition on the part of professional Christian counselors that an equipping ministry is a good use of their time, talents, and training.

Advantages of the Pastor's Counsel

Even when the pastor has capable laypeople who are available to counsel, many people will insist on seeking help from the pastor himself. Some of those people are so constituted that they will not settle for anybody but the "top man" to help them with their problems. No mere layperson will do. Because of his theological training, the pastor may indeed be the appropriate person to deal with them, sharing Scripture with them to help them see that an improper attitude may be at the heart of their problems.

At times people will seek a pastor's counsel because they see him as a father figure, or as a special representative of God, attaining a godliness that is not possible for a layperson. Whatever the reason, for them the pastor is a person of special credibility. This credibility gives the pastor a distinct advantage when he counsels them.

Part of his credibility arises from the pastor's training, experience, and reputation. People reason that a person who was graduated from a Bible college or seminary will have gained advanced skills in counseling. If the pastor also has a distinguished pastoral record and has earned the reputation of being a good counselor, it is proper for lay counselors to refer cases to him that are more difficult than they feel they can handle. The pastor, in turn, needs to recognize his own limitations and know when to refer people to a skilled therapist. Yet even when he believes that the problems of the person he is dealing with are beyond his couneling skills, he should be reluctant to turn over his counselee to an unsaved therapist unless a Christian therapist is absolutely unavailable.

Selecting Those to Counsel

Because there is such a lengthy list of potential counselees, the pastor will need to choose those counselees with whom he will work. The very title of his office as shepherd should make obvious to him that his first priority must be members of his own flock. Despite his evangelistic ambitions, all other persons necessarily must receive second priority. When we extend the shepherd image it means that the pastor may be expected to bring comfort, sympathy, discipline, and incentive to his flock first, even pampering them on occasion until they mature enough to require it no more.

In the hard world in which we live, all of us can stand special care now and then. Just as a parent may be expected to pamper a little child from time to time, so it is reasonable to expect that the pastor will pamper some of his sheep occasionally as long as it does not reach ridiculous and unmanageable proportions and consume the major part of his time. If he is to disperse extra attention to a group in his church, his focus should not necessarily be on the "squeaky wheels" but on those who work long and hard in the service of the Lord, anticipating little reward and never expecting to receive special treatment. Such people deserve extra consideration when the pastor sets up his counseling schedule.

A second category of people to receive the pastor's counseling attention are those the pastor senses are ready to respond to the gospel message. He ministers to such persons as part of his responsibility to "do the work of an evangelist," a task discussed at greater length elsewhere in this book.

How does the pastor know who is receptive to the gospel? He does so by being with people and by being sensitive to people. In rare cases someone may have referred such a person to the pastor. More often the person will have identified himself through a contact he has made with the pastor. He may have been a stranger who just appeared one day at the church office and expressed a desire for counseling. Although not all persons in this category can be seen on an extended basis, it is important for each of them to receive at least an initial interview from one of the pastoral staff to ascertain their receptivity to the gospel. Although it would be good if the church were able to provide extensive counseling to everyone who asks, when there is a limited amount of time, those who seem receptive to the gospel should receive a high priority.

Sometimes, those appearing at the church do not expect a long-term counseling relationship. Perhaps an answer to a current problem is all they desire. All who come for such help should be treated warmly and courteously and should be made to feel important, even when they approach the pastor on a basis which seems superficial to him.

Essential Qualities of the Counselor

To be a good counselor, a person must have a genuine love for people and be able to refrain from talking. I have not heard of a truly successful counselor who was not a good listener. The skilled listener will learn to ask a few appropriate questions to aid the counselee himself to find the root of his problem and decide on a proper biblical solution. However, contrary to some who use purely non-directive techniques, I do not believe that a client will be able always to define his real problem or to voice a proper solution to it unless he has been given the type of information he needs to reach such conclusions. Thus, in my opinion, the counselor needs to be more than just a good listener. He should know how to reflect back to the client what he is actually saying, and he should know how to use key questions in gently interrogating the client. Occasionally the counselor must supply cognitive data the client needs to absorb. When the client applies such information to his thought patterns, he will probably come up with more rational thinking.

Methods That Can Be Used

The biblical counselor has absolutes with which to work. In a nonthreatening adult way, it is proper for him to say, "Thus says the Lord," and at times to state categorically that the thoughts and behavior of the counselee are biblically unacceptable. Sometimes the necessary cognitive data can be supplied through homework assignments given to clients. The counselor can ask the person he is counseling to read relevant portions of Scripture and to answer pertinent questions regarding the text. Sometimes the reading of certain books or the viewing of special films will be helpful to the client as he works to alter his thought patterns. In many cases, participation in some kind of accountability group can be of healing benefit. Certain types of tests given by the counselor may reveal problems needing attention. Some tests can be administered by a counselor who has had relatively little training in their use, but other tests are more sophisticated and should be used only by the professional.

The Seriousness of the Counselee's Search for Well-Being

I am convinced that though a counselor should hear out the counselee, endless repetitions of the same story session after session may be merely an exercise in self-pity, rather than an earnest attempt of the person to find an adequate solution to his problems. I am convinced as well that if a counselee neglects or refuses to do the homework assigned to him, gives no sign of progress, or indicates an unwillingness to take concrete steps toward working with the counselor to solve his problems, counseling should be discontinued after the third session. It may be resumed then when the counselee declares his seriousness in a tangible manner.

By the third session, the counselee should have had time to establish rapport with the counselor, see him as a caring person, and share with him at least the surface concerns in sufficient detail to be ready to get at the heart of the problem. If a counselee is not willing to help himself enough to do his part, it may be that he is unwilling to deal constructively with his problems, or that the pastor is not sufficiently skilled to help the counselee progress as he should. Whichever is the cause of the client's lack of participation, painful as it may be to the pastor who wants to be "all things to all men," the pastor should point out kindly, firmly, and objectively that the counselee is not taking an active part in the solution of his problem. He should, therefore, discontinue counseling or seek the help of someone better trained in counseling.

One word of caution. In attempting to help the counselee get to the heart of his problems, it is not necessary for the pastor to become a kind of voyeur by encouraging the client to reveal all the lurid details of his background and the depths of sin through which he has come. Theological soundness alone should teach that individual sins are merely symptomatic of the major problem, which is sin itself, rebellion toward and estrangement from God. If the counselee cannot confess his sins directly to God and receive His forgiveness, it may be necessary for him to recite some of them to his counselor. There is a vast difference, however, between the pastor who hears the cathartic confessions of a person as he unloads burdens from his soul, and the pastor-counselor who prods the counselee to share things that serve only to provide sordid entertainment for the counselor.

Some Advice

Although it is not the purpose of this book to give a detailed step-by-step description of the counseling process and the proper counseling techniques, a few hints are in order. First, it is important for any counselor to maintain the attitude of a novice, always remembering that he has not begun to see anything yet. Throughout his career he will be exposed continually to new situations. In light of that, although I would encourage him to obtain the finest training possible, to read the newest substantive books and periodicals on the subject, and to gain as much help as he can from professionals, he must realize that even when science has been taken into consideration, counseling is still, in large part, an art. Though the counselor will gain expertise as he practices his art, nevertheless, in a real sense he is painting a new creative picture with every person he helps.

Second, while avoiding the use of pat answers, the counselor never should hesitate to be biblical in the advice he gives. He should avoid the thundering, condemnatory phrases with which some Christians flail sinners, but when questions arise that call for a biblical answer, it is surely appropriate for him to say something like this: "Why don't we turn to (such and such a passage) and see what it says. Would you like to read the passage? How do you suppose it relates to the problem you are now facing?"

Third, the pastor should not hesitate to use a counseling appointment as an evangelistic opportunity, despite the reticence of even many Christian professional counselors to do so. Of course it would be inappropriate for him to introduce salvation as a panacea before he has given the counselee a chance to express his problem. There is a sense in which any believer, talking to an unbeliever about his soul, first needs to earn the right to be heard. After he has listened and the counselee knows that the counselor genuinely cares for him, God will provide the opportunity for the gospel to be communicated. At that point the conversation may sound something like this: "You know, John, I really care for you. Yet if I were a physician, knew what your illness was, and withheld a medication that was sure to save your life, I would be derelict in my duty. You could conclude correctly that I didn't really care for you. Now, as your counselor, I know about something that will cure the root cause of your problems and help you work them out more effectively. Because I care for you and am not derelict in my responsibility to you, with your permission, I would like to share it with you. May I?"

Again, the pastor must know how to reach a happy medium between springing the message on a person prematurely and missing the opportune moments the Holy Spirit sends along. The pastor will find that genuine concern for the person and sensitivity to him is the key to good, effective, counseling evangelism.

One final suggestion. People tend to value that in which they have invested something. Members and regular church attenders already have invested in the ministry of the church through their time, talents, tithes and offerings. Strangers, on the other hand, have invested nothing. It may be beneficial to them to remember that nothing is free. Someone must pay the expenses of the church building—the heat and light for example—and the salaries of the pastor and his secretary. Therefore, I believe it is proper for the board of the church to suggest a fee scale graduated on the basis of the income of the counselee. Every non-member or non-attender should pay something. If the income of the counselee is so low as to make the payment of any fee prohibitive, he could be asked to exchange labor for counseling.

Because the salary of the pastor is paid by the church already, I believe it is improper for the counseling fee to go to him. Instead, a fund could be established to take care of expenses required in extending the counseling program; or the church could use the fees to satisfy the needs of poor people in the community.

Requiring a fee may substantially reduce the pastor's counseling load, but those counselees who remain will probably be much more serious about what they are attempting to accomplish than they would have been if they were allowed to receive the counseling free. Also, requiring the counselee to pay will give him a dignity not possible for the person who receives a handout.

In trying to picture the pastor's counseling role, I have attempted to describe a process where one caring human being attempts to interact meaningfully and sensitively with another. In that process the pastor listens a great deal and encourages the counselee to discover for himself answers to his problems. The pastor points his client to relevant biblical data that, when applied, will help him reorient his thought processes. Through the application of biblical principles, the counselee may discover that it is possible to alter his life dramatically and positively.

In engaging in such a helping relationship, the pastor should not be detached or cool, but instead should establish a meaningful, vital, trusting atmosphere in his dealings with the counselee. Counseling textbooks used to say that a counselor should keep himself aloof from the client and his problems, maintaining an objective attitude. Though there is a danger of the pastor's becoming so involved with the counselee and his problems that he actually assumes the client's problems, I do not believe that a counselor can help a counselee toward healing unless he genuinely cares for his client, is concerned about the client's problems, and conveys that concern to the client in some manner. Therefore, I would offer the pastor-counselor a summary piece of advice. Do become personally concerned with and involved in the life of the counselee. Laugh with him and cry with him. But remember: the problems he faces are still his. Do not let them become yours. Do not allow yourself to get so tied up in his problems that you no longer can help him discover the solutions.

Probably no aspect of ministry is as capable of producing such favorable results as that which involves one-on-one contact between the pastor and his people. Often such contact in a counseling session comes as the result of inordinate stress in the counselee's life. Studies have shown that such periods of stress often produce sufficient cognitive disequilibrium in the life of a person to work toward that person's destruction or to propel him to new heights of satisfying living. If the pastor-counselor has sufficient skills to be able to use the opportunity properly, he may find himself a partner with the counselee in effecting the most dramatic positive change the counselee ever will experience. Rather than being a perfunctory chore, pastoral counseling may be among the most rewarding, exciting work performed by the pastor in his years of service.

Questions for Discussion

1. What role does the pastor play as counselor in the midst of a wider community that includes the professional counselor, the psychologist, and the psychiatrist?

2. How can the pastor cope with the constant increasing demands on his schedule in the area of counseling?

3. What advantages does the pastor have over others in the community who are counseling?

4. What resources are available for equipping members to participate in pastoral counseling? How would you use these resources?

5. When is it appropriate for a lay person to do counseling; when must it be the pastor himself who counsels; and when should the pastor refer to a Christian therapist?

6. Understanding that there is considerable demand for the pastor's counseling services, what sort of priority system should the pastor devise when he sets up his counseling schedule?

7. When the pastor is counseling, why is it important for him to refrain from speaking a majority of the time?

8. What methods and techniques may the pastor employ to accomplish his counseling goals?

9. What should be done about fees for counseling services? Should members be charged? What about non-members? Who should receive the fees? Is there therapeutic value in charging a fee?

Helpful Resources

Adams, Jay E. *Christian Counselor's Manual.* Grand Rapids: Baker, 1973.

Clinebell, Howard J. *Basic Types of Pastoral Counseling.* Nashville: Abingdon, 1966.

Collins, Gary R. *Effective Counseling.* Santa Ana, Calif.: Vision House, 1980.

———. "Lay Counseling Within the Local Church." *Leadership* 1, no. 4 (Fall 1980):78-86.

———. *How to Be a People Helper.* Santa Ana, Calif.: Vision House, 1976.

Crabb, Lawrence. *Basic Principles of Biblical Counseling.* Grand Rapids: Zondervan, 1976.

Getz, Gene, Richard Hunt, Frank Minirth, David Seamands, and James Smith, "The Demands, Dilemmas, and Dangers of Pastoral Counseling." *Leadership* 1, no. 4 (Fall 1980):129-41.

Smith, Fred. "Common-Sense Counseling." *Leadership* 2, no. 4 (Fall 1981):111-17.

Zilbergeld, Bernie. "The Myths of Counseling." *Leadership* 5, no. 1 (Winter 1984):87-91.

Part 3
The Pastoral Tasks

The Baptism of the

12

A Biblical Description of the Pastor's Tasks

One of the exciting aspects of studying the New Testament is to discover the leeway it gives for creativity in the gospel ministry. Although the Bible is abundant with descriptions of what went on during its own times, seldom does it say that those descriptions prescribe the way we should do things today. I have found only seven prescribed categories of activity for those engaged in pastoral ministry. All of them are broad enough in description to allow for much latitude and creativity in their application. Before considering the specific tasks that a contemporary pastor is required to perform, I would like to explore those seven biblical categories.

Equipping

Ephesians 4:11-16 indicates that a principal task of the special officers given to the church is to equip the saints for the work of ministry. There has been a certain degree of misunderstanding on the part of some pastors as to the meaning of the word *equip*. The Greek word used here, *katartismos*, connotes complete adjustment to a particular situation or task. The King James translates the word "perfecting." The equipped saint, then, may be considered one who has been made perfect for the job or who has completely adjusted to it. He is completely qualified to carry on that ministry. Since the pastor is only one of several equippers noted in the fourth chapter of Ephesians, it would be logical to say that he is not to be called upon

157

to do all of the necessary equipping of the saints. His equipping duties lie principally in his particular area of responsibility, specifically in the task of pastoring, or shepherding, the sheep. It seems plausible, then, that the chief equipping duty of the pastor to his people should be the equipping of the saints to care for each other's needs: the fostering of a caring, loving, fellowship of believers.

A certain degree of pulpit teaching will be helpful in developing an appropriate caring attitude among the people of a congregation. However, the most effective equipping in this area will be done only as the pastor himself acts as a teaching model, displaying a loving, caring attitude toward his flock, and exemplifying the way his parishioners should conduct themselves. Such an attitude is better caught then taught. As a result, if the pastor intends to equip others for caring ministries, it is wise for him seldom to perform those ministries alone. Instead, he should select people in his congregation who he believes are good candidates for such a ministry and take them along with him, one at a time, as he performs shepherding tasks. Little by little he will teach them to perform the tasks themselves, and, eventually, as they become skilled, he will encourage them to equip others, too.

Shepherding

Because the term *pastor* means shepherd, and because there is much evidence that the pastor will best carry on an equipping ministry through teaching by example what it means to be an effective shepherd, it follows that the pastor himself must be involved in shepherding activities. Yet in our culture today, not all pastors are. Thus they miss out on the essence of the ministry to which God has called them. For how can a person be called a shepherd if he is not directly involved in shepherding functions?

Frequently, that discrepancy is found in those who believe that they are called to equip only by didactic teaching from the pulpit. They reason that the actual work of ministry is to be performed only by the saints, forgetting that they themselves are saints. Consequently, they absolve themselves from actual ministry responsibility, sequestering themselves in their studies, preparing pointed messages in which they harangue their people for their lack of involvement in the ministry. They fail to recognize that they are actually saying, "Do as I say and not as I do."

The pastor is to shepherd God's flock. He is to do so not begrudgingly, feeling compelled to do so, but voluntarily, willingly, according to 1 Peter 5:2. Shepherding should be one of the most desirable and gratifying areas of his ministry. If it is not, and he refuses to engage in such a ministry or engages in it reluctantly, he should not be pastoring. Moreover, according to the same verse in 1 Peter, this service is not to be performed merely for financial remuneration but is to flow out of a genuine desire to serve.

Leading

The next verse, 1 Peter 5:3, states that a pastor is called to a position of leadership. The apostle makes plain that the kind of leader he has in mind is not a dictator. The pastor should not exhibit a haughty, superior, or overbearing attitude. A leader is not someone who whips his people from behind, urging them to get or keep going. He is someone who goes in front, setting the pace and inviting his people to follow him. At the same time, he is careful not to get too far ahead. If he gets too far ahead of his people, he may discover when he looks back that no one is following him.

At the other end of the spectrum from domineering leadership is indecisive leadership, which really is not leadership at all. Unfortunately, many pastors do not exercise the discipline of planning ahead, opting instead for a fly-by-the-seat-of-your-pants philosophy. Instead of being out in front of their congregations leading the sheep to greater accomplishments, they lag behind them, hoping the sheep will not move ahead too rapidly. Worse than that many actually serve as brakes when their sheep attempt to put their dreams into action.

What happens when a pastor leaves leadership to others? Well, generally, because those "others" who must pick up the leadership are not themselves equipped for the job, the sheep get led in unwise paths or even in giant circles. The church spins its wheels rather than progresses. Inherrent in the job of shepherd is the task of leadership. A person who recoils from leadership responsibilities does not belong in the pastorate.

Preaching and Teaching

In addressing Titus, whom he called his "true child in a common faith" (Titus 1:4), the apostle Paul set forth as one of Titus's pastoral tasks the "holding fast" to "the faithful word which is in accordance with the teaching, that he [Titus] may be able both to exhort in sound doctrine and refute those who contradict "(Titus 1:9). The word Paul used to indicate "holding fast," *antecho*, carried with it the meaning of clinging or adhering to something, of exercising a zealous care for it. We who are called to preach the Word of God are to cling to that Word, adhere to it closely, and zealously use it as the basis for our teaching so that there will be no question that our doctrinal position is sound. We should do our exegesis of the text carefully and present our findings to the congregation in light of the proper hermeneutic. Our preaching is to be used for two purposes: to exhort our own people and to refute error, especially the error of those who contradict our teaching. Since the Sunday morning service almost always attracts the largest audience of any church event, it is our greatest opportunity to exercise the preaching-teaching ministry. As a result, we should spend much time and effort in careful preparation for the service so that the sermon we give is the best we are capable of presenting.

As exhortation, the pastor's message should aim for some type of decision. Implicit in any exhortation is a desire to see people begin doing something or cease doing something. Thus, our exhortation should be toward godliness, toward taking positive steps forward in the Christian life, toward doing something that God wants His people to do. Conversely, the exhortation should be aimed at encouraging people to cease an activity that is displeasing to God or behavior that impedes his Christian growth and eventual maturity. For me, preaching is a special kind of public teaching that contains elements of encouragement and exhortation. Although not all would agree with my understanding of the nature of preaching, I believe that when those elements are missing, the presentation of the sermon cannot be described as true preaching.

A cognate purpose of the preaching-teaching ministry is the refutation of error. Care should be exercised lest the sermon deteriorate into attacks on individuals or groups of people who hold erroneous views. In refuting error, it is wise to attack the error itself rather than the group or person holding the position. That does not mean that a particular group may not be identified according to its position. It means that the preacher should use the Word of God to attack ideas rather than to attack people. Especially embarrassing and painful to me are sermons in which the character of some contemporary religious leader is attacked in an attempt to refute the error of his teaching. If a person has taken any logic at all, he knows the tactic is one of the oldest and most frequently used fallacies. Citing deficiencies in a person's character rarely proves anything about the soundness of his ideas, although it may prove something about his exercise of judgment in regard to his life-style. Diatribes against people are unworthy material for the Christian pulpit.

Correcting

Second Timothy 2:24-26 states that a pastor is to be gentle when he corrects those who oppose him. The only prudent manner for giving such correction is in a personal confrontation. The pastor should speak to the offender in person, humbly lay out the problem, give the person a chance to explain, and then—quietly, humbly, but confidently—show that person from Scripture where he is wrong. Once the pastor has stated his position he should withdraw from the scene as soon as human courtesy allows, rather than staying to argue his point. He should avoid all foolish arguments, which lead to quarrels.

Two abuses of the guidelines in 2 Timothy are frequently seen in the church. Some pastors are so reticent to engage in personal confrontation that they use their pulpits to whip those whom they consider to be offenders. Thus everyone in the congregation gets the same medicine whether or not he exhibits the symptoms. The innocent person remains dumbfounded, wondering whether he has been misunderstood or whether the communication is directed toward someone else. The curious go one step further, speculating as to the intended recipient. Soon a sermon directed at one person becomes a source of gossip.

Other pastors are so quick-tempered they seldom involve themselves in corrective action with another person without the occasion's deteriorating into a shouting match. They are so insecure they believe they must make their point regardless of the decibels raised. Yet such an exchange seldom proves anything to the antagonist, except perhaps that the pastor cannot control his temper. Moreover, sometimes the correction has just the opposite effect from that which was desired. The person becomes defensive and constructs elaborate rationalizations for holding his position. Because he knows the pastor has an educational and vocational advantage over him, he may seek support for his position by enlisting others in the church to his side. The result may be the formation of a faction that opposes the pastor as long as he ministers in that church. How the church needs pastors who will control their tempers and maintain gentlemanly behavior, while not sacrificing their convictions!

Evangelizing

As far as we are able to determine, the apostle Paul addressed the two epistles of Timothy to a young man then working in the pastoral ministry. Is it not interesting, then, that though Ephesians 4 defines an office of evangelist as distinctly different from the pastorate, Paul instructs young Timothy to "do the work of an evangelist" (2 Tim. 4:5)? The reason for Paul's exhortation may have been that there was no evangelist available in Timothy's church. Thus Timothy had to do double duty.

I do not think so, however. A colleague of mine, Professor James Andrews, offers a plausible explanation. He says that the first phrase of 2 Timothy 4:2 sets the stage for the four verses that follow it. The pastor is to "preach the word," says Professor Andrews, and that ministry of preaching will find its expression in such things as reproof, rebuke, exhortation, and evangelism. In so doing, the pastor will fulfill his ministry, to use the language of verse 5. As a pastor faithfully preaches through the Bible, inevitably he will come across evangelistic passages. Those he will preach faithfully and with great vigor.

There is yet another dimension to the passage. It is folly for a pastor to exhort his people to evangelize if he is not willing to do so himself. A pastor may not feel called or qualified to occupy the office of evangelist. He may not be the best resource to equip the saints for the work of evangelism. Still, he must be faithful to his calling by preaching all aspects of the Word—including evangelism—and by serving as an appropriate model for his people in that he himself actively engages in the work of evangelism.

The apostle Paul instructs Timothy, "Do not neglect the spiritual gift within you . . . Take pains with these things; be absorbed in them, so that your progress may be evident to all" (1 Tim. 4:14-15). Paul tells Timothy never to consider himself a finished product. What excellent advice, especially for the young pastor! The gifts of the Spirit are not given to the Christian as finished products but as do-it-yourself kits. All the ingredients are there from the beginning, but a recipient, in partnership with the Holy Spirit, is required to produce the final polished product. That is a lifelong project.

In the next verse of the fourth chapter of 1 Timothy, Paul charges his young son in the faith to keep on doing these things. As Timothy continues to work toward improving his skills, his persistence and diligence will be a positive example to his people. What appropriate advice to today's pastor as well as to Timothy. In most cases the pastor today has received the finest training that Bible colleges and seminaries can provide. But this is just the beginning. His schooling only gives him some of the tools with which he may work. The polishing and learning go on. If he ever reaches the place where he feels that no learning is necessary, no improvement is indicated, he has begun the road to stagnation. The diligent pastor will take every opportunity he can to engage in some type of continuing education, either through formal courses or informally at home. As he continues to sharpen his skills, he will serve his people better and will be a model that will encourage them to become more proficient in ministry.

In this chapter we have seen that the Bible prescribes the terms of a pastor's ministry in sweeping terms, allowing the pastor a great deal of latitude and creativity in the actual performance of his tasks. In the rest of this section of the book we will consider tasks that a pastor ministering in a local church today will be expected to perform.

At this point I want to anticipate and counter objections that may be raised by the reader. Through the years when I have broached the subject of pastoral duties my classroom students inevitably have remarked, "I have no need to perform these tasks because they are incompatible with the Bible's description of the pastoral ministry. Therefore, when I become a pastor, I have no intention of performing them. If my people want to see these things done, I will let them know in no uncertain terms that they will have to do those jobs themselves."

When I hear such objections, I have great concern for the person who makes them, because I do not believe he is mature enough to carry out a successful ministry. Unless he changes his attitude drastically, both he and the church he serves will experience considerable pain. Probably his days in the pastoral ministry will be short, and, for the church that calls him, mercifully so.

Moreover, he is operating under a faulty premise. Where does he find scriptural evidence to support limiting pastoral tasks to the ones he thinks should be part of the pastoral office? Quite the contrary to his opinion, the Bible paints the picture with such a broad swath that almost any conceivable task carried on by the contemporary pastor could fit into the seven categories of ministry the Bible gives. The Bible provides an exceedingly large parameter in which the choice of how the pastor is to spend his time becomes highly subjective. If the pastor is not careful, he will confuse his personal dislikes and likes with biblical directives. For instance, there are many pastoral tasks I find extremely odious, but they need to be done. I may use any number of rationalizations to try to avoid doing them. My first excuse may be based on how busy I am. Then if I am absolutely pressed, I may try to uncover a biblical justification for my action or lack of action. Down underneath I know that I am lazy or that I am trying to avoid doing something distasteful. I know that my "biblical pronouncements" are just bluster. I am trying to bully my people with my superior knowledge of the Bible.

When I examine the Scriptures, I find that the apostles were called upon to perform tasks they did not like to do. It is probable that some of the tasks they were compelled to perform did not seem to them productive to their ministry. For example, it is likely that the tent-making business was a source of frustration to Paul and a hindrance to the ambitions he had for his ministry.

When I am honest with myself and study the Scriptures objectively and in their proper context, I am forced to admit, maybe begrudgingly at times, that there is absolutely no biblical rationale for my refusing to do the task I dread so much. Though I may not enjoy doing it, the task needs to be done. I can complain about it, I can stand on the piety of my biblical rationalities and verbally thrash my people because they will not do it, or I can plunge in and do the job to the glory of God.

My doing the job does not mean I have to perform the task forever, however. The essence of the pastoral ministry is the equipping ministry. The task that is so repulsive to me may be inviting to someone else. If I stay close enough to my people to identify someone who would enjoy doing the dreaded task, I may be able to equip that person not just to perform the ministry himself, but to train others to do it as well. If I do not have sufficient expertise in the area to equip others for the task, I may seek help within the larger Christian community. If I am the person who does the training, I will do so in steps. As the person I am training gains confidence and exhibits positive results in his ministry, I will turn the task over to him little by little, asking him only to keep me informed of his progress and supplying helpful correction to him when it is necessary.

As a result, I can become progressively less involved in that particular area of ministry, though I will make sure to engage in the work from time to time as a positive example and encouragement to my people. Then I will select another area of ministry distasteful to me and once again work my way out of a job. By doing that I will be showing my people that no area of ministry is beneath my dignity to perform as pastor. Gradually, though, I will be moving to the point where I can concentrate time and effort on areas that I believe are the most productive for me—the high-priority tasks.

Questions for Discussion

1. List the seven tasks the Bible prescribes for those in pastoral ministry. For each of these seven categories describe specific activities a pastor would perform during a given week in his ministry.

2. In the area of equipping, why is it important to seldom perform tasks alone?

3. If a pastor is going to be a true shepherd, why is it unwise for the pastor to have an attitude that says, "Do as I say not as I do"?

4. What do you think is the best position for pastoral leadership: behind, with, or in front of the people?

5. Why is it important for the pastor to engage in continuing education?

6. What would you say to the pastor who wishes to exclude certain traditional tasks from his ministry?

Helpful Resources

Browning, Don S. *Pastoral Theology: The Emerging Field in Theology, Church, and World.* New York: Harper & Row, 1982.

Oden, Thomas C. *Pastoral Theology: Essentials of Ministry.* New York: Harper & Row, 1983.

O'Meara, Thomas Franklin. *Theology of Ministry.* Ramsay, N.J.: Paulist, 1983.

Pittenger, W. Norman. *The Ministry of All Churches: A Theology of Lay Ministry.* Wilton, Conn.: Morehouse, 1983.

Shelp, Earl E. and Ronald Sunderland. *A Biblical Basis for Ministry.* Philadelphia: Westminster, 1981.

13

Planning and Conducting the Worship Service

O f the many public services in which the church participates, perhaps none is as important or visible as the Sunday morning worship service. Rarely is any other function better attended. Because people have been programmed to think in terms of Sunday morning church, the service is the one most likely to attract visitors. That reason alone would justify the church's putting its best foot forward on Sunday morning.

But there is an even more cogent reason to make the Sunday morning service the best service of the week. That reason has to do with what the church should be trying to do on Sunday morning. For centuries the church operated on the mistaken premise that the only real way to worship God was through the Eucharist. Thus, an integral part of every Sunday morning service was the observation of the Lord's Supper, the focal point of the Mass. Because the Lord's Supper points to the death, rather than the resurrection, of our Lord, somber overtones were attached to the Sunday morning service. It became an occasion for great solemnity instead of celebration. Then the reformers came into the picture and said, in effect, "Look, we've been doing it all wrong. Sunday is not the day Jesus died. It's the day He arose!"

What a wonderful realization! We do not serve a dead Christ hanging on a crucifix. Our Lord is alive. Each Sunday is the anniversary of the resurrection, not of Good Friday. Instead of being sad and somber, Sunday should be a day of great enthusiasm, exuberance, joy, and exhilaration; it should be a time of rejoicing and celebration.

Unfortunately, overtones of the past have crept back into many evangelical churches. In some places, the Sunday morning worship service is anything but a time of celebration. The pastor needs to restore the rightful emphasis to the day. In order to do so, he must make extensive plans and coordinate his efforts carefully with others who will take a leading role in the service.

The Location of the Service

Before considering the preparation the pastor must make if the Sunday worship service is to be effective, I would like to discuss the room for and the atmosphere of the Sunday morning worship service. It is unfortunate that long ago the room received the erroneous title it did. The term *sanctuary* is both inappropriate and theologically incorrect. The actual sanctuary is within the believer. That is where the Holy Spirit dwells. The room in which believers assemble is more properly called the *assembly room* or the *auditorium.*

MULTI-PURPOSE AUDITORIUMS

Some believers believe they must come to a special room to be in the presence of God, and that the room thus set apart is in some way holy. Actually, when the church assembles in any room, those who enter that room are in the presence of the living Christ. Therefore, although the room itself is not holy, when the church assembles in that room there are actions that are appropriate to the occasion and setting and there are actions that are not. My view of the nature of the room selected as the site for the worship service leads to another conclusion. After a great deal of thought concerning the room in which the church meets, I have come to believe that it is inefficient and poor stewardship for a church to construct a room intended to be used solely for the conduct of its worship.

That does not mean that I would make such a viewpoint a critical point of my ministry by insisting that I get my own way in the matter. Pastors come and go, but the people remain. They are the ones who are left to pay for the church building. Therefore, if they feel strongly that they must have an auditorium used only for worship and agree to pay the mortgage payments, they have a right to their choice. If a substantial number of people in the church are not yet ready for the multi-purpose concept when the church anticipates building, I would work carefully and quietly with the architect, encouraging him to design a room for worship that is beautiful and functional but also is capable of being converted to multi-purpose use in the future.

THE ATTRACTIVENESS OF THE AUDITORIUM

Whether or not the congregation uses a multi-purpose room or a one-purpose auditorium for its worship service, the most important factor to remember is to make the room as attractive and inviting as possible. To accomplish that in a multi-purpose room, it is advisable not to go to extremes in the number of functions the room is designed to accommodate. For example, I have seen auditoriums designed for worship that are equipped with movable seating. They can be converted easily into gorgeous banquet halls. But, I have never seen a gymnasium that proved truly satisfactory for worship services over a long period of time. At best it served as a stopgap until the church was able to erect something that was more aesthetically and acoustically suitable to worship.

Aesthetics indeed must be considered despite the opinion of some Christians that it does not matter. In part as a blacklash against liturgical groups that erected lavish and ornate church buildings, evangelicals seem to have been determined to go in exactly the opposite direction. The prevailing philosophy among some evangelical groups seems to be, "Ugly is holy." Often the resulting church buildings are poorly planned, constructed of ugly materials, and devoid of any beauty that might aid the congregant in his worship. It pleases me to see that a growing number of evangelical architects are designing church buildings that are utilitarian but still have aesthetically pleasing features.

The Attitude of the Congregation

This is an appropriate place to discuss the attitude of the congregant as he enters the room in which worship will be held. Were a person to attend on one Sunday a church that employed a detailed liturgy, and on another Sunday an average nonliturgical church, he would notice a distinct difference in the conduct of the worshipers, especially before the service itself. In the liturgical church, before the service actually began he would probably find a group of people sitting in quiet contemplation. If any conversation was going on, it would probably be brief and in whispered tones. In the nonliturgical church a strikingly different scene might greet the observer. There, most likely, he would find a group of people chatting away, oblivious to the fact that others might want everyone to be somber and quiet. It would be evident to the visitor that the people enjoyed one another. But would their conduct be an appropriate prelude to a worship service?

Many evangelicals, including some of my teaching colleagues, would say a definite "No," declaring that such informal conduct was inappropriate to the occasion. They would insist that when congregants enter the auditorium to participate in a worship service, they should be quiet and reverent. Adherents of the position often work hard to make their views known. Such devices as terse notices in the bulletin, signs at the entrance to the auditorium, and pointed announcements from the pulpit are designed to make the offenders feel guilty. As a result, people are relatively quiet for a week or two, but then the noise level gradually builds to its former level. Those who are annoyed by people who talk in the auditorium are constantly tense and frustrated when they attend worship services. The observer is likely to feel sympathy for them.

Yet I have come to the conclusion that they, not the people who offend them, are wrong. If indeed the Sunday morning worship service is the chief celebration occasion of the church, then it is appropriate for the Christian to celebrate the great joy he feels in being among other believers. In such a setting, words of greeting and pleasant conversations among Christians are not out of order but are more savorful to God than the sour countenances of those who insist on silence. I believe, therefore, that Christians should not be made to feel guilty for visiting before the worship service but should even be encouraged to do so.

Of course, that conversing should be done in good taste. Loud and boisterous conduct is inappropriate to the setting. If Sunday morning worshipers are in the presence of the Lord—and indeed they are—it behooves them to conduct themselves with the dignity befitting the occasion. Children, for example, should not be allowed to range up and down the aisles causing disturbances. But on the whole, it should be remembered that Sunday worship is a time of celebration. Healthy, vital moments of interchange between Christians are desirable and enlivening. Those who prefer a time of contemplation and silence prior to the service should be made aware that church policy encourages an atmosphere of friendliness during that time. If they insist on quiet then, they are likely to find only frustration in the church auditorium. If there is substantial friction on the subject, the church may want to set aside a prayer room where those who wish to may compose their thoughts before participating in corporate worship.

I realize that my position on this matter is a sharp departure from the traditional stance. Yet, after much thought on the subject, this is where I stand.

Characteristics of the Service as a Whole

In the actual planning of a worship service there are several important matters to keep in mind. First, the different parts of the service should be interrelated on a deep level, and transitional devices should be employed so that the congregation can move from one part of the service to another without awkwardness.

Second, a supreme effort should be made to involve the worshiper as actively as possible in the various elements of the worship service. In some churches the worshiper has become a spectator instead of a participant. That is not the meaning of true worship.

Third, a great deal of planning and care should be exercised to assure that the Sunday morning worship service does not become a one-man show. The pastor has ample opportunity to appear on the platform in a leadership role. Other members do not. There are a number of reasons for employing as many lay people as possible in the leading of public worship, even though as novices they may occasionally stumble or make errors. First, if they are given a chance to participate and are given kindly instruction, eventually they will become proficient in the task. As they become more active participants in the worship service, they are likely to take a greater interest in it. Second, by standing before the congregation in a role such as this, they are, in essence, making a public commitment of their willingness to assume the responsibilities of being a church leader. Third, it is a striking testimony to visitors for a church to have a large core of persons in it who are willing to be involved in a leadership capacity.

Fourth, participation in the service by lay adults demonstrates vividly to children that their parents are willing to assume positions of spiritual leadership within the congregation.

Fifth, lay participation sometimes uncovers people with pulpit potential who should be encouraged to train for positions of ministry leadership beyond that they are already capable of performing.

Sixth, lay leadership brings variety to the worship service and often lends a spark that would not be present otherwise.

As is the case in other aspects of ministry, it is essential that people asked to share in the leadership of the service be given the proper instruction before they are expected to engage in that ministry. At present, I am personally involved in teaching and pastoral ministries and do not have time to instruct those who participate as worship leaders. As a result, I have printed a few of my ideas on a suggestion sheet. I give the sheet to each platform participant, and I work closely with a worship coordinator. He meets with me each week and then personally contacts all of those who will lead in worship. He gives them special instruction and answers their questions. Although that is far from a perfect system, I have found that it works out satisfactorily for me.

Format and Length of the Service

What about the actual format of the service? Because the New Testament gives only a scant idea of the content of the worship services conducted by the early church and prescribes no format for the present church to follow, there is room for considerable variation and creativity. The format I will focus on here is one that has worked well for me, though I make no claims that it should be applied universally. My practice is to divide the service into three portions: fellowship, worship, and instruction. In the first, Christians interact with each other. In the second, the worshipers interact with God. In the third, God interacts with his people through the instruction of His Word.

As to the length of the service, I have adopted a somewhat unconventional pattern. There is, of course, no indication from the Scriptures that a worship service needs to be restricted to one hour in length. In fact there are many indications that the early church met for much longer periods of time. I have found that the type of service I prefer can be held comfortably in about an hour and fifteen minutes if the service begins on time.

There is a psychological disadvantage to using such a time frame if the service is not planned properly. Regardless of when the service starts, when the minute hand moves to twelve, many people automatically shut down their minds and begin to fidget, squirm, and think of other things. The problem is solved best by starting a seventy-five minute service at fifteen minutes before the hour and ending it as precisely as possible.

Another change is useful, too. In the traditional pattern, Sunday school might begin at 9:30 and end at 10:30. Morning worship might then begin at 10:45 and end at noon. For years the particular church I serve has reversed the pattern. We begin our worship service at 9:45 and end at 11:00. After fifteen minutes of coffee and fellowship, Sunday school is conducted from 11:15 until 12:15. Because people have had a chance to eat a little snack before Sunday school and the "heavy" part of the morning is already over, they do not seem to mind remaining in Sunday school until 12:15. In at least one of the adult classes, discussion of the sermon topic often consumes much of the class period.

BODY LIFE

Earlier in the chapter I expressed my conviction that, whether we like it or not, Christians will probably use the time prior to the

morning service for fellowship with one another. Rather than expecting them to settle down immediately and assume an attitude of
worship, I schedule a fellowship period or body life time at the
beginning of the service to serve as a transition between friendly
chatter and worship. The period also serves as an appropriate time to
carry on many of the miscellaneous activities that are not integral to
worship itself but are still necessary to the functioning of the church.

This warm informal period may begin with a word of greeting by
the pastor and a verse or two of a hymn that emphasizes the unique
relationship Christians enjoy with each other. Even though all the
necessary announcements are usually contained in the bulletin, if
the pastor is realistic he will recognize that many people do not read
the bulletin thoroughly. It is better to use this early portion of the
service to highlight important announcements so that later in the
service he will not need to interrupt the flow of the worship pattern
in order to do so. Immediately after the announcements, a number
of churches have found it helpful to have an informal time for the
worshipers to greet each other, with the specific purpose being the
identification of visitors. The time of greeting is ended and congregants brought together once more, by the singing of a contemporary
fellowship chorus. Then visitors to the service are introduced by
name by members of the church who made it a point to meet them.
A visitor should never suffer the embarrassment of having to introduce himself to anyone, no less to an entire congregation. The
church should train individuals who can assist the visitor over the
awkwardness of being new and can help him feel at home in the
congregation.

The fellowship period of the service is a good time to feature brief
presentations promoting various organizations of the church, such as
youth groups or children's clubs. Special care should be exercised,
however, to make sure that the fellowship portion of the service is
kept short and pertinent so that it does not become the dominant
feature of the morning, stealing time from the worship and instructional periods. Also, the initial period of the service should be well
planned to ensure that it covers all the bases. It is disruptive of a
period of worship to have someone interject, between the reading of
the Bible and prayer a sentence such as, "Oh, and by the way, we
forget to tell you in the announcement time about the Thursday
evening potluck." If an important announcement has been overlooked, it is better to use some other form of communication to
convey it to the people than to interrupt the latter portions of the
service.

If planned well, the fellowship period that begins the service will be far from perfunctory. It will produce enough warmth to foster a spirit of unity such that the congregants will worship God as a body rather than as a mere group of individuals.

Worship

THE IMPORTANCE OF CORPORATE WORSHIP

Because of the heavy emphasis on Bible teaching in many evangelical churches, the worship period has fallen into disrepute. A friend of mine, commenting on his church, said to me recently, "I can hardly wait for them to get the 'preliminaries' over so that I can hear the sermon. That's what I really come for." His statement betrays the fact that he has missed the major reason Christians gather on Sunday morning. A great portion of the Christian's Sunday celebration should focus on corporate worship of Almighty God. Certainly a person is able to worship God by himself, but that is not the same as the body assembled for corporate worship expressing its combined praise and adoration of God. Even though each Christian is an integral part of the church, he, himself, does not constitute the church. It is only when the separate members are assembled into a group that true corporate worship takes place.

Thus, in churches that have allowed the teaching or preaching period to take over the main portion of the Sunday morning service, little if any corporate worship actually takes place, to the distinct loss of that church. Corporate worship of God is a time-honored tradition dating back to Old Testament times and was practiced by the first-century church. Not only does it fulfill a unique need in man, it is a sweet savor to God. Corporate worship, then, should never be considered unnecessary or preliminary. No matter how challenging or instructive the sermon, it is not a substitute for worship.

THE VALUE OF LAY PARTICIPATION

There is one other common misconception that deters rather than facilitates worship. Proponents of the error consider worship such a solemn and important event that no one but professionals should be involved. In this case, so-called worship becomes a performance carried on by those who believe they are professionally qualified. The platform becomes a stage upon which a type of drama is enacted, and, except for their participation in the singing of one or two congregational hymns, the congregants are little more than spectators.

My view of worship is much different. To me, worship is an exercise in involvement. The worshiper should not go away saying, "Look what I got out of that service." Instead, he should be able to say, "Look what I put into that service." Rather than passively receiving entertainment, he should have been involved in spiritual exercise.

Now, of course, we cannot force people to become involved in the service, but we can provide them the means whereby they can do so if they want to. Those means should be appropriate to the church. In liturgical churches, ways of getting the congregation involved in the service are already built in. Of course they can become perfunctory, but they do not need to be so. If the worshiper approaches the liturgy with the right attitude and means what he recites when he repeats the words of the service, he may be able to engage in a meaningful time of worship. The pentecostal churches offer still different ways of involving the congregation in worship.

Those may include the raising of hands and praying out loud.

The problem over worship faced in many evangelical churches is one born out of a reaction against the extremes of the liturgical and pentecostal traditions. On the one hand, because the liturgical tradition has been decreed formalistic, and thus in error, many churches studiously avoid all traces of liturgy. Some churches even insist that the order of service he changed constantly to avoid all appearance of formality. On the other hand, because some consider Pentecostals to be fanatical, many churches avoid anything that might be construed as frenzied, including, of course, all clapping or raising of hands, praying out loud, or responding orally to the speaker. When a reluctance to engage in actions that resemble either formalism or fanaticism is combined with a platform-oriented philosophy, there is little room for the congregant to participate actively in the worship service. And because he has little opportunity to participate, he finds it extremely difficult to worship. My contention is that, as a result, in many evangelical churches little if any actual worship ever takes place.

IDEAS FOR INCREASING LAY INVOLVEMENT

How can this serious condition be remedied? A good start is to adopt a philosophy that sees the worship service as an action carried on primarily by the congregation rather than by the leadership. Traditional, time-honored means may be updated and used effectively to give the congregant opportunities to participate. Those means can include the reading of the Scriptures by the congregation, either in unison or in varying forms of responsive reading. Included as well may be meaningful litanies, which really are a type of responsive prayer. Another helpful means is to use affirmations of faith and to intersperse musical responses throughout the service. Often those can take the form of contemporary choruses that are based solidly on Scripture. Other useful choruses are those that express praise and adoration of God. Care should be exercised to see that such choruses are singable by the congregation and appropriate to a worship service. Also they should be songs the accompanist can handle. The church should use every appropriate means possible to make those who attend the service truly worshipers and active participants.

CONTINUITY AND VARIETY IN WORSHIP

What constitutes a proper morning worship service? Any number of creative formats may be used, but it is my contention that when a format is discovered that the congregation finds desirable, it should be adopted as general practice and followed as closely as possible. Of course, great variety may be pursued in the selection of hymns, choruses, and Scripture portions, but the person planning the service should keep in mind that people are usually most comfortable in situations where they know what to expect. The elements of the service should be distributed in such a way that events of the same type do not follow one another directly. It is pleasing, for instance, for a spoken portion of the service to follow one that is sung. A worshiper's attention span may be increased if, after he has been standing for a portion of the service, he is given the opportunity to sit down, and vice versa.

HYMNS

The worship portion of the morning service should also include the great hymns of praise traditional to the church. A principle of variety can be used in selecting hymns and hymn tunes. Sometimes the pastor will find that although the words of a particular hymn are appropriate for the service, the tune is not suitable. In most hymnals, alternate tunes for the hymns are listed at the back, and the pastor might use one of them instead. We need to be reminded that although we are accustomed to hearing a certain melody accompany a particular metrical composition, the words and tune probably were not composed together. In most cases they found their way to each other only later. In many cases the alternate tune would have been much more acceptable to the author of the words than the one normally used. In some churches gifted musicians are able to compose entirely new tunes that are better than those found in the hymnbook.

One other caution. Many times people believe it is necessary to sing every verse of the hymns contained in the hymnbook in order to set forth the complete story of what the writer wanted to say. Few people realize that it is likely the hymn in question originally had many more verses than the ones now printed in the hymnbook. For the sake of space, a musical editor had to leave out some verses. Since many of the verses left out filled in necessary gaps in the story the writer originally wished to convey, it is impossible for us today to know the whole story from the hymnal. In addition, some of the verses contained in the hymnal may be entirely inappropriate to the general worship theme of a particular Sunday. Therefore, the pastor should not feel compelled to use all the verses of the songs in the hymnal but should choose the verses that pertain to what he wants to accomplish on a given Sunday.

OTHER ELEMENTS OF THE WORSHIP SERVICE

Other elements the pastor may wish to include in the worship service are an invocation—an opening prayer given by the pastor or other leader on behalf of the congregation, special numbers either by the choir or by gifted individuals, a pastoral prayer delivered by the pastor himself or by a member of the congregation, an offering, a public invitation to salvation or discipleship (if deemed appropriate), and a benediction or closing prayer.

May I interject here my own concern about churches that are so reluctant to mention money that they exclude the offering from the worship, choosing to place a box in the foyer where members can place their tithes and offerings. The Bible is not hesitant to talk about money. In fact it is probably one of the most frequent topics mentioned in the Scriptures. Moreover, the Scriptures teach that where a person's money is, there is his heart also. If true worship is an exercise of the heart, then the issue most crucial to the heart should be included within the worship pattern. People should be allowed to give public expression of the extent to which they have dedicated this particular area of their life to God. The giving of tithes and offerings is an integral, important part of the worship experience and should not—pardon the pun—be short-changed.

USHERS

The subject of offerings leads naturally to the subject of ushers. Of all the people who participate in the ministry of the church, perhaps the ushers should be selected and trained more carefully than any others. Besides receiving the offering in a dignified and efficient manner, ushers should be trained to greet members and visitors alike, making each person feel welcome, comfortable, and important. In addition, ushers should be calm people trained to handle any unexpected occurrence decisively and diplomatically. If someone suddenly becomes ill, the ushers should be ready to help that person exit from the service, giving him whatever aid is possible and calling for medical help if that seems advisable.

Ushers should be prepared to deal with all forms of disturbance, distraction, and disruption—even to the point of forcibly ejecting a person from the service. When children become disruptive, for instance, first an usher should alert the parents. If the parents do not take satisfactory action, an usher should recruit an adult to sit next to the offending child or the usher should sit there himself. If the parents of an offending child do not attend services, the church should take steps to appoint surrogate parents for the purpose of helping the child learn how to behave in the church building and particularly in the worship service. If a child whose parents are present in the auditorium persists in his unruly behavior, an usher should request that the parents remove the child. If the parents refuse to do so, they should become the recipient of disciplinary action by the board, and if necessary, by the congregation. If no adult is available to assume responsibility for a continually disruptive child, the usher should gently but firmly remove the child from the worship service. If a nursery is provided for babies, there is no excuse for a crying baby being present in the auditorium disrupting either the worship portion or the sermon. The parent should be dealt with by an usher in a friendly but firm manner. Even at the risk of possibly alienating the parents, such persons should be informed of their obligations to other worshipers.

One further word concerning disruption. A visitor may appear whose behavior is considered acceptable in his home congregation but not in the congregation he is visiting. Rather than allowing him to disrupt a service, at the first sign of inappropriate behavior, an usher should approach him, appraising him of the fact that his behavior is considered disruptive in the congregation he is visiting. If he persists in his behavior, he should be urged to leave. If he still persists he should be assisted in leaving. We are, after all, conducting a worship service appropriate to a particular congregation. Distractions and disruptions are an affront to the congregation and to a God who insists that everything be done "decently and in order."

At the end of a worship service, the ushers should open the necessary doors, greet people once more, make it a point to talk with visitors, and remain close by to assist people in any way that is appropriate. People chosen for ushering should be cordial, level-headed, even-tempered, teachable, and willing to dress themselves appropriately for the occasion. In many churches a coat and tie is considered part of the proper attire for anyone involved publicly in the worship service. Dress requirements, of course, will vary from church to church and from one part of the country to another. The important point is that the ushers should wear clothing considered acceptable in that location for that particular occasion.

Preaching the Word

LENGTH

Were I to give one piece of advice to an inexperienced preacher I would have to say, "Limit your sermons to twenty minutes each." Many times the novice pulpiteer is so excited about the opportunity before him that he tries to make every major point he can think of in the course of one sermon. Undoubtedly there are accomplished orators who can hold their audiences spellbound for hours at a time. Our young pulpiteer, however, usually is not one of those. Having preached sermons appropriate to seminary classmates who enjoyed complicated theological concepts as much as he, the young preacher seldom considers that the terminology he uses and the concepts he discusses will attract little interest among the people he serves. At this point his theological training is still a liability instead of an asset because he has not yet learned to translate what he has learned into terms that apply directly to the people. For an inexperienced speaker to limit his remarks to twenty minutes may be an exercise in careful discipline. When he does so, however, he will find his audience much more willing to come back for more.

STYLE

As to message style, recognition should be given to the fact that there are differences between teaching and preaching. Although there should be instructional points in every message preached, teaching per se may be somewhat passive, with the teacher merely explaining what the text means. Preaching, on the other hand, should contain some degree of exhortation. The listener should not only be taught the meaning of the text, but he should also be challenged to apply it in tangible, practical ways to his life. The essence of preaching, to my way of thinking, is that it is designed to move the hearer toward some type of decision, to initiate some kind of positive change in his life. That is the primary reason I place the sermon at the end of the service instead of the middle. It is my goal to have everything in that service progress in orderly fashion leading a person to the desired decision. The sermon is the climax toward which the entire hour builds.

EXPOSITORY PREACHING

Though I am not opposed to topical preaching and use it from time to time for special events, I have found that expository preaching as a pattern has suited me best. That preaching, however, should not be confused with verse-by-verse exposition. In expository preaching, the preacher selects a passage, studies it to determine its structure, organizes his major points around that structure, and constructs an outline that moves the hearer in logical fashion toward the major theme of the passage. Instead of tacking an application to the end of a verse-by-verse commentary, expository preaching weaves the application into each point being considered. My own preference through the years has been to select a particular book of the Bible and preach through it passage-by-passage in more or less orderly fashion until I reach the end of the book. When the Word is presented in a systematic fashion such as this, almost inevitably it will present a balanced diet and meet a great many spiritual needs that may be overlooked when the Word is preached in more random fashion.

YOUNG CHILDREN AND THE SERMON

Throughout my years of experience I have found that although some parents are convinced it is desirable for young children to be present in the worship service, it is better to excuse them to junior church activities before the sermon begins. A number of my friends have argued this point with me, saying that it is good training for a small child to sit through a sermon. My question to them always has been, "Good training for what—to learn that church is necessarily an unhappy and boring place where you have to listen to things you don't understand, and where you have to remain still when your body tells you to squirm?" God's Word is too precious and important for it to be used to bore anyone. Undoubtedly there are countless numbers of adults who would never consider going to church because they remember it as an unpleasant experience. In many cases if we explored the situation further, we might find that when they were small children, their parents required them to sit quietly through sermons which were, for them, unintelligible and boring.

BECOMING A SKILLED PREACHER

Once a person has completed his training for the pastoral ministry and enters the active pastorate, becoming proficient in the pulpit is much like becoming a good swimmer or automobile driver. It takes a great deal of practice. The way to become a good preacher is to preach, and unfortunately a person never seems to get enough opportunities to do that while he is in Bible college or seminary.

In assessing his skills and working toward improvement, the pastor will find that videotaping his messages is a helpful tool. Also, positive suggestions by diplomatic members of the congregation often aid the blossoming preacher if he is secure enough to receive those suggestions as being helpful. My most valuable appraisals have come from my long-suffering wife, even though her comments about my sermons in the first years of our marriage taxed our relationship because I was so insecure and easily threatened. Through the years I have found that she has a superb sense of what should or should not be done in a sermon. When I follow her advice in regard to sermons, inevitably I discover she is right.

Unfortunately, it may be well into a person's first pastorate before he can ascertain whether he should be preaching on a regular basis or pursuing some other phase of Christian work. If, however, he feels a burning compulsion to preach and believes he cannot be happy unless he is preaching, he should give that aspect of his ministry one of the highest priorities. He should work long, hard hours preparing and hone his delivery skills through constant practice until he is sure that preaching is one of the strongest areas of his equipping ministry. Because the pulpit represents the pastor's most public appearance and because it is likely that he reaches more people from the pulpit than in any other aspect of his ministry, he should determine to give the pulpit ministry the very best he has, or he should leave the pastorate. If he remains a pastor, he should realize that the sermon he preaches on Sunday morning may have greater impact than anything else he does the entire week.

THE INVITATION

Following the sermon, an invitation should be given if it is appropriate to the topic, and the service should be closed in a positive and dignified manner. Some comment is necessary concerning the public invitation. In some churches an evangelistic invitation is as much a part of the morning service as is the sermon. To neglect giving an invitation is tantamount to committing professional suicide for pastors ministering in such churches. The candidating pastor should try to discover the feelings and practices of the church before he agrees to become pastor. If he is comfortable with always giving an invitation, and all other factors seem to be right, he should consider the call to that church favorably. If, however, he is opposed to giving an invitation every Sunday, he should make his feelings on the subject clear to the church while he is still a candidate. He should refuse the call if the church insists that he do something he is convinced is ethically wrong. The philosophy of extending an invitation each week is born out of a mentality in which the church considers the pastor its sole evangelist. Each member assumes that he fulfills his evangelistic obligations by paying the salary of the "pro" hired to win people to Christ. In such a setting, often the most in evangelistic practice that can be expected of the church member is for him to invite a friend to church so that the friend may hear a gospel message.

Although an evangelistic invitation may be successful and even desirable at times, it is a rather recent method in the long history of the church. The historical and biblical text of discipleship is not walking the aisle but being buried in the waters of baptism. Unfortunately many people believe that they have taken the only public step necessary when they respond to an invitation. As a result, it rarely occurs to them to follow the Lord in baptism or in church membership. Many of these, in turn, remain immature during the entire course of their Christian pilgrimage.

If an invitation is given, it should be given in an honest, straightforward manner in which the one extending the invitaton specifies clearly and carefully the kind of commitment he is asking potential respondents to make. When the sermon is edificational in nature, and the application of the Scripture lesson calls for a certain type of commitment from the Christian, that commitment should be specified very clearly. Likewise, an invitation for baptism or church membership should be equally clear. When an invitation is given for salvation, I view it as manipulative to ask persons to respond in a series of successive steps, for example, to raise one's hand, then to stand in one's place, and then finally to come forward. Instead, the person who is being invited to make the decision should be told in a simple and straightforward manner that he will be expected to come forward as a public declaration of his faith in Jesus Christ as Lord and Savior.

The pastor should state the expectations he has from the very start of the invitation, and he should indicate that leaders of the church will be on hand to meet with respondents and aid them in the decisions they are making. When an evangelistic invitation is given, personal workers of both sexes should take their Bibles and move quickly to the front of the auditorium, assuring the inquirer that he will not have to stand there alone. At that point it may be helpful for the congregation to rise and sing a hymn. If the hymn has multiple stanzas, the pastor may want to pause between the second and third stanzas and repeat the invitation.

If during the singing of the last stanza, people continue to come forward, the pastor might pause again for a few minutes, giving ample opportunity for those who still wish to respond. Under no circumstances should he attempt to manipulate his audience or to attract them forward through some subterfuge or emotional device, such as attempting to lay a "guilt trip" on them. Always he should be direct, honest, and convincing, extending the invitation clearly and concisely but leaving the ultimate result to the Holy Spirit. After all, it is the Holy Spirit of God, not any human agency, who convicts a person of his sins and calls him to repentance and faith. He does the converting. We are only tools and never should attempt to take over the job that can be performed effectively only by the Master Craftsman, especially if our taking over involves using deceptive and overly-persuasive human sales techniques.

In the course of my own pastorates I have always been fortunate enough to serve in churches that left to my discretion whether or not to extend a public invitation and what the purpose of that invitation would be. I personally would feel uncomfortable were I required to give an evangelistic invitation every Sunday.

CLOSING THE SERVICE

Despite the fact that it is traditional and thus an affront to those people today who want to abandon the traditional altogether, a benediction is a dignified and scripturally proper way to end a worship service. The words of an appropriate benediction tie the service together and send the participants away on a positive note. Following the pronouncement of the benediction, I favor the practice of observing a few moments of quiet music and a moment of meditation while the pastor and perhaps his wife make their way to the narthex, where they can greet visitors and make themselves available to members of the congregation.

The practice of greeting worshipers after the service is for the express purpose of being able to add a warm, human touch to the event, not so the pastor can receive adulation from the congregation. People like to be able to give a personal greeting to a man who has an impact in their lives through his sermons. In churches where the pastor slips away after the sermon without personally greeting the people, his action can be interpreted as aloofness on his part. Some members of the congregation may never understand that their pastor cares for them as persons. If a pastor is alert to people and the signs they give, he may gain a great deal of understanding concerning their needs just through his brief exposure to them following the morning worship service. Then, too, people with immediate needs will be able to alert him to the fact that they need to spend a few moments with him in private. A quick retreat into the pastor's study may ascertain the particular question or problem, and arrangements can be made on the spot to meet further with the person if the situation demands.

In summary, every consideration in the planning of the Sunday morning worship service should be made with the view in mind that it is the great celebration service of the church, that each Sunday is the anniversary of the resurrection, and that, in addition to being the most important service for many in the church, it is also the sole contact with the church and its message for many members and visitors. Every effort should be made to see that, in every single thing done in the context of the morning service, the church, its leaders, and its people put their best foot forward.

Questions for Discussion

1. What significance to the worship service is the fact that Sunday is not the day on which Jesus died but the day on which He arose?

2. Of what importance is the place of worship and the atmosphere of the service? Why is it inappropriate to call the place of worship a *sanctuary?*

3. Under what circumstances would you use the church auditorium for purposes other than worship?

4. How much importance do you give to aesthetics in the design of a place of worship?

5. Some members prefer that the minutes just prior to the beginning of the worship service be spent in quiet meditation. Others enjoy engaging in conversation and fellowship. How do you resolve the two approaches?

6. What value do you see in involving lay people in the worship service as participants rather than observers? How may that be done? Compose a suggestion sheet you could use to guide lay people in conducting themselves, should they have the opportunity to participate in the worship service.

7. How long should a worship service be? Is there an ideal length of time?

8. What value is there in beginning the worship service with a time of fellowship? What are the key elements that make up a body life time during the worship service?

9. How much of the actual Sunday morning service should be devoted to worship? What is worship, and why is it important to you?

10. Is it possible to incorporate some liturgy into the worship service of a nonliturgical church? How would you accomplish that without its becoming perfunctory?

11. What role should the usher play in the ministry of the church? What qualities should an usher possess?

12. Of what importance is preaching to the ministry of the church? What is the difference between topical and expository preaching? What steps may a pastor take to improve his preaching?

13. Children hold an important place in our hearts and lives. At what age should they be encouraged to attend worship services?

14. What is your approach toward public invitations? Defend your position.

Helpful Resources

Patterson, Ben. "Worship As Performance." *Leadership* 2, no. 3 (Summer 1981):49-52.

Hoon, Paul W. *The Integrity of Worship.* Nashville: Abingdon, 1977.

Huff, Ronn, Bruce Leafblad, Roger Pittelko, Bob Schmidgall, and Sherm Williams. "Worship: Preparing Yourself and Your Congregation." *Leadership* 2, no. 3 (Summer 1981):112-13.

O'Day, Rey, and Edward A. Powers. *Theatre of the Spirit: A Worship Handbook.* New York: Pilgrim, 1980.

Pollock, Shirley. "Sunday Morning Worship Innovations." *Leadership* 3, no. 1 (Winter 1982):101-4.

Rayburn, Robert G. *O Come Let Us Worship.* Grand Rapids: Baker, 1980.

Segler, Franklin M. *Christian Worship: Its Theology and Practice.* Nashville: Broadman, 1967.

White, James F. *Christian Worship in Transition.* Nashville: Abingdon, 1976.
————. *New Forms of Worship.* Nashville: Abingdon, 1971.
White, Lyla L. "Worshipers Make the Worship Service Work." *Leadership* 2, no. 3 (Summer 1981):88-91.

14

Sunday Evening Services

Recently, Jewish friends of ours, knowing that my family and I had a deep interest in their religion, invited us to celebrate a Sabbath meal with them. We arrived just before sundown and participated in the lighting of the candles, the traditional blessings, the reading from the Torah, and a delicious meal. The ceremony, along with the meal around which it was organized, was a significant part of their worship pattern.

Historical Overview

Jews often worship at night, and perhaps it was no accident that some of the earliest meetings of the Christian church were held at night. The Last Supper, instituted before the actual birth of the church, was held in conjunction with the Jewish feast of Passover, traditionally celebrated at night. Thomas experienced his first encounter with the risen Christ in an evening meeting, according to John 20:19. On at least one occasion, Paul preached so long into the night that one of his listeners fell asleep, toppled from his perch, and lost his life, only to be revived (Acts 20). When Peter was in jail, an evening prayer meeting was held in his behalf (Acts 12:5-12).

In addition to the precedent for meeting at night established by the Jewish culture, there were probably even more pragmatic reasons for the early church to do so. The first undoubtedly arose from the fact that the day on which Christians chose to worship, Sunday, was an ordinary work day. Employers of Roman or Jewish background would have little patience with new believers who insisted that they be granted the privilege of taking off from work on Sunday just because of their religious convictions.

Second, it is likely that Christians met at night because it would have been dangerous for large numbers of them to gather in the daytime, except perhaps during evangelistic ventures held periodically in Solomon's porch of the Temple. Even there, however, they were not safe.

Third, Christianity was a countercultural movement and had to operate in a clandestine manner. A visit to Salzburg, Austria, reveals that Rome was not the only place where Christians met in catacombs. Far below the earth, where their songs and praise were masked from view and from hearing, they could realize some degree of safety. Passage in and out of the catacombs was best done at night.

After the time of Constantine, when Christianity became the religion of the empire, Sunday became a holiday, and the custom of meeting on Sunday evenings seems to have been abandoned except among bands of evangelical dissidents. The meetings of the dissidents were clandestine. It is probable that they met in the evening not because they chose to but because they had to in order to escape persecution.

In early American history, the Puritans met on Sunday morning and on Sunday night. It would be interesting to know whether their Sunday evening meetings arose because of custom born out of persecution or came about because the people really were as pious as reported. If the latter is true, one meeting a Sunday simply would not have sufficed.

What then is the origin of the Sunday evening service in more modern times? We can only speculate, because historical records on the matter are not complete. In the revivals of the eighteenth and nineteenth centuries and even into the twentieth century, services often were held at night. Since those meetings were held during the week as well as on weekends, the working schedules of people precluded their attending on weekdays. Their decision to meet in the evening on Sundays, may simply have been a case of following the pattern established during the week.

On the frontier, where people such as Wesley had to travel during the daytime, and where people were engaged in survival pursuits during the daylight hours, evenings were probably the only time possible to hold meetings. Again, the pattern established during the week may have been the genesis of the choice to meet on Sunday evenings.

Even more recently, in grandpa's day, when life was slower and less complicated than now, numbers of the faithful lived in homes and communities clustered around the church building and centered their lives in the activities the church offered. To people whose normal work week entailed six hard days of labor, the seventh day was delightfully different. It was a day in which they could refresh their bodies and recharge their souls. The church provided spiritual nourishment and refreshment and an accepting social climate in which people of like background and theological persuasion could build their social life. To the factory worker surrounded all week by those hostile to his Christian witness and to the isolated farmer separated by his job from human companionship, the fellowship of the saints was the tonic to the soul that enabled him to survive. Moreover, in an age when Christians were restricted in conscience and pocketbook to but few choices in entertainment, the church provided a modest type of entertainment that was comfortably within the bounds of conviction and budget.

Remembering that background, remembering that Christian books were written chiefly for intellectuals, remembering that radio and TV had not yet been invented, it is not difficult to see how Christians of an earlier day felt that one spiritual and social encounter a Sunday was not enough and opted strongly for an evening service in addition. The need was bolstered also by the fact that large numbers of domestic workers, such as my own grandmother, were required to work on Sunday. Surely the church must meet their needs as well! And so the evening service became a permanent fixture and became a success. To people of simple tastes and demands, of limited financial means and social opportunities, and of severely restricted choices of entertainment, a Sunday evening formula of gospel hymn singing, a musical presentation by a person of modest talent, and what the average person today probably would judge a mediocre sermon by the pastor rounded out their day. It was just what they needed, and they went home satisfied.

That satisfaction was short-lived, however. With the preaching emphasis of Moody, Billy Sunday, and other evangelists of the late nineteenth and early twentieth centuries, the church once more was awakened to its evangelistic responsibilities. Because evangelism appeared to be an item of curiosity among the people at large, and because numbers of the curious were flocking to evangelistic meetings, many pastors and congregations thought the church should capitalize on the phenomenon and hold services in which there would be a systematic and regular evangelistic appeal. The evening service was the natural time for that to happen. Entertainment choices still were limited, and the tactic seemed to work. For the most part evening services were well-attended, and a fair number of people responded to the evangelistic invitation.

Even in the early thirties, however, Sunday evening attendance had begun to fall off, according to my father. It became exceedingly difficult to attract the unconverted to Sunday evening evangelistic meetings. With little or no unsaved people attending, it was hard for the preacher to sustain a message of evangelism each Sunday evening, and it was boring for regular attenders to listen to such messages Sunday after Sunday. The advent of radio contributed as well to the decline in attendance at Sunday evening services. Moreover, during the early forties all coastal cities had to observe lighting brownouts and blackouts because of World War II and consequent danger from submarines. Inland cities dimmed their lights to conserve energy, gasoline rationing limited automobile travel, and many churches decided that for the duration it was too difficult to hold evening services.

The real threat to the evening service was yet to come. Our present era probably began in the fifties with the widespread utilization of television. Man now had a source that brought professional entertainment right into his living room. Little effort was required of him except that needed during commercials to entice him out of his chair to the refrigerator. Accompanying the rise of television were other important developments, all of which worked together to change man's life more in a relatively few years than it had been changed in centuries. As a result, as we view man today in the mid-twentieth century, it is impossible not to make some sobering observations. Man's work load has been lightened, and his hours of work shortened. He has more leisure time than ever before in history and more sources than he can bear to tell him how to use that time. The automobile has given him mobility. He no longer needs to live close to his place of employment or his church. An eroding of ethnic group distinctions has widened social opportunities for him. Higher wages and modern technology have enabled him to take advantage of a variety of entertainment sources, some within his own home, making him more sophisticated, if not more discreet, in his choices. Also, the church is no longer man's sole source of spiritual life. Home Bible studies, Christian radio and TV, along with well-written, lay-oriented Christian books offer him a great choice of spiritual resources.

At this point, the reader of this book may be thinking, "My word. Why the lengthy discourse on the evening service? He did not give such a commentary on any other service?" The answer is that the evening service, more than any other program of the church, is under attack at this time. It is appropriate to ask where the evening service fits into the life of modern man. Is the service merely a vestige of quieter days when life was slower and less complicated, or does the service have valid application today? Are churches holding onto the service for traditional or sentimental reasons, or does it satisfy a genuine need for today's Christian? Many churches have abandoned the Sunday evening service, stating that the family already has too many demands on it. Other churches have discarded it in the hope that the period it formerly consumed will be used by Christians for times of fellowship with each other. In many cases, however, that is not happening. Consequently, it was with some dismay that I heard a pastor friend confide recently that he was making a strong effort to get his church to abandon their Sunday evening service so that the members of the congregation would have more time for witnessing. If his church cancels its evening service, will his goal actually be realized?

In contrast to the opinion of my pastor friend, I believe that few church members spend an inordinate amount of time in church activities. Furthermore, I believe that in an age when the church has been fragmented by the many demands of society, it would be tragic to abandon a ready-made opportunity for members of the body to interact meaningfully, as is at least possible in a Sunday evening service.

Causes for Decline

Why is it that Sunday evening services flourish in some churches and drag in others? It could be a difference in the attitude of the people, but more likely the answer lies in the amount of forethought and effort put into the service. Many pastors new to the ministry do not have "barrels" of sermons on which to draw for such purposes as evening services. Sermon preparation is not an easy task. To prepare a sermon properly takes a great deal of time. In former days, the life of the pastor was less hectic. Fewer demands were made for his time. As a result, many men were able to spend long hours visiting with their people or studying the Word, preparing for the various sermons and Bible studies they were called upon to provide each week. Moreover, by and large people were not nearly as well-educated or as sophisticated as they are today, nor were their problems, on the whole, so complex. Society's demands and pressures were not so rigorous. Life moved more slowly, and people did not experience the high degree of change encountered today in a world dominated by what Alvin Toffler has called "Future Shock." In earlier days, therefore, the pastor's preparation may have been much easier.

These days, the demands upon people are enormous, and the pressure for the pastor to supply the answers to their questions from the Word is staggering. Recently I asked a speech teacher from a nearby university, "Realistically, how many truly good speeches can we expect an experienced public speaker to produce in a year?" His answer was, at the most, seven. Yet congregations are asking their pastor to produce, on the average, forty-seven sermons a year for use in the morning service alone. My professor friend thinks that is an impossible task. If, in addition, a pastor is called upon to produce another forty-seven sermons for the evening service and still another forty-seven for the midweek service, the church has assigned to him a task he cannot possibly perform.

The consequence is that the average pastor approaches the evening service with dread. The service that results is something like this. A half-hearted attempt is made to inspire the faithful through the singing of the old gospel songs. Because the pastor has had little time to prepare for the hymn-sing, many times the format consists of singing favorites requested by members of the congregation. The instrumentalists may or may not know those hymns, but, at least, they are game for a try. Interspersed with the singing may be a few so-called spontaneous testimonies, generally given by those persons who find silence uncomfortable. An offering is taken. Then it is time for the pastor. If he has a sermon barrel left over from the last church he served, the message he preaches may or may not be passable.

And what if he is near the bottom of that barrel? It is my firm belief that in many cases when the pastor finds himself at that point, with many pressing duties and no time to prepare three sermons a week, he finds also that he hears a mysterious "call" of the Lord to move on. At any rate, many who attend the traditional Sunday evening service once or even twice find it an experience in drudgery. Outside of a few faithful ones—those who are present every time the church building is unlocked and who are faithful to the pastor no matter how painful the experience—the rank and file shows its discontent by staying away from the service. No wonder there is pressure on the part of many people to bury it.

Revitalizing the Evening Meeting

The evening service does not have to be like that. Yet to make it otherwise is going to take careful planning and the marshaling of the most gifted individuals the church has. If the pastor is going to change the evening service from a vestige to a venture, he is going to have to be freed from other duties so that he can spend time in that pursuit. There is much he can do to make the service better. Even if the church insists on retaining a traditional preaching service, the format can be made much more inviting than the service described above. In almost every church, there are people with platform abilities who do not often get a chance to exercise those skills. Such people may be assigned the responsibility for establishing and executing a meaningful and enjoyable evening service. With input from the pastor and other church leaders, the evening service can be transformed into something people look forward to instead of dread.

When planning the format of the service, it is wise to remember that it damages a service to hold it in an auditorium too large for it. An effort should be made to choose a room appropriate to the size of the crowd attending, to make that room as attractive as possible, and to use the room until forced to seek larger quarters. When the room is crowded out, the effect on the congregation will be exhilarating.

In contrast to the traditional evening service, there is a way to hold a service that will truly suit the needs of the congregation. The rest of this chapter describes such a way, though a word of caution is in order first. Rather than introducing the new format as a complete package and effecting change all at once, often it is better to move into the format gradually, employing one new element for a while before introducing the next. Be assured, however, that even if the move to the new format is made in measured steps, there will be those in the congregation who will not like the new arrangement. They will complain, even to the point of stating that they do not think the pastor is working hard enough. Unfortunately, they may make up the majority of the persons who were faithful attenders of the evening service under the old format. It may not be easy to quiet such people. It is possible, however, that by the time their protests become significant, the pastor will have been fortunate enough to have an evening service so successful it will have attracted enough persons who are grateful for and excited about the new evening service to outnumber the protesters.

EMPHASIZE FELLOWSHIP

Though he is surrounded by people most of the time, modern man is desperately lonely. He cries for in-depth relationships with others. The church of Jesus Christ should be the happy exception in this lonely society. Yet church after church goes through the motions of greeting visitors at the door or exchanging handshakes during the morning service, while visitors and sometimes long-time members go away as lonely as they came in.

Sunday night is a convenient time to create a climate in which people with like interests can discover each other and begin a life of meaningful interaction. The church can hold periodic hospitality nights on which the families of the congregation are assigned to various homes of other members. The evening service that night could be conducted in each host home and could consist of a short Bible study, hymns, prayer, and the recounting of God's work in individual lives. Thus, instead of meeting at the church building for one large service, the church would go into the community for many smaller services, providing Christians an opportunity to know and appreciate each other better.

One of the most valuable tools in creating a suitable climate for fellowship is food. Sunday evening programs, whether in the church building or in the homes of members, should give as many opportunities as possible for people to sit down and eat together. The early church set a valuable precedent, which should be reestablished.

Another helpful tool for promoting fellowship is a carefully planned time of testimony in the evening service. Such times help alert people to those who are kindred spirits. Rather than planning times of testimony merely as spontaneous occasions, the alert pastor who knows his people can prepare members of the body to relate their experiences in a concise and meaningful manner.

The church that is convinced that creating an effective fellowship climate is important will use many other ways of creating such a climate.

EMPHASIZE INSTRUCTION

Sunday night is an excellent time to meet some of the diverse instructional needs of the contemporary Christian. It is a fine time, for instance, for the pastor to present a series of talks on doctrinal issues, speaking in an atypical, non-pulpit manner and using appropriate audiovisuals. Church history is also a pertinent topic for the setting. Many Christians do not know who they are in relation to their Christian heritage.

The evening service is a good occasion to conduct a year-round missionary conference, devoting a Sunday night each month to presentations by missionaries themselves or to quality missionary films, both types of programs informing church members as to the diverse, worldwide outreach opportunities now open to missionaries.

A great many attractively-produced instructional film series are available in which some of the foremost experts on a number of important subjects report vital information in an entertaining manner. Since many of the films are oriented toward adults, it may be a good idea to plan an alternate program for children on the nights the films are shown, offering an earlier private showing for children's workers so that they do not have to miss the information contained in the film. An increasing number of videotapes offer an even wider instructional selection to be used with smaller groups.

EMPHASIZE INFORMATION

Dialogue usually is not possible in the morning service. In the more relaxed, informal setting of the evening service, however, there is excellent opportunity for members of the congregation to request clarification on issues the pastor has raised in his morning sermons. A question box at the rear of the building and a periodic "pastor on the spot" program will enable members to receive answers to questions of importance to them that have been raised but not answered in the pastor's sermons. Besides the written questions, spontaneous verbal questions from the congregation will help the pastor clarify issues still further.

Sunday evening is the time to use panels, forums, symposiums, and guest speakers to explore subjects important to the Christian community at large. Many experts are happy to volunteer their services for such presentations so that they and their ideas might become better known. Sunday night is an appropriate time for organizations within the church, such as youth groups and children's clubs, to share with the congregation the ministry in which they are engaged. Matters of denominational importance are pertinent topics for Sunday evening, and often audiovisual presentations are available from the denominational headquarters for such use by a local church.

EMPHASIZE INSPIRATION

There is not a Christian alive who does not need a periodic shot of inspiration to help him through the work week. Sunday night can be a wonderful vehicle for producing such a boost.

The Sunday evening service is exactly the right time for people to join in praise and thanksgiving for all that God has done for them during the week. It is a good time to make known prayer concerns to brothers and sisters so that prayers may be offered on the spot and later at home, as Christians engage in intercession for each other.

Sunday night is an excellent time to praise the Lord in song. Centuries-old hymns of the church may be sung, or more contemporary expressions of faith and praise may be used. Sometimes solo, duet, ensemble, instrumental, and choir numbers on a common theme may be interspersed throughout the service, for an entire evening of musical inspiration. On other occasions, major choir works will provide blessing and incentive to a congregation. Periodic guest artists and singing groups also add to the inspirational life of the church.

If guest artists or singing groups are asked to perform at the church, be sure it is clear ahead of time what financial remuneration they expect. Also, it is wise to listen to a performance tape ahead of time to ascertain that the type and quality of music is appropriate to the tastes and needs of your particular congregation. To make sure of the authenticity of the Christian testimony of the artist or group, references should be required if the artist or group is unknown to the pastor or congregation.

In planning the use of musical resources from outside of the church itself, care should be exercised to see that there is a sufficient amount of time to advertise the event properly. Also, such an event should fit into the overall church calendar. As a pastor, I have received numerous requests from soloists and groups to appear on the spur of the moment, placing a great deal of pressure on me to respond favorably, even if the time is not convenient with my congregation. Except for nationally-known Christian artists, who because of their name alone would draw a crowd, and who, because of the urgent need of a booking would agree to come on the basis of a love offering, I have learned to say no to the "tyranny of the urgent," despite the musical abilities of the artist or group soliciting the booking.

EMPHASIZE THE LORD'S SUPPER

Who has not experienced the frustration of trying to fit the Lord's Supper into an already crowded morning worship service? The result is that the ordinance—which should be worshipful and meaningful—becomes hurried and perfunctory. By moving the Lord's Supper to a Sunday evening and making it the focal point of the evening, it is possible to elevate the Lord's supper to the place of prominence it should enjoy in the church. (Much more about the ordinance is contained in a later chapter dealing exclusively with the two ordinances of the church.)

There is still another use that can be made of the Sunday evening service. But it is one that requires a congregation with a charitable

spirit who, instead of attending the service only for their own benefit, would agree to come as partners in equipping others for the work
of the ministry. In many churches there is a group of men—some
young, some old—who harbor the secret desire to preach. However,
because there is no opportunity for them to preach, they have no
chance to receive the guidance of the body as to whether they have a
valid gift that should be developed. Sunday evening is a wonderful
time to allow them to test their abilities through the delivery of a
short message.

The pastor or other staff member should work with the men ahead
of time, giving them helpful suggestions concerning content and
delivery. Before a novice preaches in front of a congregation, he
should be required to preach that same sermon before a select group
of seasoned people who will be able kindly to critique him, giving
him helpful points on how he can improve. It may be exceptionally
helpful for the same group to rate the sermon as it is delivered to the
congregation, so that the novice may gain still more advice concerning strong and weak points. He will then be able to do better the next
time he has a chance to preach.

The men selected to preach should be instructed to limit their
presentations to twenty minutes. After all, even charitable people
have a limit to their endurance, especially since inexperienced
preachers are not as interesting or instructive as they imagine. After
a person has been allowed to preach three or four times over a
reasonable period of time, the board of the church may want to make
a formal evaluation of his potential. At that time, he should be
encouraged to pursue training that will enhance his skills, or he
should be told in a gracious and gentle way that his gifts lie in areas
other than preaching. If the latter advice is offered, he will not be
invited to preach anymore in the evening service.

In deference to the evening service and the quality of program
sought, I would like to suggest that when novices preach, those
planning the service should take into consideration the fact that the
skills of the novice may still be modest. They should take greater
care in planning the earlier portions of the service so that they contain enough important and meaningful events to assure that even if
the sermon turns out to be terrible, the people will come away
feeling that the service itself was a success.

This chapter has revolved around the fact that the people of God
need to be together as a body more often than just the Sunday
morning service. Thus, while it is true that some of the time the
people need to meet in small groups so that they can get to know
each other, that need for small-group meetings does not replace the

need for the body to meet as a whole. The evening service provides a ready-made opportunity for the church to meet as a whole in a setting less formal than is the case with the Sunday morning service.

Problems concerning the evening service have arisen in large part because it is sometimes treated as an unimportant appendage to the program of the church. When important things take place in the evening service, people will consider the occasion important and will elect to attend. Rather than giving up on the evening service, more emphasis needs to put on it. In some cases, a major overhaul is necessary. In others, slight modifications will give it exactly the sparkle it needs.

The bulk of this chapter has pointed out many of the meaningful things the church should be doing and has noted that Sunday evening is an ideal time for doing them. Although the suggestions made in this chapter are not meant to be exhaustive, they are numerous enough so that a church employing only those suggestions would discover that, far from having too little material to supply meaningful Sunday evening programs, it did not have available enough Sunday evenings in the year to do all it wished.

Questions for Discussion

1. What are the cultural, historical, and practical reasons for having Sunday evening services?

2. How does the evening service fit into the life-style of modern man? Is it merely a vestige of quieter days when life was slower and less complicated? Are we holding onto it for traditional or sentimental reasons, or does it satisfy a genuine need for today's Christian?

3. Why is it that the Sunday evening service flourishes in some churches, though it declines in others?

4. Is it unrealistic to expect a pastor to be the main item of attraction on Sunday evening when he has already prepared and delivered a major address that day?

5. What alternative programming possibilities are there for Sunday evening services?

6. Utilizing the suggestions found in this chapter, develop alternatives to the traditional Sunday evening program. Plan a distinct program for each Sunday evening in the next year.

15

Midweek Activities

In recent years probably no activity of the church has come under harsher criticism than the midweek service. Yet, in many churches, when a concerted effort is made to replace the midweek service with an alternate activity to take place outside the church building, often a small but powerful group within the church voices such strong disaproval the effort is sabotaged. Never mind that few of the protesting group attend the midweek service on a regular basis. It is more likely that one of the reasons for their protest is that many of them attach special meaning to the church building itself. They are convinced that it is a "holy" place and that nothing of true spiritual significance can take place outside of its walls.

Moreover, those same people often have a stereotypical idea of the pastor and his role. Perhaps their view has grown out of the memories they have of a model pastor they knew in their childhood. Impressions of the past, of course, are easy to color in a rosy hue. If those people even admit that the pastoral role has changed, they deny that the change was for the better. In their way of thinking the pastor should be visiting his flock or sitting in his office "minding the store," so that when they call to voice the smallest grievance, he will be there to listen sympathetically. His ministry to the community at large is an unnecessary luxury to them. "After all," they are heard to say, "who pays his salary anyway?"

One of the things that counts with them and for which they pay his salary, is that he conduct three services a week and prepare a sermon for each. Any less activity on the pastor's part signifies to them that he is lazy and does not want to do the job to which he was called. Even if he is extremely busy and can demonstrate that from his calendar, they will take him to task if there is any deviation from the three-sermons-a-week routine.

Tactics for Bringing About Change

The pastor can respond to the problem in one of two ways. He may decide to fight the complainers because, after all, he knows what is best for the church and for his ministry. Surely only he knows how to utilize his time for maximum effectiveness in accomplishing the tasks he believes are important. In taking such a firm stance, he may get his own way, only to learn—perhaps many months later—that he won the battle only to lose the war. By taking an unbending approach in dealing with the stubbornness of an unrelenting group, he will have drawn up battle lines and established the persons in the group as his enemies. He can be certain that in the future they will oppose any action he wants to take. Eventually a tug of war may result. Because the people he is battling are likely to be tithers, they can carry on an effective game of "starve the preacher," and he will find it necessary to distribute his résumé.

Be Patient

In sharp contrast to such a hostile approach, he may decide on quite a different tactic. At least for the first few years of his ministry, until he has established his credibility, he may decide to humor the group and go along with their wishes. Even though few show up for midweek service, he will do his best to relate meaningfully with those who do. He may select a passage of Scripture, for instance, prepare a brief meditation, and deliver that meditation with as much aplomb possible, considering his busy week and the few people who have come out to hear him. He may then encourage the assembled saints to spend the rest of the period in prayer for specific needs in that congregation and across the world. Depending on the number present, he may encourage them to divide into smaller groups or he may ask them to remain in one group for prayer.

Recognize a Plurality of Interests

Many readers may suspect at this point that I have retreated in my thinking to the dark ages. They may balk at what I have written, saying, "I object! What my church really needs is small groups meeting in homes. That's the way the body interacts meaningfully." I agree with their position, but nevertheless I insist also that what their congregation more likely needs is a program that retains the traditional midweek service even while it sponsors home Bible studies. Because the majority of the members do not come to the church building for a midweek service, the church would not be competing against itself in offering an alternative activity. Those persons who are prohibited by the demands of their employment from attending the midweek service can attend neighborhood groups that meet at times convenient for them. Perhaps the particular groups they will join will be those that meet near their own homes, eliminating transportation problems and expenses. In addition, those who do not appreciate what they believe is the more formal climate that prevails in the church building may enjoy the more relaxed atmosphere of a home.

What I am trying to emphasize is this: Instead of trying to impose uniformity, and defensively claiming that all nonconformists are rebellious, the church needs to address the question of pluralities, ministering to as many groups as possible in surroundings and using methods with which they are comfortable. The church that insists it will conduct only home Bible studies, for instance, is not facing up to the fact that some people do not enjoy such activities and will not attend. For those people, a midweek service at the church building is far more desirable. Despite my firm belief in home Bible studies, I must ask, "Why can't the church be sufficiently thoughtful and flexible to minister to the needs of those who want midweek services as well as those who support the home approach?" Why should the church try to force everyone in the congregation into conformity? Why should it not offer options so that people can make choices according to what is meaningful for and desirable to them?

Perhaps one of the reasons the church has striven to enforce conformity in the past is that many people are threatened by those who think differently than they. They view such persons as threats. Therefore, even though it would be desirable to offer a variety of activities, the church seeks uniformity and conformity, and defends its position by citing the biblical requirement for Christians to be submissive.

There is perhaps another reason, a cultural one. For years we in North America have been caught up in the myth of the melting pot, believing that a receiving culture grows strong as the contributing cultures lose their identity in the larger culture. The view is, of course, the height of cultural chauvinism. I am happy that in recent years, it has been proved that when immigrating people retain their cultural identity within the receiving culture they actually enrich the receiving culture rather than weaken it. How sad my life would be if there were no taco stands, and I had to restrict my fast-food diet to the all-American hamburger. In some cases the church has not caught up with this philosophical change. It fails to prove the variety of programs it should to meet the divergent needs of the various groups of people who look to it for spiritual leadership.

However, even the combination of two methods I have suggested probably is not adequate. People with divergent interests need an even greater variety of opportunities. Some people, perhaps, will find neither the midweek service nor Bible studies to their liking but will find meaningful interaction among fellow choir members, Sunday school teachers, softball team members, or ushers. Often people who perform tasks together develop meaningful relationships with each other. It would be logical to encourage such groups of people to meet together for Bible study and prayer, at a time convenient to them.

CONSOLIDATE THE SCHEDULE

Another concern to consider is that the church, in whatever format it adopts for its program, should do its best to see that it does not fragment the family or require family members to be away from home an excessive number of evenings. To avoid such a development, many churches try to schedule the majority of their activities on a single evening of the week. Some of those churches meet as a whole for a brief time of Bible study and prayer. Then the group disperses into interest and age groups. In other churches there is no general assembly time. People arrive at the church building and immediately report to their appropriate groups. Each of the individual groups conducts its own time of Bible study and prayer.

Some churches go one step further and prepare a tasty but inexpensive meal for individuals attending midweek functions. A nominal fee is taken up to meet expenses, and the housewife is freed of the task of rushing to feed her hungry family before they leave for church activities. Of course, the idea of conducting all of the church's midweek activities simultaneously suggests that the church is large enough so that people do not have to double up on responsibilities. In a small church, a person might be forced to choose between serving as a children's club leader or singing in the choir, which would amount to having no choice, because he would be needed for both.

The Pastor's Role

With such a variety of events possible, what is the pastor's role in all of this? I believe that it is proper for him to expect to conduct personally the Bible study or prayer meeting held in the church building. That does not mean that he needs to feel compelled to prepare and present a sermon or Bible study topic personally each time. In fact, if the pastor does not face major objections to such a plan, the midweek service would be an excellent time for lay persons with potential for being excellent speakers to try their wings. In churches where such a practice has not been tried before, the pastor may want to introduce the concept gradually, at first utilizing such individuals no more than once a month and then gradually increasing the frequency. Regardless of who actually delivers the devotional message or conducts the Bible study, it is advisable for the pastor to be present in the service and to take an active leadership role of some kind. In addition to attending the midweek service, it is wise for the pastor to drop in from time to time on each of the other groups that meet during the week. It is in the casual atmosphere of such groups that he may make his most rewarding contacts with people.

This chapter has presupposed the traditional rather than the non-traditional church. That is because traditional churches account for the majority of churches to which a pastor can expect to be called. A young pastor might prefer a non-traditional church, but there are few of them around. He might have to wait a long time before finding one in which to minister. In addition, there really is no such thing as a completely nontraditional church, except for maybe a few brand new ones. Given a little bit of time, each church forms its own traditions, even though those traditions may be different from the ones practiced by the churches most people would label "traditional." In the traditional setting—which I suspect represents the great majority of churches—the pastor, in close coordination with other church leaders, is wise to promote and develop as diverse and varied a midweek program as possible to meet the plurality of needs within his congregation.

The pastor should not suppose that it is necessary for him to run all of those programs himself, or else he will be bogged down hopelessly with that task alone. With the exception of the midweek service at the church building itself, all other activities I have mentioned should be placed into the hands of other competent leaders. If there are no "competent others," the activity should not begin until the pastor or another trained church leader has equipped an enthusiastic and willing lay person to supervise the activity. Although the pastor cannot be expected to run all of the activities in his church personally, his occasional presence at each one of them will show his keen interest and concern and will allow him to interact meaningfully with a variety of people in an atmosphere more casual and relaxing than is usually the case in a church building. Each such contact will be valuable to the pastor in his effort to get to know his people more thoroughly so that he may serve them more skillfully.

Questions for Discussion

1. What is the expectation of most congregations regarding the midweek program of the church?

2. What options are there besides the typical midweek prayer meeting? How would you advise a pastor to provide for the needs of a larger group of his congregation without alienating those who feel that a traditional approach is necessary?

3. What is the value of diversity in planning the midweek programs of the church?

4. What are the strengths and weaknesses of conducting all of the church's midweek activities on a single night?

5. What role should the pastor play in the multiplicity of other activities that occur during the week in addition to the traditional prayer meeting? How may the pastor show interest and concern for those who participate in those activities?

Helpful Resources

Dilday, Russell H. *Prayer Meeting Resources.* Vol. 1. Nashville: Convention Press, 1977.

Griffin, Em. "Influencing Others to Pray." *Leadership* 3, no. 1 (Winter 1982):41-46.

Matthews, C. David. *Prayer Meeting Resources.* Vol. 2. Nashville: Convention Press, 1978.

Patterson, Ben. "The Central Work of Prayer." *Leadership* 3, no. 1 (Winter 1982):114-17.

Tatum, Scott L. Herschel H. Hobbs, and Harper Shannon. *Prayer Meeting Resources.* Vol. 3. Nashville: Convention Press, 1981.

16

Special Events

It is wise to use special events to build a spirit of expectancy in a church. Such a spirit is desirable because human beings are so constituted that often half of the fun of a given event is the anticipation leading up to that event. Although the pastor should avoid planning so many special occasions that members of the congregation are inundated with church activities, a wise pastor is aware that there is a psychological advantage to planning enough special events to make people feel they are part of a local body where important and enjoyable things are happening.

Planning Intelligently

The judicious planner keeps many things in mind. First, he plans around the activities of the surrounding community. Is that community sports-minded, for instance? Despite the undying loyalty of his congregation, he may find any church event sparsely attended when it conflicts with a major athletic event in which there is keen community interest. Such a time is not the proper one for testing the loyalty of the congregation.

Are there other major events in the secular or the religious community that appeal to large numbers of the congregation? If there are, why should the parish knowingly plan a competing program, especially when the church finds the event already planned to be an acceptable activity for its people? Why not instead cooperate in those acceptable events and plan activities that will not compete with them.

Second, in addition to cooperating with events already on the calendar, the wise planner will capitalize on seasonal opportunities. Many churches experience a summer slump when a significant number of members are vacationing. Despite a drop in attendance, activities can be introduced to make the summer enjoyable to those who remain. Events to be maximized in the summer are ones that are built around outdoor activities but that can, nevertheless, shift to a "plan B" in case of inclement weather. Sunday evening services held in a park, with a potluck or homemade ice cream social to follow, can contribute greatly to the fellowship life of the church. An old fashioned Sunday school picnic with a well-planned schedule of games and contests for all ages or an all-church campout may be valuable to the church if only because those who participate will have a chance to get to know each other better.

How does the proper planning for such events take place? Although I am opposed to overloading the church with standing committees, I am a firm and enthusiastic proponent of forming ad hoc committees, that meet over a relatively short time for a specific purpose only and then are disbanded when the purpose has been accomplished. Such committees are not burdened by having to consider a great many concerns. As a result they can devote much energy to a specific event and bring that event to fruition with considerable vigor. After a period of rest, the people who formed the committee, or an entirely different group of people, can concentrate their energies on a new project.

Seasonal Activities

SUMMER

The creative mind will construct a variety of pleasant and meaningful church summer activities. However, some practical guidelines should be observed.

1. Church-wide events should include enough activities to appeal to a wide variety of people. Some people, for example, are sports enthusiasts, whereas others enjoy more sedentary pursuits. Children are likely to enjoy activities entirely different from the ones that attract adults. The committee planning such events should take care that no one is left out.

2. As much as possible, summer events should be interspersed throughout the season instead of being concentrated in one period. If

too many activities are planned too close together, they will wear the people out. As a result, attendance at each event will be a chore instead of a joy.

3. Groups wanting to sponsor events in which only select people would care to participate should plan those events in close conjunction with the overall church calendar so that they do not compete with church-wide activities. For instance, a particular group may find waterskiing highly enjoyable, but the sport may not have as wide an appeal as a Sunday school picnic in which the majority of the church could participate. The activity with the greater appeal should receive the first priority. The event with more limited appeal should be scheduled at another time.

Summer is a wonderful time for teaching events such as vacation Bible school, day camps, five-day clubs, church camps, and children's crusades. Care should be exercised in planning these events to assure that they are entertaining and contain enjoyable activities. Children who spend the entire school year in a stuffy classroom considering "heavy" topics will not delight in repeating the scenario in a church classroom during the summer.

FALL

Other seasons of the year present opportunities for meaningful and happy special events. Several weeks into the fall, when attendance has picked up again, may be a good time for a special evangelistic emphasis or an informative Bible conference. Although evangelistic services or Bible conferences used to be held over a week-long period, recently, many churches have found great success in planning activities that are concentrated into a shorter period of time, such as a weekend.

CHRISTMAS

Christmas is a wonderful time of the year for special events. When those events include public performances by children, many adults will attend who ordinarily would not be found in church. Personally, I have found it wise to plan and promote a variety of special activities during the early weeks of December but to keep the number of church events to a minimum during the Christmas period itself. The pressures of office parties, school events, Christmas shopping, and dozens of other demands make the Christmas season itself a pressure-laden time for many families. It is best when the church can alleviate the condition rather than complicate it.

NEW YEAR'S EVE

New Year's Eve is a time when many Christians feel lonely, especially if they are relatively new believers. The church has the opportunity to present a wholesome, happy alternative to what the world offers on that night. Some churches plan an elaborate progam on New Year's Eve that includes a meal, films, a guest vocal artist, a special speaker, and a comprehensive youth program lasting well into the next morning. Other churches have experienced success in a round of activities taking place in a variety of homes. Sometimes those activities include table games, video games, home movies, refreshments, and periods of fellowship. Such a relatively unstructured evening allows families to come and go as they desire and provides a meaningful way for them to share the holiday with their Christian brothers and sisters.

WINTER DOLDRUMS

After the excitement of Christmas, things tend to slump in January and February. Then is the time to plan events designed specifically to lift people out of the doldrums. Concerts and banquets are good tools for the purpose. In addition, the church might encourage fellowship among believers by arranging for series of events that a number of people attend together. For instance, the church might purchase a block of tickets for a sporting or a cultural event. Refreshments following the occasion will round off a pleasant evening when Christians have taken time to relax together.

EASTER

The focal point of the early spring is, of course, Easter. Even though in essence every Sunday is a celebration of the resurrection, the Easter season should be used to bring the Blessed Hope of the church into sharp focus. In order to highlight Easter Day properly, however, the church must emphasize the events leading up to it, focusing especially on the tremendous sacrifice the Lord made on the cross for our salvation. For centuries the church did that in a period of the church year called Lent. During Lent, Christians were encouraged to give up something in order to help them remember what the Lord gave up for them. It is unfortunate that many evangelical churches, in reaction to what they termed "dead formalism," included Lent among the items to be discarded. The idea of Lent is a sound one. Since the earliest days of the church it has drawn attention to the events leading up to the cross and has given the Christian an occasion to engage in some degree of voluntary sacrifice. Considering the opulent life enjoyed by the average North American Christian today, the idea of setting apart a season when Christians attempt to get back to the essentials, through some voluntary form of fasting or through abstaining temporarily from some form of pleasure, is pertinent. Those who participate will receive the moral benefit of discipline and the spiritual benefit of having been helped to concentrate on the Lord in a more intense manner, at least for that short period of the year.

A number of evangelical churches are rediscovering Lent. In addition to encouraging their people to engage in voluntary acts of sacrifice, some congregations hold a special series of midweek services during the period. At least one church with which I am acquainted, one located near a downtown shopping mall, holds a special service each Wednesday noon during Lent, inviting prominent guest speakers to offer their observations concerning the cross. The church publicizes the Wednesday services widely in the adjoining business community, and the results have been gratifying.

During Holy Week itself an even more intense focus on the cross may be desired. The custom of observing Maundy Thursday Communion is being revived once again, sometimes in conjunction with a Passover seder conducted by a Hebrew Christian or Old Testament scholar. Good Friday presents a unique opportunity to focus on the oneness in Christ that was brought about by the Lord's sacrifice on the cross. In places where it is no longer practical to hold a joint midday service, evening services held with other evangelical churches can be effective.

In order for people to realize the full impact of its meaning, Easter itself must stand out in sharp contrast to the events preceding it. It should be a day of jubilant celebration. Many of the hale and hearty will want to arise early to attend the sunrise service every community seems to have available. Or, because food is an integral part of celebration, others might want to begin Easter festivities by participating in a sumptuous Easter brunch with the rest of the family of God. When stomachs are full, humor runs high and spirits soar. Such a feast can do wonders for the morale of a mother who has had barely enough time before church to dress her brood, no less to feed them. Being released from the responsibility of cooking on that one morning will make Easter Day a time of celebration for her.

There are many creative ways of handling the Easter service itself. One church I know of dismisses Sunday school and holds one large praise celebration on Easter morning that includes a great many musical numbers, a children's message, and a short sermon by the pastor. Churches following a more traditional approach will want to use the best musical resources available. Musical numbers by choirs, soloists, instrumentalists, and small groups should be interspersed throughout the service, and the congregation should be given many opportunities to join in singing the great Easter hymns of praise. Easter and Christmas are occasions for the shortest sermons of the year (in some cases, that alone will be cause for rejoicing on the part of the congregation). Also, Easter and Christmas are occasions when it is appropriate for the pastor to include a clear evangelistic thrust in his sermon. Extended altar calls, however, are usually not right for such occasions. It is not the prerogative of the church to exploit non-Christian visitors and make them feel uncomfortable. It is the obligation of the pastor, and through him, the church, to make the message of the gospel clear, to extend a polite invitation, and then to leave the rest to the Person of the Holy Spirit.

SPRING

Once Easter is over, generally the weather begins to improve markedly. Usually, however, people are not yet able to take vacations. Thus the period proves to be the time of highest attendance in the church year. Spring is therefore a good time for an evangelistic thrust, a Bible conference, or a missionary conference. Be forewarned, though, that unless such events are planned, advertised, and executed properly, they can be the dullest of the year. Great care must be exercised to see to it that they are exciting events. Also, those scheduling the events should make sure that they take place well after Easter but early enough in the year so that they do not compete with the array of events that seems inevitably to surround school graduations. When spring conferences can be scheduled to coincide with Pentecost a dual function is realized. The local church benefits from the conference, and it gets a chance to celebrate the birthday of the church universal in a festive and special manner, thus linking itself with its heritage.

Activities for Small Groups

This chapter has dealt primarily with church-wide activities. Along with those, throughout the year it is important to promote activities by smaller groups whose members have common interests. Adult class parties, choir retreats and outings, seminars, workshops, weekend retreats, and deacon and elder retreats all may enhance the fellowship life of Christians and be valuable opportunities to equip the saints for the work of ministry.

Devotions in Church Activities

Here I would like to share a matter of personal concern. It seems to me that in the last few years there has been a tendency to insist that every activity involving church members include a devotional as a part of the program. To some pious souls the devotional serves as some sort of excuse to condone the fact that Christians are having a good time, as if having a good time were inappropriate. In some circles, the devotional inevitably contains an evangelistic thrust, the hope being that a Christian will bring along an unsaved friend or even a spouse who is not a Christian and that that person will hear and respond favorably to the gospel message. May I state as emphatically as I know how that Christians do not have to manufacture an excuse for having a good time together. As a matter of fact, they should have a good time almost automatically every time they get together. After all, who has a better reason to live in a constant state of celebration than Christians? Joy should be the essence of the Christian life. In addition, non-Christians will remain much more open and receptive to the gospel if they are not constantly subjected to a hidden agenda in the church events they attend. Moreover, probably the most impressive witness that can be made to a nonbeliever is for Christians to demonstrate their love for one another and to take obvious enjoyment in being with each other.

The world depends on various crutches—including drugs and sex—to bring people to the point where, supposedly, they are relaxed enough to enjoy one another. The Christian finds it relatively easy to be outrageously happy with other joyous Christians. That happiness is a puzzle to the world. It finds it hard to understand but often so compelling it feels it must discover the answer. Why do Christians enjoy being with each other so much? Why is it that they look after each other so well when one of their number has a need? Such conduct is appealing to the world because it is so rare in the world. But after all, do not the Scriptures indicate that the feature that should most distinguish believers from the world and make them intriguing to the world is the extravagant love they show to one another? May such love be the intent of the special events we plan for the church. If love is evident among us, we will be excited groups of Christians being built up in the faith, and the social events we plan will have evangelistic side-benefits. A healthy, happy, excited group of Christians always has been an irresistible force in the world.

Questions for Discussion

1. What value do special events have in the life of a church?
2. What factors should the pastor take into consideration when he plans special events?

3. How does the proper planning for such events take place? Make a list of guidelines to use in your planning of special events.

4. Review your experience in the church and list the various types of activities that can be enjoyed within the context of the church.

5. What may a church do to enhance traditional Christian holidays and community events and keep them meaningful?

6. Make a list of the special religious days on your church's calendar. Expand your list to include religious days normally associated with liturgical churches. How might a church bring life and meaning into its fellowship by revitalizing special yearly events such as Lent, Pentecost, and Maundy Thursday?

7. What danger is there in having a hidden agenda for the non-Christian who attends a church event?

8. Why is it unnecessary to have a devotional time at every special event?

Helpful Resources

Allen, R. Earl. *Days to Remember: Sermons for Special Days.* Grand Rapids: Baker, 1975.

Barron, Vance. *Sermons for the Celebration of the Christian Year.* Nashville: Abingdon, 1977.

Church Management: The Clergy Journal. Annual Planning Issue. Each year this journal offers suggestions for enhancing the year's activities through careful planning and through using the lectionary.

McCarthy, Brian. "Two Cheers for the Three-Year Lectionary." *The Christian Ministry* 11, no. 2 (March 1980):35-36.

Wood, Charles R., ed. *Sermon Outlines for Special Days and Occasions.* Grand Rapids: Kregel, 1970.

Youngblood, Ronald. *Special Day Sermons.* Grand Rapids: Baker, 1973.

17

The Lord's Supper and Baptism

Many seminary graduates move to a church similar to the one in which they grew up and never receive exposure to the way other denominations perform a variety of rituals. Such a protected atmosphere was not to be my lot. Upon graduation from seminary, I went immediately into the Army chaplaincy, where I found a variety of ways of doing things that seemed within the bounds of Scripture, even though they did not resemble very closely the practices I had learned growing up. During my first Sunday morning service on active duty, for instance, my colleague insisted that I be properly robed, since that was the way they did things there. Three times that Sunday he and I entered a chapel packed with perhaps four hundred basic trainees per service and offered the Lord's Supper. Confused because I did not see the customary racks with the Communion glasses, I was handed a gold chalice by my colleague. It was divided into two sections, one containing wafers, the other containing wine. I was told to follow the leader as he invited row after row of men to the altar rail, dipped a wafer in the wine and laid it upon each man's tongue. That was intinction, I was told, the only way Communion could be served so many men in such a short time.

The Lord's Supper

Procedures Vary

What is the proper way of serving the Lord's Supper? I do not know if there is one, and short of transporting an entire congregation to Israel, finding the site of the upper room, and inviting people to recline on mats around a table (which probably should be round, not oblong as in Leonardo da Vinci's painting), and thus to partake of Communion, no doubt versatility and flexibility constitute the best rules of thumb. Many people find solace in Communion only if it is taken at an altar rail. Others insist that it must be served to them in the pew. Some of those partaking in the pew insist on kneeling. Others think that sitting is more appropriate. Still others choose to observe Communion in conjunction with a "love feast" and therefore participate in it as they sit around tables in the social hall of the church. A growing number of people, wishing to get back to what they believe is a New Testament model, celebrate Communion at home with choice Christian friends. It probably does not matter where or how members of the church celebrate the Lord's Supper as long as the observance is done with dignity, calling forth and making plain the designed purpose, showing "the Lord's death" until He comes.

ELEMENTS

What about the elements to be used in Communion? Some denominations insist that to be absolutely correct, the beverage must be wine. Others state categorically that Jesus never would have partaken of an alcoholic beverage. I recall being in an isolated outpost in Korea some years ago. It was the Sunday to serve Communion, and we searched that little Army compound for some kind of suitable beverage. We had our choice of only two, tomato juice or pineapple juice. Believing that the use of tomato juice would have made the symbolism a little too vivid, I opted for pineapple juice, and although a substitute beverage was used, we had a Communion service that was both reverent and meaningful.

What *is* the appropriate beverage? I believe that our Lord used what was handy on the occasion. Following His example, some form of fruit juice probably is appropriate to symbolize His blood as long as it is used sincerely and reverently. Friends of mine, lacking any other beverage, celebrated communion once using coffee. Because coffee is a type of fruit, maybe that is not too farfetched after all. When considering a matter such as this, a good rule of thumb is to ask the question "What has this church been accustomed to using?" and "Are there people with really strong feelings concerning this?" If the pastor himself has strong convictions, he should find out the feelings of the church concerning the issue before he agrees to become pastor and not accept the pastorate with the idea of making abrupt changes when he gets there. If, for instance, the church is accustomed to using wine and he has strong convictions against it, perhaps he had better turn down the call rather than being embroiled in contention from the start of his ministry.

The same rule of thumb applies to the bread. Some churches insist on unleavened bread. A member prepares the bread fresh before every Communion, or the church purchases a commercially-produced wafer of some type. Despite the fact that they generally taste horrible, the wafers are easy to procure, store, and use. Other congregations do not care if the bread is leavened or not. Sometimes they purchase commercial white bread and cut it into little cubes. My own preference is to have a member of the congregation bake a loaf of wheat bread and leave it uncut. The bread is served fresh at Communion. There is a beautiful symbolism in having the pastor take the whole loaf and break it into as many pieces as are necessary to accommodate all of the serving platters, and then having each communicant in turn participate in the breaking of the bread, by tearing off for himself a small bit of the portion of the loaf in the serving platter passed down his pew. When I mentioned this system to a member of my family, she was shocked, feeling that by doing this we were exposing people to germs. I could not bear to tell her that a number of churches go one further step and have each member drink from the same chalice. That really would have upset her. However, under normal conditions, I do not believe anyone is going to become ill from breaking a small piece of bread from a common loaf. However, the comment of my relative illustrated to me once more than our ministry must be in contextualization. It is wise to know the territory before launching any crusades to change the status quo.

The Setting of the Communion Table

As far as the setting and utensils of the Communion table are concerned, I think the utensils should be shiny and the setting elegant. The church I presently pastor designates the setting up of Communion to the deacons. As a result, the Communion utensils, though clean, do not sparkle. They are placed directly on the Communion table instead of on a white tablecloth, and they are covered by paper instead of linen napkins. I could compare the arrangement to the type of table I would set at home were I to do so for guests. My wife, however, is far more genteel. When she sets the table, the result is elegance. I think that we should mirror such elegance at the Table of the Lord. Soon I hope to be able to break the news gently to my deacons that it would be a good idea if they let the ladies set up the Communion table. If the Lord is to be our honored guest, then our setting should reflect the respect with which He deserves to be served.

There may be a person in the church with sewing or embroidery skills who could prepare Communion linens as a service to the Lord. Likewise, I have known others who saw as their task the laundering and pressing of linens so that the Communion table had an attractive appearance.

The condition of the utensils is important, also. These days, most trays are made of aluminum. After a short time they become streaked and dingy, and often it does not occur to anyone that they need polishing until the person in charge of getting the Communion elements ready rushes into the building to prepare them. Often there is no time for polishing. To reiterate, utensils used for Communion should sparkle in a way that is appropriate to the honored guest. If they are beyond help with a good aluminum polish, they ought to be buffed. If even that does not help enough, they should be replaced.

HANDLING THE UTENSILS

In handling the utensils, the pastor should do so with dexterity, avoiding all clinking sounds whenever possible. A cloth on the table will help to muffle clattering sounds. If trays containing small Communion glasses are used, the pastor should learn to grip the trays with both hands. When he stacks them, he should extend his fingers slightly beyond the bottom of the tray being stacked so that his fingers will serve as a cushion between the upper tray and the one into which it is being lowered. Then he should withdraw his fingers gradually, allowing the tray on the top to settle into place gently, thus eliminating for the most part any sound. In churches where Communion is served in the pews, and the pew racks contain holders for Communion glasses, it is important that the church purchase commercially-produced rubber liners for the holders or line the holders with felt. Few things insult my aesthetic sense more than the clackety-clack of Communion glasses being placed in the pew racks once the element of the cup has been consumed.

DISPOSAL OF THE ELEMENTS

Before considering the details of the Communion service itself, I should like to comment on the matter of the disposal of the leftover elements following the service. I used to insist that all the surplus of the elements used in the Communion service be destroyed. The bread was burned and the juice was poured down the drain. In view of the hungry all over the world, I can no longer justify such action. I feel now that the bread should be trimmed and given to a family in the church. The trimmings should be put out for the birds. I believe also that the leftover juice should be consumed. However, I think that the consumption of the bread and the juice should be done discreetly and at home. It offends people to see children running around the church munching on the Communion bread. Again, if the idea of consumption is offensive to a significant number of persons in the congregation, I would opt for destroying the leftover elements.

PLACEMENT ON THE SCHEDULE

For me, the timing of a Communion service is important. For instance, I do not like to see Communion tacked on to the morning service. When that happens, there is little time for meditation on the meaning of the Lord's Supper. The observance becomes a race with the clock. If Communion is included as part of the morning worship service, the other portions of the service should be shortened drastically, especially since Communion itself is a significant form of worship. If necessary, even the sermon should be shortened, so that the Lord's Supper may be given the honor due it, and so that the worshipers will not feel hurried.

Actually, I do not care to hold the Lord's Supper in the morning at all. At times, I have said facetiously, "Who ever heard of the Lord's breakfast? A supper should be served at night." I prefer to celebrate the Lord's Supper in the evening and to make it the entire thrust of that service, seeing to it that the hymns, Scripture readings, and prayer follow a Communion theme. At present I conduct Communion in the morning one month out of three to accommodate those who are not able to attend the evening service. I much prefer the evening setting, however.

THE SERVICE ITSELF

Many creative ideas may be used as part of the Communion service. Those include public testimonies, a variety of Scripture readings, messages in music, drama, slides and film clips that dramatize our Lord's sacrifice, and soft organ music as an aid to prayer and meditation. A congregational hymn telling about the cross might be sung prior to the serving of the Lord's Supper itself, so that the worshipers may focus their attention on the theme being considered.

Just before Communion is served, it would be appropriate to read a specific passage of Scripture concerning Communion, such as the one found in 1 Corinthians 11. If the passage in 1 Corinthians is used, it will give the pastor a natural lead-in for comments about the condition of the heart of a person wishing to take Communion. Instructions should be given that Communion is the Table of the Lord. Only those who know Him as their personal Savior and Lord and whose hearts have been made right before Him ought to partake of the Communion elements. Time should be allowed for communicants to pray silently, confessing their sins to God. If the right atmosphere prevails, members of the congregation may want to move quietly to the side of those they have wronged or against whom they have harbored ill feelings and ask their forgiveness. In many churches, at this point a deacon, elder, or server is requested to ask God's blessing upon the elements being served. The bread is served first and then the cup. After the serving of the cup another prayer on behalf of the congregation is appropriate. In large churches, where the serving of each element takes a long time, often there is special music or the reading of relevant Scripture passages during the actual passing of the elements. In other churches the time is used as an opportunity for the communicants to spend an extended quiet time with the Lord.

Many churches take up an offering for the poor immediately following the Communion service. Then a hymn is sung, and the congregation is dismissed with prayer. For sentimental reasons, I like to use the hymn "Blest Be the Tie That Binds" and have the congregation sing it while holding hands.

Because Communion tends to produce an atmosphere of great warmth, not only toward the Lord but toward other Christians, I believe that it is good to have a time of fellowship and refreshment directly after the Communion service.

Because Communion is one of the more significant worship experiences of the church, it should be well-planned and carried out with excellent taste. Also, it should include some degree of variety to keep it from being routine. Here is a wonderful opportunity for the pastor to enlist those in the congregation with creative minds to help him construct Communion services that are imaginative and yet worshipful and inspiring.

Baptism

In a later chapter I will deal at some length concerning the proper utilization of warm occasions in general—those occasions that unify

and please a congregation. They create a unique and cozy atmosphere that, built upon properly, will promote and solidify a spirit of
unity among the people. In this chapter, I will deal with a specific
one of those occasions, Christian baptism.

Baptism represents victory. Its very symbology tells a story of
death to the old self and resurrection in Jesus Christ. Yet it also
represents humility. Since the earliest days of the church, baptism
has been a person's initial test of discipleship. Examined in human
terms the whole process is ludicrous. There is nothing gracious or
beautiful about a person's being immersed in water and coming up
looking half-drowned. Humanly speaking the act is degrading—and
that may have been the exact point Jesus was making when he required it.

The humility implicit in baptism is evident in the history of the
observance. The act did not originate with Jesus or even with John
the Baptist. It was an act of ceremonial cleansing required of all non-
Jews who were converting to Judaism. The unique application that
John, and our Lord, made was that Jews—who felt no prior need for
such an act—degrade themselves to the position of the despised
Gentiles and agree to endure the action themselves. Thus, from the
very beginning of the Christian era, baptism was a test of human
pride.

And so it is today. If a person is willing to go through a public act
as humiliating and degrading as baptism, maybe, just maybe, our
Lord can trust him with some of the greater tasks and responsibilities of the kingdom. As an initial test of discipleship, baptism says
to the world and to the church, "This person is for real. He is indeed
a genuine follower of the Lord Jesus Christ." It proclaims that Satan
has been defeated.

A baptism is great cause for celebration within the church. If the
baptism is of a person who grew up in the church, it is a victory for
the Christian parents and for the Sunday school teachers and others
who helped lead him to Christ and who nurtured him. If the baptismal candidate is a person who was saved because of the witness of
the church or of one of the members of the church, the occasion is
likewise a time for great rejoicing, because it proves that the outreach program of the church has been successful. Though the church
may find itself in many "no win" situations, baptism is always a "no
lose" proposition. It always is a cause for rejoicing.

Because baptism is such a warm and positive experience, I believe
that it, along with the dedication of babies, should be observed as
often as possible. The typical church, such as the one I grew up in,
would differ from that practice. Inevitably, such a church saves up its

baptismal candidates. When there are a sufficient number, an instructional course is held, which the candidates are required to attend. At the end of that course, the candidates are given certificates of completion, are baptized, and immediately are voted upon for church membership. Many church publications still list new members under two categories—"by transfer" or "by baptism." I have had a terrible time with such terminology over the years, insisting that after a person is saved, he should then be baptized immediately. Baptism is a separate and distinct act from being voted into church membership, even though many churches may require baptism as a prerequisite for church membership.

The process of saving up candidates may have its logistical advantages as far as the church is concerned. The church does not have to go to the expense and bother of cleaning out the baptismal tank, filling it, and heating it. However there are more drawbacks than advantages to insisting that a candidate for baptism wait until a number of persons can be baptized with him. Those drawbacks apply to both the candidate and the congregation. First, by requiring him to wait, the church dulls the edge of the candidate's spiritual enthusiasm.

Let me illustrate. For many years my wife and I have been caring for foster children as part of our ministry. The first of these, my son Randy, was extremely resistant to the gospel, on the surface at least, for a long period of time. What we were unaware of, however, was that he really had been listening carefully the whole time. When he finally made his peace with God and experienced a glorious conversion experience, two days later he came to me and said, "Dad, doesn't the Bible command all Christians to be baptized?" I told him that I believed baptism was a universal test of discipleship. His comeback was this: "OK, then I want to be baptized the Sunday after next when Grandma, my aunts, and cousins are in town. I want to show them what kind of a change Jesus had made in my life." I said, "Well, son, you know that it is the custom of our church to require a candidate for baptism to take a thirteen-week membership class. He is then baptized, voted upon, and becomes a member of the church." Randy's response was characteristic Randy. "Dad, I don't know about all that other garbage. I'm not ready to talk about church membership yet. I just know I want to be obedient to Jesus. Will you fix it with the deacons so that I can be baptized when Grandma comes?" I did, indeed "fix it" with the deacons, most of whom knew how very far Randy had come in his pilgrimage of faith. It seemed for a while that one old stalwart was going to hold out. However, in the end, even he capitulated, and I had the joy of baptizing my son, to the accompanying tears of joy expressed by a congregation who, once again, rejoiced because Satan had been dealt an important defeat.

Through the years, then, I have come to the conclusion that baptisms should occur as soon after salvation as a new Christian knows the reason why he should do it, and before he loses the initial glow of his newfound faith in Christ. After he is baptized, he is encouraged to enter "basic training." Upon completion of that phase—which may be accomplished by many means, only one of which is the pastor's class—he is presented to the church for membership. I have followed this pattern for a number of years. Although friends predicted that if I did not tie baptism to church membership I would experience a serious dropout rate because of newly baptized persons' neglecting to become members, I have had a better completion record than my colleagues who practice the other procedure.

May I interject a word of warning at this point. The young pastor, especially tends to want to change the world overnight. On matters such as baptism—over which the church as a whole may have strong feelings—the pastor should be advised to initiate change very gradually, and not at all until a great deal of teaching has been done on the subject, the people have been able to consider the proposed changes and discuss them extensively, and the pastor senses that a strong consensus in favor of the new procedure has formed. Even then, the pastor should not initiate such a change independently. He should do so only when his board is solidly behind him and votes decisively for him to proceed.

As is no doubt obvious, the mode of baptism I refer to is the total immersion of the believer, the person who has established a personal relationship with Jesus Christ and therefore knows Him as Lord and Savior. Because my own experience has been with baptism by immersion that is the procedure I will describe in this chapter. Every denomination of which I am aware accepts that form of baptism and permits its pastors to practice it even though it may not be the prevailing method in the denomination. Therefore, the discussion of the subject in this chapter should be helpful even to those who have never been asked to baptize a person by immersion. Perhaps sometime in the future they will be called upon to immerse, and at least they will be acquainted with the mechanics of the procedure.

LOCATION

I am convinced that baptism is performed best outdoors in a lake or stream. In such a location, baptism gives a dual testimony, one to the church and one to the world at large. I have been involved in outdoor baptismal services where curious onlookers asked such pointed questions that they were led to Christ as a result of the public testimony offered by baptism. To restrict baptism only to an outdoor setting, however, limits the number of baptisms and the frequency with which baptism may be performed. Because of the restrictions of climate alone, it is a good idea to have a baptistry in a church building. The need is emphasized by the fact that many times the church slows down to a lower key in the summer and steps up its efforts during the fall, winter and spring. As a result, the greatest number of conversions come at a time of the year when most localities are experiencing cold weather, the very time an indoor baptistry would be most desirable.

SAFETY FEATURES

When a baptistry is designed, the design should include several safety features. The stairs and bottom of the tank should be coated with an abrasive, non-skid surface. Sturdy handrails should be installed in stairways leading into and out of the baptistry. The baptistry itself should be spacious enough and so designed that there is no danger of a person's hitting his head on the sides of the baptistry or on the steps when he is baptized.

The water temperature of the baptistry should be comfortable—the person being baptized should not have to endanger his health because the water is too cold. Some sophisticated baptistry systems have a circulating heater that keeps the temperature of the water constant. Other churches use a simple immersion heater that can be plugged into 220-volt current and lowered into the baptistry several hours before the baptismal service. The church should be extremely careful in the way it uses such a device. The worker preparing the baptistry should see to it that he handles the heater only after it has been unplugged. Under no circumstances should the heater be in the baptistry during baptism. Because an immersion heater heats the top layer of water hotter than the rest, the person preparing the baptistry should stir up the water and distribute the heat before the baptistry is used.

Recently I read an article about a man who sued a church for a fall he had suffered following his baptism. Despite any doubts we might have concerning his spiritual attitude, the man was correct. The church was culpable. It seems that the dressing rooms were quite a distance from the baptistry. After baptism the candidates traveled down a long hallway in which an eager church official, concerned about the carpeting, had laid a slippery plastic runner. The man in question hit the runner, slipped, and suffered a painful fall. It is too bad when a church cares more about its carpeting than the safety of people.

DRESSING ROOMS

If at all possible, the dressing rooms should be spacious, adjacent to toilet facilities, and equipped with curtain-like partitions that can be drawn to provide privacy for those changing. Separate dressing rooms should be provided for men and for women. Because the rooms will not be used for dressing on a regular basis, it is advisable to equip them as classrooms as well, so that the space is not wasted. A non-skid indoor-outdoor carpeting on the floor will make the rooms attractive, functional, and safe.

CLOTHING

Baptistry clothing is an important consideration, especially for women. Men may wear a pair of washable slacks and a shirt. Socks will provide additional insurance against slipping. Many churches have a collection of white cotton robes to be worn by women in the baptistry. It is my earnest recommendation that if such robes are used the women be fully clothed under the robes. Light-colored slacks and a blouse under which are a full set of underclothes allow for a more discreet exit from the baptistry.

PROCEDURES

There are many kinds of elaborate baptismal gear available to the pastor. Also, some baptistries now are so designed that the pastor actually stays outside of the tank while he performs the baptism. Through the years, I have chosen to dress in the same manner as the men candidates. I have someone else begin the service with prayer and a song. During the last verse of the song, I make my way into the baptistry. Baptism is the next item on the program. Following baptism, a staff member or lay leader proceeds with the worship service and I have more than adequate time to get into dry clothing in time for my part of the worship service. Because the service begins on a high note, a warm experience, I find that the spirit of the rest of the service usually is even more positive and exciting than usual. Thus baptism sets the tone for the entire morning.

Other churches reverse the procedure. I have known of churches who believe in baptizing immediately after a person responds to the invitation. In such churches, the baptistry is always filled and heated, and baptism is the very last order of worship, sending everyone home on a high note.

As to the procedures for the actual baptism, it is my policy to meet with the candidate before baptism to ascertain that he knows the full implications of what he is doing. Prior to the baptismal service itself, I take the candidate through a dry run, letting them know exactly what I am going to do and how I am going to do it. Initially, I step into the baptistry alone, read or recite from memory a passage appropriate to baptism, and give an explanation of what baptism is and why we practice the mode that we do. Then I step back and assist the candidate into the baptistry, again for purposes of safety. The candidate is given the opportunity of confessing his faith in Christ and the reason he wants to be baptized. At this point it is important to remember that their fear of water will make some naturally timid people even more afraid. When I sense that, I address the person directly, asking him such questions as, "Do you know the Lord Jesus Christ as your personal Savior and Lord? Are you being baptized as an act of obedience to Him?" To each of the questions, he need only to respond in the affirmative. Then I baptize him, "In the name of the Father, and of the Son, and of the Holy Spirit." After helping him rise from the water, I pray for the individual, thanking God for the step of faith taken and asking Him to make the person a faithful and fruitful disciple. I assist him out of the baptistry and exit myself when the last person has been baptized.

Although my convictions confine me to practicing baptism by immersion, the Bible does not spell out the details as to exactly how baptism is to be done. If baptism is to be reminiscent of funeral practices, it is important to note that those too, differ around the world. There are places in the Orient, for instance, where people are buried upright in a sitting or kneeling position. All this is a prelude to saying that there may be other valid ways of baptizing than the one that tips the person over backwards in the water. In fact, in my study of church history, I have found good cause to conclude that early Christians were baptized forward in a kneeling position. For example, if one examines the baptistry at the cathedral at Pisa in Italy, which is purported to date back to the fourth century, it is evident that immersion indeed is possible in the main portion of the baptistry, but not if the candidate is in the backward prone position.

I prefer to baptize forward for a number of reasons. First, it requires the candidate to kneel before his Lord. Second, it allows him to have his legs in such a position that he can get up at any time. Thus baptizing forward is much safer than the backward position. Third, it allows a person to be baptized without the danger of his ingesting water. When he comes up, the water runs off naturally. If you chose to use this method take certain precautions. First, make sure that the water level is sufficiently deep to cover the entire person with water when he knees and bends over. Second, instruct the person to kneel and tip forward far enough for the water to cover him. When the moment for baptism occurs, have the candidate place his palms together. Arrange the person so that he faces to your left, grasp his wrists with your left hand and place your right arm around his back, supporting it. Assist the person as he kneels and then tips forward until the water covers him. Using your left hand, assist him in rising from the water.

When you use the backwards position, have the candidate place his palms together. Then grasp his wrist with your left hand, supporting his back with your right arm. Walk the candidate forward enough in the baptistry to assure that if there are any steps behind him, he will not hit them when he is baptized. As you tip him backwards, the candidate should bend his knees, thus assisting in the process. As he proceeds backwards, he should raise his hands to his face and clasp his nose as he goes under the water. Then assist him upward to his feet and offer him a cloth to wipe his face.

The backwards method is fairly difficult, and the pastor should practice it ahead of time if he can find a willing victim. Even after a person has become proficient in the method there are potential problems. Tall people or heavy people are extremely hard to baptize in this way. In addition, some people are so built that when they go over backwards, their feet rise immediately to the surface. When the pastor uses the backwards method he needs to be ready for any exigency.

Some evangelical groups baptize three times, one for each member of the Trinity. Forward baptism is especially helpful to such groups. Again, however, a precautionary word. Despite the pastor's own preference for a particular baptismal form, when he begins at a new church, he would be wise to see what the church has done before and how important it is to the people to continue doing things that way. A pastor should ease into the practice he prefers only after there has been a much discussion of the subject and the board advises him that the matter is no longer an item of contention.

BAPTISM BY LAYPERSONS

Recently several new considerations have arisen considering baptism. As we have returned to a sounder concept of the priesthood of all believers, the question has been raised by lay persons, "If I'm really a priest, why can't I baptize members of my household?" Why not indeed? There do not seem to be scriptural injunctions against it. In churches I have served, not only have laymen baptized members of their households, but also deacons and other lay persons have had the pleasure and honor of baptizing people they consider their spiritual sons and daughters.

BAPTISM OF THE HANDICAPPED

Questions inevitably arise about the baptism of handicapped people. A procedure increasingly followed for persons who cannot walk is for them to be lowered into the baptistery in their wheelchairs. Then they are lifted out of the chairs by several people assisting the pastor, or the water level is set high enough to allow the pastor to perform the baptism by leaning the person forward in his wheelchair. Even old age in itself is not an excuse for not being baptized. I have known people in their eighties and nineties who have followed the Lord in this manner and have found baptism to be a wonderful, spiritual experience.

THE SIGNIFICANCE OF THE ORDINANCES

In this chapter, I have explored the administration of what many evangelicals have come to call the *ordinances.* Other churches may call these observances *sacraments* and in so doing indicate that observing them constitutes a means of grace for the believer. Some groups insist, for instance, that the elements of Communion become the actual body and blood of our Lord. Others would say that He is, instead, mystically present in the elements. In their sharp reaction to such groups, many evangelicals have gone overboard the other way, treating the ordinances in a manner so casual as to be nearly profane. Whether or not our Lord is or is not present in the elements, He certainly can be present in a special way to the believer as he partakes of Communion. Even though most evangelicals do not consider baptism necessary for salvation, the New Testament gives sufficient evidence that it is a test of discipleship, so much so that in many New Testament passages, salvation and baptism are mentioned in the same breath.

Neither Jesus, nor His disciples, nor the early church took the ordinances lightly. They are important parts of Christian worship and should be conducted with the greatest possible reverence and dignity. Properly used they can be a tremendous aid to the believer's everyday life and to his pattern of growth in Christ. Moreover, by the message they convey, they may be the means of dramatically portraying the gospel story to those who have not yet become Christians.

Questions for Discussion

1. What is the proper way to serve the Lord's Supper? What essential routines must be a part of the observance? Is it possible to have flexibility and versatility and still "show the Lord's death" until He comes?

2. What constraints do you think are necessary in regard to the type of beverage and the type of bread used for Communion?

3. What significance do the elements have in the Communion event?

4. What can the pastor and deacons or elders do to see to it that the weekly or monthly repetition of the Communion service does not become merely an empty tradition?

5. What is the proper order of events in a Communion service?

6. What is the significance of baptism in the ministry of the church? What does baptism represent for the church? What does it symbolize for the believer? What does it say to the world at large?

7. Is there any importance in a candidate's being baptized relatively soon after his conversion?

8. What is the relationship between baptism and church membership?

9. What responsibility does the church have to ensure the safety of the candidate during baptism.

10. What procedures would you institute or follow in order to make sure that baptism is a meaningful event?

11. Is it permissible for lay people to baptize? What is the basis of your opinion?

12. What value do you give to the ordinances of the Lord's Supper and baptism? How may we conduct these ordinances so as to maintain the highest possible reverence and dignity?

Helpful Resources

Beasley-Murray, G. R. *Baptism in the New Testament.* Grand Rapids: Eerdmans, 1973.

Greet, Brian A. *Broken Bread in a Broken World.* Valley Forge, Pa.: Judson, 1972.

Johnson, Gordon G. *My Church.* Arlington Heights, Ill.: Harvest Publications, 1982.

Leitch, Addison H. *This Cup: Communion Meditations.* Grand Rapids: Baker, 1982.

Lumpkin, William L. *Meditations on Christian Baptism.* Nashville: Broadman, 1978.

McEachern, Alton H. *Here at Thy Table Lord.* Nashville: Broadman, 1976.

Marty, Martin E. *Baptism.* Philadelphia: Fortress, 1977.

Morris, Henry M. III. *Baptism: How Important Is It?* Denver: Accent, 1978.

Rayburn, Robert G. *What About Baptism?* Grand Rapids: Baker, 1979.

Wallis, Charles L., ed. *Complete Sourcebook for the Lord's Supper.* Sourcebooks for Ministers. Grand Rapids: Baker, 1978.

18

Evangelism

Elsewhere in this book we have alluded to the fact that the single, overall purpose of the church is to glorify God and that one of the primary ways of glorifying God, according to the Bible, is through evangelism. It is a sad commentary on the church, therefore, that in many cases there is so much emphasis on edification the emphasis on evangelism is minimal.

Evangelism is synonymous with mission, the overriding term that encompasses local evangelism, regional evangelism, and worldwide evangelism. As I define it, evangelism is the proclamation of the gospel message in such a way that people commit their lives to Jesus Christ as Lord and Savior and become responsible members of a local church. In New Testament times, it was inconceivable for a person to become "saved, period." In the same breath it describes a person's salvation, the New Testament tells also that as the result of his salvation the new convert was expected to declare his faith by being baptized. Likewise, there seems to be no question that he was expected to identify immediately in a responsible way with a local church. Moreover, the New Testament seems to assume that once a person had become a Christian, it was a natural thing for him to speak of his faith to others.

Rationalizations for Not Evangelizing Locally

WORLD MISSIONS SHOULD COME FIRST

In our day many excuses and rationalizations are given for churches who do not have comprehensive plans of evangelism. One of those, unfortunately, is couched in world mission terms. It sounds something like this: "People in North America have had such a great opportunity to hear the gospel, whereas men and women in other lands have had no chance at all. We must stop spending our efforts and money on people in North America and make world missions our major emphasis." I agree wholeheartedly that the local church must have a vision for world mission, but its commitment to the foreign scene must be balanced by a commitment to carry on the mission God has given it to win those in its own community.

Indeed, the ability of a church to increase its support to world mission often will be in direct proportion to the size of its congregation. I remember my father's sharing with me how, during the days of the Great Depression, the denomination with which he was affiliated insisted that its churches contribute 50 percent of their budgets to world mission. At the same time the churches were priding themselves in such action, their buildings were a disgrace and many of their pastors and families were nearly starving. The churches themselves became a deterrent to the spread of the gospel in their own communities. Moreover, 50 percent of a budget of $1,000 does not amount to very much. Had the churches been allowed to establish firm bases in their local communities, even though the percentage they gave to missions might have decreased, the overall amount of their support for world missions probably would have increased dramatically.

It is a common saying among church growth experts that the proof of a church's determination to grow is the amount of money it allocates in its budget to local evangelism. I am afraid that many evangelical churches fall far short of what they should be doing in this area.

THE PASTOR-TEACHER IS NOT EQUIPPED

A rationalization given by some local churches that do not engage in evangelism comes from the pastor's study. Its lyrics are as follows: "Don't expect me to be involved in evangelism. I am the pastor-teacher and am responsible only for edifying the saints." Timothy must have been caught up in the syndrome, for though church leaders all around him were evangelizing on a regular basis, it was necessary for Paul to tell Timothy, "Do the work of an evangelist" (2 Tim. 4:5). It is interesting to note that there was not even a bit of discussion as to whether or not Timothy was equipped for the task, or whether evangelizing was designated to him under the division of labor spelled out in Ephesians 4:11. In his pastoral position, he merely was expected to do it. Why? Because the pastor is the most visible role model a congregation has. If he expects other people to do as he says, he must build an atmosphere of credibility by agreeing to do personally what he tells others people they should do.

THE SHEEP, NOT THE SHEPHERD, GIVE BIRTH

Another version of the same rationalization is this: "I am the shepherd, and, after all, who is expected to give birth to the baby lambs, the shepherd or his sheep?" In so identifying himself, the pastor forgets that he occupies a dual role. Though he is indeed an undershepherd, subject to authority of the Great Shepherd, he is still, himself, a sheep. Even though he may have unique qualifications and a specialized job description, that does not absolve him from the responsibilities placed upon all sheep, and evangelism is one of these.

THE PASTOR WILL DO THE JOB

Some rationalizations take an entirely different course, placing most of the evangelistic responsibility on the pastor. The church member reasons thus: "It is the pastor's job to see that people are saved. After all, isn't that what we are paying him for?" Such people often believe that their evangelistic responsibilities have been satisfied if they give regularly to the church, maybe even tithe a little. Occasionally they may go so far as to invite a neighbor to a special church event. They are upset when the pastor preaches other than an evangelistic message, claiming that when he does so he is not "preaching the gospel." They insist also that an altar call be given every Sunday. "After all," they say, "what if someone came who was unsaved and didn't have a chance to get saved?" Yet ironically, though they insist that evangelism is the pastor's business, they do not actually want him to spend much time approaching non-Christians. Instead, they expect him to carry on a careful schedule, visiting each of the saints on a regular basis, so that he may wipe away all emotional sniffles and soothe any feathers that have been ruffled over matters of little consequence.

I am convinced that the persons God calls to pastor such "evangelistic churches." are special individuals with superhuman patience. To survive and conquer indifference to evangelism, a pastor must compromise, not theologically but methodologically. Of course, he can stand on his rights, insist on his own way, and experience a short and rocky tenure at the church. Or he can begin his pastorate by including an evangelistic thrust as a portion of every message, but making sure to feed his sheep more and more with the meat of the Word. Initially he may find it necessary to give an evangelistic invitation every Sunday, but as his people grow in the Lord and engage in personal evangelism themselves, one day his leaders will come to him and say, "Pastor, why do you have to give an invitation every Sunday?" He may reply, "Do you really think that is too often? Maybe I should only do it when I preach an evangelistic message. What do you guys think?" When he decreases the number of invitations and complaints arise, he may then respond, "The deacons would like me to try it this way for a while." Inevitably, a few die-hards from the old camp will continue to express their dissatisfaction. The patient pastor who digs in for a sustained ministry at that church probably never will be able to change the minds of those people. All he can do is to love them extravagantly and trust God to deal with them adequately.

No One in the Church Has the Gift of Evangelism

While we are exploring the list of excuses given by churches for a lack of evangelistic outreach, why don't we look at this one: "Our church doesn't engage in evangelism because no one has the gift of evangelism." That is a most interesting observation, especially since nowhere in the entire Bible is such a gift listed. Furthermore, the New Testament contains only three direct references to people called by the title *evangelist*. In Acts 21:8, Philip is called an evangelist; Paul says in Ephesians 4:11 that God has given evangelists to the church; and in 2 Timothy 4:5, the passage we have addressed already, Timothy was told to do the work of an evangelist.

After studying Ephesians 4:11 as carefully as I can, I have become convinced that the gifts spoken about there are function gifts, positions given to the church as a division of labor, and that God calls certain people at specific times to occupy those positions and carry out the function of equipping the saints in a particular area of service. Thus, there is room for latitude within the kingdom of God. A person does not necessarily have to perform the same function for life. He may be a teacher for a while or even spend part of his life serving as an evangelist.

Although I do not believe that evangelism is a gift granted to the evangelist personally by God, the Lord does equip a person with gifts compatible with his office. The noted platform evangelists, for instance, undoubtedly have the gift of exhortation. Personal workers such as Dawson Trotman and Bill Bright no doubt were given the gift of persuasion. The point I am making is simply this: a local church cannot base a lack of a program of evangelism on the fact that no one in that church has the gift of evangelism—especially when one cannot prove from Scripture that there is such a gift.

The Elect Are Chosen Already

Probably an excuse given on theological grounds has proved more damaging than many of the rest put together. That excuse is this one: "Because God has already elected those who are to be Christians, no matter what we do or don't do, it will have no effect on whether or not people come to Christ. If they are part of the elect, nothing can keep them from being saved. If they are not part of the elect, there's no chance for them anyway." If first-century Christians, however, held to the view of election quoted above, they certainly did not act like it. Quite the contrary, they demonstrated a great sense of urgency, exerting all the strength they had to win everyone they could to faith in Jesus Christ. Therefore, whatever election means in all of its complexity, there is no New Testament evidence to suggest that it absolves the believer of the responsibility of communicating the gospel message with the lost.

Everyone Has Been Elected

Equally absurd and without scriptural basis is the claim that everyone has been elected because of the death of Jesus Christ. Those who hold such a view do away with the possibility of human choice's entering into consideration. According to them, we are saved whether or not we choose to be. They see no need for structured programs of evangelism, because they see evangelism as merely the process of announcing the good news that man already is saved so that mankind can rejoice in the news and alter his life-style accordingly. But because everyone, by their definition, is saved already, there is no urgency to spread the gospel.

Living Godly Lives Is Enough

Finally, some churches use this excuse in ignoring evangelism: "If we merely live godly lives before our neighbors and the light of Jesus shines through us, then the testimony of our lives alone will be enough to bring our neighbors to Christ." There are two problems with that excuse. First, it is extremely difficult to live one's life before one's neighbor with such consistency that the neighbors will never discover a flaw in our lives. Second, even if we were able to live such a life, the neighbor could spend years observing that life, constantly noting that our example was admirable, and could still die without Christ. A fact that the Christian often forgets is that if a friend or neighbor is going to become a Christian, someone is going to have to show him how.

A Program for Evangelism

Having discredited the most common excuses for not evangelizing, I would like to explore a feasible program for the local church, noting at the same time that because no two local churches are entirely alike, the implementation of the program will vary, depending on the personality of the church being considered. My first piece of advice is this: Do not put all of your eggs in one basket. Just as there are varieties of churches and varieties of people, effective evangelism requires a variety of methods. Although some churches use only one method, to the detriment of their program of evangelism other churches use so many methods they find it impossible to do anything well. There needs to be a happy balance between the two extremes, and that balance will vary according to the size of the church, the assets available to it, and the different types of unsaved people God sends its way.

When a pastor begins his ministry in a church, he may find a successful program of evangelism already in progress. It is wise for him to support, enhance, and encourage those working in that program. He should urge them to continue their work, and he should do what he can to help them make the program even stronger. After a year or so, he should take inventory of how many additional workers he can count on to join him in still another method of evangelism. Then he should identify a group of unsaved people in his community whom he feels his people can reach. He should search out a strategy suitable for winning that group of people. Then he should become equipped himself in the appropriate technique so that he may equip his people, or send someone in his congregation to be trained, or bring in an outside equipper to provide the training he and his people need to do the job.

After he and his people are proficient in the new method and are using it successfully in winning people to Christ, the pastor may want to turn over the supervision of the program to someone else, while, once again, he looks around for willing workers, identifies a group of people to be won, searches out a proper strategy to reach the group, and receives the training necessary if he and his people are going to practice the new strategy successfully. As time goes on, he can begin still another program, and another, and so on, until he reaches the limit of the assets of his congregation. In addition, periodically he may decide to bring in a proclamation evangelist for an evangelistic crusade. Always the pastor should try to steer a middle course between two few and too many evangelistic efforts.

Getting a Church Excited About Evangelism

VISITATION EVANGELISM

Up until this point we have been quite idealistic. Now let us get practical. A young pastor fresh out of seminary and enthusiastic about making known the gospel goes to a church where for years there has been little emphasis on evangelism. Where does he start? First, he must remind himself that if he is going to maintain a peaceful pastorate he must deal wisely with those of the saints who demand coddling. If he is able to find out who they are and can give them a fair amount of attention, he probably will be able to keep them satisfied while he puts his evangelistic strategy into operation. While being sure to give the proper attention to all the saints, he should select a few key individuals to disciple intensively. One or more of those persons will accompany him as he begins his program of visitation evangelism.

In that program he should call on persons who attend services regularly but are not actually members and present them the message of the gospel. Besides regular attenders, his list should include "fringe" people—unsaved spouses, relatives, friends and neighbors of church members, or people whose children attend church activities. During such visits, it may become apparent that the disciple has far greater powers of persuasion than the pastor. Gradually, the supervision of the program will pass from the pastor to that disciple. The new leader of the program will disciple still others as they help him carry out the ministry of visitation evangelism.

FRIENDSHIP EVANGELISM

At the time he begins a program of visitation evangelism, the pastor may want to begin his own personal program of friendship evangelism. Establishing a model for the rest of the congregation to follow, the pastor and his wife should identify two or three non-church families in their neighborhood and attempt to establish a close relationship with them. Throughout their contacts with those neighbors, the pastor and his wife should keep two goals in mind. First they should remind themselves that friendship in itself is a proper Christian motive. They should try to establish meaningful friendships, regardless of whether or not the people they are dealing with ever become Christians. Second, they should keep in mind that they really do want to win their neighbors to Christ. They should not be hesitant to explore all avenues of reaching those God sends their way. If they explore such relationships carefully and sensitively, eventually they may discover an opening for an evangelistic home Bible study or for some other meaningful spiritual encounter with the new friends. Some of their new friends may receive Christ and become vital members of the church.

In any evangelistic effort, probably it is valid to assume that the number of actual conversions realized will be in direct proportion to the number of evangelistic contacts made. And often the deciding factor as to how many evangelistic presentations are successful is the quality of the relationship the church member has established ahead of time with the people to whom he presents the gospel. A person is more apt to respond favorably to an invitation to become a Christian if the one extending that invitation has earned the right to be heard and has proved himself a trustworthy and credible friend.

Friendship evangelism can be a long and tedious process. However, those who engage in it on a regular basis indicate that periodically there are major breakthroughs. When one member of a family comes to know Christ, many of his extended family and friends may join him. If the pastor can win even one family to Christ and then can disciple that family to the point where they are ready to win and disciple another family, a multiplication process will have begun that can have far-reaching repercussions in the community. As each new family is added to the church the vitality they bring will begin to wake up a sleeping, lethargic church, producing life once more. If other church families catch the pastor's excitement and follow his example, the results can be overwhelming. The lesson to be learned here, then, is that a program of evangelism does not have to start with a great deal of fanfare and superhuman effort. It may be very small at the start and mushroom into something tremendously effective.

When a pastor decides to add a new program of evangelism it is wise for him first to determine either that the old ones are well established and successful or that they were unsuccessful and consequently discontinued. There are many programs a church can engage in, depending on the type of people it feels are ripe to be won. The strategy used should be the method most likely to win a particular group of people. Visitation evangelism may be successful for one group; friendship evangelism for another; and still other methods may work for other groups of people.

EVANGELISTIC CRUSADE

One method rarely discussed these days is the evangelistic crusade. Though it lost favor for a while, today it is experiencing a comeback. Yet these days it is often dressed in more modern and varied fashions than its traditional predecessor. In most places life moves too fast to engage an evangelist for a prolonged series of every-night meetings in a local church. Instead, many evangelists offer a variety of special events from which a church may choose. Those events include concerts, banquets, children's meetings, and youth meetings. The evangelist is brought on the scene for a week at the most, and he aids the church in holding a variety of programs likely to attract unchurched people. Besides providing an avenue for the non-Christian to come to Christ, crusades give the believer a period of time to focus his attention on evangelism and an opportunity to take the small, initial step of working up enough courage to invite an unsaved neighbor to an evangelistic event. An evangelist friend of mine likens the entire spectrum of evangelism to the edge of a sword. Evangelism occurs all along the cutting edge, but crusade evangelism is the thrust point that gets the cutting action going.

Strengthening Evangelism Through the Leadership Structure

ASSOCIATE PASTOR: PERSONAL EVANGELISM

So far, I have been describing one-pastor or one-elder operations. That, I believe, is realistic since it is the type of situation to which a majority of pastors will find themselves called. Even if he is called to a church that features a so-called multiple eldership, in many cases he will find those elders not properly trained or qualified for the job and functioning essentially as deacons. When a church grows large enough to add the third staff person (after the pastor and the church secretary) I believe it is wise that he occupy the office of evangelist. In most cases, his will not be a ministry of public proclamation from the pulpit. Instead, the church should select a person with persuasive powers who is well-grounded in the Word and has well-developed skills in evangelism. Also, he should know how to disciple others so that he can equip them to do the work of evangelism.

SENIOR PASTOR: PLATFORM EVANGELIST
ASSOCIATE PASTOR: SPECIALIST IN EDIFICATION

Still another model needs to be considered. There are churches that have enjoyed a constant, sound teaching ministry for many years and where the people are mature in the Lord—but they have received little encouragement to evangelize. As a result, there has not been much evangelistic effort going on. A church such as this may want to call to its senior pastorate a person with great evangelistic zeal and skill. Because the ministry of the church has been weighted toward edification for such a long time, his may be exactly the ministry needed to bring the church back into balance.

If the person whose primary emphasis is evangelism continues in the church for an extended period of time, the church should then call an associate pastor who understands and is sympathetic with the thrust of the senior pastor but whose ministry is primarily edificational. His teaching ministry might occupy the core of the Sunday evening service. As a result, those who are converted to Christ through the evangelistic efforts of the senior pastor and the people he is able to equip for the work of evangelism, will not be left as babes but will be given the meat of the Word, so that they can grow to maturity.

The Pastor Is the Leader in Evangelism

This chapter has given only a thumbnail sketch of the points of involvement a pastor can use in the ministry of local evangelism. Though the work of the pastorate is primarily edificational, and though the pastor may believe that he is not called to the office of evangelist, in most cases he will be called upon to do the work of an evangelist as a model for his people and as a means of equipping others for the task. Above all, the pastor is called upon to provide the type of leadership that makes certain that the ministry of the local church does not swing from the extremes of being only evangelistic or only edificational. Instead, the church's ministry must maintain a happy balance where evangelism and edification are in close harmony, to the end that God may be glorified.

Questions for Discussion

1. Define evangelism. How much emphasis should evangelism receive in the overall program of the local church?

2. List some of the reasons frequently given for not having a comprehensive program of evangelism. How would you refute those rationalizations?

3. What strategies would you use to organize a program of evangelism in your church? Do you agree with the author that it is more effective to have a variety of programs than to have a single program? Why or why not?

4. You are just beginning your ministry at a new church. There has been little emphasis on evangelism. How should you proceed?

5. What is friendship evangelism? How would you utilize that approach to evangelism within the context of the overall program of a local church?

6. What is meant by the statement "The number of actual conversions realized will be in direct proportion to the number of evangelistic contacts made"?

7. What are the pros and cons of evangelistic crusades? Do you think that mass evangelism has a place in today's church? If so, how would you make mass evangelism a part of your overall approach to outreach?

8. If you were to add a third staff member (after the pastor and the church secretary), would that person occupy the office of evangelism? Why or why not?

Helpful Resources

Aldrich, Joseph C. *Lifestyle Evangelism: Crossing Traditional Boundaries to Reach the Unbelieving World.* Portland, Oreg.: Multnomah, 1981.

Coleman, Robert E. *The Master Plan of Evangelism.* Old Tappan, N.J.: Revell, 1964.

Gerber, Virgil. *God's Way to Keep a Church Going and Growing.* Glendale, Calif.: Gospel Light, Regal, 1973.

Kennedy, D. James. *Evangelism Explosion.* Wheaton, Ill.: Tyndale, 1970.

Lewis, Larry L. *Organize to Evangelize.* Wheaton, Ill.: Victor, 1980.

Little, Paul E. *How to Give Away Your Faith.* Downers Grove, Ill.: InterVarsity, 1966.

Metzger, Will. *Tell the Truth.* Downers Grove, Ill.: InterVarsity, 1981.

Packer, J. I. *Evangelism and the Sovereignty of God.* Downers Grove, Ill.: InterVarsity, 1961.

Peters, George W. *Saturation Evangelism.* Grand Rapids: Zondervan, 1970.

19

Weddings

John the beloved apostle closed his gospel with the words "And there are also many other things which Jesus did, which if they were written in detail, I suppose that even the world itself would not contain the books which were written" (John 21:25). Because the activities of our Lord on this earth were so many and varied, it is likely that only the most important ones were recorded in the pages of Scripture. How significant then, that the apostle John dedicated such a large portion of third chapter of his gospel to a description of the visit of our Lord to the marriage feast at Cana of Galilee. Moreover, the wedding must have been an important event to our Lord, as well, for He chose it as the occasion for performing his first public miracle.

The High Estate of Marriage

The Bible sets high moral standards for God's children and describes the institution of marriage as honorable and blessed. Hebrews 13:4 is one of the many such verses. It asserts: "Let marriage to be held in honor among all, and let the marriage bed be undefiled; for fornicators and adulterers God will judge." In the epistle to the Ephesians, the fifth chapter, the apostle Paul elevates marriage to its zenith, describing the marriage union as the highest type of human relationship, akin to the relationship Christ enjoys with His church. If that statement were not enough to elevate marriage to a most significant position, Revelation 19 puts the capstone on all biblical portions regarding marriage when it compares Christ's final union with His church as a marriage feast.

In light of the high esteem in which God holds marriage, should the church and its pastor view it any lower? In the past few decades, disastrous things have happened to the philosophy of the permanency and sanctity of marriage, a philosophy that our culture used to affirm, even if many did not put it into practice. All kinds of justifications and rationalities have arisen, even from the lips of clergymen, to foster the attitude that remaining married is only an option, even for the Christian. Thus, some couples taking wedding vows today promise only to "love, honor, and cherish as long as our love shall last."

If it has not been stated loudly or clearly enough in other books, let it be stated here emphatically: *Divorce is not a Christian word.* God's design for His children is not that they should bail out when the going gets rough, but that they should choose carefully ahead of time, should select a mate who fits God's standards for them, and should live with that mate until God calls one of them to be with Him.

Now, of course, there are exigencies born out of severe circumstances. Sin can take its toll in the life of a marriage partner to the extent that his or her actions make it impossible for the two to live together. Sometimes, for the sake of the very life of a partner and the lives of the children, a partner will need to separate herself or himself from a spouse. Sometimes the moral values of one of the marriage partners can become so perverted that it is necessary for the other partner to remove him or her from day-to-day contact with the children because of the negative example that person sets. Even in the latter instance, however, we have the biblical example of the prophet Hosea searching out every pit and brothel in town trying to find his beloved Gomer. Yet, divorce is not a Christian word. Every other possible alternative needs to be explored before considering this desperate and unchristian solution. The Bible seems to indicate only two situations in which divorce is even to be tolerated. Matthew 5 seems to permit it in a relationship where one of the partners is adulterous. First Corinthians 7 seems to leave divorce as the final undesirable option to a Christian mate whose non-Christian partner has deserted.

Laying a Solid Foundation

MODELS IN THE CHURCH

In the church of Jesus Christ, preparations for marriage should begin early in its teaching program. Implicit in that program of training is the appropriate choice of teachers, so that the children may have suitable models to observe. Even though it may sound extremely retrogressive on my part, I do not believe that a person with marital or moral skeletons in his closet is a fit choice to model the Christian life for others, unless there is long-term evidence that God has helped him to lick the problem completely. Therefore, those teaching others should be chosen with care.

The pastor, as well, should put and keep his own moral house in order and should work constantly to make and keep his own marriage relationship a suitable model for others.

EXPLICIT INSTRUCTION

As young people near the marrying age, clear, concise instructions should be given as to the sanctity of Christian marriage and the Christian responsibilities inherent in choosing and uniting with a life partner. From the pulpit, in youth meetings, and through counseling sessions with young people who are dating, the pastor and the youth sponsors should point out that God has certain standards and moral expectations for Christians. In imposing them, God does not do so as a killjoy but as a loving heavenly Father who wants his children to experience the best life has to offer. Because He made us, He of all people knows what actions ultimately will make us happy and which ones will overwhelm us with problems. When we do things the way we were designed to do them—that is, do them according to God's guidelines—then we have the greatest chance of experiencing happiness. When we ignore or refuse to follow God's guidelines, the ultimate result always is tragedy. Thus, just as a loving earthly father warns his children concerning impending physical danger, God the heavenly Father advises His children in areas of impending spiritual danger. He does that through His Word and through the counsel of godly older friends who care enough to share such truths with teens.

LONG-TERM EDUCATION

Ideally, marriage counseling is not something that takes place in a few sessions before the wedding. It is a long-term process of Christian education that does not terminate when the couple gets married. Instead, it continues in adult classes and through clear, biblical teaching from the pulpit. That teaching reaches its ultimate fruition as the union of two Christians is blessed with children and the couple themselves become teachers and models of the seriousness, the sacredness, and the permanence of marriage.

If the process is carried on faithfully and consistently, Christian young people will in great part select Christian partners and behave in a scriptural manner; they will need little formal marital counseling by the pastor. The problem is that the process is seldom carried on in the manner God intended. Inconsistencies often arise, models become faulty, teaching is poor, choices of partners are less than optimal, and the couple standing before the pastor are often not what the Bible and the church would declare an ideal match.

MARRIAGE COUNSELING IN ORDINARY SITUATIONS

How many counseling sessions should a pastor conduct with a couple before marrying them? The answer to that, of course, depends on the couple. In cases where both young people are members of the church, are well known to the pastor, have received the proper training in the church and at home, and have observed couples whose marriages model the biblical pattern, the pastor will probably schedule only two sessions. One of those will be devoted to the details of the wedding. The other most likely will be a quiet informal session in the pastor's home, well after the "PK's" have gone to bed.

Sitting in the living room or around a table in the dining room or kitchen, the pastor and his wife will share with the engaged couple, as intimate friends, what marriage has meant to them, how they have got over some of the rough spots, and how they have been able to draw closer to one another. Rather than being a typical, pedantic instruction session, the occasion should be one where warm friendship grows still more solid and where the bridal couple feel free to ask questions of an intimate nature. As the questions arise, both the Scriptures and the experiences of the pastoral couple are valid sources of reference. The problem I have seen with many pastors is that they lock themselves into a pattern of premarital instruction, even if a large portion of the curriculum is unneeded by or inappropriate for a particular couple. As a result, couples who do not need the "full shot" find much of the material superfluous and a waste of time—and as a result they lose patience with the pastor. In other cases, the "full shot" may not be nearly enough. A couple with severe problems may require more guidance than the pastor has available in his curriculum, and though the pastor thinks he has done a good job, the couple moves into marriage with many vital issues unsettled.

What is the happy solution? Probably it is to find out how much instruction the couple needs and attempt to give them that much. In counseling couples with whom he is not fully acquainted, the pastor may decide to use some of the personality indexes and marriage

inventories that are now available. Many of them may be administered by the pastor after he has had a day or two of training concerning their use. By using the indexes and inventories and by meeting
personally with the couple, the pastor can determine whether or not
the kind of counseling and instruction needed is within his capabilities. A number of excellent guides to premarital counseling are available as well. Many of the finest of those have come from the pen of
my good friend, H. Norman Wright. Some of Dr. Wright's guides are
accompanied by sets of helpful audiovisual presentations.

In some cities, groups of evangelicals band together to conduct
centralized premarital classes. As young people express their marriage intentions, they are channeled into those well-prepared and
skillfully-taught classes. The pastor deals with the couple personally
only in the last session or two before the wedding itself. In many
places, Christian counseling clinics provide such services to local
churches.

MARRIAGE COUNSELING IN MORE DIFFICULT SITUATIONS

There may be instances where the pastor knows from the beginning that he is "over his head" because of the number and complexity
of the problems expressed by the couple. In such cases, he would be
wise to refer the couple to a trained counselor at the very outset. If
they refuse to attend and the pastor believes that the proposed marriage is clearly a mistake, as graciously as he can, he should refuse to
marry them. Regardless of who the couple is, the pastor ought to tell
them at the outset of the counseling sessions that although he cares
for them, he will make no commitment to marry them unless he
feels that action is right for both of them. In some cases it may take
several sessions before he finds out whether in good conscience he
can marry them.

Reasons for Refusing to Marry a Couple

Who can the pastor refuse to marry? He is justified in refusing to
marry any couple that insists he marry them on the spur of the
moment without prior counseling sessions. Sometimes the pastor is
so afraid of offending anyone or of turning someone away from the
church, that he will honor the demand of the rude and the importu-
nate. If such people had any genuine regard for the church or the
pastor to begin with, they would never have approached him in that
manner. The truth is, often such people want to find a gullible pastor
they can bully into performing a marriage on demand. A pastor who

stands firmly but kindly on his convictions probably will not alienate such people from the church, and he may even gain their respect if he explains the reason for his refusal.

In addition, the pastor should refuse to marry any couple when doing so would violate his own theological convictions. Especially is this pertinent when one of the partners is a Christian and the other one is not. In biblical terms there is absolutely no justification for such a union, and the pastor should not be a part of it under any circumstances. He should, however, meet with the couple, explain to the non-Christian why he, as a pastor, cannot perform the ceremony, explain the gospel to him or her, and attempt to lead that person to Christ. However, he must be careful to see to it that the unsaved person is not merely "going through the motions" in order to get the pastor to perform the ceremony. In such cases it may be advisable to delay the ceremony long enough to determine whether or not the fruit of the Spirit really is a product of that person's life.

The pastor may refuse to marry a couple where one of the partners has gone through a messy divorce and the circumstances are not all clear. If there is a large element of doubt, a negative response is the safer of the two.

Finally, a pastor may refuse to marry a couple if he believes that their motives for marriage are wrong or that they are incompatible in personality.

In all cases of refusal, the wise pastor takes time to affirm the value of the persons he is dealing with, and he expresses his personal concern for them. In some instances where deep friendships are involved, he may even elect to attend the wedding and reception to indicate his friendship for the couple even though he, in good conscience, cannot perform the actual ceremony.

Planning for a Wedding Ceremony

THE CHARACTER OF THE CEREMONY

In recent years, wedding ceremonies have taken on almost every conceivable form. Ceremonies have ranged from weddings performed while the participants were floating to earth in a parachute to underwater weddings in which the participants wore snorkels. The prevailing philosophy seems to be that the wedding day is the bride's day, and therefore she should have anything she wants. The problem is that many practices are not a fitting part of a Christian worship service though they would be appropriate in a number of other settings. If the officiant is a minister of the gospel, he should engage in only a Christian worship service if he agrees to officiate at a wedding. More bizarre wedding services should be conducted before a judge or a justice of the peace.

When he meets with a couple to discuss wedding plans, it is helpful for the pastor to make his convictions plain from the start. The fact that he is being called upon to perform the ceremony implies that the couple is invoking the blessing of Almighty God on their marriage. Even though the ceremony itself may be planned and performed creatively, it should be characterized by great dignity.

A Christian wedding, especially one held in a church building, is a worship service rather than a mere ceremony. Because an integral part of worship is music, the music for a wedding should be selected with care. Anything that would be considered appropriate for a regular worship service probably is a fitting choice for a wedding. Conversely, many secular, contemporary songs about human love are not appropriate for a worship service and should be relegated to the more informal setting of the reception, if the couple insists that they be used. Vocalists should be instructed to conduct themselves as they would in a worship service. The wedding is not a performance. Their choice of songs, dress, and style of singing, and their decorum, should reflect the worship setting.

The wedding ceremony itself may be simple or elaborate. Probably the only really essential elements are the reading of Scripture, a brief sermon, the repeating of the vows, the giving and receiving of rings, a prayer or two, and the pronouncement of the couple as husband and wife. Other elements that may be added are vocal numbers, congregational singing, the lighting of a unity candle, the processional, the benediction, and the recessional. The length of the ceremony has nothing to do with the degree of commitment of the couple or with the validity of their marriage.

As Christian young people observe the weddings of others, many times they see meaningful, creative features they want to incorporate into their own weddings. If the feature is appropriate to a worship service it is fitting for a wedding, although I do not recall a wedding in which an offering plate was passed.

Many helpful books concerning wedding ceremonies and other church events are published by a variety of denominations and independent publishers. I have referred to those in the chapter on the pastor's tools. It is good for the pastor to have several handbooks in his library so that when he is called upon to perform a wedding, he can add variety to the service.

THE WEDDING COORDINATOR

Early in a pastor's ministry, he will discover that he is bogged down enough in details not to want to get involved in the intricacies of wedding planning. That is best left to others. A helper that will prove invaluable to him is a person those in many Jewish communities would call a *Yenta*. Loosely translated the term means "busybody." The traditional Yenta served as a matchmaker between the two young people and their families, and she arranged the details of the wedding, coordinating its various details.

In modern times, a Yenta, or wedding coordinator, is just as important to the ministry of the church. The person who performs the service should be adept at planning weddings of all sizes and complexities. She should know the best place to buy a wedding gown and where to rent male formal wear for the most reasonable price. Often she can save the bride's family a great deal of money by guiding them to wedding cake bakers, flower arrangers, caterers and photographers—all of whom she knows are competent but reasonable in price. Usually, she should have a corps of women at her disposal who are accustomed to planning, setting up, and serving receptions, utilizing the church's social facilities and equipment. She should be sufficiently versed in weddings to be able to anticipate what is needed, down to the quantity of nuts and mints at the reception. She should be able to work out the details so smoothly that the wedding party and parents can relax completely.

It is she who recruits staff for the guest book and gift table, according to the wishes of the family. It is she who signals the organist that the time has come to start the processional, who makes sure the ushers seat the mothers properly, and who starts each of the female attendants and the bride on their journey down the aisle at the precise moment agreed upon beforehand. During the ceremony, she makes sure that the photographer does not create a disturbance in his zeal to snap pictures. She positions members of the wedding party in the proper order in the reception line, and generally she sees to it that all phases of the wedding celebration go smoothly. Finally, she arranges for cleanup after the festivities, and she remains long enough to see that it is all accomplished. Such a woman truly is worth her weight in gold and certainly is a valuable ally of and assistant to the pastor. She should be paid an honorarium commensurate with the valuable service she renders.

If such a person is not available, the pastor himself may have to work closely with the couple, taking responsibility to remind them of the many details concerning the upcoming wedding. As he gets to know his people, though, inevitably he will find someone who has a special interest in weddings and who would love to be trained to serve as a wedding coordinator. Usually women desire such positions. However, before he confirms anyone in the position, it is in the best interests of everyone that the pastor know with certainty that she is a diplomatic person whose manner would calm rather than excite the members of wedding party, who will be excited enough by the many pressures the wedding places upon them. Also it is important that the wedding coordinator be someone who can work in harmony with the pastor, so that the couple receives one clear signal instead of two competing ones.

THE WEDDING HANDBOOK

The pastor's second valuable ally in wedding planning is a little booklet. The booklet, which he will have written, should state the wedding policies of the church, including financial responsibilities. (If the church has one policy for members and another for outsiders, he should prepare two booklets, each one oriented to the target group.) The booklet should contain a list of whom to pay and a suggested amount for each. Also, it may contain a statement outlining the meaning of a Christian wedding, the kind of ceremony that should be observed in a church building, and guidelines in selecting music. In addition, the booklet may describe the responsibilities of the pastor, and it may outline church policies regarding photography, smoking, the throwing of rice, and cleanup procedures. Marriage application procedures should be contained in the booklet, along with checklists noting the responsibilities of the bride and her family, the responsibilities of the groom and his family, and the responsibilities the wedding couple together must attend to before the wedding. A booklet such as this will save the pastor much time and will prove to be a valuable guide for the bridal couple.

THE PASTOR'S RESPONSIBILITIES DURING THE EARLY PLANNING

Besides counseling the couple, the pastor should work closely with the wedding coordinator to see to it that the proper arrangements are being made and that they are in keeping with his and the church's philosophy of ministry. In the weeks immediately preceding a wedding, emotions can run high and misunderstandings occur. It will tax the pastor's diplomatic abilities to keep things running as smoothly as possible during that period.

The Rehearsal

The rehearsal is sometimes the most edgy event of all. If at all possible, the rehearsal should be held the night immediately preceding the wedding day. The pastor should be on the scene well ahead of time, and he should be the epitome of calm and personal organization. A humble and confident attitude will allay many tensions. He should be sensitive to the emotions and fragile relationships of the families—mothers who are domineering, strained relationships, future in-laws who are not yet comfortable with one another, "cold feet" on the part of the wedding couple, and nervousness generated by being involved in a public event. The pastor should be relaxed and professional. This is his turn to be in charge, but he should not be pedantic or overbearing. Many times appropriate humor will defuse a potentially explosive situation.

Alone or with the help of the wedding coordinator, the pastor should line up the participants and go through the ceremony step-by-step, informing each person of his responsibilities. After going through the entire ceremony, he should go through it again completely. This time the wedding party will be more relaxed and are likely to remember better than the first time what they should be doing. During the rehearsal the pastor should remember that he is a faithful friend, not an army drill instructor. He should be ready for anything and not panic when it happens. He should be encouraging, and he should keep his instructions clear and simple. During the rehearsal, he should assure the couple that if they forget anything or make a mistake the next day, he will help them over their difficulty. If the couple have composed their own vows and plan to memorize them, it is helpful for the pastor to have a copy of the vows so that he can prompt them if they forget.

The wise pastor brings the marriage license to the rehearsal and obtains the necessary signatures before the rehearsal is finished. Such action will preclude uneasy moments the next day, if someone forgets the license. If at all possible, the pastor should clear his calendar so that he can attend the rehearsal dinner, should he be invited. The dinner is an ideal time for him to become acquainted with out-of-town guests. Sometimes he will receive a clear invitation to attend the event. Sometimes the invitation will be unstated but attendance expected of him. Other times he is not expected to attend. If in doubt, he should inquire judiciously of the groom. If the answer is nebulous, the pastor should forget about attending. He will enjoy the time relaxing at home with his own family.

The Wedding Day

On the big day itself, the pastor should be properly attired and present at the church building or other wedding location at least a half hour ahead of time. He may have been able to convince the wedding couple to abandon a long-standing superstition and pose for the wedding pictures well ahead of the wedding ceremony, a courtesy to guests who would be inconvenienced by a long wait if the photography was done between the wedding and the reception.

A last-minute check makes certain that all details are cared for. The pastor delivers the signed wedding certificate to the father of the groom and instructs him to give it to the groom after the service. The pastor positions himself with the groom and his party and leads the procession of men to their designated places. With dignity, and yet in a friendly manner, the pastor greets the congregation and leads the couple step-by-step through the wedding ceremony.

An important part of that ceremony is the sermon. It may be in two parts: one addressed to the couple, reminding them of the responsibilities they owe to each other; and one directed to the congregation, instructing them as to the meaning of Christian marriage and inviting them to affirm or to renew on the basis of a personal commitment to Jesus Christ their marriage commitment to their mates. It would be good for the pastor to state clearly that a truly happy marriage will occur only as a man and wife commit themselves and their relationship to Jesus Christ as Lord and Savior. I believe sincerely that no wedding message should be without an evangelistic thrust. However, the gospel should be presented in a friendly, nonthreatening, and noncondemning manner. A wedding is not the appropriate time to grind theological axes. It is the time to make plain the meaning of Christian marriage.

After the pastor has pronounced the couple husband and wife and has introduced them to the congregation in their new entity, he follows the wedding party as they recess down the aisle, or he finds his way out of the auditorium in the most graceful way possible. He may want to be the first guest in the reception line, offering his congratulations to the participants and the parents. His wife may want to join him as they greet people at the reception itself. When he feels it is proper, he will slip away quietly. Soon after the couple has returned from the honeymoon he should visit them in their new home and perhaps invite them to his home for dinner or dessert. In that way he will be recognizing them in their new identity and will encourage their active participation in the church. If there are other couples in the church who are about the same age, he may want to encourage them to plan activities with the new couple to help them adjust to their new status and, at the same time, find their place in the church family.

Few activities of the church present such an opportune time to get close to people as the wedding. If the pastor is warm, caring, and personable to the couple and their families in the period prior to the wedding, and if he conducts the ceremony itself with beauty, dignity, and warmth, even though he is not the most creative person in the world, almost everyone will remark, "Wasn't it a lovely wedding?" and the pastor will be held in esteem by those who attend.

Two more hints may be helpful. First, the pastor should remind himself to mail in the marriage license promptly, or everyone— including himself—will be in trouble and his reputation be ruined. Second, if an honorarium is offered to him, he should accept it graciously. If there is none, however, he should never ask for one, nor should he wait around at the reception hoping to receive one. That is beneath the dignity of his office. Prior to a wedding, if the bride and groom are members of the church and ask him how much his fee is, he should simply tell them that his performing the wedding is part of his duties as their pastor. When instructing outsiders, it is proper for him to stipulate a fee for his services. He should never attempt to collect it, however. Instead he should view his part in the wedding as a service to the Lord, trusting fully that the Lord is faithful and will meet the financial needs of His servants.

Questions for Discussion

1. What place is the institution of marriage to have in society and in the church? How would you evaluate the current status of marriage in your place of ministry?

2. What is your attitude toward divorce? Should it ever be condoned? Are there instances where divorce is permitted? Explain your position.

3. What course of action would you recommend to the local church so that concise instructions may be given as to the sanctity of marriage and the Christian responsibilities inherent in choosing and uniting with a life partner?

4. How many counseling sessions should a pastor conduct with a couple before marrying them? Should a pastor refuse to marry a couple who will not cooperate with a program of premarital counseling?

5. Under what other circumstances should a pastor refuse to marry a couple?

6. What should characterize the Christian wedding ceremony? How is it different from secular weddings?

7. What are the essential elements of a Christian wedding?

8. What role can a wedding coordinator play in assisting those who wish to marry?

9. What value is there in writing a clear statement of wedding policies and suggestions in booklet form? What information might such a booklet contain?

10. List the responsibilities of the pastor following his decision to marry a couple.

Helpful Resources

Ellison, Stanley A. *Divorce and Remarriage in the Church.* Grand Rapids: Zondervan, 1977.

Laney, J. Carl. *The Divorce Myth.* Minneapolis: Bethany, 1981.

Lewis, Fay O. *The Christian Wedding Handbook.* Old Tappan, N.J.: Revell, 1981.

Palmer, Marjorie. *Bride's Book of Ideas.* Wheaton, Ill.: Tyndale, 1980.

Rock, Stanley A. *This Time Together: A Guide to Premarital Counseling.* Grand Rapids: Zondervan, 1980.

Swaadley, Elizabeth. *Your Christian Wedding.* Nashville: Broadman, 1966.

Wheat, Ed. *Love Life for Every Couple.* Grand Rapids: Zondervan, 1980.

Wright, H. Norman. *Premarital Counseling.* Rev. ed. Chicago: Moody, 1981.

20

Funerals

Several years ago my wife, children, and I were enjoying a rare weekend in our hideaway cabin in the Midwest when, to our surprise, friends drove into our driveway. We knew that they had driven many miles to see us, and we were delighted although somewhat puzzled at their visit. Our delight soon turned into sorrow, however, when they explained their mission. They were there to tell us that my father had been felled by a fatal heart attack. Hours later that same night my wife and I found ourselves at the home of my parents in Southern California in the arms of my mother, who was comforting us more than we were consoling her.

An Example of Neglect

There are times when my mother is a bit excitable but never in times of emergency. When really difficult times come, she can always be counted on to be a rock. In the hours after my father's death, she had taken care of all the necessary details, even to the alerting of the pastor, the setting of the funeral date, and the arranging for transporting the body to its final resting place, our family plot in the East.

All of that she had done without help, except for the supporting love of neighbors. Because my father was a well-known religious leader in the Southwest, his many friends needed to be notified so that they could attend the funeral. It was Labor Day weekend, though, and there was no way to notify most of them until the following Tuesday. That prolonged the process, delaying the funeral until Wednesday.

Because there was such a long period between the death and the funeral, I thought that my mother's pastor and other church leaders would take the opportunity of calling on Mother several times to provide support and comfort. At that time, I, also, was a pastor in the denomination. Because I was a brother pastor, I thought, surely my mother's pastor would make a courtesy call at her home, for that reason alone. To our amazement, in the five days between my father's death and his funeral, no one from the church visited us. The pastor telephoned once to inform us that the church was planning a buffet dinner for members of the family and special guests following the funeral service. The gesture was a fine one and was much appreciated. But it did not take the place of a personal visit.

On the morning of the funeral, when our family arrived at the church building, the pastor ushered us into his office, spelled out the details of the funeral, and then proceeded to tell us of himself and of some of the publications he had written recently. No words of comfort and assurance were offered until the funeral ceremony itself.

Following the funeral, my mother, sister, and I accompanied the body to New York for burial. My mother stayed on in New York for several weeks, visiting with relatives. When she returned to California, no effort was made by anyone in the church leadership to visit her or to comfort her. Months passed, a change of pastors took place, and still no visit. Knowing how hard it was for my mother to handle her grief alone, finally, in desperation, I wrote to the new pastor, pleading with him to minister to my mother. Again, months went by. At last he visited her. The visit was unannounced, however. He came on one of those rare days when she was entertaining company, and it was not a convenient time for her to talk with the pastor. He never returned.

Members of that church were astounded months later when my mother joined a church of a different denomination closer to her home. They were heard to say, "How could she do a thing such as that? Doesn't she have any loyalty?"

An analysis of this illustration reveals that the pastors and the church involved demonstrated some good points and some bad ones. The public details—those things that would be noticed by the public—were done rather well. I am sure, for instance, that those attending the funeral were struck by the beauty and order of the service and by the fact that the church was generous enough to give the family and guests a fine meal after the funeral. In the more private details, however—those things pertaining to the initial and continuing needs of the grieving—both the pastors and the church would have to receive a very poor grade. Yet the more private matters were the ones the family members considered especially important.

Probably there is no greater need for a pastor's ministry in a person's life than when that person experiences the death of a loved one. No other opportunity in life gives the pastor a better chance to minister to people.

Concern Translated into Action

FOLLOWING A SUDDEN DEATH

What should the offending pastor have done if he was to have been truly helpful to my mother and the rest of us in the family? First, when word reached the pastor of my father's death, the pastor should have canceled all appointments and visited my mother immediately. After comforting her, praying with her, and perhaps reading an appropriate Scripture passage containing words of comfort, he should have offered to accompany her to the funeral home of her choice and, once there, should have helped her make the necessary arrangements. Because he knew that a number of hours would elapse before out-of-town family members would arrive, he should have arranged for someone in the church to stay with my mother in the interim. He knew that the airport was many miles from my mother's home and that a person in grief should not be called upon to drive such a long distance. He should have arranged with church members to provide transportation from the airport for arriving family members.

In view of the fact that a number of days were to intervene between the death and the funeral, the pastor should have made at least one visit to my mother's home after family members had arrived. Also, he should have made arrangements for church leaders to check in with the family from time to time to provide comfort as needed, and for church members to provide meals for the family until the funeral. Sometime before the funeral itself, he should have sat down in person with the family and asked them what details they would like to have included in the funeral service. The pastor in question did so only briefly by phone. During the viewing of the body at the funeral home, church leaders—including the pastor—should have made personal visits. They did not. Prior to the funeral itself, the pastor should have encouraged the family to speak concerning their needs, instead of asking them to respond to his ego needs by reading the pamphlets he had written.

In the weeks my mother was absent from California, a phone call from her pastor would have been encouraging to her. Upon her return, a personal visit by the pastor was in order. During that visit, he could have ascertained her needs, including the need for financial and legal counsel, and subsequently helped her to obtain the needed services. Thereafter, a personal visit each week, either by the pastor or by another church leader, would have proved helpful, until at least the first six months of my mother's bereavement was past. Then at least one visit a month would have been in order until the first anniversary of my father's death. None of these visits should have been unannounced. All should have been by appointment only.

Meanwhile, other resources of the church should have been mobilized to encourage my mother to venture forth into the mainstream of life once again. Even if she turned down invitations initially, church members should have been encouraged to follow up on her until she began taking the first halting steps toward a more normal life. In my mother's case, no such care took place—and her subsequent response of finding and joining another church was an appropriate one.

THE DEATH OF A TERMINALLY ILL PATIENT

In the example above, my father's death was unexpected. There was no way the pastor could have anticipated it. However, there are times when it is obvious that a person is terminally ill. As the time of death approaches, it is important that the pastor keep in close contact with the family. Regardless of whether the patient is at home, in a hospital, in a nursing home, or in a terminal care facility, the pastor should visit the patient as frequently as possible. When the actual deathwatch begins and it is obvious that the person will expire in a matter of hours, the pastor, a church leader, or an intimate friend of the family should be with family members at all times. Because of other demands, the pastor will not be able to be there the entire time himself. Nevertheless, he should keep in close contact with the person designated to stay with the family. As death approaches rapidly, the pastor should cancel other appointments and be with the dying person and his family. No one ever should be required to die alone, and no family should find it necessary to experience bereavement alone.

In dealing with a dying person, even though that person may appear to be comatose and unaware of what is going on around him, care should be exercised in what is said. Often he is aware of every word that is spoken. Thus it is advisable to speak to him as if he understands everything being said. If he is not a Christian, the plan of salvation should be presented to him in simple and direct terms, even though he is not capable of giving any visible or audible response. As a person nears death, the family and pastor should gather around him and join in prayers committing him to God. If he is a radiant Christian, it may be an appropriate time to close the hospital room door and join together in singing some stirring hymns of the faith. There have been incidents where the dying person could not speak but actually was able to join in singing the hymns. What a way to be ushered into the presence of the Lord! Family and pastor should remain with the patient until he dies.

Immediately following the death of the patient, the pastor should spend as much time as necessary at the scene of death with the family, grieving with them and giving them words of encouragement and comfort. At this time it would be appropriate for the pastor to read a pertinent Scripture portion and to pray with them, but only if and when the family appears ready for him to do so. When the family leaves the place of death, it is proper for the pastor to leave as well. If the death occurs at home, the pastor may leave as soon as he senses the family feels it is the right time for him to do so. If they express a further need of his presence, he should stay as long as is necessary. He may then follow procedures similar to those I outlined earlier in the chapter, as the church begins to respond to the needs of the bereaved.

THE DEATH OF A NEWBORN

When a newborn baby dies, the pastor may want to make sure that the mother is not alone in the hospital during the funeral service. In addition, special effort should be exerted to meet the needs of the father. He may be the most forgotten person in the drama. Following the death of a baby, it is good for the pastor to put the family in contact with a sympathetic and sensitive family that has experienced the same kind of grief.

Making Arrangements at the Funeral Home

If the family accepts the offer of the pastor to accompany them to the funeral home to make the necessary arrangements, the pastor should gently but sensitively steer the family away from making funeral arrangements that will result in prohibitive costs to them. If they insist on lavish funeral arrangements, the pastor should back out of the picture as graciously as possible, allowing family members to make their own decisions. If an argument arises between family members concerning funeral arrangements, the pastor should try to segregate the opposing figures and help them to resolve their disagreement. When arguments arise, usually the funeral director is sufficiently experienced and skilled to offer valuable assistance in resolving them.

The Typical Funeral Home Service

OVERVIEW OF THE SERVICE

Details of the funeral service itself should be made with the wishes of the family in mind. However, often the service will include the following elements:

An organ prelude
Opening words of Scripture
Prayer
Vocal solo (optional)
Reading of the obituary
The eulogy (optional)
Vocal solo (optional)
Short sermon
Prayer
Benediction

The entire service should last from twenty to thirty minutes. Because its sole purpose is to provide comfort and hope for the living, it should be designed specifically for those attending the funeral service. Comments in detail on some elements of the service follow.

ORGAN PRELUDE

If the organ prelude is to be a recorded one, the pastor should make sure he talks with the funeral director ahead of time concerning the kind of music that will be played. Increasingly, the recorded music used by funeral directors is secular in nature and is offensive to many Christians when used in the setting of a Christian funeral. The time spent selecting appropriate music will be worthwhile.

OBITUARY

Because the funeral service is a time for remembering the deceased, the reading of the obituary is a convenient way of reminding those at the funeral of the details of his life. There have been instances where I believed I knew the deceased quite well, but found in preparing the obituary that I did not know him as well as I had thought. Additional, interesting facts concerning my friend came to light that were of great value to me in helping me to know him even better. Often the funeral director will use facts gleaned from the bereaved to compile an obituary for publication in a local newspaper. That information will be helpful to the pastor in preparing the obituary he will deliver at the funeral. In the time preceding the funeral, the pastor will want to gather with the family and get them to reminisce about the deceased. Many stories and facts that will bring a human interest element into the obituary and the eulogy can be uncovered in this way.

Generally, the obituary is a factual statement containing vital information about the deceased, such as the date and place of his birth, the number of children he had and their names, and the names of his parents and siblings. Consequently, it does not go into detail concerning the virtues of the deceased. Yet, the facts can be presented in a warm, interesting manner, so that even in the obituary, those at the funeral can get a more personal picture of the deceased than given by the obituary in the newspaper.

EULOGY

A eulogy is a short speech in praise of an individual. I have designated it as an optional feature, because sometimes the individual being buried has lived so negative a life it is extremely difficult to find reasons for praising him. No doubt most people have heard the story of the widow who stopped the pastor in the middle of the eulogy and asked the funeral director to open the casket. The eulogy was so positive that the dear widow wanted to be sure that the person being buried was, indeed, her husband. In such a case, it often is better to move directly from the obituary to the next portion of the service.

Eulogies sometimes are the most effective when more than one person participates. I have attended services in which many friends of the deceased expressed what he had meant in their lives. Many times even little anecdotes have been recounted, some of which contained considerable humor. Though a funeral ought not to consist of a series of jokes, it is not at all out of line at a funeral to share bits of humor that are representative of a person's life and that may help the bereaved to remember him as he actually was. Such humor, shared in taste, may provide a heartwarming experience for those who are mourning. Often I have heard relatives say, "This is just the way John would have liked it."

Following a service in a funeral chapel, it is proper for a pastor to join the family of the deceased and stay with them until the casket has been placed within the hearse. If there is to be a committal service at the cemetery, the funeral director will probably request that the pastor ride to the cemetery in the front seat of the hearse. The committal service will be covered in later paragraphs.

The Church Funeral

RATIONALE FOR HAVING A CHURCH FUNERAL

In my earliest years, I lived in an extended family situation in our ancestral home in the East. When I was a small boy, it was the custom of my family to hold home funerals. In those days and in that culture, as soon as the body was embalmed, the funeral director delivered it in its casket to the family home. There the body lay in state for several days, while friends and relatives came to view it. The funeral itself was conducted in the home itself or in the church, depending on the number of people who were expected to attend. Few funerals were conducted at the mortuary.

To this day, I have dreams of the body of some elderly relative lying in state in the front parlor. The practice certainly made the fact of death realistic to the children in our family, especially when one of us got up at night to go to the bathroom and found a family member standing vigil with the body. I am glad that the practice, by and large, has been discontinued. Even now it would give me spooky feelings to return to that house.

I am sorry, however, that church funerals no longer are common. Although funerals at mortuary chapels are convenient for funeral directors, such funerals actually deprive the family of a significant gathering in the more natural environment of the meeting place of the church. I hope that the trend will soon revert to the church funeral. There are several reasons for my wish. First, a funeral chapel is an unnatural place, signifying that death is an unnatural occurrence. But in the life of a Christian many significant, natural occasions of life occur within the church building. It is fitting, therefore, that the final event take place there as well. Second, even though funeral directors may be the kindest and most generous people in the world, funerals conducted in mortuary chapels are on the turf of the funeral director, and, consequently, to a great extent he sets the game plan. Because of that, the service I suggested earlier in the chapter for use in a funeral chapel is significantly different from a typical worship service conducted in a church building. Yet, granted the physical limitations of the funeral chapel, the service I outlined is appropriate for that setting.

Far greater freedom can be exercised in a service conducted in a church building. The musical instruments church instrumentalists customarily use in regular worship services are there, for instance. The congregation feels greater freedom to sing and worship in surroundings that are familiar. In his own natural setting, the pastor does not need to feel constrained by time. He, rather than the funeral director, is in charge. It is appropriate for him to say to the funeral director, "Here is where I want you to place the casket. Close the lid five minutes before the service, and I will signal you when it is time for you to take charge of the body." The pastor may then proceed without restraints of time except those that are proper to decorum.

OVERVIEW OF THE SERVICE

A service conducted in a church building can be a memorial service or a funeral. In the former case, the body is not present. In the latter, it is. A memorial or funeral service in a church building can take on the form of any other worship service. Songs of praise to God in thanksgiving for the life of the deceased can be sung, and the service can include any other feature normally part of a church worship service. Even though I have never seen it done, I do not think it inappropriate for the congregation to be called upon to give an offering. The offering could be designated for the specific needs of the family or for a memorial fund through which some special project in memory of the deceased will be completed. For example, a special purchase for the church might be made, or the money might be used to fund a charitable project in which the deceased had expressed an interest.

SERMON

Funerals and weddings are the church occasions the greatest number of non-Christians are likely to attend. Therefore, it is not only proper but desirable that the funeral sermon always contain the gospel message in clear terms. The message should be presented in a polite, nonthreatening manner. It is not right to harangue the bereaved or attempt scare tactics to propel them into the kingdom of

God. A simple explanation of the gospel message, including the necessity for a person to commit his life personally to Jesus Christ as Lord and Savior, and a simple step-by-step description of how a person may do that will suffice. If an invitation is given, it should be one where the inquirer is asked to respond inwardly. Generally in our culture, altar calls at funerals are in poor taste.

If the deceased was unsaved, it will not help the family for the pastor to dwell on the fact. Besides, the pastor does not know that the deceased was unsaved. Despite outward evidence, he may have had an experience with God that nobody else knew about. It will be sufficient for the pastor to say, "Having gone through the experience of death, if John were here now, this is the advice he would give to the rest of us." From there, the message of the gospel can be made plain.

Again, let me emphasize that the sermon should be brief. Those who have been bereaved are in pain, and often that pain is intensified by the emotional setting of the funeral. It is best for the pastor not to prolong their suffering by giving a lengthy exegetical presentation. Although such a sermon might convince some of those attending of his scholarly ability, it will not provide the word of comfort the bereaved need. It is likely, in fact, that the words of the Scripture will prove far more comforting than the sermon itself.

One other observation. A funeral sermon is not the time for pious platitudes or pat answers, even if they are logical and biblical. It is a time to bring words of comfort and hope to people who are hurting. Various pastors' manuals containing model funeral services can be helpful to the pastor, especially if he is a novice. However, after a person has been in the pastoral ministry for any length of time, most generally he will be able to plan a service that is unique to himself and that is more comfortable to him than those he finds in books.

Graveside Committal

When the pastor arrives in the hearse at the cemetery, he should get out of the vehicle and stand by the rear of the hearse until the coffin is lifted out. Then he should walk slowly at the head of the coffin, leading the way to the grave site. At the grave, he should stand at the head of the coffin. If he is wearing a hat, he should remove it. The graveside service follows.

GRAVESIDE SERVICE

The service at the grave will usually contain the following elements:

Words of assurance from the Scriptures
Words of committal
Prayer of comfort for the bereaved
Presentation of the flag (if appropriate)
Benediction

WORDS OF COMMITTAL

The words of committal may simply be a statement such as this: "In that God has ordained that the soul of our beloved brother be returned to Him, we commit his earthly body to the ground: earth to earth, ashes to ashes, dust to dust, looking forward to the resurrection when we shall be united with him."

PRESENTATION OF THE FLAG

In the event that the deceased is a veteran of military service, his coffin may be covered with a flag. In a nonmilitary funeral, the funeral director will fold the flag and give it to the pastor who will present it to the next of kin, saying, "Mrs. Jones, it is my privilege to give you this flag in behalf of a grateful nation."

AFTER THE SERVICE

Following the graveside service, the pastor will want to linger informally with family members and friends of the deceased until the funeral director signifies it is time to return to the funeral home or church building. If the pastor's wife has attended the graveside services or if there are friends present who offer him a ride, he may want to forgo the trip back in the hearse. In that case, he may stay at the cemetery as long as he wishes, departing only when he feels that the family has no further need for his services.

Services for Nonchurch Families

If the deceased and his family were members of the pastor's church, he should observe follow-up procedures similar to those outlined earlier. Today, however, a pastor will sometimes be asked to perform funeral services for families who do not have any church connection. When he receives such a request, the pastor should visit the family, giving them whatever comfort he can. During that visit he may talk with them concerning the details they wish to include in the funeral service. If they are still too pained to talk about the funeral, he can return later to complete the arrangements.

The services held in the funeral chapel and at the grave site may differ in content but probably not in format from those already suggested. Following the funeral, the pastor should make one and perhaps even two visits to the family. He might ask a church member living in the same neighborhood as the bereaved to try to establish a meaningful relationship with them.

The pastor should not be overly optimistic about the results of such contacts. The family was unchurched prior to the funeral and probably will remain so afterwards. There is a ray of hope here, though. Often if the family has further need for a pastor or a church, they will seek to meet that need through the only pastor with whom they have had religious contact. As a result, sometimes ministries to such families bear fruit eventually.

Fraternal Rites and the Christian Funeral

Recently one of my students asked if there were occasions when a pastor should refuse to perform a funeral, as for example in the case of a funeral that was to be followed by the rites of a secret fraternal organization. In response, I told him that throughout my ministry I have held that a funeral is designed primarily to minister to the living, not to eulogize the dead. Therefore I do not refuse to perform a funeral unless something of major importance demands that I be out of town. A funeral is a singular opportunity to edify the saints and to share the gospel with the lost.

Yet though I do not want to miss opportunities for ministry, I do not participate in ceremonies I believe are unbiblical or spiritually offensive. If I am informed that a secret organization is to perform its rites in conjunction with a funeral I am scheduled to conduct, I arrange with the funeral director and the family to hold my service first, to make it plain to the congregation when that service is over, and then to slip out of the room while the fraternal organization carries on its rites. Afterwards, I return to minister to the family.

Likewise, in regard to a committal service at the cemetery, I arrange to conduct my service first and then to remove myself from the gravesite, perhaps retreating to the front seat of the hearse, until the secret rites have been performed. When they are over I return to the gravesite and continue ministering to the family for as long as my presence is needed. This is a formula the pastor can follow to take advantage of a ministry opportunity while not violating his conscience.

Cremation

Cremation of the body is again becoming more common. In such cases, the pastor may want to begin to begin the committal service immediately after the funeral. Following the committal service, the funeral director will usually transport the body directly to the crematorium. On some occasions the pastor will be asked to conduct the committal service at the actual place of cremation. On rare occasions, the family will ask the pastor to officiate at an additional service held when the ashes are interred or scattered.

Memorial Services

If a memorial service is desired, the family may want to have a short graveside service before the memorial service. The committal service should be brief, but because it is the initial contact the family will have with funeral procedures it should be longer than the committal service described earlier.

Other Occasions

The scope of this book does not allow for the treatment of military funerals, mass funerals, or the burial of a child, but valuable information concerning them can be found in pastors' manuals and funeral manuals, several of which should be part of the pastor's library. In the case of a military funeral, the pastor should consult military officials in his local community for any unique requirements.

Dealing Gently with the Flock

In closing the chapter I should like to return to the illustration with which it opened. The omissions of the pastor we studied there were probably not what we would call "professional" omissions. They were deficiencies in human relationships. Perhaps the pastor was a product of his training. At one time professionals, pastors included, were advised to stay aloof from those they served so that they could maintain an attitude of objectivity. The rationale was that it was too exhausting for a people-helper to get emotionally involved with the problems of his clients.

Such an approach is wrong. No one can remain emotionally detached and be a successful pastor. In Matthew 10, Jesus spells out the difference between a true shepherd and a hired hand, suggesting that the objectivity of the hired hand amounts to indifference, for when the pressure is on he does not hesitate to break and run. He may perform perfunctory duties well. But as far as really caring for the sheep—forget about that.

The true shepherd is dedicated to his sheep and involved with their welfare. He will even give his life for them. The very meaning of the word *pastor* is shepherd. We may never be asked to give our lives for our sheep, but a willingness to do so must be there if we are to be authentic in our calling. That commitment means we will do more than view our people with cold objectivity. Instead, we will love them, care for them, and be sensitive to their needs.

Most of the things I have suggested the pastor do for the bereaved are merely common sense actions any thoughtful person should take on behalf of someone with whom he is close. A person who cares for others will make it his business to know and respond to their needs in every way possible. A person who aspires to be a pastor must like people and be able to participate genuinely in their joys and in their sorrows.

A pastor may be an articulate speaker, a superb exegete, a competent administrator, a skilled educator, a gifted evangelist, and an impressive person; he may be physically attractive, charismatic in personality, persuasive, and gregarious. But if he does not truly love his people or does not demonstrate that love through tangible, personal effort on their behalf, he is merely a hired hand—and eventually will be revealed as one.

The pastor's acts of kindness may never gain public attention. They are not the more visible forms of his ministry. But during crisis periods in the life of church members and friends, the private demonstrations of concern he makes may be the actions of his ministry that are the most important and beneficial to the sheep. A pastor can be forgiven for occasionally "laying an egg" in the pulpit or for an administrative faux pas. If the people are convinced that he really loves them, they will overlook many inadequacies. A pastor ministering in this way will always gain the hearts of his people.

There is no more strategic place for a pastor to convince his people that he loves them than in his ministry to them before, during, and after a funeral. This is the time for him to cancel other obligations in order to give himself unreservedly to those who have been bereaved. This is the time for him to marshal the resources of the church to meet the needs of those who are grieving. When the church and the pastor minister empathetically, by and large the bereaved will not take the course of action my mother did. They will have no need to join another church. They will already be where they belong.

Questions for Discussion

1. In what ways can the pastor provide support and comfort for those who are bereaved?

2. Why is the initial visit to the home of the bereaved so critical?

3. What services can the members of the church provide up to and following the funeral?

4. What is the importance of grief in the healing process of the bereaved? How can the pastor aid the bereaved during the grieving process?

5. What are the essential elements of the Christian funeral service?

6. How should the pastor and his people respond to the terminally ill? What ministry can they provide before and following death?

7. What special problems come up in dealing with the comatose patient and his family?

8. What is the difference between the role of the funeral director and the role of the pastor? How may they aid each other?

9. What do you see as valuable in the obituary and the eulogy [when it is used] as parts of the funeral service?

10. What are the essential elements of the committal service?

11. How would you include the gospel message in a funeral sermon? What precautions would you take in making such a presentation?

12. How can a pastor be a shepherd to those who are bereaved?

Helpful Resources

Bachmann, C. Charles. *Ministering to the Grief-Sufferer.* Englewood Cliffs, N.J.: Prentice-Hall, 1964.

Bailey, Robert W. *The Minister and Grief.* New York: Hawthorn, 1976.

Bell, Peggy, and Clayton Bell. "A Look at Grief." *Leadership* 1, no. 4 (1980):40-51.

Meyers, C. D., and R. A. Myers. "Clergy and Funeral Directors: An Exploration in Role Conflict." *Reformed Review* 21 (1980):343-50.

Clark, Geoffrey L. "The Pastor's Problems: IV. Ministering in Dying." *Expository Times* 92, no. 6 (1981):164-66.

Doka, Kenneth. "The Funeral Service: Grace in Grief." *Currents in Theology and Mission* 9 (1979):235-38.

———. "Resources in the Parish on Death and Dying." *Currents in Theology and Mission* 6, no. 3 (1979):165-67.

Gibbie, Kenneth L. "Preparing Parishioners for a Pastoral Visit." *Leadership* 2, no. 4 (1981):55-58.

Horton, William D. "The Pastor's Problems: XV. Funerals." *Expository Times* 94, no. 4 (1983):104-7.

Irion, Paul E. *The Funeral and the Mourners: Pastoral Care for the Bereaved.* Nashville: Abingdon, 1979.

Mitchell, Kenneth R., and Herbert Anderson. *All Our Losses, All Our Griefs: Resources for Pastoral Care.* Philadelphia: Westminster, 1983.

Morgan, J. H., and R. Goering. "Caring for Parents Who Have Lost an Infant." *Journal of Religion and Health* 17 (1978):290-98.

Richards, Lawrence O., and Paul Johnson. *Death and the Caring Community: Ministering to the Terminally Ill.* Portland, Oreg.: Multnomah, 1980.

Stone, Howard W. *The Caring Church: Guide for Lay Pastoral Care.* San Francisco: Harper and Row, 1983.

Sullender, R. Scott. "Three Theoretical Approaches to Grief." *Journal of Pastoral Care* 33, no. 4 (1979):243-51.

Taylor, Michael H. *Learning to Care: Christian Reflection on Pastoral Practice.* London: Anchor, 1983.

Vail, Elaine. *A Personal Guide to Living with Loss.* New York: John Wiley, 1982.

Manuals

Allen, Earl R. *Funeral Service Book.* Grand Rapids: Baker, 1974.

Biddle Perry H., Jr. *Abingdon Funeral Manual.* Nashville: Abingdon, 1976.

Poovey, W. A., ed. *Planning a Christian Funeral: A Minister's Guide.* Minneapolis: Augsburg, 1978.

Rest, Friedrich. *Funeral Handbook.* Valley Forge: Judson, 1982.

Sigler, Franklin. *The Broadman Minister's Manual.* Nashville: Broadman, 1969.

Wood, Charles R., ed, *Sermon Outlines for Funeral Services.* Grand Rapids: Kregel, 1970.

21

Services of Child Dedication

Whether the local church is experiencing calm or stormy periods, interspersed within those periods are special moments that foster warmth and oneness among people. A service of child dedication is one of those moments. All of the vital ingredients are there: parents pledging themselves to bring up their children in the way of the Lord—a circumstance that has a solid biblical precedent (Luke 2:21) and that brings warm sentimental feelings to observers; a congregation affirming that it is willing to help the parents discharge their responsibilities; and last, but far from least, a beautiful, cuddly baby. Such an occasion should melt the hardest hearts.

Because a service of dedication is such a warm, unifying moment in the life of a church, I have often wondered why in many churches it is observed so rarely. The typical pattern seems to be to wait until a number of children accumulate or until a special day, such as Mother's Day, comes around and then perform a mass dedication. The practice detracts from the personal aspects of the occasion and possibly even contributes to the noise and confusion factor as well—one crying baby seems to encourage his peers to do likewise. Moreover, the practice deprives the congregation of enjoying throughout the year warm events that would bring them encouragement and delight.

It is my feeling that just as a person ought to be baptized as soon after he is saved as possible, so a baby should be dedicated as soon after he is born as possible. Both observances are events of great significance to the congregation and should be performed often.

Commitment the Parents Make

Rightly understood, the service of child dedication is primarily an event in which the parents commit themselves before God to bring up their child in the "fear and admonition" of the Lord. Even before the service, as the pastor counsels the parents, he should make plain that the ceremony itself carries no magic, no saving grace. The child himself will be no better for having gone through it, unless the parents mean what they say when they are called upon to make their commitment.

Commitment the Congregation Makes

Despite the fact that the parents willingly and wholeheartedly make a commitment in good faith, it is extremely difficult for them to carry out such a large assignment all by themselves. This is where the community of saints comes in. Because believers are part of the family of God, genuine family responsibilities accrue to every Christian. Each believer has the responsibility to do all he can to aid parents in the church in the rearing of their children. In a Christian service of child dedication, that obligation should be made plain to the congregation and to the parents.

Commitment the Godparents Make

In addition to the general congregational responsibility, it is advisable, as well, to invite more specific sharing of child-rearing responsibilities. When my father was a child, godparents were selected prior to a child's dedication or christening. When the child was brought before the congregation for dedication, those people pledged themselves to take a special interest in the child all the rest of his or their lives. In my father's case, a warm relationship developed between him and his godparents. They were together with him often, including notable occasions such as Christmas, his birthday, and various graduations. They never missed presenting him a gift at such festive times. When he needed it, they were available for counsel. In the event that all members of his family who could take care of him were to die, the godparents were pledged to raise him as one of their own. That was an extraordinary demonstration of faithfulness, for, in my father's case, his godparents were not even Christians.

It is too bad that this marvelous tradition has died out. How appropriate it would be to resurrect it within the context of the community of people who know Christ as Savior. Thus, when a couple brought their child to be dedicated to the Lord, they would not stand alone. In addition to being surrounded by a congregation that agreed to join them in spiritual child-rearing responsibilities, they would be accompanied by another Christian couple, perhaps close friends or relatives, who before God would make the same commitment as the parents. That couple would assume a great deal of responsibility in partnership with the parents in the spiritual upbringing of the child. They would agree to stay close to the child, to provide help and counsel as he needed it, and to be with him on all special occasions. They would agree also to take over complete parental duties and, if the parents should die or some other tragedy rendered them incapable of caring for their child. The Christian community would be called upon to support the godparents or sponsors in the job of bringing up the child.

In a day when the nuclear family holds such a prominent position, we have learned that it is difficult for such a family to operate by itself. We need the concept of the extended family. Yet because our society is so transient, the generations may live large distances from one another, and often one generation will not take responsibility for the other. How appropriate it would be for us to renew the concept of the extended family—this time a family composed of brothers and sisters in Christ who possess genuine love for one another and who agree to be responsible for each other.

Overview of the Service

A service of child dedication should be short, to the point, and conducted in the beginning moments of a worship service. Following the invocation, the congregation should be invited to sing a verse of an appropriate hymn at which time the parents and the sponsors bring the child to the front of the auditorium to be dedicated. For the dedication itself, the pastor may wish to follow a format similar to the following:

The reading of an appropriate passage of Scripture

The outlining of the biblical admonitions pertaining to the raising of a child in a Christian family

A careful delineation of the responsibilities the parents, the sponsors, and the congregation are expected to carry out

Pointed questions directed to those three groups of people, asking them to affirm verbally before each other their willingness to carry out the responsibilities required of them

A prayer of dedication for the child, sometimes given with the pastor holding the child in his arms and laying his hand on the child's head

The presentation to the parents of a certificate of dedication

The singing of a hymn of celebration, giving the congregation the opportunity to rejoice in the occasion and allowing the parents and sponsors the chance to make a graceful exit so that the child may be placed in the church nursery

The Value of Dedication Booklets

Often pastors who are new to ministry do not know what to say and do on an occasion such as this. A visit to a local Christian bookstore will reveal a number of attractive booklets that contain a certificate of dedication and the text of a service, should the pastor decide to use it. Also, some of the booklets contain a page on which to enter vital statistics, such as the name of the child, the name of his parents, the date of his birth, and the date of his dedication. If the pastor gives the parents the booklet, they will have a record of the event and a copy of the actual service that was used.

Booklets such as this should be selected with great care concerning their content and their appearance. The church should not try to save pennies on an item so relatively inexpensive as this. The dedication is an important event in the lives of the parents and the child, and the appearance of the booklet or certificate should reflect the importance and dignity of the occasion.

One more comment concerning the certificate is appropriate. There have been occasions when birth records have been lost and when government agencies have accepted baptismal or dedicatory certificates in lieu of official birth certificates. Parents should be advised, therefore, to keep the dedication certificates in a safe place.

The Reception Following

In the liturgical tradition, the christening of a child was an event of such importance that relatives and friends from miles around would attend the ceremony. Following the church service, the extended family and special friends visited the home of the parents, or, if their home was too small, the home of another family member, where a nice dinner and lavish desserts were served. Often the extended family spent the rest of the day together in fellowship and reminiscing. Such occasions promoted the feelings of loyalty and solidarity the families enjoyed. The party that followed the dedication demonstrated the importance of the event itself and drew families closer together.

In a day when huge geographic distances often separate the members of our extended families, we may draw upon the concept of the family of God's being our extended family in any particular location. Consequently, to demonstrate the importance of the event being celebrated and to promote family loyalty and solidarity, it is appropriate for the parents of the child being dedicated to hold a reception following the church service. They can hold it at the church building or at their own home, to which special friends and fellow members of the body are invited.

Role of the Service in Counteracting Cultural Trends

The church today is plagued by the impersonality that characterizes the culture around it. It needs as many occasions of warm, intimate fellowship as possible to halt the trend toward impersonality. A service of child dedication is one such occasion.

In addition to being impersonal, our culture is addicted to change. Often the primary target for attack has been tradition. Certainly tradition can be limiting. But when our traditions are examined and the original goals they were designed to pursue discovered, it is evident that many of the traditions now under severe attack had tangible and practical advantages. Therefore, rather than discarding old traditions only to establish new ones that may not be even as good, we would be wise to examine our traditions, find out what is good about them, and then revamp them to reach their original, desirable goals.

In this short chapter, I have attempted to do just that. As a result, I have examined old traditions outfitted in new clothes. It is sad that the old traditions were discarded in the first place. It is my prayer that in their new clothes they will serve us better than ever before.

The thesis of this chapter has been that a service of child dedication is one of those few, rare, warm occasions that unite a church in a special way. Let us not downplay the importance of the event or the benefits on our people it may have, by treating it in a perfunctory manner. Instead, let us elevate the occasion by investing it with as much pomp and ceremony as our nonliturgical form allows. In addition, let us involve the extended family of the church as much as possible in the sharing of child-raising responsibilities. Finally, because the occasion is indeed a time when the extended family should be celebrating, let us encourage the parents to host a celebration in honor of the occasion, thus in joyous spirit promoting the solidarity of the family of God.

Questions for Discussion

1. What are the ingredients that make a service of child dedication a special time in the life of a church?

2. What is the advantage of having services of child dedication often rather than scheduling them once or twice a year?

3. Who are the participants in a service of child dedication? What duties do the participants have from God's viewpoint? In responding to the question, consider Deuteronomy 6:6-7; 1 Samuel 1:28; Luke 2:22-23; 2 Timothy 3:15; and Mark 10:14.

4. What value do you see in the tradition of having godparents?

5. List the key elements of the service of child dedication. Find a child dedication certificate in a local Christian bookstore, and then design a dedication service with its use in mind. Think of a specific couple in your church as you prepare the service.

6. What might a church do after a service of child dedication to add to the warmth and fellowship of the occasion?

Helpful Resources

Aldridge, Marion D. *The Pastor's Guidebook: A Manual for Worship.* Nashville: Broadman, 1984.

Keating, L. A. *A Service of Dedication for Parents and Little Children.* Valley Forge, Pa.: Judson, 1943.

Part 4

The Pastor's Administrative Tasks

22

Planning and Managing

The starry-eyed young pastor who reports to his first church expecting to do little else than study and preach the Word is in for a rude surprise when he finds out how many administrative duties confront him. Whether he likes it or not, the program of the church will not "just happen," nor can he ignore those duties and hope lay people will take care of them. In many churches lay people have not been trained sufficiently to carry out such duties, and they are looking to him to provide the necessary direction.

Overview of the Duties

PLANNING

Chief among his duties is planning. Although it is good to involve as many people as possible in the goal-setting process of the church, it will often be necessary for the pastor to teach his people how to set goals and to instruct them as to the kinds of goals a church should be setting. After proper goals are set, the pastor as principal overseer must be a facilitator, aiding the various committees in adopting plans to accomplish their goals, helping them set timetables for doing so, and then reminding them of those timetables as the months progress toward the time when the goals should be reached.

IDENTIFYING AND REACHING GOALS

Along with helping the church identify and reach goals, the pastor should oversee the preparation of a coordinated church calendar. Suggestions for programming are contained in other chapters of this book. Though others in a church are involved in the planning of events, the incentive and direction for putting together the overall calendar must rest in the hands of the person who has the broadest knowledge concerning the many activities of the church—the pastor.

OVERSEEING THE CHURCH OFFICE

The pastor must also oversee the efficient operation of the church office and the support it gives the membership. If a church secretary is chosen carefully, he or she may relieve the pastor of much of that responsibility. A good church secretary serves as an administrative assistant, keeping up on details that affect the entire congregation and informing the pastor of the dozens of details that may escape him, especially in a medium-sized or a large church.

It was one such secretary, Carol Williams, who taught me the value of a really good church secretary. Even after these many years she still carries on a most effective ministry in a church I once served. In every way she is an integral part of the pastoral team of that church, and she has kept more than one pastor from embarrassment.

In return for such service, the pastor should champion the cause of his secretary, making sure that his or her working conditions are pleasant and that he or she has decent equipment with which to work. In turn, the pastor should insist that the secretary present the same type of servant image that he himself is expected to exhibit. A secretary who is to be an essential part of the ministry team must be pleasant and even-tempered. She or he should view ministry to people—even difficult people—as service to the Lord.

MANAGING FINANCES

Along with other, more routine, administrative functions, the pastor is usually called upon to take an active part in business matters involving figures and finances. Some pastors view such responsibilities with relish and enjoy them as much as anything else they do. They have strong gifts in the area of finance, and God may send them to just the right place for them to exercise those gifts. Others of us face such duties with a sense of panic. My best advice to the pastor or the prospective pastor is this: If you are not particularly gifted in this area, don't worry about it! If every pastor were required to keep a statistical account of everything that went on in and a running tally of the financial condition of the church, I would not make it in the pastorate. But, in actuality, I love the pastorate, and thank the Lord that He has sent others to keep such records for me. My major concerns in this area are these: Are we in the black or in the red? Are we growing or declining in size? More sophisticated figures than those are beyond me. Maybe since I am at last computerized, I will soon discover software programs designed to help people such as myself.

Church Government

DEACONS, ELDERS, AND PASTORS

In other chapters it is asserted that though the church is an organism rather than an organization, it still must be organized if it is going to survive. Although nowhere does the New Testament give an ideal or prescribed model of church government, when one studies the early church, it is clear that each assembly had at least one elder and a group of people called deacons. According to Scripture, the latter category, at least, was for women as well as for men (Rom. 16:1). Although the Scripture does not specify exactly what the deacons are supposed to do, it does give a good indication as to the kind of persons they are to be (1 Tim. 3).

Clear requirements are given, however, as to the type of person an elder should be and as to the duties he should perform. In an earlier chapter the seven kinds of duties the Bible assigns to elders were considered at some length. Because one of the duties of an elder is the oversight or leadership of the congregation, the biblical words *episcopos* (overseer) and *presbuteros* (elder) may be seen as referring to the same office. Because the Bible indicates, in addition, that every elder has pastoring responsibility (1 Pet. 5:1-2), it is safe to conclude that elders are to be considered the members of the pastoral staff. (Although the Bible gives some indication that elders were paid for their services, I do not think that it thereby requires that the persons serving as elders should be paid.)

Keeping in mind the view that elders are to make up the pastoral staff and the fact that Ephesians 4 appears to refer to specialization and division of labor among elders, it seems safe to conclude that there is a distinctive office of pastor. The person who occupies that office exercises an overall undershepherding function among the flock and among his fellow elders.

One more point should be made concerning the office of elder. The pastor is not the only elder in a church who should be required to receive training commensurate with his responsibility or to undergo the process of ordination before he is considered a bona-fide elder. Every elder has shepherding functions. Therefore, it is reasonable for a church to require that every elder receive special training and be ordained for the task.

THE IDEAL LEADERSHIP PLAN

What is the ideal church leadership plan? Every church is unique and God allows for great creativity. However, I would always opt for a one-board church whose board was made up of elders, the equipping ministers, and deacons, the serving ministers. Because Ephesians 4 specifies that all Christians should be involved in the work of a deacon, I believe that the special leaders called deacons should be the persons in a church who supervise its serving ministries. Thus those who serve on the board as deacons are not the only ones with ministering responsibilities; they are simply those who supervise those in the church who carry out such responsibilities.

Deacons and elders should be assigned to as few standing committees as the church can establish and still get its work done. Those committees, in turn, should be made up principally of the persons who supervise activities in the area in which the committee functions. The committees should report back to the church board, not so that the board can approve or disapprove their decisions, but so that the board can coordinate the program of the church. If the church has a minimum of standing committees, all the good workers are not wasted by making them committee members. Thus more Christians are freed from committee responsibilities so that they can engage actively in the work of the ministry.

A word needs to be added here in regard to a commonly-proposed concept, the idea of equality of elders where no one has an overall coordinating function. I do not believe that such a model can be supported by biblical directive or by biblical example. In my opinion, everywhere in Scripture the Lord asserts the necessity for one individual to take charge in any given situation. Human beings become confused when that does not happen. As I have already intimated, I believe the pastor is the one designated by God to take such leadership in the church.

Church Discipline

The principal passage referring to church discipline is one of only two passages where our Lord speaks about the church. The subject of church discipline, therefore, must have been especially important to Him.

In Matthew 18, the Lord sets the pattern whereby the church is to discipline an offender.

First, the person who has been offended or the person who is most affected by the offense should approach the offender personally. That requirement is an important one. In some churches, the offender never gets to interact with his accuser. The news about his offense is given to the pastor, who then is supposed to exercise discipline. That is not the intent of our Lord's directions. As pastor, I would go so far as refuse to take action of any kind unless one who was offended or who noticed the offense went personally to the offender and dealt with him brother to brother.

Second, if the offender and the accuser are not able to resolve the situation, then others—preferably officers of the church—should accompany the accuser when he approaches the offender for the second time. If that action does not succeed, the offender should be brought to the church for action. Once again, may I stress that the desired biblical end product for church discipline always is full restoration. Church discipline is not intended to be a way for the pastor to rid the church of those who oppose his programs.

Before leaving the subject, it would be good to examine the examples the Bible gives of people who should receive the most severe form of church discipline—expulsion and the withholding of fellowship. Matthew 18 does not give clues as to the kind of sin necessary to call forth that action. It does picture a person with an unrepentant heart. In the second scriptural passage dealing specifically with church discipline, 1 Corinthians 5, the offender is described as openly and flagrantly practicing an unspeakable sexual sin, incest. In 2 Thessalonians 3:6, 11, the third passage frequently referred to on the subject, Paul says that people who live unruly or disorderly lives and who refuse to follow the directions of Scripture are to be considered for discipline along with those who refuse to be employed but instead act "like busybodies."

Nowhere do the passages say that those who express a concern that the pastor's methods and programs are not correct should be meted out discipline.

In the light of Scripture, perhaps it would be good for many churches to establish a policy of discipline more biblical than the one they now follow. Always, the rule of thumb should be to follow the biblical practice of disciplining carefully and lovingly with the goal of reaching restoration. If I seem to have repeated myself here, it is because I have. The point seems to have been lost by a majority of churches today. Churches either do not discipline at all, or when they finally resort to discipline, they do so with the idea of getting rid of the troublemaker rather than of restoring him.

Church Management

The essence of the elder's function as an overseer is to see that the job gets done. That does not mean that he should do everything himself. Through the years, I have noted a succession of so-called managers who spend long hours in their offices pouring over every detail and trusting no one but themselves to make major decisions. I am not impressed by such persons, because I am not convinced that they spend their time wisely.

There are times when the pastor's schedule reaches almost unbelievable proportions. But usually when that happens, he himself is to blame because he has not apportioned his work properly or because he has not had the ability to say no to nonessential events and functions. There are times when circumstances defeat his best efforts to establish a normal life. However, such circumstances are far less frequent than many pastors are willing to admit. Although in the early part of his ministry a pastor is called upon to perform many services he deems undesirable or not the best use of his time, it is not the sign of good management if he continues to perform those functions permanently. The mark of a good manager is his ability to share the work, to equip others to take over certain duties, and to function as the inspirational part of a team effort. The manager who is constantly involved in petty details may impress people by how hard he works, but he certainly does not impress anyone by how skilled a manager he is. The pastor who is able to survive a long and successful ministry is one who is able to manage his time and talents appropriately. He schedules his day so that his time is spent reasonably, and he equips his people in the exercise of their ministry rather than working as a lone ranger. He sees the work of the ministry accomplished but does not feel that he has to do it all himself.

The Pastor As Shepherd

In closing this section, I want to speak to the kind of manager God wants His servant the pastor to be. God does not want the pastor to be the type of person who places unusual demands on his people, nor does he want him to be the type of person who gets impatient when someone makes a mistake. Instead, the Lord wants the pastor to be a loving shepherd who encourages his flock, helping them to get up when they fall down, and urging them on to greater accomplishment through his loving spirit when they fall short of their best. Instead of criticizing them and castigating them for their insufficiencies, the pastor after the Lord's heart tells his people what was good about what they did, and then he suggests constructive ways they can do even better. There is a great deal of difference between a shepherd who tries to whip the sheep into submission and the gentle encourager who leads the sheep into ever greater accomplishments. The latter is the kind of shepherd Jesus is to us and the kind He expects us, and undershepherds, to be to the rest of His sheep.

Questions for Discussion

1. What is the role of the pastor in planning and managing? What traits characterize a good manager?

2. What does it mean when we say that the pastor is to serve as a facilitator in the process of planning and managing the church's program and activities?

3. Why is it important to have a coordinated church calendar?

4. How may the church secretary serve as an administrative assistant to the pastor? What qualities should he or she possess in order to be successful?

5. How should the government of the church be organized? Do you agree with the author's viewpoint? What changes would you make in the way the church you attend is organized? Why?

6. What is the biblical pattern for church discipline? What is the purpose of church discipline? Give an example of how you would apply the process of church discipline in your church.

Helpful Resources

Church Administration: A Journal for Effectiveness in Ministry. Sunday School Board of the Southern Baptist Convention, 127 Ninth Ave. N., Nashville, Tenn. 37234.

Dayton, Edward R., and Ted W. Engstrom. *Strategy for Living: How to Make the Best Use of Your Time and Abilities.* Glendale, Calif.: Gospel Light, Regal, 1976.

Engstrom, Ted W., and Edward R. Dayton. *The Christian Executive.* Waco, Tex.: Word, 1979.

Gangel, Kenneth. *So You Want to Be a Leader.* Harrisburg, Penna.: Christian Publications, 1979.

Merrill, Dean. "Doing vs. Managing: The Eternal Tug of War." *Leadership* 3, no. 2 (Spring 1982):30-37.

Sanders, Oswald J. *Spiritual Leadership.* Chicago: Moody, 1974.

Schaller, Lyle E. *The Change Agent.* Nashville: Abingdon, 1972.

———. *Parish Planning.* Nashville: Abingdon, 1971.

23

Promoting Good Public Relations

For a number of years I have shopped at a major retail firm that has a liberal policy on returns. Of the hundreds of purchases I have made at their stores, on only a few occasions has it been necessary for me to return an item. When that happened, even though the item was used, if it had displeased me, the company—without hesitation—took immediate remedial steps, offering me the choice of a refund or a comparable item. The retailer believed that it was better to lose money on certain items occasionally in order to maintain good relationships with its customers.

Despite my satisfaction with that retailer, last Christmas an advertisement in the paper enticed me to try another store where a bicycle was on sale for an extremely good price. I purchased the bike for one of my children. It lasted only a week before major structural defects emerged. When I returned it to the store where I had purchased it, I found that the new company, in sharp contrast to my favorite company, had a very conservative return policy. Instead of refunding my money or offering me another bike, the store required me to take the bike to a repair point many miles from my home to see whose fault it was that the bike had failed. When I told the clerk that traveling the long distance to the repair point was inconvenient for me, the store offered to ship it there—at my expense, of course. I protested, but to no avail.

As I write this chapter, many weeks have passed. There is still a question as to who is going to pay for the repair of the bike. Regardless of who does, it is obvious to me that my child is stuck with a piece of merchandise that is inferior in quality. It is apparent, too, that although the second firm's return policy is more conservative than the first's, and though the second firm probably will save a few dollars on a broken bicycle, in a long run its policy will have cost it a great deal. Surely it has lost the income my patronage might have given it, and it has lost the business my recommendation might have brought it. I intend never to shop there again.

If good public relations is important to a retail firm that specializes in commodities people already think they must possess, how much more important is good public relations to the church, an institution that must prove its value to a skeptical world.

Christ's Command to Love One Another

What is the church's most valuable public relations principle? Jesus spells it out in John 13:35, where He says, "By this all men will know that you are My disciples, if you have love for one another." It is interesting to note that Jesus did not say that believers were to show love to non-Christians, as important as that is. Instead, He asserted that believers were to show love to fellow Christians. The early church practiced what Jesus taught. In modern terms, the love they had for one another was as impressive a means of good public relations as could be found. Indeed, that kind of love they exhibited was so attractive to nonbelievers that they gossiped about it in astonishment, telling one another how wonderful the love Christians had for each other was. As a result, in a world where the type of love the Christians had was unknown, unbelievers found the message it conveyed nearly irresistible. People came to the Lord by the thousands.

I have often speculated that if in our age non-Christians witnessed the same kind of conduct on the part of Christians, we might expect the kind of results the early church experienced. Undoubtedly a major public relations statement would be made by the church if its members began in earnest to behave in a loving manner toward one another.

The Pastor's Role

CARING FOR HIS FAMILY

The pastor, of course, is usually the key to developing such an attitude in a congregation. As in many other areas of concern, it is necessary for him to model the desired behavior. The beginning point for modeling is with his own family. If he is judged to be negligent of or rude to his family, he will be a negative model for his people and non-Christians also will take careful notice. He must be doggedly persistent in the pursuit of treating his family with care and consideration. Though he may do well 98 percent of the time, because of his position as a pastor, nonbelievers will be alert to any slip. They will be more impressed with the pastor's 2 percent rate of failure than with his 98 percent rate of success. The pastor, therefore, must be extremely careful when he deals with members of his family in public. That does not mean that his children should be undisciplined in public places. It means that the pastor should watch his temper and discipline his children rationally and quietly without a display of temper on his part. It means, also, that he and his wife should avoid arguing or airing their differences in public. The same principles of behavior apply, of course, to others in church leadership roles.

MEETING RESIDENTIAL NEIGHBORS

Though Christians may show a profound degree of love for one another, the presence of a church in a local community can be one of the community's best kept secrets unless the church finds ways to alert the population to its existence. How does a church make its presence known in a community? Whether a pastor likes to admit it or not, for a majority of persons, the pastor is the personification of the particular church he serves. Therefore, it will be valuable to the church and to him, if he establishes visibility within the community.

A good way for him to do so is to make certain strategic visits early in his pastorate. What do the neighbors think of the church? Visits to homes near the church property may reveal that the neighbors have no ideas concerning the church, that they view the church with some degree of approval, or that they are adverse to the church because of an action the church people took some years before. The pastor can get valuable ideas from the neighbors concerning the way the church can improve its public relations image in its own neighborhood. His visits may result in valuable support for the church when neighborhood backing is needed for property variances to put in a parking lot or to increase the size of the church building. More important, the visits will identify for the neighbors a person and a group of people upon whom they may feel comfortable to call in times of trouble.

SUPPORTING COMMERCIAL NEIGHBORS

In addition to visiting the residential neighbors, it is important for a pastor to visit the commercial neighbors. Nearby bankers, lawyers, and business people are important persons for a pastor to know, and it is good for them to become acquainted with the church in this manner. Some of them may come to the aid of the church in times of need. However, the relationship is a two-way street. If the church expects to receive support in the future, it is wise for the church to purchase supplies from neighboring businesses, to do its banking at a nearby bank, and to patronize, as much as possible, professionals in the neighborhood who offer services needed by the church. For example, if the church expects to receive free advertising in the local newspaper or to have free announcements read on local radio stations, it should be prepared to purchase commercial advertising with those media as well. It is wise for the pastor to deliver such paid advertising copy himself and to become acquainted with the people who control those media sources.

PARTICIPATING IN LOCAL ORGANIZATIONS

In the town in which he resides or in a nearby town there are likely to be prominent civic organizations such as Kiwanis or Rotary. In order for his church to become known in the area, it is helpful for the pastor to join one of those organizations. In other locations, a membership in a local athletic club may be helpful in getting acquainted with the community. If his convictions permit him to do so, it may be valuable to the pastor for him to join a local association of clergymen. In so doing, he will become aware of the religious picture in the area, and he will learn about resources outside his church that may benefit the program of his church. In addition, both he and his church will become better known in the religious community.

External Public Relations

NEWS MEDIA

One of the best ways a church can become known is through its special events, especially if they are newsworthy. Those events may include evangelistic crusades, special speakers, holiday events, missionary conferences, athletic events, film showings, banquets, award ceremonies, and anniversary celebrations. They may include events planned by church organizations, such as children's clubs, the women's missionary organization, or the youth group. Many times when information on church events reaches the media in a form that includes a special human-interest angle, editors are happy to feature the story free of charge.

Recently, in a town close to ours, three hundred volunteers from numerous churches in a particular denomination converged on a small sister church for a weekend and erected a complete church building. The local congregation paid for most of the materials. The rest were donated by interested friends. The sister churches supplied all of the labor and the building was dedicated debt free. The story made the front page of our newspaper and was shown on the newscasts of three nearby television stations.

Probably there are many stories of human interest that newspapers and radio and television stations would be happy to feature. The church itself needs to recognize the newsworthiness of those stories and report them promptly. In so doing a church that might have remained obscure can become well known in its community.

OUTDOOR SIGNS

Besides the use of the media, there are other effective ways to make a church visible within its community. One of these is to place a well-designed outdoor sign at a strategic place outside the church. The copy on the sign should be catchy, and it should be changed often. Caution should be observed to include items that will appeal to human interest and to state legibly the times of the major services. Additional care should be taken to make sure that the information on the board is current. Few things are as frustrating to visitors as to arrive at church at the time advertised on the church sign only to find that the hour of the service was changed but not the time listed on the sign. Many church growth experts think that if a church is visible from the road and strategically located, its most effective means of advertising, by far, is an outside sign or bulletin board, especially if the sign or board is attractive and kept up-to-date.

THE YELLOW PAGES

Probably the second most effective means of making a church known in a community is through an ad placed in the yellow pages of the telephone book. There is where most newcomers to a town look if they are at all interested in finding a church home.

BROCHURES AND BUSINESS CARDS

Other effective means of introducing the church are attractive, well-printed handouts describing the church and its ministry, and the business cards used by staff members. The church should take care to see that all publicity pieces are visually appealing and not too wordy.

Internal Public Relations

Along with external public relations devices, the church will find a number of internal devices helpful in promoting good public relations within the membership itself. In general, the rule of thumb is that the larger the church, the more redundancy in means of communication is necessary to keep its people informed of its activities. The means of communication can include the church bulletin and a church newsletter.

CHURCH BULLETIN

For the sake of visitors, the church bulletin should contain a complete, concise order of worship. When a visitor attends a church service, he should not have to be embarrassed by having to guess at anything. Every item of the worship service should be listed so that he knows what he is going to be called upon to do. The bulletin can contain a list of prayer concerns and a calendar for the week that lists pertinent church activities. The bulletin should be typed clearly, and it should be proofread by at least two people to catch misspellings or grammatical errors. If at all possible, the temptation to mimeograph or reproduce by ditto machine should be avoided. Money spent having the bulletin printed or having it reproduced by a high-quality copy machine is money well-spent. It tells the reader, "This is an important publication aimed at an important reader."

NEWSLETTER

With the exception of the order of worship, a church newsletter may contain many of the items of interest contained in the Sunday bulletin. In addition, newsworthy articles by members of the congregation, pointed cartoons, letters from missionaries, a note from the pastor, pertinent denominational news, and news about organizations within the church are among the items that may be added. The publication should be attractive and professional in appearance, and its contents should be positive and constructive. In such publications humor used appropriately will build up the reader's interest. The publication offers members of the congregation opportunities to discover skill in the graphic arts or in writing that can be employed to great advantage in promoting good public relations for the church. Also, through the newsletter, budding amateur photographers can begin to develop additional skills to be employed in the ministry of the church.

KEEPSAKES, BULLETIN BOARDS, AND CHURCH DIRECTORIES

Other effective means of internal public relations are handouts of lasting value, such as bookmarks and calendars, and various well-placed bulletin boards that carry church directories and various items of information. Church directories in book form containing pictures of church members are valuable in helping people get to know one another. Still another means of internal public relations is an extended calendar outlining church events over a long period of time.

SETTING UP A PUBLIC RELATIONS PROGRAM

When a pastor begins a new ministry, occasionally he will find in a church a well-organized group of people already engaging in a successful program of public relations. In that case, all he has to do is learn from them, share some of his ideas with them, and help replace them when they move out of the community or out of that particular church job. In most cases, however, he will find no such organization. He will be fortunate if there is even one person in the church who will type and reproduce the Sunday bulletin. In that situation everything he does will be an improvement, and he can assume that initially, at least, most of what is done, he himself will do.

If he is wise, he will identify those in his congregation who have writing, typing, and artistic skills, and who have initiative and imagination. He will disciple those people, confide his dreams to them, and encourage them as they begin, at first hesitantly and finally with confidence, to take over a most exciting and rewarding ministry of the church so that he may devote his time to other tasks. As important as public relations is, he must remind himself continually that he is called not only to the ministry but to equip and encourage others to engage in vital ministries of their own.

Questions for Discussion

1. Why is it important for a church to be concerned with good public relations?
2. What is the church's most valuable public relations principle?
3. What effect does the pastor's behavior and that of his family have on the public relations image of the church?
4. How may a church make its presence known in a community?
5. List specific ways the pastor and congregation can improve the public relations image of the church. Which of those are the respon-

sibility of the pastor? Which are the responsibility of the congregation?

6. What strategies would you employ in using the media as a vehicle for advertising the church?

7. What devices would you use to promote good public relations within the church? Why is it important that attention be given to this area?

Helpful Resources

Clark, Ida M. "Tips for Telling It Better Via the Church Newsletter." *Church Administration: A Journal for Effectiveness in Ministry* 24, no. 10 (July 1982):25.

Crockett, David W. *Promotion and Publicity for Churches.* Wilton, Conn.: Morehouse-Barlow, 1974.

Knight, George W. *How to Publish a Church Newsletter: An Illustrated Guide to First Class Editing, Design and Production.* Nashville: Broadman, 1983.

Reid, Russ. "Making the Media Work for the Local Church." *Leadership* 5, no. 1 (Winter 1984):30-32.

Sumrall, Velma, and Lucille Germany. *Telling the Story of the Local Church: The Who, What, When, Where and Why of Communication.* New York: Seabury, 1979.

24

Handling Correspondence

One of the most annoying experiences a pastor will have is facing the huge amount of mail with which he is inundated every day. Christian organizations and groups of all kinds and secular organizations, as well, constantly solicit support for their causes from the pastor. The temptation is to discard unopened most of the unsolicited mail.

Classes of Mail

JUNK MAIL

The only problem with discarding mail is that occasionally even junk mail contains interesting news items the pastor can use as sermon illustrations. Sometimes the information will pertain to particular areas of the world in which the church has missionaries. At other times a vital social issue may be explored. Many times the very magazine I intended to throw away unopened has provided an illustration that made a valuable contribution to my ministry by allowing me to comment in depth on a subject I really was not conversant about before. The trick is to learn to skim through materials quickly, discard what is not pertinent, and then abstract and file those items that might be helpful in the future.

Another kind of correspondence deserve a bit more attention because it is addressed personally to the pastor and is signed personally by the sender. The problem is it is often misaddressed. If any division of responsibility exists among the staff of the local church, much of the mail the senior pastor receives is actually intended for someone other than he. Yet in the eyes of the public—which does not understand the inner workings of the church—the responsible person to contact in any case regarding the church is the senior pastor. Though they may not know who else is on the staff, they do know about him. Thus whatever the appeal, they are likely to contact him. Moreover, even people who know there is a division of labor within the church often hesitate to address vital issues to assistants, on the assumption that if a person goes right to the head man he will have the best chance of getting some action.

Pastors of all people should do their best to practice proper etiquette. To do so brings honor to the Lord. If he receives a personal letter, the pastor should write a personal note in return, even when it is necessary for him to forward the letter he has received to someone else for appropriate action. Because the answering of letters is time-consuming, the pastor ought to compose a form letter, the substance of which may be retained in the computer or given to the secretary. As each inquiry of the type just mentioned arises, the form letter is made personal by the addition of the appropriate name and address, and it is typed anew. Its contents can be something like this:

> Dear _____ ,
> Thank you for your recent letter. I regret that I will not be able to handle this matter personally. In this church we are involved in a team ministry, and the team member responsible for this particular area is _____ . I have taken the liberty of forwarding your letter to him. You should hear from him shortly.
>
> Again, thank you for writing. May I extend to you a hearty invitation to worship with us when it is convenient for you to do so.
>
> Sincerely,
>
> Joe Fickle
> Senior Pastor

The original letter and a copy of the pastor's note is then forwarded to the appropriate church leader. It is now his responsibility to correspond with the inquirer.

Still another form of correspondence arrives all too frequently at the pastor's desk: personal letters that either extend an invitation to the pastor or ask him a question. Regardless of the topic or the question, etiquette demands that the pastor write a personal reply. If an invitation is extended, sometimes he may write a short note on the letter itself with a word of personal greeting and a short reply. At times the note may be as brief as this:

> Dear Paul,
> Thanks for inviting me. I'm swamped at present and just can't make it. Please ask me again.
>
> Sincerely,
>
> Joe

In some cases there is no easy way out. The pastor must "bite the bullet" and write as long a reply as the subject of the letter requires. In all cases, replies should be written promptly. Again, may I emphasize that pastors who do not answer their mail are guilty of crass rudeness. Such behavior is akin to saying to the correspondent, "I am important and my time is important, but you are not important enough for me to waste my time answering your letter." Perhaps more clergymen are guilty of this kind of rudeness than any other. That is why I am stressing the subject so much.

Letters the Secretary Signs

There is one other area of concern. If a pastor has a secretary, he should not delegate to him or her the task of signing his personal correspondence, except on rare occasions. If he will be out of town by the time the secretary gets the letter typed, he should include within his letter a statement reading something like this:

> By the time Anne gets this typed, I will be out of town. However, I didn't want to delay having my letter reach you. Please excuse the fact that Anne is signing it in my absence.

There are several reasons for a pastor's signing his own correspondence. One is a practical reason. The pastor, like other professionals, is subject to malpractice litigation. If the secretary misunderstands him and includes the wrong type of information or advice in a letter, the pastor can find himself in legal trouble. Even if no one sues him, a mistake in a letter may be a major source of embarrassment for the pastor.

The second reason for his signing letters is the fact that the clergyman who routinely leaves such details to his secretary is guilty of the kind of rudeness that says one of two things to the correspondent. Either it says, "Look, I'm trying to impress you with the fact that I have a secretary and she performs all these little perfunctory chores for me," or it says, "I'm sorry. You just aren't important enough for me to spend my time proofreading and signing my correspondence to you." Regardless of the thought behind the pastor's delay in writing, the receiver of the letter will be neither impressed nor pleased by such tactics. The pastor who signs his own correspondence personally demonstrates his respect for the persons to whom he writes, and he has the satisfaction of being able to double-check that the letters were transcribed accurately.

Letters That Ought Not to Be Written

Before closing this section of the chapter, perhaps it would be of value for me to recount something I have learned through personal experience. When I was younger, I had the habit of firing off angry letters of condemnation on matters of concern to me. Some of those letters were so fiery they should have been written on asbestos. Instead of making my point, they often alienated the recipient and made an enemy out of him. It took me years to realize that "a gentle answer turns away wrath" (Prov. 15:1). It was possible for me to express my concern in a kind, gentle, and positive way. In all cases, letters of mine that were kind but firm made much more impact than the literary tirades.

There is a second lesson to be learned concerning letters on sensitive subjects. In many instances, correspondence probably should be avoided entirely. On issues that are extremely controversial and that involve a serious difference of opinion between oneself and another person, personal contact is always the best approach, a telephone conversation is second best. Correspondence in these instances is third best but should be rational, polite, and objective. Accusations of all kinds should be avoided. The other person should always be given the benefit of the doubt. Two key sentences might be these: "Apparently there has been some misunderstanding on this issue. Could you clarify the matter for me?" In all cases, the contents of the letter should be such that the writer will not be embarrassed to read it two years later. A person's reputation may be damaged by his feisty letter writing—and the tragedy is that such letters may not even represent him accurately. They may simply reflect the fact that he has not yet learned to use written words in a gentle, Christlike manner.

Help with Spelling and Grammar

Some pastors have a terrible time with spelling and grammar. They should never allow anything to get out of their offices until it has been proofread by a grammarian. Inevitably letters with major mistakes in spelling and grammar create in the reader a poor impression of the writer. Surely God has placed within the body someone with gifts in this area. Your asking such a person to help you with your letter writing will be a profound example of the members of the Body of Christ working as a unit to accomplish the work Christ has for His church.

Questions for Discussion

1. What kinds of correspondence will you be required to handle as the pastor of a church?

2. What value is there in reading junk mail?

3. Think about the various types of formal correspondence you need to prepare as pastor. Compose form letters that can be used for some of that correspondence. Take special care with the form letters to recent visitors, to those who have suffered bereavement, or to the parents of a new baby.

4. Why should a pastor sign his own letters?

5. If a pastor absolutely must send someone a letter of condemnation, what principles should guide him as he writes? What steps can be taken in lieu of writing?

Helpful Resources

Adams, Walter H. *Church Administration: A Handbook for Church Leaders.* Austin, Tex.: Firm Foundation Publishing House, 1979.

Anderson, James, and Ezra E. Jones. *The Management of Ministry.* New York: Harper & Row, 1978.

Lindgren, Alvin and Norman L. Sawchuck, *Management for Your Church: How to Realize Your Church Potential Through Systems Approach.* Nashville: Abingdon, 1977.

25

Conducting Church Business Meetings

How should the pastor run a church business meeting? The answer, of course, is that he should not.

There are several good reasons for that. One is that when items of business are presented to the congregation, it should not appear that they are necessarily the ideas of the pastor or that he is attempting to railroad his ideas into adoption. Another reason for having someone else lead a business meeting is that it propels a layman rather than the pastor into the limelight and gives the lay leader an aura of credibility and authority before the people that will aid him in being a part of the leadership team. Also, if the pastor is in the audience during a business meeting, he will not immediately be identified with the conflict, should the discussion heat up. As the discussion moves back and forth the pastor can collect his thoughts and, if necessary, step in to steer the discussion toward a more reasoned, peaceful, and on-target dialogue. There will be times in a business meeting when the disparity of opinion is so great the pastor, as mediator, may need to suggest that the church delay action on the issue in question. If he were also leading the meeting it would be difficult for him to exert a moderating influence.

Besides being a mediator, the pastor may have a great impact on the church business meeting through the help he provides the moderator of such meetings. In churches I have pastored, there has been little need for me to supply such help. However, I realize that throughout my own pastorates I have been unusually blessed with a corps of lay people such as few pastors know. The persons leading business meetings in those churches have been bright, articulate, and well-organized; they have known exactly what agenda items needed to be considered, and they were able to move the discussion along at a reasonable rate. Having been a member of other churches, I know that that is not always the case. The pastor often must provide much help to the layperson leading the business meeting.

When some of my own children have had to sit through a typical business meeting, they have remarked, "Dad, church business meetings must have been invented by a sadist. How much torture is a person expected to endure?" The pastor can help change that. Church business meetings do not have to reflect the philosophy of the Marquis de Sade. With the correct organizational structure, a carefully prepared agenda, and a leader who has been briefed by the pastor on a few vital techniques, the meeting can be sweet, relatively short, and even—at times—a blessed experience.

Running the Meeting

Policy, Not Minutiae, Should Be Taken Up

Organizational structure is of utmost importance. It is said that in ancient Athens the people practiced what we would call pure democracy. Meetings were almost a constant occurrence, and the people themselves voted on every minute issue. In our society we do not have the time or patience for that type of democracy. Even if we had the time or patience to attempt to run the country on the Athenian model, we could not succeed: the country is too large, the government is too big, and the issues at hand are too complex. Only in the local church, it would seem, is pure democracy still possible. However, in congregations where it is practiced and where frequent business meetings are called to discuss and vote on minuscule matters, often an aura of frustration, dissension, and division is evident.

How strange that is. Many local churches select competent businessmen to carry on the financial matters of the church. In the secular world those men have authority to spend hundreds of thousands of dollars. The church places them in a supposedly responsible position and then makes them seek board or congregational approval for every expenditure exceeding fifty dollars. Thus, responsible, creative men who could be leading the church in constructive pursuits, must spend their time in endless meetings discussing trivia. Is it any wonder that many competent people refuse to hold leadership positions in the churches?

The organizational structure should be so constructed that when a person is given responsibility he is also granted commensurate authority to carry out that responsibility. For instance, the deacon responsible for property should not have to call a board meeting or go before the church for permission to replace a faulty valve in a toilet in the ladies' room. He should be given authority to make decisions and authorize expenditures up to a reasonable amount established by the church. Likewise, the Sunday school superintendant should not have to seek permission of the Christian education board or committee to purchase crayons and scissors. If it is within his budget and the money is available, he should be allowed to make the expenditure.

On items requiring a large amount of money, board, or even church approval may be necessary, but that should be the exception rather than the rule. If the church roof is leaking, if it can be repaired within budgetary limits, and if the money is available, the deacon in charge of property should be able to authorize the repair. However, if a new roof is needed, that may require a major expenditure not anticipated in the church budget. Congregational approval will probably be needed. The major point here is that the church should set reasonable parameters within which decisions may be made by responsible people, thus avoiding a crowded agenda and frequent business meetings.

FLEXIBILITY SHOULD BE THE RULE IN SCHEDULING MEETINGS

How often should a business meeting be called? Many churches choose to do so once a quarter. However, the constitution should stipulate that if there is no important business to be brought before the congregation the "quarterly business meeting" can be conducted through printed report of the "state of the church." The report could be distributed among the membership for informational purposes. To attempt to hold a quarterly business meeting in the summer months, for instance, usually is folly unless pressing business matters need to be considered. One of the quarterly business meetings can serve as the annual meeting of the church. In most states an annual meeting is required, by law, of every corporation—profit or non-profit—operating within the state.

Planning the Meeting

PREPARE THE CONGREGATION FOR THE ISSUES COMING UP

In planning for any business meeting, several important factors should be kept in mind. The first is that all crucial and potentially volatile issues should be presented to the people many weeks ahead of time for their discussion. If the particular issue is controversial enough, special meetings should be held well before the actual business meeting, where the leaders can explain to the rest of the church, in a careful, logical way, why the action is being proposed. If the leadership discerns that a consensus in favor of the issue has not developed, it should cancel the business meeting or remove the offending item from the agenda of the meeting, so that the congregation will have more time to think about and discuss the matter more fully.

The annual budget should be worked on as many months ahead of time as possible on the basis of projections made from the current budget. If necessary, a special meeting should be called prior to the annual meeting for the purpose of discussing the budget.

What I am insisting is that no item on the agenda of a business meeting should be a surprise to the people. Each issue should have been debated ahead of time so that the business meeting itself is a time for the taking of votes and acting on items of business in an efficient manner.

SEE THAT PROPER BUSINESS PROCEDURES ARE FOLLOWED

To facilitate orderly meetings, whoever moderates the meeting should become familiar with *Robert's Rules of Order.* The procedures in that little book need not be adhered to slavishly, because most churches are somewhat more relaxed than the organizations in mind in *Robert's.* Nevertheless, the Bible calls for the church to conduct its affairs "decently and in order," and at least some of the procedures in *Robert's* should be followed by the local congregation.

It is wise for the pastor to be familiar with proper business proceedings himself, not actually to chair business meetings but to aid others in doing so. In some churches skilled leaders and parliamentarians are able to move a business meeting along so smoothly that the wise pastor stays out of the way, observes, and learns. In other churches, the leadership needs to be discipled in this area. At times the pastor and his layman will be learning together. In such cases, it will be helpful for the pair to read and discuss the procedures outlined in *Robert's* and to observe such rules in action. The meeting of the local city council or the annual denominational gathering may be valuable places of observation. A visit to the business meeting of another church may be helpful, too. If this is done, however, it is courteous to call ahead, explain the situation, and request permission of the pastor of the other congregation.

SUSPEND BUSINESS TEMPORARILY IF TEMPERS RISE

Even though the best possible plans are made and the most appropriate procedures are followed, from time to time a tense moment will arise in business meetings and tempers will flare. A skilled moderator should sense what is happening and suspend business temporarily while the congregation has a chance to stand, perhaps sing a song, or even to take a short recess. Should tensions continue to mount, and the assembly is clearly not of one mind the moderator should call for prayer. If, after considerable time in prayer, the tension still is not resolved, it is wise to call for the tabling of the offending issue or to dismiss the meeting to reconvene at another time. During the interim period the leadership can hear out those in the congregation who still are angry and perhaps alleviate their concerns. If a member continually brings strife and disruption to business meetings, he should be admonished by the leadership, and, if necessary, he should be disciplined according to the guidelines contained in Matthew 18.

PLAN THE AGENDA WITH HUMAN NEEDS IN MIND

Rather than beginning a business meeting abruptly, it is better to start with a stirring hymn, prayers by several godly leaders, and—perhaps—an inspirational message in music by a skilled musician. If it appears that the meeting will last well over an hour, it is good to plan a recess so that people can stretch and refresh themselves. After the reading of the minutes and other perfunctory chores, important issues should be taken up early in the meeting so that the people can discuss them while their minds are still fresh. Routine matters should be relegated to later in the meeting. When a financial report is given, it is important for the people to have a printed copy of that report in hand. Also, it is wise to have the figures printed on a transparency and projected on a screen. If that is done, the person using the transparency should have ascertained before the meeting that the smallest letters and figures are visible from the last row of seats. Otherwise the transparency should not be used.

Recently churches have found that a wonderful addition to their church business meeting is to project color slides taken of the various church activities during the year. Thus, when the report of a particular committee is given, the members of the church will see not only pictures of people working in that program but also will see pictures of those benefiting from the program. Pictures of people in action will bring back happy memories of the events for those who participated and will portray to others the effective ministry the church is having in the lives of people.

REMEMBER THE VALUE OF BREVITY AND RELEVANCE

In planning the agenda for a business meeting, the moderator should make certain that no matter is brought before the congregation that can be settled properly and amicably at a lower level. If there are reports to be given, they should be presented to the congregation well ahead of time in printed form. During the meeting itself, reporters should be held to presenting a short, succinct summary of their written report. As the moderator and the pastor work together ahead of time with them, those giving reports will learn to abbreviate their remarks and yet tell the important details of the story.

END ON A SWEET NOTE

It is always good to end a lengthy business meeting on a sweet note. Refreshments such as pie or homemade ice cream are always incentive enough to keep many people at the meeting until the last item of business has been discussed. The fellowship following a business meeting also helps to make the occasion pleasant and memorable. When any event ends with a time of meaningful fellowship among Christians, nothing could be better.

Questions for Discussion

1. What role should the pastor play in the church business meeting?
2. What are the arguments for and against the pastor's participating in the church business meeting as moderator or chairman?
3. Think back on your church's recent business meeting. What were the vital elements of the business meetings that were successful? What can you do to make your church's business meetings more successful? What can you do to see to it that the business meeting is not unnecessarily long or characterized by conflict and unrest?
4. If you were the pastor of a church, would you have business meetings only as often as required by law or would you meet more often?
5. Describe procedures the moderator can use to handle controversial or potentially volatile issues. Suppose you were sitting in on a

business meeting in which tempers began to flare. How would you handle the situation?

A Helpful Resource

Roberts, General Robert H. *Robert's Rules of Order.* Reprint. Old Tappan, N.J.: Revell, 1983.

26

Supporting Christian Education

Recently a pastor friend of mine was bemoaning the fact that the program of Christian education in his church was a disaster. As he described the symptoms, the answer became obvious to me. "Why don't you conduct a teacher-training program?" I asked. He replied, "I would have to take one before I could conduct one."

He then told me that the seminary from which he had graduated placed a heavy emphasis on the learning of biblical languages and exegetical skills, but the students considered Christian education a kind of joke. He had slept his way through a boring required course in the history and philosophy of Christian education, figuring that he would never need that information in the parish. As a result, he chose other than Christian education courses for his electives, never pausing to learn anything about learning theory or methods of teaching and learning. Subsequently, although he envisioned himself a Bible teacher, he was able to teach only through the methods he had observed in those who had taught him. If he had been asked to use a means other than lecture or large group discussion, he would have been at a loss.

The Value of Christian Education Courses

May I make clear to the reader of this book: *Christian education courses are not an unnecessary luxury in seminary. They may well be the courses that give the student survival strategies for the pas-*

torate. Once again we are attacking the prevalent fallacy that if a person is able to excel in pulpit oratory or is a gifted expositor, he will succeed in the pastorate. That philosophy is taught by those who have no real concept of what the pastorate is all about or who have a limited view of the church, having been exposed only to atypical situations. Although there is a trend towards specialization in every other facet of life, the pastor of a local church cannot be a specialist.

It has been reported that 95 percent of North America's churches consist of two hundred fifty members or less. Many of those churches are struggling hard to support even one staff member. A majority of the churches are filled with lay people who have not been equipped properly for the work of the ministry. The novice pastor will find that the church he serves, rather than needing a specialist, more than likely needs a general practitioner who can carry on the many phases of the ministry at the same time he equips others to join him. If he is committed to a superior Christian education program, he will find that he is the one who must equip others in this vital area of the church's ministry whether he wants to or not.

The Importance of Christian Education

Why is Christian education—or church education, as many people are labeling it today—so important? After all, many churches do not consider it important. They say that the principal teaching ministry should occur in the pulpit. Everything else is supplementary. They say also that it is wrong for the Sunday school to have usurped the responsibility of Christian parents to train their children in the things of the Lord. To an extent I would agree with them—but not entirely, for there are significant questions they are not able to answer.

FILLS NEEDS NOT MET BY THE SERMON

For one thing, educators tell us that the people in any given group will be in differing stages of personal development. It is arrogant and foolish for any pastor to insist that all of his people fully understand all of his sermon, or to insist that they survive on its contents each week as their sole spiritual food. No sermon is able to do that. Even for adults, there needs to be a variety of educational experiences each week. In the case of children, Piaget and others have been helpful in telling us that children are not able to reason in abstract terms until they reach a certain developmental phase in their lives.

Because the pulpit ministry is primarily abstract and directed mainly to adults, it is an exercise in futility, and will alienate children from the church, to force them to sit through long sermons. Sunday school and junior church are not babysitting ventures but are vital parts of the Christian education of a child. They should present truths in a setting the child is comfortable with, and they should use methods appropriate to the child's learning abilities and interests.

INSTRUCTS WHERE PARENTS CANNOT

Now, let us consider the question of the church's usurping the responsibility of Christian parents to train their children in the things of the Lord. The fact is that the job simply is not getting done. First, Christian parents have not been taught how to give the necessary training. Second, many parents are not mature enough in their own spiritual lives to be sufficiently motivated to do the job. Third, in our day the phenomenon of the stable, two-parent Christian household is becoming increasingly rare. A great many of the children the church ministers to are living in situations other than the traditional one. Although solid Christian teaching is sometimes offered by the parents of those children, that is probably the exception rather than the rule.

Even in a household where there is a stable family situation and the parents strive faithfully to teach their children spiritual values, the church should not bow out of the job. It should consider itself a rich resource for reinforcing and solidifying the teaching the children receive at home. The reinforcement of spiritual values by persons other than the parents will have value in itself.

Components of a Successful Christian Education Program

Having then advanced the view that the church ought to have a Christian education program of superior quality for persons of all ages, it is logical to ask, What components are necessary to bring that about?

GOOD TEACHING

The first necessary component is good teaching. The question has often been raised as to whether good teachers are born or made. The answer is both. It is interesting to note that those who are "made" teachers, those who train to become teachers and even teach in the public school system, are not always the best teachers in the ministry of the church. Just because a person has trained for a specific voca-

tion and is proficient in the use of its tools does not necessarily mean
he has a spiritual gift in that area. In order to become maximally
effective in the work of the church, a person should be exercising a
spiritual gift. Though a professional teacher may have teaching
skills, if he does not have the gift of teaching, he will not be the best
teacher in the education program of the church.

Conversely, if a person given the gift of teaching by the Holy Spirit
never develops or refines that gift, he will never effectively exercise
it. It is the task of the church to identify people who have potential
giftedness in the area of teaching and aid those people in developing
their gift. In training people for teaching roles in the church, it will
be helpful if the pastor has the gift himself and is able to share his
teaching skills with others who may have the gift.

Therefore, he ought to prepare himself in several ways to be a
teacher of teachers. First, he should take as many Christian education courses as possible while he is in Bible college or seminary.
Especially helpful are those courses specializing in methods of teaching and learning. If he does not have the opportunity to take such
courses before he graduates, he would be wise to return to his school
after graduation to complete them.

Second, he should arrange to serve a teaching apprenticeship under
an experienced teacher so that he can learn from observing a master
teacher in action and from having that teacher observe him. An
essential part of my seminary training was a practicum course where
I was required to teach two days a week in a Christian preschool. I
probably learned more about teaching methods in that course than in
all my previous studies.

Third, if he is truly interested in improving the Christian education programs of the churches he will serve, the pastor should gain
experience in teaching at different age levels in the Sunday school so
that he can observe firsthand what methods work best for what ages.

Fourth, the pastor should avail himself of every Christian education seminar he can attend until he becomes proficient in Christian
education skills and knowledge. Even after he becomes an expert, he
should attend seminars and workshops from time to time so that he
keeps his knowledge and skills up-to-date.

Once he has gained the knowledge and skills he needs, the pastor
may choose to train teachers himself, to select other people to train
them, or to engage in a combination of the two methods. If he lives
close to a Bible college or seminary, he can arrange with his church to
send prospective teachers in the church to courses the schools offer.
If the church is able to hire, part-time or full-time, a competent,
experienced minister of Christian education, the senior pastor

should turn the major responsibility for teacher-training over to him. Or it may be feasible for a small church to "borrow" a Christian education specialist from a larger church to aid the smaller church in training its teachers. Yet even that arrangement may not be possible. For a good portion of my years in the ministry I have been located in places where I was the sole source of Christian education expertise. At those times I was especially grateful for the knowledge I had gained through my studies and experience.

In the event that a pastor has to train his own teachers, where does he start? Fortunately there are many materials on the market that will be helpful to him.

Filmstrips, especially, are abundant, and they are well-constructed tools for the purpose. For a number of years I have found that the "Successful Teaching" series produced by the Moody Institute of Science (Whittier, California) is extremely valuable in the training of teachers. In addition, the International Center for Learning, a subsidiary of Gospel Light Publications, has produced a number of excellent filmstrips geared to the different age groups in the Sunday school. Accompanying the filmstrips are well-written books discussing in detail the characteristics of the particular age group being considered and focusing on ways to help the student learn. An older, now out-of-print filmstrip series produced by Scripture Press, "Royal Commission," is often available from filmstrip rental sources. Though the pictures are dated, the material is good.

Increasingly, videotapes are being used for training Sunday school teachers. James Dobson's tape on discipline in the classroom, a series of eight teacher-training tapes produced recently by Lowell Brown, and videotaped courses produced by Western Conservative Baptist Seminary in Portland are all marvelous tools for the pastor-trainer.

Once a teacher-trainee has successfully completed a basic training course, he or she should be assigned to an experienced teacher for an internship program. In churches where such master teachers are not available, the pastor himself may need to be a model, or he can set up a teacher-training program in conjunction with a church that has master teachers who serve as models and supervisors. However a pastor goes about training master teachers, once they are on the job they can take over the task of discipling interns and of conducting the church's teacher-training course.

In one church I pastored I got the Christian education board to agree that every prospective teacher had to receive training before being given a teaching position. Next, a rule was passed requiring existing teachers to observe a sabbatical quarter after teaching a certain amount of time. During the sabbatical, they had to complete the teacher training course successfully. At the end of the course they were evaluated as to whether or not they could return to a class as teacher. Before we began the teacher-training series we were always having difficulty finding teachers. As the course began to be conducted on a regular basis, we developed a surplus of trained teachers. Prospective teachers went on a waiting list, and we were able to choose from the best. Even if the person being considered was a teacher in the public school system, he was required to complete our teacher-training course, so that we could evaluate more carefully whether or not he or she was gifted by the Holy Spirit for teaching.

RECEPTIVE LEARNERS

The second ingredient in good teaching is receptive learners. In large part, the receptivity of a particular learner will depend on the skills of his teacher. However, that is not always the case. There are children who for physical or emotional reasons are extremely difficult to control in the classroom. For that and many other reasons, it is important that no teacher be required to work alone. In every case a team of two or more teachers should work together, sharing the teaching hour and using complementary skills. While one teacher is actively engaged in teaching, another teacher can focus his attention upon a potential troublemaker.

There have been times in my experience when one child or a group of children were impossible to handle until we added a tough but loving man to the staff. Disciplinary problems usually ceased immediately. If a child insists on being disruptive and cannot be controlled, his parent should be required to attend class with him or he should be expelled from Sunday school.

The wise pastor will not do the expelling himself. If an expulsion is made, it should not be a surprise to a parent. Conduct reports citing the offending action should precede such drastic action. Many times the church is reluctant to expel a child from Sunday school because it is afraid the action will offend someone and cause him to leave. Even if that happens, it is far better than allowing a child to continue to disturb the other children and the teachers. In the case of Christian parents who do not take action to bring the child under proper discipline and then make trouble in the church when their child is expelled, I believe the parents themselves are fitting subjects for disciplinary action under the provisions of Matthew 18. Clearly they are sinning in not following biblical principles in bringing up their child. Likewise by defending him when his behavior is clearly unacceptable, they are not showing him a proper biblical example.

Still another factor needs to be discussed. In order to carry on a really successful program of Christian education, suitable curriculum is a necessity. Where does one find a curriculum that fits the particular needs of a particular local church? The answer is, of course, that such a curriculum does not exist. It does not exist because Christian education materials are extremely expensive to produce. To produce them at all, curriculum firms must appeal to a variety of needs and a broad spectrum of churches. They cannot build any denominational distinctiveness into the material.

The mistake many churches make is to receive these materials exactly as they are and not even try to adapt any of them to the particular needs the church has. Thus, Sunday schools become franchise outlets instead of originals. Sometimes the content of the curriculum speaks to the particular educational needs of the church; sometimes it does not. Nevertheless, the church maintains a faithful schedule, quarter-by-quarter purchasing the same material and using it unthinkingly in its educational program. It rarely supplements the material with anything distinctive to its denomination. And what is the result? The church produces franchise Christians who give little evidence of belonging to a church in any way different from any other church. If the members are questioned as to the doctrinal and methodological distinctives of their own denomination, they cannot pass the test.

The Pastor's Role in Selecting Curriculum Materials

Where does the pastor fit into the picture? Up to this point we have spoken of his heavy involvement in the training of teachers for the church. He may have to take on such training early in his ministry because excellence in teaching is so important to the church. Likewise, early in his ministry, before he gets bogged down in other tasks, he should work with the people who are involved actively in the Christian education program to set up curricular goals, examine existing brands of curriculum, and—along with the teachers who will use the curriculum—choose materials that will help the Church meet its specific educational goals. That may mean purchasing materials from one curriculum source or from several. It is probable that the church will need to supplement the material with denominational publications. In many cases, it will need to ask someone to write additional curriculum materials. The latter, however, is an extremely difficult task and neither the pastor nor any of his members should attempt to do it unless they are experienced in the field of Christian education, understand in detail the characteristics and needs of the age group for which they are writing materials, and are absolutely positive there are no commercially-produced materials the church can adapt to meet its goals.

If he is fortunate enough to have a full-time minister of Christian education, the pastor should do his best to see that the minister of Christian education does not waste his time and talents on such perfunctory tasks as ordering supplies and staffing classes. That kind of activity is ideal for the volunteer, lay Sunday school superintendent. The principal tasks of the minister of Christian education should be the training of teachers and the selecting and writing of curriculum.

What about the many churches that do not have a minister of Christian education? In them a large part of the task will fall to the pastor. It is a most important task and requires quality and a positive attitude on his part, but the results will be worth it. A superior Christian education program may be one of the church's most important assets.

The pastor should not consider running the Christian education program a task he will need to perform forever. As is the case with many other jobs, it can be given to other people in the church as the pastor disciples them. Gradually he can work himself out of his Christian education job, being available then only to provide general direction while qualified saints carry on the work of the ministry in this vital area.

Questions for Discussion

1. Discuss why Christian education or church education, as many people are labeling it today, is so important.

2. Why is it not possible for the pulpit ministry to meet all of the educational needs of the people in the church?

3. How would you answer those who say that the Sunday school is usurping the responsibility of Christian parents to train their own children?

4. What components are necessary for the church to develop a superior program of Christian education for all ages?

5. Review suggestions made in the chapter of ways a pastor can prepare himself to lead an effective Christian education program. What strategies do you plan to employ in being an effective supporter of the Christian education program of your church?

6. What can the pastor do to train his own teachers? What outside resources are available to him?

7. What can the pastor do to see to it that his teachers have receptive learners?

8. How important is curriculum to a successful Christian education program? What suggestions would you make to the pastor or teacher who wishes to write his or her own curriculum?

Helpful Resources

Brown, Lowell, comp., and Frances Blankenbaker, ed. *Christian Educator's Manual.* Glendale Calif.: Gospel Light, 1979.

Brown, Lowell. *Sunday School Standards.* Glendale Calif.: Gospel Light, 1980.

International Center for Learning. *Teacher Training Manual: A Manual for Providing Ongoing Pre-service and In-service Training in Any Size Sunday School.* Glendale Calif.: Gospel Light, 1982.

Kilinski, Kenneth K. and Jerry C. Wofford. *Organization and Leadership in the Local Church.* Grand Rapids: Zondervan, 1973.

Leypoldt, Martha. *Learning Is Change.* Valley Forge, Pa.: Judson, 1971.

McDonough, Reginald M. *Working with Volunteers in the Church.* Nashville: Broadman, 1976.

Richards, Lawrence O. *A Theology of Christian Education.* Grand Rapids: Zondervan, 1975.

Rogers, Charles A. *Recruit . . . Train . . . Plan . . . Building a Christian Education Staff.* Glendale, Calif.: Gospel Light, Regal, 1979.

Stewart, Ed. *How People Learn: Guidelines for Bible Teaching.* Glendale, Calif.: Gospel Light, Regal, 1978.

Wilbert, Warren N. *Teaching Christian Adults.* Grand Rapids: Baker, 1980.

Zuck, Roy B., and Gene A. Getz. *Adult Education in the Church.* Chicago: Moody, 1970.

Zuck, Roy B., and Robert E. Clark. *Childhood Education in the Church.* Chicago: Moody, 1975.

27

Aiding the Youth Ministries

Youth ministries can be the most rewarding or the most frustrating facets of the church's program. In many churches, as soon as sufficient financial support is available, the first staff member added after the pastor will be the minister of youth.

Crisis over Church Youth

Many times the minister of youth is hired when the church is in a state of panic. No one in the church knows what to do with teenage kids. The parents have exhausted their resources and many of them have had to admit that their efforts have not been successful. The young pastor, steeped in lofty theological concepts, thanks to his extensive training, has become accustomed to older people and more mature ideas than teenagers are capable of handling. Often he has far outpaced his own teenage years and no longer has much tolerance for the immaturity and childish behavior he sees in teenagers. Because he has not reached the point in life where he has teenagers of his own, he probably does not understand teenagers, nor does he care to. Therefore, his attitude toward them often is, "I wish that these kids would get on the ball spiritually, clean up their act, and begin to act maturely."

In actuality, he is asking for the young people to deny their youth and act as adults, a demand that puts the young people in an impossible position. Were they to emulate the behavior of the somber Christian adults sometimes held up as their models and refrain from the spontaneity and silliness characteristic of teenagers, their peers would ostracize them. Yet when they mimic adult sophistication, adults may refuse to take them and their ideas seriously. They are, after all, "just kids," and what do kids know about life?

Perhaps I have cast the young pastor in the wrong light. Undoubtedly there are many pastors who have kept close to the teenage scene during the period of their theological education. However, those are rare. Recently, as a member of a camp board, I looked in on a high school camp. The speaker had been well known as a youth leader before he went to seminary. For that reason he was chosen as a speaker for the camp. As I listened to him, it was obvious that his seminary education had been a real handicap to him as far as youth work was concerned. He was having extreme difficulty communicating with the high-schoolers. The concepts he was preaching were so involved theologically they were not even interesting to me, much less intelligible to the teenagers who had to listen to him.

Frequently a church hires a young pastor fresh out of seminary because it believes that, along with his other attributes, he will be successful with youth. In reality, he is often the poorest choice of a person to work with youth. A younger person who has not been steeped in theological jargon or an older person who has or has had teenagers of his own would be far better. One of the most successful youth pastors I have known reached his peak in youth work at age fifty-five.

Back to the problem of our typical church. The young pastor the church called was not the answer to the youth problem that the church anticipated. Yet it is too early for them to expect him to leave—so what does the church do? It is obvious that families in the church are still suffering because of problems they are having with their young people. The public school certainly has not helped the situation. Even placing the children in Christian schools has not resulted in much improvement in their behavior and attitudes. The only agency left is the church—but because the pastor is of little help, the parents think there is nothing left for the church to do but to "trust God to supply the money" and launch out into a program they hope will reclaim their errant youth and keep the rest from going astray. The church decides to hire a youth pastor. The decision is justified on the basis that "after all, the youth are the future of the church."

Statistics show that youth are not the future of the church. In this age of excessive mobility a majority will leave and establish residence elsewhere. Evangelism is the real future of any church. Although youth problems call attention to themselves, youth ministries are not the highest priority of the church, and only rarely should the second staff member hired be a youth pastor. Nevertheless a church does have a responsibility towards its youth and it is appropriate for the pastor to help the church respond to that responsibility.

The Key Ingredient: Caring Adults

What should be the pastor's attitude toward youth ministry, and what should be his role in supporting it? The first thing he can do is to spend time with teenagers in a nonthreatening environment, to find out about their needs and to analyze how their behavior is related to meeting those needs. There are a number of good books and films that will be helpful to the pastor as he attempts his analysis.

Second, the pastor should learn how to relate to youth as persons who have worthwhile thoughts and valid things to say, even though their actions may seem strange to adults. Third, he should identify adults in his congregation who understand teenagers and who will agree to receive the training they need to give them the skills to begin and direct a worthwhile youth program. Sometimes the pastor will have to lure adults out of prominent positions in the church so that they will be free to devote the amount of energy needed to make a youth ministry a success. The key ingredient to a successful youth ministry is not curriculum or program but adults who are able to establish a meaningful relationship with teenagers.

Meeting the Needs of Teenagers

Know What's on Their Minds

As the program is formed, the pastor should understand that, by and large, teenage youth are not fit recipients for obscure theological discourse. There are more pressing matters competing for their attention. They include the following:

1. Coping with physical growth
2. Intellectual maturation
3. Growing in independence and responsibility
4. Forming an identity
5. Developing in sexuality
6. Experiencing new emotional stimuli and mixed feelings
7. Facing new values

8. Reordering family relationships
9. Responding to society
10. Responding to God[1]

BUILD SOLID RELATIONSHIPS

Those of my children who already have passed through their teenage years tell me that it is difficult and sometimes frightening to be a teenager, even under the most ideal of home situations. The curriculum for teenagers, therefore, should speak to their needs. The problem is that they may never express their needs until they learn to trust their adult sponsors. For this reason, a program for teens should start out casually and relationally. Later on there will be plenty of time for content when that content arises naturally out of the questions the teens ask.

MAKE THE SUNDAY SCHOOL CLASS THE CORE

The core around which activities for teens should be organized is the Sunday school class. The persons who teach that class should be the ones who lead the teens in social events. At least at first, the Sunday school class should be conducted in a low key manner. Although there is an hour or so to fill, perhaps a good part of that hour should be spent in athletic activities or even in eating hamburgers and drinking Cokes at a nearby fast-food restaurant. Discipline should be permissive and casual. The sponsor should treat the teens as adults as much as possible, bringing horseplay to a halt only when it gets unruly, ends up injuring people, or makes a disturbance for others. Young people should be allowed the exuberance of being young and of being loud, as long as such behavior does not injure or disturb others.

HOLD SOCIAL EVENTS FREQUENTLY

Social events should be held often and should consist of the things the teens express an interest in doing, not necessarily the things the sponsors enjoyed when they were young. Activities of a past generation should not be discarded automatically, however. Sometimes they are unique to a teenager who has not experienced them before. A moonlight cruise or an old fashioned hayride may be sufficiently novel to receive their enthusiastic support.

1. From Merton P. Strommen, *Five Cries of Youth* (New York, Harper & Row, 1974).

BE TOLERANT OF THEIR MUSIC

If adults are going to relate to teenagers, one thing they must learn to do is to tolerate their music. That does not mean that the adult has to enjoy or appreciate it. Another chapter in this book considers in detail the problem each succeeding generation has with the music of the generation following it. The youth sponsor may have firm convictions against the particular style of the music the young people listen to. He may believe even that it is sinful. Surely he will be able to substantiate his convictions by referring to some of the lyrics of the songs, just as my parents did with the songs of my generation. But the sponsor will soon realize that he must reach the teen where he is, even though he may not appreciate where the teen is. The sponsor will find, further, that as the teen matures spiritually he will become more discerning in his choice of music, although the sponsor may never see him abandon the objectionable music altogether.

ENCOURAGE RESPONSIBILITY

I have already intimated that a successful youth program is built primarily upon relationships, the chief of which is the relationship between the teen and his sponsor. I have stated further that those relationships are enhanced by a low-key teaching approach, a variety of fun activities, and a disciplinary approach that is permissive, unless the teen's activities injure others or disturb them seriously.

However, all of the activities I have named do not necessarily build maturity in the teen. In order to accomplish that goal, methods need to be adopted that are fun for the teen but still require him to exercise responsibility. Some youth sponsors have discipling programs in which teens who demonstrate a responsible action are asked to disciple other teens. Other youth sponsors have developed singing groups that give teens the opportunity to sing for other teens and for adults and the opportunity to prepare and deliver brief testimonies. The responsibilities such singing groups place on the teenagers in them often results in their demonstrating responsibility in the whole range of their activities.

Athletics is also a helpful means of involving teenagers. Before events, teams gather to pray, and often during halftime they give their testimonies. A side benefit of using athletics as a means of developing responsibility is that simply by playing the game in a sportsmanlike manner they have the opportunity to back up their verbal testimonies. Still other teens will agree to help lead Bible studies for their peers. In having to prepare in this manner, often a young person will become much more conversant with the Word than if he were merely a student in a Bible study group.

In all his planning the sponsor should be cautioned that just as athletic teams are not for everyone, so, too, musical groups or Bible study groups may not be for everyone. Any youth sponsor who builds his entire program on only one activity will necessarily exclude a great many teens who have other preferences. It is good for a program to be varied.

Reaching Unchurched Teens

What if a church wants to set up a program for unchurched teens? If that is its desire, it probably should set up an entirely separate program for those young people and staff it with different personnel than run the edificational program for teenagers already in the church.

It should do so for several reasons. Christian teenagers are not necessarily mature enough initially to be involved in a program to reach unsaved young people. When they are involved, the result can easily be the deterioration of their own spiritual condition. Also, the setting and methods of approach that are most attractive to unchurched teenagers are not always the ones most helpful to church young people. A colleague of mine recently left a church where he had been a longtime member. He did so because the youth program of the church was so geared to unsaved teenagers that his daughter found it impossible to receive help in her Christian growth.

The program for unchurched teens should be set up with the goal of integrating new converts into the edificational youth group as soon as the new believers are mature enough. The members of the edificational youth group could be given instruction in making the newcomers feel at home—something not always easy for teenagers.

The Beginning of a Successful Youth Program

Where does a successful youth program start? Certainly not with the teenagers who already attend a church. To start with them is merely a stopgap measure until a more thoughtful program can be put into operation. In order to start a really successful youth group the church needs to begin with children when they are very young. Using the vehicles of the Sunday school class and midweek club programs, the church should place the children in primary groups that will remain intact throughout the next several years and will serve as the basis for the teen program.

Recent studies in organizational behavior have pointed to the desirability of forming and utilizing the primary group, a group of people who learn to know each other, work with each other, and identify with each other in a special way. Unfortunately, both the public school and the Sunday school are more likely to break up rather than strengthen a primary group.

Let me illustrate. First grade was an exciting time in my daughter's life. She became fast friends with her classmates, and, under the direction of an excellent teacher, the class became a homogenous working unit. After first grade, summer passed, and my daughter looked forward once again to attending school with her former classmates. To her dismay, very few of them were members of her new class. The children in her first grade class had been divided among several classes, and new children were added to her class. She had to learn to know a great many other children. It took the majority of the school year for the teacher to weld the class into a homogenous working unit. What a shame! Schooling was hampered because the teacher had to overcome the inertia caused by the formation of a new primary group. In my daughter's case the pattern was repeated with each successive grade, even though empirical evidence exists to prove that forming entirely new classes every year is not the best tactic.

We have fallen prey to the same erroneous philosophy in the church. As a result, each year we promote children out of one grade and into another—where they must become acquainted with an entirely new group of children. A child will put up with the arrangement until about junior-high age. By that time he has developed some degree of independence. He says to himself, *I don't have to put up with this anymore. I'm just not going to come.* He then becomes a church dropout.

There is a viable solution to the problem. Suppose the church identified a group of first and second graders as the "ambassadors." Suppose the church kept that group intact over the years and always referred to it by the same name. Suppose members of the group attended club and Sunday school functions under that name, no one ever was promoted out of the group as the group progressed in age. That particular group of people would become fast friends and would learn to count on one another. Group solidarity would be so strong that when the youngsters in the group became teenagers, they would be bound to one another. If, in addition, the group retained the same set of sponsors as the years progressed, the sponsors would have no problem establishing relationships with teens, for those relationships already would be there.

In a personal conversation, Lyle Schaller told me that when this strategy is practiced in a local church, group members become so loyal to the group it often stays intact until the young people are married and are raising children.

What if a sponsor had personality difficulties with a child from the time that child was young? The answer is, of course, to have a large enough teaching team so that others within the team can relate to that particular child. A large teaching team also allows for teachers who need to move out of the community. With a large enough team, even though there will be turnovers, they will not happen all at once. More gradual transitions can be made, and although new teachers will move in, the students will never be without a teacher with whom they have enjoyed a long-term relationship. If the teachers—who are at the same time sponsors for club and social activities—are promoted as they remain with the same group of children, the teachers may become specialists in relationships with a specific group of people instead of becoming experts in relationships with a specific age group.

The idea I have proposed may sound revolutionary to a church that has practiced another format for a long time. Therefore, the pastor must be extremely careful about how he promotes it. He may introduce the new way of doing things in this manner: "I have just read about an exciting new concept. It sounds great and I think we should try it as an experiment. If it doesn't work, we can always go back to the old way and nothing will be lost. Why don't we start with the present junior class in Sunday school, and designate them a permanent group within the church. As they progress through junior high school and high school we can compare their retention rate with our past results and see how we do. Anyone game to try it?" Almost any worthwhile concept can be introduced into the church if it is offered on a trial basis first. If the new way of doing things works well, almost always it is retained.

The Pastor's Responsibility

The subject of youth ministries is a broad one requiring much study. My intention in this chapter has been to introduce the subject, to lay a few ideas before the reader, and to stimulate him into a more complete investigation of the subject. Although the pastor may in no way see himself as a youth pastor, he is nevertheless pastor to all people—and that includes the young people. If he is to minister successfully to that segment of his congregation, he is going to have to know them, to become acquainted with how they think, and to

learn what they consider important. As the chief undershepherd of
his people, he will be called upon to supply ideas concerning this
area.

When the pastor is asked to supply ideas, he can take one of three
approaches. He can claim ignorance, suggesting that ministry to
youth is beyond his area of expertise. Usually a congregation will not
be satisfied with such a reply. He can act the part of an expert and
offer all kinds of solutions out of his ignorance. People may try those
solutions for a while. He may be in luck because some of them
actually will work. In the long run, however, he will be found out. Or
he can study the area as carefully as possible and seek the help of
anyone who can supply him information about how teenagers think
and act so that he can help his congregation conduct a successful
youth program. Armed with such information, he can identify and
begin to equip other adults to become youth sponsors. When the
pastor reaches the end of his own knowledge he can turn to experts
outside his church to continue the training, so that continually his
youth sponsors will become more proficient in what they are doing.

In no case should the pastor overlook the area, hoping that the
problem will go away or that someone will step in and bail him out.
His people will look to him for overall guidance and leadership.
They will not expect him to supply all the answers to all problems.
However, they will expect him to know where to find the answers.
The youth ministry of a church is one that causes great concern
among the members. The wise aspirant to the pastorate will learn all
he can about conducting a successful youth ministry.

Questions for Discussion

1. Do you agree with the author that "only rarely should the
second staff member hired be a youth pastor"? Why or why not?

2. What qualities should a youth pastor possess? Give reasons for
your answer.

3. What strategy would you use to familiarize yourself with the
youth of your church?

4. How would you assist key adults in your church in a ministry
of establishing meaningful relationships with youth?

5. The author lists ten crucial needs that must be addressed by a
church that wants to meet the needs of youth. How might the youth
ministry of your church respond to those needs?

6. What strategies and attitudes are necessary for success in
working with young people?

7. Why is it important in working with youth that discipline not

be heavy-handed but be permissive and casual?

8. What role can music and sports play in a ministry to youth?

9. Considering the author's comments regarding evangelism and outreach, what would you do to reach unsaved youth?

10. Describe the author's concept of the primary group. What advantages and disadvantages do you see in basing the church's youth program on primary groups?

Helpful Resources

GENERAL

Benson, Warren S., and Roy B. Zuck, eds. *Youth Education in the Church.* Chicago: Moody Press, 1979.

Hoover, Kenneth H. *Learning and Teaching in Secondary School.* Boston: Allyn and Bacon, 1979.

Reed, C. Edwards and Bobbie Reed. *Creative Bible Learning for Youth: Grades 7-12.* Glendale, Calif.: Gospel Light, 1977.

Richards, Lawrence W. *Creative Bible Teaching.* Chicago: Moody, 1970.

Towns, Elmer. *Successful Youth Work.* Glendale, Calif.: Gospel Light, 1966.

COUNSELING

Blees, Robert A. *Counseling with Teen-agers.* Philadelphia: Fortress, 1965.

Frellick, Francis I. *Helping Youth in Conflict.* Englewood Cliffs, N.J., 1965.

Irwin, Paul B. *The Care and Counseling of Youth.* Philadelphia: Fortress, 1975.

RESEARCH STUDIES

Muuss, Rolf E. *Theories of Adolescence.* New York: Random House, 1975.

Strommen, Merton P. *Profiles of Church Youth.* St. Louis, Mo.: Concordia, 1963.

———. *Five Cries of Youth.* New York: Harper and Row, 1974.

Zuck, Roy B., and Gene A. Getz. *Christian Youth: An In-depth Study.* Chicago, Moody, 1968.

28

Improving the Music Ministry

Music is a supreme gift from God able to inspire, to bless, and to thrill man in a way no other art can. Since the beginning of time, music has been part of the soul of man. Even today, when a tribe is discovered that has had little or no contact with the outside world, almost inevitably that isolated group of people will have some kind of music.

Music has played a prominent part in every new religious revival or awakening. Some of the most productive days of the church musically, for instance, were the times of the Wesleys in Great Britain, the era of the Reformers in Europe, and the late-nineteenth-century revival period in North America. It is difficult to imagine how effective the message of John Wesley would have been without the music of his brother Charles. Undoubtedly the monumental hymns written by Charles Wesley reached the people and broke down their resistance so that the Holy Spirit could convict them through the words of the preacher.

If we examine more recent times, who knows how much the effectiveness of Moody would have been diminished if he had not been able to call on Mr. Sankey to stir the hearts of people through his dramatic rendering of the intensely moving gospel songs of his day. I am certain that the ministry of Billy Sunday would not have been as effective had it not been for the music of Homer Rodeheaver.

Several years ago I spoke to a person who had committed his life to Christ as a result of a Billy Graham campaign. He told me, "I could hardly wait for Graham to stop talking and give the invitation so that I could go forward. I made my decision as Mr. Shea was singing."

Choosing Christian Music

CONTROVERSIES ABOUND

Were we to survey what may be called the great local churches of the world, almost invariably we would find that they were churches with good music programs. If we assumed that good music programs contribute significantly to the building of great churches, and we knew that we wanted to be involved in the building of a great church, the first step we would take in reaching that goal would be to find out what constituted a good music program. At the end of our search we would probably conclude that the essence of a good music program is good music. And that is precisely where we would experience most of our problems.

It is difficult to uncover a congregational definition of what constitutes good music, because choice of music is a matter of taste. Most congregations have numerous individuals and groups whose tastes differ markedly from each other. Unfortunately, each of those individuals or groups is likely to feel that its particular taste reflects the most important, the most spiritual, and the most effective type of Christian music. Surely that kind of music should be used exclusively in the services of the church. In a church with which I am acquainted, a group of middle-aged, well educated people think that no hymn of value was written after 1700 A.D. In this same church is a group of younger people who think that all really worthwhile church music was written after 1960. Yet another group thinks that the only valuable songs are the gospel songs of the late nineteenth and early twentieth centuries. They are the "good old hymns" they grew up with.

It is a fact that whenever God creates something valuable and beautiful for man to enjoy, Satan tries to spoil it. In the church, if he can't figure out any other way, he will try to get Christians to quarrel about the beautiful things God has given them. Consider Satan's tactics regarding the gift of music. For centuries, music, which was given for the conversion of sinners and the edification of saints, has been a battlefield of the church. Musicologist friends have told me that throughout the church's history, each generation has found the musical tastes of the next generation unacceptable and, as a result, often has declared them unspiritual. The music of the Wesleys was considered outlandish and worldly by churchmen of their day. Some declared that such poor substitutes for church music never would survive. Likewise, many of the great works of Bach were based on contemporary secular melodies not considered fit for use in public worship. It is impossible to compare the gospel songs of the late nineteenth- and early twentieth-centuries with the musical theater of that day and not notice similarities in the music. Likewise, any analysis of some of the early works of John W. Peterson in the mid-twentieth Century will reveal a striking resemblance between his work and the tunes popular on the Broadway stage then. In each successive period, many members of the older generation viewed the new styles of music as frivolous and unworthy for use in the worship of the church.

Today the battle still rages. The styles of music once considered frivolous or revolutionary are represented now by songs in the most sedate hymnbooks. Yet many in the younger generation today are ready to drop the work of the previous twenty centuries on the grounds that the only relevant music is the music being written now. What can be concluded from the fluctuation in appreciation a piece of music undergoes? If one generation's revolutionary music is the hymn of the establishment in the next generation, how is the pastor to select music for his church that has genuine value?

First, the pastor should remember that it is difficult to argue that any particular musical form, regardless of its kind of harmony or its rhythm, is intrinsically sinful and inappropriate for church use. The music may be too loud for the pastor's tastes. It may include harmony that displeases him. In many ways it may be unacceptable to his ears. But those things in themselves do not give him the right to condemn the music when it may be the precise medium to communicate the gospel clearly to a young person today. Of course, any art form can be perverted and used to Satan's advantage. But that is not necessarily the case with the music the pastor dislikes.

Second, the pastor should remember that the fact that many religious songs do not survive the generation in which they were written does not mean that none of them will. Consider the hundreds of songs written by the Wesleys. Relatively few of them are known to us today. Fanny Crosby wrote more than eight thousand poems, many of which were set to song by composers. Proportionate to the number of songs she wrote, comparatively few have survived to the present. Perhaps in another generation even fewer will ever be heard. Yet many did survive. And how much we would miss not being able to sing "To God Be the Glory, Great Things He Hath Done," or "Blessed Assurance, Jesus Is Mine."

What is good Christian music? It is the combination of words that are biblically sound and music that is appropriate to the words and to their intended purpose. In authentically Christian songs the words and musical score work together to accomplish the one purpose God has for His church on earth: bringing glory to Himself. If the music does not glorify God, it is not good church music. God has directed the church to glorify him through two basic means: evangelism and edification. We must ask ourselves, "Does this song convert the lost or edify the saints?" If the answer is no on both counts, then the song should be discarded as unworthy of being called Christian music.

There is still one more important consideration. We must ask ourselves, "Is this song appropriate to the occasion, to the setting, and to the specific group of people who will hear it?" Major problems arise in church music when we define our own favorite style of music as being the only worthy style and then try to impose that style on others who do not share our views. For instance, it is probably extremely foolish to force teenagers to sit through a concert given by an operatic tenor who rolls his R's as he sings the old standbys in church music. It wouldn't hurt the teenagers at all, on the other hand, to hear a single selection sung in that manner from time to time in an attempt to broaden their musical tastes.

Similarly, it would be equal folly to insist that the elderly ladies of the Philathea class be required to attend a youth-oriented concert where amplifiers blare, drums pound, and nearly unintelligible lyrics are sung.

A problem arises when the young people and the elderly worship together in the same service. When that happens, we rack our brains, asking, "How do we satisfy both groups?" There are two possible solutions. We can conduct two separate services where the music in each is entirely different, or we can combine the traditional and the contemporary in a single service, but do so in a way that is not offensive to either group. In deference to other brothers and sisters in Christ, those who are younger should agree to listen without complaint to the good old songs. In deference to the young people, the person who sings those songs should have a contemporary-sounding voice, use a modern style of singing, and sing from arrangements that capitalize on contemporary musical techniques. That may be done without sacrificing the words or the music of a song. Those who are older should agree to accept contemporary songs as long as the melodies are not offensive to their ears. Again, in deference to the older people, young people can agree to toned-down versions of their music. The amplification can be turned low and the drums and bass minimized.

When concerts are designed specifically for young people, those in the older generation who may be upset by loud music ought to stay home, allowing the young people to pull out the stops and perform the music in a way that appeals to their generation. The young performers should agree to stay away from actions that are bizzare, or that will result in an adverse testimony, or that will not bring glory to God.

Still another factor to consider in judging if music is good for use in church is whether or not it is appropriate to the occasion in which it will be used. If the principal purpose in the morning service is worship of Almighty God, then slushy, sentimental, subjective songs are inappropriate. The pastor or music director should opt for the great objective songs that speak of God or of His marvelous attributes.

If the occasion is not a worship service, other kinds of songs may be perfectly appropriate. Care should be exercised to see that the songs are theologically correct, however. In addition, those selecting songs should be aware that there are a number of songs with excellent lyrics whose melodies are either difficult to sing or do not fit the words. How many of us have galloped merrily through such lovely, sentimental words as, "Years I spent in vanity and pride," completely missing the meaning of the words because the beat conveyed a frivolous mood. If the lyrics of the song convey a serious message but the tune does not, it might be a good idea to find an alternate tune or to avoid the song as much as possible. One of the greatest contributions of contemporary song writers has been their ability to take songs of yesteryear with good lyrics, and write sparkling, meaningful, contemporary tunes to fit the words.

Performing Christian Music

EXCELLENCE IN PERFORMANCE

The ability to minister effectively through music is a gift of the Holy Spirit and is akin to the gift of prophecy in its forth-telling aspect. If that is true, then many churches practice a double standard in their treatment of music. Most churches agree that the exposition of scriptural truth is so important it should be proclaimed from the pulpit by the most qualified person available. Churches do not let just anybody preach. They check out the character of the speaker and try hard to discern if he has the proper preaching skills. Maybe the church cannot always locate a Spurgeon to deliver the morning message, but at least it will use the best it can find.

But the situation changes when it comes to music. Although the proclamation of God's Word through music is of no less importance than the proclamation through preaching, in many churches music is treated as less important. Rather than selecting the best musician they have and, therefore, using a fewer number of people more frequently, many churches allow almost anyone to render a "special number," even if he is incompetent or untalented. An excuse frequently given is that the church wants to build up people and thus give them this opportunity to minister. More often than not, the congregation is the loser. What is even worse is that a person selected in this manner often gains an unrealistic picture of his own abilities. Every time he presents a musical selection, the experience becomes an ego trip for him instead of an opportunity for ministry. I have seen people who have deceived themselves so badly in this area that they have erroneously considered music their principal spiritual gift. As a result, they have refused to perform any other ministry in the church. The sad thing is that they turned down ministries for which they were qualified in order to take up a ministry that fed their egoes but was one for which they had absolutely no qualifications.

THE GLORY OF GOD AT THE FOREFRONT

There is another aspect to the story. Recently, the Christian community has been plagued by religious music superstars who travel from city to city filling huge auditoriums and exacting extremely high fees for their services. I have no problem with gifted Christian artists being paid respectable sums so that they can live comfortably. But when they become wealthy through performing Christian music and begin to attract a following to themselves that is almost cultic, then I am compelled to raise objections. That raises the question: Is it legitimate to use Christian music as an entertainment medium? History reveals that the question is not new. Not too long ago, when I was rereading a biography of John Newton, who ministered in the eighteenth century, I was comforted to find that he wrestled with the same problem. The following was reported of Mr. Newton and his colleagues:

> None of them approved turning Westminster Abbey into a concert hall for commemorative production of Handel's Oratorio, the suspension of worship so that thousands of careless dilletantes might admire and criticize the musical rendition and accompaniment of words which fell on unheeding ears.[1]

1. Grace Irwin, *Servant of Slaves* (Grand Rapids: Eerdmans, 1961), p. 356.

After wrestling with the problem of Christian music as an entertainment source, whether performed in a church building or a civic auditorium, Mr. Newton mounted the steps of his pulpit at Olney, England, and proclaimed:

> It is probable that those of my hearers who admire this Oratorio may think me harsh and singular in my opinion, that of our musical compositions this is the most improper for a public entertainment. But while it continues to be equally acceptable whether performed in a Church or at a theatre, and while the greater part of the performers and of the audience are the same at both places, I can rate it not higher than as one of the many fashionable amusements which mark this age of dissipation. Though the subject be serious and solemn in the highest sense, yea for that very reason, yet if the far greater part of the people who frequent the Oratorio are evidently unaffected by the Redeemer's love and uninfluenced by his commands, I am afraid it is no better than a profanation of the name of the Son of God afresh. You must judge for yourselves. If you think differently from me, you will act accordingly.[2]

Should the local church sponsor concerts in its building or in an auditorium where Christian music is used as an entertainment source? I think that it is important to declare once and for all that Christian music as entertainment definitely is inappropriate, either as a part of a worship service, or as a substitution for a worship service. How do we judge whether or not music rendered in a worship service is entertainment or ministry? The attitude of the musician often is a good indicator. Why is he performing? Is it to bring attention to himself or his message, or is it to bring glory to God? Does his music fit into the mood of the service and contribute to the ultimate purpose of the service, or is the music an end in itself? Does it draw attention to itself, or is it an integral part of the worship service?

Although I try not to use music as an entertainment source during a worship service, I am not opposed to the use of Christian music as entertainment in other settings. Indeed, as I view the other forms of entertainment available today, I would recommend Christian music as a far more acceptable form of entertainment for Christians than those others.

However, before I would sponsor such a concert, recommend it to my people, or allow my church to host it I would ask certain questions. Does the life of the performer honor the Lord? Are the lyrics of the songs sound theologically? Does the performer honor the Lord

2. Ibid., p. 358.

Jesus Christ in his speech and actions on stage? Are his remarks constructive? Are his financial demands reasonable? Is the performer supportive of the local church? If I receive satisfactory answers to those questions, and if the concerts do not compete with the program of my church, I may be willing to endorse them.

The Administration of a Church Music Program

A prevalent custom among many churches is to elect a music committee from the membership at large. That committee is given the responsibility of setting up and administering the music program of the church. I believe that such an arrangement is unfortunate. It tends to set up a power block within the church. That block may be oblivious to the philosophy of ministry held by the pastor, and it may promote music inappropriate to the mood and message the pastor wants to create. Or it may engage musicians who perform rather than minister, and thereby create sources of tension within the body. Besides, I believe that generally the church is "over-committeed" to the point that many people who could serve as effective workers spend their time instead on meetings of committees and boards.

If the church can afford to hire a competent minister of music, part-time or full-time, it should do so. However, such a person should be hired only with the express approval of the pastor, and he should carry on his work under the pastor's direct supervision. Of all staff members, he should be the one who works the closest with the pastor. The music the minister of music plans for the worship service should contribute rather than detract from what the pastor hopes to accomplish. Also, musical programs should be in keeping with the overall thrust of the program of the church as the pastor envisions it. I have observed churches where the music program grew so powerful it became the tail that wagged the dog. The minister of music built an empire and became untouchable, even by the pastor. In one case, the pastor was forced to resign because he could not get along with the minister of music.

If the church finds it necessary or desirable to form a music committee, the committee should be composed of those people who engage in musical ministries: the choir director, the instrumentalists, and perhaps a coordinator who arranges a schedule of those who will minister in music during worship services and other special events. The committee should be under the supervision of the music director, rather than having the committee supervise him. If there is no music director, and the church desires to appoint a standing committee of this type, I believe that the committee should be under the direct supervision of the pastor.

The person chosen to direct singing in the public meetings of the church should be approved by the pastor; he should agree to work in close partnership with him and under his supervision. In many churches, the same person will serve as minister of music and choir director and will lead the singing at public services.

As a guide for pastors and for potential music leaders, a denominational committee recently published an extremely helpful ethical guide for pastors and ministers of music. An adaptation of it is printed below.

Dos and Don'ts for the Music Director

1. Remember that the pastor is the shepherd of the flock. He is the number one man of the church organization—as ordained by God. It is your responsibility to support him in deed and in prayer.

2. Choose music that supports the pastor's messages. Consult with him three to four weeks in advance to find out what the main thrust of his messages will be.

3. Pay close attention to him when he is preaching. Remember, your example will be followed.

4. Invite him to speak to the choir on occasion. Also invite him to choir specials and other functions of the music groups.

5. Tell him when his messages have been especially challenging or of special blessing to you.

6. If you have disagreements with the pastor, discuss them openly with him. Keep lines of communication open.

7. It would be most helpful if you and the pastor had a weekly prayer time together.

Dos and Don'ts for the Pastors

1. Listen attentively when the anthem is sung. Sing with the congregation on the hymns.

2. Tell the director of music when the choir has particularly blessed you.

3. Allow the director to plan the music of the services with you.

4. Plan messages three to four weeks in advance, if possible. The director of music must rehearse his anthem three weeks in advance, so it is imperative that he know the basic thrust of your messages that far in advance.

5. If you disagree with the music director concerning the music program or philosophy, discuss those areas of disagreement with him or her.

6. Do not tell the director what anthems to sing or not to sing. If he is not competent enough to have a good sense of values in his choice of music, he should not be on the staff. Suggestions are welcome, but continued suggestions usually are not appreciated nor necessary.

7. Occasionally it is a good idea to take time during the service to tell the congregation how much you appreciate the work of the choir or choirs. A real booster from the pulpit is worth a dozen from the pew.

8. Take an interest in and be willing to help with the choir school. Remember that enthusiasm for the program will be contagious and will be a real encouragement to all who participate in the music ministry of the church.

The pastor can be a valuable recruiting agent for the church choirs, because he is in a position to know new families and those already there. With that knowledge, often he is more likely than anyone else in the church to know if there is musical talent in a particular church family. Also, the pastor is in a good position to see to it that members of the choir are not drafted out of the choir for service in other activities in the church. Because of their willingness to serve, choir members are often put in other important positions in the church. As a result, through overwork, they are lost to the choir. Positions of responsibility outside the choir should be filled by persons who lack the ability to sing.

A time set aside where the music staff can pray together will solve many problems. The old adage that the choir is the battlefield of the church is not true. In the unity of the Spirit the choir can be a true spiritual power in the church and a source of heartwarming and encouragement to the pastor. Prayer vigilance, sacrificial work and time, and the fulfillment of Philippians 2:1-13 is the price that must be paid if real harmony is to exist.[3]

How Do I Begin?

At this point many relatively inexperienced pastors will have the urge to say, "The music program of my church is a disaster. How do I begin to improve it?" The answer clearly is to work slowly, carefully, and sensitively. No area of change in the church offers more emotional overtones than this one. The pastor should work in close partnership with the minister of music or music director to accomplish the following:

1. Use the best you have as much as you can, and help those persons obtain training so that they can become even better.

2. Set up a variety of singing groups, and encourage the ones who

3. *Directing Music in the Church* (Arlington Heights, Ill., n.d.). Pamphlet produced by the Music Commission, Board of Christian Education, Baptist General Conference.

are more modestly talented to express their ministry of music through one of those groups.

3. As soon as possible, begin an academy of music where young people of the church can obtain musical training of varying kinds.

4. If some of the less talented insist on solo performance, steer them toward singing in the more poorly-attended church events.

5. As more gifted people join the congregation, ease them into a performance role on a regular basis.

6. Work toward establishing a system of choirs and ensembles that are graded by age and ability. The abilities of the respective groups will then determine how often and upon what occasion a particular group will sing in public.

7. If there is an elected music committee, work slowly and carefully toward passage of a constitutional amendment that eliminates it, along with other undesirable committees, and places supervision of the music program under one qualified person who will work closely with the pastor.

It may be that the pastor and the church will have to live under circumstances that are less than ideal for a long while until the music program evolves gradually into what it should be. If a pastor is patient and loving, he will be able to shape and mold the program gradually without injuring the feelings of his people. He will thus preserve the unity of the body and eventually will realize nearly what he wants. If he moves precipituosly in this area, however, he is almost certain to bring calamity upon himself and shorten his pastorate.

God has given the church the wonderful gift of music. In most local assemblies, however, the music falls far short of reaching its potential effectiveness. Sometimes major overhauls need to be made. Yet because music is an area of intense emotional involvement, the pastor who wishes to bring about major change must be sensitive, discreet, and patient. Too often the music program of the church becomes a battlefield and the pastor a casualty. Even if major change is needed in the music program of the church, if it is put into effect in a hasty manner, it will be costly for the church and for the pastor. The name of the game for the pastor is most definitely this: Slow down. In so doing, you may be able to stay in that church long enough to bring about changes in the music program even greater than the ones you had initially hoped for.

Questions for Discussion

1. What is the importance and the role of music in the ministry of the church?

2. In view of the many possible styles of music, how does a pastor decide what music to use in the services of the church? Why does the matter of musical taste present a problem for many churches?

3. Review your experience in church ministry. Has music ever become an issue of conflict among church members? Why was this so? What could have been done to remedy the situation?

4. Explain what the author means when he says that good Christian music is "the combination of words that are biblically sound and music that is appropriate to those words and to their intended purpose."

5. How does a pastor or minister of music determine whether a song is appropriate to a particular situation? Give several examples.

6. What dangers does a church face when there is a difference of opinion over music? How would you resolve such a disagreement between two groups in the church that have strong and opposing opinions in regard to musical style?

7. What standards would you impose upon those who wish to exercise their musical gift by presenting a special number? What responsibility does the person in charge of the worship service have to see to it that those who participate musically are sufficiently talented and adequately trained to make a positive contribution to the service?

8. Do you agree with the author's position regarding the use of Christian music as entertainment? Why or why not?

9. What suggestions would you make to a new minister of music as he endeavors to administer a church music program? What might he do to encourage the pastor? What would you hope the pastor would do to support and encourage the minister of music?

10. You are the new pastor of a relatively small church. What initial steps would you take in beginning a music program? What precautions should you take?

Helpful Resources

Delamont, Victor L. *The Ministry of Music.* Chicago: Moody, 1980.

Ellsworth, Donald P. *Christian Music in Contemporary Witness: Historical Antecedents and Contemporary Practices.* Grand Rapids: Baker, 1980.

Hustad, Donald P. *Jubilate! Church Music in the Evangelical Tradition.* Carol Stream, Ill.: Hope Publishing, 1981.

Osbeck, Kenneth W. *Singing with Understanding: Including 101 Favorite Hymn Backgrounds.* Grand Rapids: Kregel, 1979.

Sims, W. Hines. *Song Leading.* Nashville: Convention, 1969.

29

Encouraging Fellowship

Recently a husband and wife were expelled from a church near where I live because they had allegedly engaged in malicious gossip and slander against the pastor. After that rather dramatic action had been taken, the board of the church took further steps. The couple were sent a letter instructing them they no longer were welcome in the public services of the church unless they came to the pastor and deacons and repented of their sins. Second, all members of the church received a letter telling them that they were to have nothing to do with the couple. If they saw them on the street or in a grocery store, members of the church were to turn their backs and were not even to talk with the offending couple. A stern warning was attached to the note indicating that if any member or friend of the church was observed having any interaction with the couple, he or she would be disciplined by the pastor and the board.

There were at least two glaring mistakes made in the instance just cited. First, the words of our Lord in Matthew 18, the chapter that the church supposedly based its discipline upon, were greatly misunderstood by the congregation. The end product to which all scriptural passages on discipline lead is the restoration of the offending member. In Matthew 18:17, Jesus says that if an offending Christian "refuses to listen even to the church," the very worst that should be done him is for him to be to the church "as a Gentile and a tax-gatherer." The leaders of the disciplining church no doubt took the verse to mean that when a Christian will not respond positively to the steps the church has available to it for discipline, the offending person should be treated as an unbeliever. In searching further, undoubtedly they came upon 2 Corinthians 6:14, which indicates that a believer is not to have fellowship with an unbeliever. Because their concept of fellowship was hazy and nebulous, the church leaders confused fellowship with contact. They concluded that the Scripture taught that an erring brother was to be shunned utterly.

Logic alone should convince us that we are not to avoid all contact with unbelievers. If this were the case, how would we have the opportunity to win them to Christ? Likewise, if the desired biblical end product of church discipline is restoration, how can believers help to restore a person they avoid having any contact with? I am convinced that such quandaries occur mainly because many churches today are in a situation similar to that of the disciplining church described above. What constituted genuine Christian fellowship never had been defined. As a result, probably little genuine fellowship was taking place in the church. The closest the church could come to understanding fellowship was to equate it with contact.

Bringing About Fellowship

ENCOURAGE OPPORTUNITIES FOR CONTACT

Contact is a necessary precondition for fellowship. A church wishing to foster fellowship needs to begin its quest by promoting and encouraging opportunities where contact can take place. The effectiveness of those contacts in promoting fellowship may depend in large part on the type of atmosphere the church creates. Is the church conducive to fellowship? What do visitors notice when they attend the first time? In his course on church growth entitled "Let the Church Grow," Dr. Winfield Arn includes a worksheet for students of church growth to use in analyzing the atmosphere into which visitors come when they attend the student's church. Arn asks the student if he has ever wondered what someone thinks who walks into his church for the first time. Arn suggests that the student picture himself as a first-time visitor and answer the following questions:

1. What are your first impressions of the church based on the building, parking lot, and immediate environment?
2. What happens when you first enter the building? What are your impressions based on the people you first meet—ushers, members, greeters.

3. Do you feel comfortable or uncomfortable as you first come in?

4. Are you ignored by most of the people?

5. Do you feel you are wanted, appreciated, and cared for? Or are the words "Good Morning" the first and last ones you hear?

6. What are your impressions of the worship service? Of the Sunday school?

7. Is there spiritual excitement or dynamic in the service and among the people? Or is the service contrived and little more than a series of rituals?

8. When the service is over, what happens?

9. Is it easy to feel as though you could become a part of the church, or does it appear that it would take considerable effort to do so?

10. After you have left, do you have any desire to or reason for coming back?

11. During the following week, was there any interest shown in you by the pastor or by laymen? Were you thanked for coming to the church? Did you feel as though the "Thank you!" was personal and meaningful?[1]

After a person makes the initial visit to the church, the people of the congregation need to foster continued contact with him in order to promote genuine fellowship. That is the philosophy underlying much of what is contained in this book, and the reader will find in many chapters a number of concrete ideas for encouraging contacts between people.

DEFINE FELLOWSHIP

Even after a consistent program is initiated whereby people come in contact with one another, genuine fellowship is still one step away. In order to encourage fellowship, it should first be defined properly. The biblical term is *koinonia.* Arndt and Gingrich define *koinonia* as "association, communion, fellowship, close relationship (hence a favorite expression for the marital relationship as the most intimate between human beings . . .)."[2] If fellowship, by definition, is an intense, close relationship, and if relationships such as that did not

---

1. Winfield Arn, "Let the Church Grow: A Self-contained Course in Church Growth," Handout, Week #7 (Pasadena: Christian Communication, n.d.).
2. William F. Arndt and F. Wilbur Gingrich, *A Greek-English Lexicon of the New Testament and Other Early Christian Literature* (Chicago: U. of Chicago, 1957), p. 439.

exist in the church that disciplined the erring couple, it is easy to see how the church mistook fellowship for the only experience they really knew about, contact, and disciplined their members by withholding contact. In doing so the church demonstrated its ignorance of a key scriptural principle. As a result, the discipline it imposed used exactly the opposite methods and obtained exactly the opposite results than those referred to in the Scriptures.

DEVELOP CLOSE FRIENDSHIPS

The essence of genuine Christian fellowship is an intimate relationship between fellow believers. An intimate relationship does not develop automatically. It must be nourished. Nor does it develop quickly. It is predicated upon believers' spending time together on a regular basis. Whereas frequent contact can and should occur between many believers, one person cannot have genuine fellowship with a great many other believers. Fellowship is an intensive kind of relationship. It takes a great deal of time. It is giving, and it is demanding. Human beings are so made that they are incapable of supporting many relationships of high intensity for long periods of time. Therefore, although all Christians in the church should have fellowship within the church, each believer must select only a very few people within the body (besides his own family members) with whom he will agree to form a close relationship. (Need I add here that with the exception of one's spouse, those close relationships should be developed with persons of one's own gender?)

SEEK THE LORD WHOLLY

Besides planning for opportunities for contacts leading to fellowship to take place, the pastor needs to encourage people to seek the Lord in ways that will make fellowship with other Christians possible. As I examine the famous Communion passage of 1 Corinthians 11, I see that at least one of the implications of verses 28 and 29 of the chapter is that broken fellowship with God results in broken fellowship among men. In the case where a person is being disciplined by the church, it is superfluous to state that members of the church should not have fellowship with the person being disciplined. If members of the church remain true to their relationship with God, and if the discipline of the church is just, scriptural principles indicate that genuine fellowship between the offender and other members of the body is not even possible. If the church is correct in its discipline and a member continues to have fellowship with the disciplined person, there may be legitimate question as to the spiritual condition of the person who continues to fellowship with the offender. Again, I am talking about fellowship, not mere contact.

The Essence of a Fellowship Relationship

THE "ANOTHERS"

What is the essence of the fellowship relationship between two believers? The Bible defines the relationship as a system of "anothers." A partial list follows.

Christians engaged in a fellowship relationship should
1. Confess their sins to one another (James 5:16)
2. Forgive one another (2 Cor. 2:6-8)
3. Bear one another's burdens (Gal. 6:2)
4. Restore one another when sin has been committed (Gal. 6:1)
5. Refrain from judging one another (Rom. 14:13)
6. Love one another (1 John 4:7)
7. Comfort one another (1 Thess. 4:18)
8. Encourage one another (1 Thess. 5:11)
9. Edify one another (1 Thess. 5:11)
10. Discipline one another (Matt. 18:15-20)
11. Pursue peace with one another (Rom. 14:19)
12. Teach one another (Col. 3:16)
13. Admonish one another (Col. 3:16)
14. Pray for one another (James 5:16)
15. Stimulate one another to love and good deeds (Heb. 10:24)
16. Be harmonious, sympathetic, brotherly, kindhearted, and humble in spirit, and bless one another (1 Pet. 3:8-9)
17. Eat with one another (Acts 2:46)
18. Share material possessions with one another (Acts 2:45)
19. Touch one another (Gal. 2:9)
20. Give money to one another (Phil. 4:14-15)
21. Suffer with one another (1 Cor. 12:26)
22. Rejoice with one another (1 Cor. 12:26)
23. Meet one another's needs (Rom. 12:13)
24. Talk and sing with one another (Eph. 5:19)
25. Refresh one another (Rom. 15:32)
26. Serve and work with one another (Phil. 1:27)
27. Speak truth to one another (Eph. 4:15)
28. Provide examples for one another (Phil. 3:17)
29. Sympathize with one another (1 Pet. 3:8)

30. Greet one another (Phil. 4:21)
31. Submit to one another (Eph. 5:21)

ASSIST ONE ANOTHER IN SPIRITUAL GROWTH

One of my former students, John Morrison, summed up the goal of fellowship in a paper he handed in to me. In it he said that as Christians fellowship individually with one another, they should have in mind that they are to assist one another "to be God's man and God's woman, motivated, matured and equipped in the Spirit, doing God's work in His way at the place of His appointment, together with His people." Morrison went on to add that the purpose of group fellowship is to produce a person who is "a functioning member of an authentic community in Christ; participating in a sharing, caring, praying fellowship, helping each other to know and do the will of God and to identify gifts and ministries."

SHARE WITH ONE ANOTHER

A colleague of mine, J. Grant Howard, has defined fellowship as the "giving, receiving, and/or sharing of material or immaterial things on a personal basis between believers based on the common bond of Christ."[3] He describes the importance of fellowship in these terms: "Fellowship is God's provision for building up believers in Christian maturity by meeting their individual needs through personal interaction with other members of the Body of Christ."[4]

USE CHURCH ACTIVITIES AS A BASE FOR FELLOWSHIP

If both those men are correct in their conclusions regarding fellowship, then genuine Christian fellowship transcends the cups of coffee shared in the fellowship hall of the church building between Sunday school and the worship service or even the interaction of people at the monthly potluck dinner. Those occasions are merely contact points the church uses to foster fellowship.

DEVELOP RELATIONSHIPS OF MUTUAL DISCIPLESHIP

As we look over the biblical requirements of fellowship and the definitions Morrison and Howard have offered, fellowship begins to

---

3. Adapted from J. Grant Howard, "Fellowship," class handout (Portland: Western Conservative Baptist Seminary, n.d.), p. 2.
4. Ibid., p. 13.

look much like a process of mutual discipleship. And indeed it should, because discipleship and fellowship are one and the same. In order for fellowship to work in the life of the believer, Dr. Howard suggests that the believer make it his objective to develop:

an awareness of a wide variety of his own needs
an understanding of how fellowship can help meet those needs
the ability to tell others of the needs he has that might be met through fellowship
the ability to find out the needs of other believers that might be met through fellowship

THINK OF FELLOWSHIP AS BEING HOLISTIC

Dr. Howard cites physical, mental, social, and spiritual needs that can be met through fellowship, thus looking at the process in a holistic rather than one-dimensional way.

BE REALISTIC IN ESTABLISHING FELLOWSHIP GOALS

Thus far we have identified what fellowship is, have looked at some of its components, and have considered what the person involved in it may expect to gain from it. In addition, we have insisted that it is the task of the pastor to make sure that the church presents as many opportunities for contact between persons as is possible, so that they will get to know one another and be able to identify those individuals with whom they would like to have the type of intensive interaction we have labeled genuine Christian fellowship. We have insisted, as well, that because genuine fellowship is a demanding and intense relationship between persons, it will be impossible for everyone in the church to be involved in a fellowship relationship, though the church should try to involve every person. In determining how many of those relationships he is capable of developing, a person should consider the time he has available and the type of person he is. He may be able to handle only one, or at most two or three, fellowship relationships, if he is committed to quality in those relationships.

The Pastor's Role

INSTRUCTING

Up to this point, however, I have not addressed the question "How does the pastor help bring all of this about in his congregation?" One answer arises out of the fact that intense interaction between people seldom will happen automatically just because they come in contact with one another. People must be instructed in the meaning of true Christian fellowship and must know that it is an indispensable part of Christian growth. Furthermore, they should be taught that genuine Christian fellowship is not a novelty but is the norm for the successful Christian life. They should be shown how to use the social occasions of the church to identify people with whom they can form such a relationship, and they should be told what they should be doing and accomplishing in the relationship once they begin. Again, Dr. Howard offers practical suggestions for helping people to know one another in a more personal way:

1. Feature pictures of people in the church directory, on bulletin boards, in newsletters, in new-member rosters, on bulletin boards at camps and retreats, and in camp and retreat newsletters.

2. Feature biographical sketches in the bulletin, in the church newsletter, in fact sheets on new members, and on church bulletin boards.

3. Schedule time in church for personal testimonies and interviews. Give people the opportunity to let others know basic information about themselves.

4. At baptisms include time for the persons being baptized to tell something about themselves.

5. At Sunday school socials ask some of the members to tell something about themselves, or schedule interviews to be held before the entire group that will introduce one or several of the class members. Use mixers to get the entire group acquainted with one another.

6. Schedule informal home gatherings where church members can get to know one another.

7. Use questions that help people know each other better.

8. Encourage people to let others in the church know what God is doing in their lives. A period during the worship service can be saved for spontaneous and planned reports.

9. When a person in the group is moving, ask him to tell the group how God led him to make that decision.

10. When a new family moves to the community and begins to attend the church, have them give a brief report to the church on how God led them to that city, that job, that school, that area of town, that church.

11. Set aside time during church for people to make brief reports on significant events that have taken place in their lives. Reports can

be made on graduations, promotions, elections, recognitions, retirements, engagements, marriages, the birth of babies, accidents, surgeries, tragedies, and miracles.

12. Encourage people to let others in the body know their needs.

13. Encourage people to act specifically to meet the needs of others in the body.

14. Explore ways small groups can be used to increase fellowship.[6]

MODELING

All the teaching, planning, and encouraging in the world can degenerate into manipulation of people unless the pastor himself believes in what he is proposing. If he is aloof from his congregation and does not practice some of the biblical "one anothers" listed earlier in this chapter, his people will soon discover that he wants them to follow him in what he says but not in what he does. The best teacher is the one who demonstrates what he desires in the lives of others by practicing it in his own life, so that people can see his theories in action. It is best, therefore, for the pastor to establish fellowship relationships himself. Perhaps he will want to do so with a few hand-picked leaders in the church with whom he feels he can enjoy a life of mutual accountability. If he is part of a multiple staff, he may want to establish a close relationship with a fellow staff member, remembering as he does so not to confine such relationships to staff members, lest he not have a chance to teach the principles of fellowship by example to those not on the church staff. In some cases, he may choose to relate to another pastor or to a denominational executive in this manner, especially if the church has many troubles and it appears that no one in it is mature enough to enter into a fellowship relationship with him. He should learn to relate to his wife in this way, realizing that she is designed to be his best friend and can be his greatest teacher if he does not let his male pride get in the way.

Through the years the Lord has given me the privilege of discipling a succession of young men whose hearts were eager for the ministry. I have had the joy of seeing many of them go on to successful pastoral ministries of their own. Recently I had a chance to spend an afternoon with one of those young men. He told me, "More and more I find myself unconsciously choosing to do things the way you did them when we were together." I do not know if that is good for him or for his church. I do know that it is gratifying to me that

5. Ibid., p. 29.
6. Adapted from J. Grant Howard, pp. 5-7.

someone saw enough that was attractive in my ministry to want to adopt a portion of that model.

Biblical Fellowship Is the Goal

What I have proposed in this chapter is a radical departure from the practice in many churches. Too frequently fellowship consists of staring at the back of the bald head of the man in front of you during a Sunday school class, or of talking casually with someone while you both are standing in the social hall during the break between Sunday school and church or of engaging in small talk with the person sitting across the table from you at a potluck. I am suggesting instead that churches return to the biblical idea of *koinonia*, which involves establishing intense, meaningful, and lasting relationships among Christians.

I believe sincerely that if churches did this, Christians would have no problem "bearing one another's burdens" because they would already know about one another's needs, and would care enough for each other to take constructive action to see that those needs were met. Also, I believe that most Christians would have no need for psychiatrists or psychologists. Their counseling needs would be met by fellow members of the body who were so sensitive to those needs that problems never had a chance to grow huge and overwhelming. Were we to return to the New Testament norm in fellowship, our churches today—like their first-century counterparts—would be irresistible.

Questions for Discussion

1. What constitutes genuine Christian fellowship? What is your definition? What characteristics of Christian fellowship would you like to encourage in your church?

2. Describe the conditions necessary for encouraging Christian fellowship in the local church.

3. Examine the list of responses that Christians engaged in a fellowship relationship should have toward one another. On a scale of one to ten, how does your church rate on each of the thirty-one possible responses?

4. What is your reaction to this statement: "Fellowship begins to look much like a process of mutual discipleship"; it involves establishing intense, meaningful, and lasting relationships among Christians"? What part does the mutual accountability of discipleship play in Christian fellowship?

5. What steps would you take in your church to help bring about true Christian fellowship? List practical suggestions.

6. How would you, as pastor, attempt to model the concepts of Christian fellowship in your own life?

Helpful Resources

Banks, Robert. *Paul's Idea of Community: The Early House Churches in Their Historical Setting.* Grand Rapids: Eerdmans, 1980.

Halverson, Richard C. *A Living Fellowship: A Dynamic Witness.* Grand Rapids: Zondervan, 1977.

Hinkle, Joseph, and Melva Cook. *How to Minister to Families in Your Church.* Nashville: Broadman, 1978.

Leonard, Joe, Jr., ed. *Church Family Gatherings.* Valley Forge, Pa.: Judson, 1978.

Martin, Ralph P. *The Family and the Fellowship: New Testament Images of the Church.* Grand Rapids: Eerdmans, 1980.

Schaller, Lyle E. *Assimilating New Members.* Nashville: Abingdon, 1978.

30

Motivating for Stewardship

The word translated "steward" in the New Testament denotes a person who manages a house. Inherent in the definition is the idea that the person called upon to manage a house is responsible for managing the assets of that house as well. Frequent Bible passages refer to the fact that Christians are expected to manage well that which God has given to us. That includes our time, our talents, and our finances. In addition, the Bible makes clear that we are not to use those resources only as means of meeting our own or of satisfying our desires, but should use them as tools to carry on the work of the kingdom of God.

As a Christian, I actually own nothing. It all belongs to God. But that does not mean that God expects me to live as an ascetic, always on the brink of poverty, unless the condition is unavoidable. Continuous living in poverty by the Christian negates the truth that God meets our needs and deals with us out of His abundance. The fact that God owns everything that is temporarily entrusted to me means that I am not going to allow those possessions to dominate my life or become overly important to me. If my automobile is smashed through no fault of mine, God knows about it. It is not my car to begin with, but His. Perhaps He knows it was time to retire the car, or perhaps if it had not been wrecked in that way, something far worse might have happened—members of my family might even have been injured severely.

It is not enough to say, "Everything I have belongs to God," unless the statement is translated into action. If the statement is true I need to ask, How I am using my resources to help carry on God's ministry in this world? and, How I am responding to people in need? After all, the Savior said that when I minister to one of the least of those, I am ministering to Him.

Stewardship is a way of life. A good means of beginning that way of life is for the Christian to observe the principle of the tithe. I know that there are many reasons for arguing that the tithe is an Old Testament concept and not for those who live in the New Testament age. Nevertheless tithing has a place in the Christian life. Though tithing is not compulsory for the Christian it is a good place to start the adventure of stewardship with the Lord. By tithing, I mean the giving of not only a tenth of one's income but a tenth of one's time as well to God for His use in the work of His kingdom. It has been said that if every Christian only tithed, the budgets of every church and every mission organization in the world would be oversubscribed. If, in addition, mature Christians practiced proportionate giving, the church would be looking for constructive ways to spend its finances.

Stewardship Must Be Caught and Taught

Discuss It Openly

The concept of Christian stewardship must be caught as well as taught. In order to do both, pastors must stop being apologetic about it. In some churches the concept of money is such an offensive word that giving is done clandestinely. Such churches refuse even to pass the offering plate, opting instead for a box in the narthex into which people place their gifts in secret. That seems to negate entirely the Old Testament and New Testament concepts of giving, for, in both, giving was a part of public worship. If the church is apologetic about asking people to give of their time and money to God, it does them a great disservice and may even facilitate their missing out on an opportunity that offers tremendous adventure and blessing to the Christian.

Be an Example

In addition to speaking without embarrassment concerning giving, the pastor should teach about giving through personal example. If the pastor leads the way, the people are likely to follow him. It has been my custom for many years to tithe or to do better when I could. Some years ago, the church I was pastoring needed to build but was overwhelmed by the large indebtedness remaining from its last building project. That indebtedness was in the form of bonds, and the church struggled for years to rid itself of it. If the church was to move off dead center, I knew that it would have to hurdle the obstacle of the bonds. At last an idea occurred to me. My wife and I had been saving to purchase a new television set. Although we would enjoy the set, it was not a necessity. One Sunday as I closed my sermon, I issued a challenge to my congregation. If only half of the families of the church made a one-time sacrificial gift, over and above their regular giving, of the price of one television set, the church could wipe out its bonded indebtedness completely. As a testimony that I was not asking my congregation to do something I myself would not do, I wrote out a check on the spot for the cost of one large-screen television set and placed it in the offering plate. Within five months, the church had retired its bonds and was able to make plans toward building. During the period, I did not place an excessive emphasis on giving but merely handled passages on stewardship calmly as I preached my way through a book of the Bible.

ENCOURAGE TITHING OF RESOURCES

Through the years, as God has directed me to preach on stewardship passages, I have challenged my people to undertake two adventures. The first is tithing. So sure am I that God will take care of His people with the nine-tenths left after a person tithes that I have dared my people to try tithing initially for only three months. I have told them that if they found at the end of the period that God had failed to help them get along well on the other nine-tenths, they should cease the experiment. What has been the result? In many cases, the people to whom I have issued the challenge have become life-long proportionate givers, often exceeding the tithe.

ENCOURAGE SUPPORT FOR MISSIONS

The second challenge I have given my people is in the area of faith promises for missions. Although I have seen many large churches, I have never seen a truly great church that was not a great missions church. The affluent branch of the church of Jesus Christ, which is located primarily in North America, has been made affluent so that it can provide the necessary finances to reach people in the rest of the world. There is no such thing as a mature Christian who is merely a North-American Christian. In the very act of becoming mature, the Christian begins to see the world as Christ sees it, and he cannot help but become a world Christian. As a result, I issue the challenge to my people: "How would God like to see you exercise your responsibilities as a world Christian? Does he want to see you go to a foreign field? I pray that many in this congregation will do so. But many of you are not called to go. What does God want of you? You are called to give. You may plead, 'I am giving all that I can already.' If that is your condition, I would like to issue a challenge. Will you trust God to provide a certain amount over and above your regular giving each month for missions? How much can you trust him for—a dollar a week? Surely He can provide that amount. Why don't you pray about it and make a commitment between yourself and God?" Then I explain that if every Christian in our church and in our sister churches gave only a dollar a week toward missions, the budget of our denominational world missions program would double in one year.

As a result of that appeal, Christians I know have taken part-time jobs, on a temporary basis as God provided them, just so they could give extravagantly to missions. In churches where I have issued the two-pronged challenge, the missions giving has even tripled in a single year—and local expenses not only have been met, but there has been money to spare. When people get a vision of how much fun giving can be, it becomes contagious.

ENCOURAGE TITHING OF TIME

So far, I have spoken only of the giving of money. Were a pastor able to excite people as to the possibilities of tithing their time, the church would have to invent creative ministries to utilize the man-hours offered by its people. In that case, no doubt evangelism might have a good chance.

Making Use of the Money

Once the foundation for increased giving has been laid, what should the church do with that money? Out of the increase in tithe income, it would be good for the church to do something about its responsibility to evangelize its neighborhood. It should hire a staff member whose principal effort is given over to expanding the church's work in evangelism and to the equipping of others for evangelistic effort. If the church takes such a step, it will soon need to make more decisions as to how to spend money, for as more people find Christ as Savior and grow in Him, the more money will be given to the church.

Concerning faith-promise giving to missions, the church should concentrate its resources on the support of a few key persons instead of giving a little to a great many people. One of the problems missionaries on furlough face is that they have to make the rounds of so many supporting churches, they exhaust themselves. How much better if they needed to report only to one or two churches! Giving to denominational missionaries is, I believe, a priority item, because it generally is the area in which the church will realize the greatest amount of control as to what goes on. Next, support should be given to missionaries who are members of the church and who made their commitment to missions in the church, even though the mission they serve may not be connected with the denomination.

While I am listing potential recipients of missions giving, let me make a plea for seminaries and Bible colleges. Without these schools the church would have no way of training pastors or missionaries. Because the schools depend on the gifts of God's people for their very existence, they should receive a significant sum from the missions budget of the local church. It is a shame that many churches that are generous to foreign missions causes often give a trifling amount to Bible colleges and seminaries. A good idea for churches to consider is to designate a faculty or staff member of a Bible college or seminary as its missionary-trainer and agree to supply all or a large part of that person's yearly salary, just as the church would for any other missionary.

One further matter needs consideration. One of the areas of heartbreak that I have seen as a seminary professor is that often a church will endorse young men and women as they enter Bible college or seminary to train for the ministry, will agree to pray for those persons, but will fail to support them financially. Through many years I have seen the young people struggle to support families, minister in churches, and receive proper biblical training. How much easier the effort would be if, when a church commissioned a young man for study for the ministry, it also declared him a staff member and paid him a living wage from the missions budget during his years of study. Surely the young pastor—whose memory is fresh with the struggles he went through—will be able to present an acceptable argument to his church, so that those following him into the ministry will not have to endure what he did.

Rather than the bane many people picture stewardship training to be, it can be a great blessing. As people begin to watch what God can do through their concentrated giving, that giving can become a great thrill and privilege for them, instead of an unpleasant responsibility. But first, to get going, they need to respond favorably to that responsibility.

This section would not be complete without reference to deferred giving or giving through one's will. Large amounts of money that ordinarily would be swallowed up in taxes can be given to God's work if a person knows how. The pastor can make deferred giving easier by inviting Christian men to his church who can show the people how, through arrangements made in their wills, they can go on serving the Lord on earth even though they themselves are already in the Lord's presence.

Questions for Discussion

1. What do you believe is the Bible's teaching with regard to stewardship?

2. List specific ways you are using your resources to help carry on God's ministry in the world.

3. What procedures would you use in the collection of the church's tithes and offerings? Explain why you would approach the collection in that manner.

4. Suggest ways in which you, as a pastor, might, by personal example, lead the way in the area of personal stewardship.

5. What approach would you suggest for the promotion of stewardship in the local church? How often do you feel the pastor should preach specifically on that topic?

6. If tithing extends beyond the area of money, what is your response to the concept of tithing one's time and talents?

7. Design a stewardship emphasis program for the church you attend. Describe the program and how you will carry it out during the course of the next year.

Helpful Resources

Burnett, Joseph D. *Capital Funds Campaign Manual for Churches.* Valley Forge, Pa.: Judson, 1980.

Ford, George L. *All the Money You Need: A Guidebook for Christian Financial Planning.* Waco, Tex.: Word, 1976.

Bartlett, L., and Margaret Hess. *How to Have a Giving Church.* Nashville: Abingdon, 1974.

Johnson, Douglas W. *The Tithe: Challenge or Legalism.* Nashville: Abingdon, 1984.

White, John. *The Golden Cow: Materialism in the 20th Century Church.* Downers Grove, Ill.: InterVarsity, 1979.

31

Leading a Building Program

Among veteran pastors is an ancient adage that the best way to shorten a pastorate is for the pastor to lead a congregation in a building program. But though building programs pose problems, they may be exceedingly beneficial to the life of a church. Besides resulting in new facilities that help the church carry out its mission to the community in a more adequate manner, building programs may provide other fringe benefits. Lyle Schaller, among others, points out that a building program may unite a congregation around a common goal. As a result, old-timers, whom Schaller called "pioneers," and relative newcomers, the "homesteaders," often are enlisted to work side-by-side on the common project. Deep friendships develop, barriers are broken down, and a church may sense a oneness it has not known in many years.

Conversely, there are dangers in a building program. Sometimes the building in which a church meets is perfectly adequate. However, it may not be as prestigious in appearance as the pastor, some other church leader, or a segment of the congregation desires. Pressures are placed upon a congregation to build, the resulting structure becomes a monument to a man or to a group of people, and the congregation is saddled with indebtedness that cripples its ministry for decades.

Reasons for Building

SMALL AUDITORIUM, LARGE CONGREGATION

There are a number of instances in which it is probably wise for a congregation to build. One of those is when the church has stretched the limits of its building so far that there is no more give, and yet the size of the congregation continues to increase. The problem of having too many people is almost always one of the nicest problems a church can face. However, even in that situation, if the church has functional, attractive facilities, and if it can meet the needs of its people by conducting multiple services and multiple Sunday schools, it should do so, rather than building a new auditorium merely to enable its people to meet in one room at the same time for worship.

The building of mammoth, costly auditoriums for occupancy for only one hour on Sunday morning and one hour on Sunday evening is poor stewardship, and it is a luxury few churches can afford. Often the argument is given, "We want to be able to see everybody and talk to all our friends, and we can't do that if we have two services." That is foolishness. There is a point at which a congregation grows so large that even if the auditorium were large enough to accommodate everyone, it would be impossible physically for each person to greet everyone else.

Another reason for waiting to build new church facilities is that studies have shown that when a church adds a second service, the total number of worshipers at the two services combined almost always exceeds the number attending a single service. That is especially true if one of those services is held concurrently with Sunday school.

Caution is in order at this point, however. There are instances where there is such a groundswell of enthusiasm and support for a building program on the part of the people that despite the pastor's desire that the money go to missions, he is best advised to get out of the way and let the people do what they want or to resign so that new leadership can guide the people more appropriately. In many instances, the excitement of a new building will stimulate people to give as they have never done before. In the long run, rather than taking money away from missions, the building program may result in an increase in the missions budget because the people will have discovered through the building program the enjoyment and satisfaction of meeting personal stewardship responsibilities.

DETERIORATED BUILDING

Another occasion when it may be deemed advisable to build is when the present facility has deteriorated to the point where it is no longer efficient and cost-worthy. Some churches may operate under the delusion that it is cheaper to patch and repair an obsolete, poorly planned, and poorly constructed building rather than to replace it. The truth may be that although the amount of money needed to construct a new building is sizeable, compared to the amount needed for upkeep and repair of the old structure, a new building may actually be more economical.

When the church is deciding whether to renovate or to build anew, it should consider whether the old building is an architectural treasure or an historical landmark. If it is, it may be wise for the church to restore the building or to sell it to a group that will preserve and appreciate it. On the other hand, if it is just an ugly old building, several other questions need to be asked. Is it in an extremely desirable location? Is it accessible to the membership? Is there plenty of parking? Then, perhaps, consideration should be made to razing at least the uneconomical portions of the old building and rebuilding on the same site. Does the site offer potential commercial value? If so, perhaps an equally accessible site is available at another location. It may be beneficial to the congregation to sell the old site and relocate. Sometimes a business wants the site so much it will pay the church enough for the land alone to enable the church to relocate, erect a new facility, and find itself free of debt.

If the church decides to sell and relocate, care should be exercised to determine that there is widespread backing for such action. At no time should it be construed as merely the idea of the pastor to which a simple majority of people agrees reluctantly. Even an ugly building may be considered sacred by people who attach sentimental value to it because the spiritual highlights of their lives took place in it.

An Ugly Building, a Small Parking Lot, and a Poor Location

Still other reasons to build are when a building is admittedly so unattractive it repels newcomers, when there is no possibility of expanding the parking lot to meet the needs of a larger congregation, or when the building is extremely poorly located. A church I once pastored met in a building located on an obscure side street that was almost impossible to find. The building was hemmed in by homes on all sides, and the owners refused to sell. Moreover, the parking lot was extremely limited, and the auditorium was unattractive. Even with all of these things against it, there still were people who attached sentimental value to that building. In such cases the watchword for the pastor is, "Go slowly." It is better to let the impetus for moving come from a groundswell of interest within the congregation.

Finally, a congregation should consider the possibility of moving when the neighborhood changes so rapidly and drastically in character that businesses replace all of the former housing or the new neighbors are so different from the membership that integration of the two groups is impractical.

Here I am not talking about the Christian ideal. Theoretically, we should be able to make everyone feel at home in our midst regardless of his culture, race, or ethnic background. The sad fact is, however, that no matter how hard we try and how sincere we may be, some people are not going to be comfortable worshiping with us. Conversely, we would like to think that all of our own people are mature enough to feel comfortable with a person no matter how different he may be. However, that is not a realistic expectation. Thus, when newcomers with complexions and customs different from ours start to attend our church in any great numbers, often we can expect to see an even greater exodus of the old guard.

At that point, a church has to decide whether it chooses to minister primarily to its changing neighborhood or to its present membership. If it decides the latter, a move almost always is the answer. If the church decides to stay and minister to the neighborhood, it must face the fact that the new neighbors may not be able or eager to support the church to a level sufficient to keep it in business. Therefore, when the choice is made to minister primarily to the new neighbors, the church should make concise plans as to how the ministry will be funded. It may decide to begin a daughter church in a location more convenient to its present membership. The pastor will have to decide whether to stay or to go with the daughter church.

The "Musts" of a Successful Building Program

If, for any of the reasons above or for other reasons a church decides to enter into a building program, the pastor is advised to consider the following matters.

Encourage the congregation to hire the very best church architect possible. In the chapter in which I discussed the morning worship service, I alluded to that need. Care should be taken to see that the architect is in sympathy with the church's philosophy of ministry so that he can design a building not primarily to exhibit his artistic tastes but to serve well the program needs of the congregation. Insist on a list of his former projects and encourage the building committee to make on-site inspections of those buildings. Interview the pastors who have worked before with him to see how well he works with pastors and churches and to see how functional his buildings have proved to be.

When the architect is engaged, be sure he supplies complete preliminary sketches and plans so that the congregation knows what the building will look like and is able to approve or disapprove what the architect proposes. Before signing a contract with him, make certain that he agrees in writing to conform to all local codes, to secure all necessary building permits, and to include within his fee a reasonable number of on-site inspections even above those called for in the code. Be sure that the architect has a clear understanding as to the extent and kind of volunteer labor that will be employed in erecting the building. A statement to that effect should be in writing.

The biggest mistake any church can make in a building program is not to hire a competent, experienced architect. A church that fails to do so may save money initially, but it will lose much more money eventually because of structural defects, poor design, unattractiveness of the resulting building, and wasted space. I place special emphasis at this point, having gone through and viewing the disappointing result for two disastrous building programs that were undertaken without engaging an architect.

Before recommending the name of a particular architect to the leadership of the church, the wise pastor does some careful investigating to find out if he is the kind of person with whom the pastor can work amicably. Several questions need to be answered. Is he a pleasant person? Despite the fact that the architect is extremely competent, he may be a bear to work with. The pastor already has enough problems and will experience even more as the building program progresses. He does not need to add hostile interchanges with the architect to the list.

Is the architect cost conscious and yet capable of designing an attractive building of superior quality? Do his buildings have aesthetic appeal? Does he consider himself a part of the team, and will he work in harmony with a congregation in which almost every member considers himself a part of the management? Is the architect a person who "makes ripples," or does he smooth over troubled waters? Does his personality exude confidence to the extent that people find him credible and trust his judgment? A competent, credible, understanding architect will be the best friend a church has in such a crucial period in its history. Undoubtedly, an architect who designs well, works harmoniously with people, and charges a fair price is worth every penny the church pays him.

BE SURE THAT PRESSURE TO BUILD COMES FROM THE CONGREGATION ITSELF

Make sure that the pressure to erect a new building arises from the grassroots as a people movement, rather than being pressed upon the people by the pastor or church board. That does not preclude sound teaching from the Scripture by the pastor as he leads the people into new areas of thinking. It means that rather than attempting to use the pastoral office or pulpit to whip the people into submission, the pastor should lead them into creative visions of what can be, and then show them the way their visions can become realities.

ESTABLISH A SOUND FINANCIAL BASE BEFORE BUILDING

Lead the congregation in establishing a sound financial base before encouraging them to attempt a building program. Often it is easier to get people to give to special projects of a concrete nature, such as a new building, than it is to encourage them to engage in a pattern of regular, responsible stewardship in behalf of the ongoing ministry of the church. Unless the pattern of faithful, regular giving is established, the church will face crushing financial pressures in spite of the fact its income will probably increase dramatically to meet building costs. Even though a building program will attract people to give who have never given faithfully before, the general expenses must be met. People should be taught to give in order for the program of the church to continue. It is ludicrous to erect a building in which nothing can take place because all of the money is designated for the building.

ENGAGE A GENERAL CONTRACTOR ON A PROFESSIONAL BASIS

The pastor should lead the church in the selection of a general contractor who will provide overall supervision for the project. Even if the contractor is a member of the church, the matter should be approached in a businesslike manner, and he should be required to submit a firm bid that includes a guaranteed price for the building as specified in the plans. If changes are made as the building progresses, the congregation should be prepared to pay extra for those changes. The contractor probably will require drafts of money from the church as various supplies are purchased and as subcontracts are completed. Be sure that the church receives proper receipts for those purchases and proper releases from the subcontractors, so that when the building is finished there are no outstanding liens against it because the general contractor juggled the funds. If volunteer help is anticipated, have the contractor include such provisions in his bid. If volunteer help fails to materialize as expected, provisions should be made for the general contractor, with the permission of the church, to hire additional people as needed.

In many cases, churches have made the sad mistake of serving as their own general contractor. Many times, when that happens, the pastor or some other church leader ends up becoming responsible for letting subcontracts, employing laborers, purchasing materials, and seeing that those materials are on site as needed. Often the person (or persons) responsible for those tasks does not have the necessary contacts to assure the securing of reputable subcontractors and the procuring of quality materials at the lowest possible prices. Inevitably when the pastor or other staff member carries on those functions, other important parts of the ministry suffer to the real loss of the church. When a willing volunteer takes on the job, no matter how skilled he is, there is no way to keep him accountable. If a capable volunteer serves as general contractor, insist that he be paid, even though he may turn back most of his paycheck to the church. Most important, no matter what his relationship to the church is, be sure that he is competent before engaging him.

EVALUATE THE LOCATION THOROUGHLY

In erecting any building, a prime consideration is location. Cheap land may prove costly in the long run because it is difficult for visitors to locate or because the subsoil is unsuitable for building upon and may require costly preparation. When it purchases land, the church should be fully aware of zoning regulations in the area to be sure that when others move into the neighborhood the buildings they erect will not depreciate the value of the church's property.

Before the church even purchases a piece of land, an architect should be consulted as to whether or not the land is adaptable to the purpose of erecting a building such as the church envisions it should have to meet its needs. Potential full-site development also should be considered at that time. Will the site be large and adaptable enough to continue to meet the expanding needs of the congregation in the years to come? Even though it may cost the church a considerable sum, it is wise to have the architect lay out an entire plan of development so that the congregation can look it over and decide if it is really what they want. If it is, this is the time to exercise the option

to buy, which had been written up several months before. Generally
a congregation remains in one location for a long time. Before purchasing the site, it is wise to find out if the people really like it and if
they are happy with the possibilities it offers. A well-located site and
the attractive development of the site may be some of the best advertising a church enjoys.

PLAN TO BUILD AS LARGE AS POSSIBLE

Plan to build as large a building as you are able to. Enclose everything that is built and make it look finished and attractive from the
outside even though a portion of the inside remains unfinished. Use
permanent-appearing walls to segregate unfinished portions from
the finished portions, so that there is no easy access into these areas.
However, before taking that route, the church should have a firm
plan in mind, including a timetable and sound financial arrangements, for the completion of the building. Again, let me emphasize,
do not allow unfinished areas of the building to be an eyesore either
from the interior or the exterior of the building. If the unfinished
portions are unsightly, they will be a source of discouragement to the
congregation and annoyance to the neighbors.

CHOOSE A REPRESENTATIVE BUILDING COMMITTEE

Assist the church in choosing a large building committee representative of as many different segments of the congregation as possible.
The building committee should select from its membership a small
executive committee and empower it to make the everyday tactical
decisions necessary to keeping a building program going. It is wise
for the building committee to work in close cooperation with the
architect and to do most of its work prior to the actual construction.
It is extremely disheartening for a congregation to see a building
program stretch on and on because actual building must cease while
decisions are made. If most of the decisions are made ahead of time,
then building can progress fairly rapidly and people will not experience exhaustion and disappointment.

REALISTICALLY ASSESS THE AMOUNT OF THE VOLUNTEER LABOR YOU WILL
RECEIVE

In many extensive building projects, the joy that should be experienced from using a new building has been supplanted long before by
the sheer exhaustion of a prolonged building program. Especially is
this true when a church plans to use volunteer labor but assesses the

size of its volunteer labor force too optimistically. In such an instance, not only do those who volunteer their time experience "burn out," but their efforts as workers are lost from other ministries of the church, sometimes for a long time, sometimes forever.

Don't Expect More from the New Building Than It Can Give

Churches must not take for granted that new buildings, in themselves, will automatically attract newcomers. The congregation must be made up of people who are attractive to visitors when they come. In order to attract visitors to a church, an aggressive, evangelistic outreach to the ministry area almost always is needed. Finally, when newcomers do become a part of a congregation, it is realistic to expect that they will not always share the same sense of urgency and dedication toward paying off the mortgage as the people who incurred the debt.

Questions for Discussion

1. List the advantages and disadvantages of a building program.
2. What factors should be considered in determining whether to remodel or to relocate a church?
3. How would you justify a church's decision to move out of a changing neighborhood?
4. What is the value of hiring a competent church architect? What considerations should be made during this process?
5. What role does the general contractor play in the building of a church? What measures should be taken to insure that the person chosen for the position is well-qualified?
6. What role does a building committee play in the process of erecting a new building?
7. Why is it important that the decision to erect a new church building be one that arises as a grassroots movement within the church?
8. How would you propose that a church finance a building project? Would you feel comfortable with borrowing a large sum of money, or do you feel compelled to go "strictly by faith"? Defend your position.
9. Why is the location of the church building important? What considerations should be made in regard to the choice of a site?
10. What are the general principles by which you will be guided to insure unity and harmony during the course of your building program?

Helpful Resources

Anderson, T. Lee. *Church Property/Building Guidebook.* Nashville: Convention, 1980.

Bowman, Ray, ed. *Church Building Sourcebook.* Kansas City, Mo.: Beacon Hill, 1982.

Crowder, Rowland T. *Designing Attractive and Functional Southern Baptist Church Buildings.* Nashville: Convention, 1976.

Jernigan, Jules Donald, A.I.A. *Quest for the Rainbow: Basic Guidelines for Building Churches.* Grand Rapids: Baker, 1975.

McDonough, Reginald M. *Leading Your Church in Long-Range Planning.* Nashville: Broadman, 1979.

Mitchell, J. Patrick, J. Patrick Mitchell and Associates, architectural firm, Kirkland, Washington. J. Patrick Mitchell is a dedicated Christian and a superb church architect.

Smith, Roland A. *Before You Build Your Church.* Nashville: Broadman, 1979.

Conclusion

Of all the words in the English language perhaps none is as ambiguous today in interpretation and application as the word *pastor*. It is not that no one knows what a pastor is and does. It is that if we were to question everyone, we would likely find a profusion of differing role pictures and expectations.

Who then is a pastor? Is he uniquely gifted, an extraordinary person with limitless abilities? When he takes off his shirt does he have a large *S* on his chest? We can safely say that he is not such a person. He is, most often, an ordinary person who has realized the direct call of God to a unique ministry in behalf of the church.

Rarely is his a specialized ministry. Almost always the person God calls to the pastorate is required to occupy a position akin to the general practitioner in medicine. Rather than concentrating most of his time on one area of ministry and becoming extremely proficient in it, the average pastor is required to do a great many things fairly well.

Remember that You Need to Grow

Many of the things the pastor needs to be able to do have been covered in some depth in preceding chapters. At first glance the novice pastor or prospective pastor may wonder, *How in the world can I ever do all of those things?* The problem faced by professors in seminaries and Bible colleges is similar to that faced by the pastor.

The professors ask, "When will we ever find time to teach prospective pastors how to do all the things they will be called upon to do in the pastorate when we must also teach them Greek and Hebrew exegesis, theology, and church history?" There is an answer, of course. I shall never forget the words of wisdom given to my classmates and to me by a kindly professor as we were about to graduate from seminary. He said, "Remember, commencement means just that. It is a beginning, not an end. Here in seminary we have been able to give to you a few basic tools that, if used carefully and wisely, will enable you to tackle most of the tasks you will find in the pastorate. Remember, too, skill increases the more you use a tool. Do the best you can from the beginning, but do not consider yourself a finished product. You've only just begun!"

Be Modest

In recent years we seem to have overlooked modesty. Because of the increasing demands and costs of a theological education, the graduate may think of himself as being far superior in ideas and training to his parishioners. He is not necessarily correct. Even three or four years of intensive theological education do not begin to compare with the training gained by a saint who lives a lifetime in close harmony with the Lord and in service to His church. Therefore, the recent graduate needs to be more modest in his expectations of himself. He should admit that he is a novice in many areas and needs the wise counsel and support of the more mature saints.

Churches, as well, need to have more modest expectations of recent seminary or Bible college graduates, realizing that the man they call to be their pastor will need their understanding and patience and the latitude to spread his wings and learn in a supportive and nonjudgmental atmosphere. Pastor and people alike need to remember that just as submission to authority is a two-way street in the church, discipling, as well, needs to go on in two directions: pastor to people in areas in which he is specially equipped; people to pastor in areas where members of the congregation have gained expertise through years of priceless experience. Even when the pastor becomes a seasoned veteran, he should always maintain the attitude of an amateur willing to learn from the marvelously gifted saints with whom God surrounds him.

Do Your Best

As a general practitioner, he cannot possibly hope to excel in every task that falls to him. Inevitably, he will perform some tasks better than others. However, whatever he does should not be done casually or haphazardly. Whatever is worth doing at all is worthy of his best effort.

Love Your People and Preach the Word

Rather than attempting to continually impress his people with his giftedness, the pastor needs to remember two basic factors that will place him in high esteem with his people. Those two factors are the real bases of this book.

1. The pastor should love his people extravagantly. If they are convinced from his tangible performance that he genuinely loves them, it is often easy for them to forgive many of his inadequacies. This kind of love evidences itself in the degree of sensitivity he demonstrates for them. It surfaces in his ability to spend time with them and really enjoy them as people, not as potential means for accomplishing his programs. It comes to light more dramatically as his people find that their pastor is quick to assume the blame for something that goes askew, humbly admits that he does not have all the answers, seeks and honors their opinions, hurts with them when they hurt, and is quick to ask their forgiveness if he feels he has failed them. Such a pastor does not go to a church exuding the impression that he knows it all. He is, instead, the type of person who states very frankly, "God has given us a great many people, all of whom are gifted. This accumulated giftedness, working in harmony together, is what makes up the genius of the church. I am much humbled that God has called me to a position of leadership among such a superior group of people. I'll share what I know. You share what you know. Together we'll discover what God wants us to be and do. Together with God we'll work to bring about what he wants to accomplish through us as a body."

2. The pastor should preach the Word faithfully. That involves honest handling of the Word of God. Too many people use the Word of God as a whip to bring other people into line. Or they use the pulpit to grind axes. The pastor must learn that the Bible supports theology, not necessarily methodology. The Bible has a great many things to say to people about their deportment and about how to mature spiritually. However, the Bible does not necessarily enjoin a congregation to give blind adherence to the pastor's pet governance structure, projects, or methods. The pastor must be faithful to engage in exegesis so that his people will know what God is actually saying; he should try not to fall into the trap of using isogesis in an attempt to get his own way.

Keep Things in Perspective

Many years ago the sage to whom this book is dedicated said to me, "Although I often get tired *in* the Lord's service, I never get tired *of* the Lord's service." The pastorate is a sterling example of the type of service to the Lord best representing that statement. The kind of ministry one experiences in the pastorate is widely varied. It is also so intensely interesting that it is hard to imagine anyone's ever getting bored with the position. Probably there is no more interesting or challenging position on earth.

However, a pastor must constantly guard against becoming so tired he is exhausted as he engages in the many activities that make up his ministry. Because the pastor often finds himself in an integral, vital relationship with so many people, he may come to view himself as being indispensable to them. In addition, he may become overwhelmed with the success philosophy of our age and think of his value as lying in how well he does in his job.

Thus he may see himself as being adequate only as he reaches what he feels to be success in the ministry.

Each of the factors I have just mentioned, combined with the unreasonable role expectations placed upon a pastor from a variety of sources, may tempt the pastor into putting an inordinate amount of time and effort into his ministry. As a result, he may neglect to take care of the needs of his own family properly, and he may drive himself to the point where he burns out. Unfortunately, it is precisely at that point that he will find out how dispensable he really is.

There are pastors who, far from being overly ambitious, are not ambitious enough. They spend too much time with their families, perform too few services for their churches, and are too solicitous of themselves. Both the extremes of ambition and indifference must be avoided if a person is to succeed in the pastorate.

Be a Faithful Undershepherd

Who then is a pastor? He is an undershepherd of God called to feed, lead, and serve a group of people making up a local church. His duties are many and varied, and, in order to do his job properly, he must be a jack of all trades. Seldom does God call extraordinary men to carry on the ministry. More often, He calls ordinary men who are extraordinary in their faithfulness and obedience to Him. It is no accident, therefore, that the Bible does not spell out many of the specifics of the job to which God calls the pastor. Instead, it lists character traits. Could it be that it is more important to God what a pastor is than what he is able to do?

Whatever the answer to that question, it should not be an excuse for slothfulness on the part of the pastor. Though he may not be supremely gifted, the New Testament parable of the talents teaches that God expects each of us to use the talents we have and invest and develop them to their maximum possible effectiveness so that the kingdom of God may be advanced.

Throughout my life I have borne a number of titles. Each has carried a certain degree of honor with it. However, if I were forced to choose my favorite among them, I would select the title *pastor* as the most honorable and rewarding of all. The pastor's job is rewarding, honorable, varied, tough, and interesting. If you are certain that God has called you to it, consider yourself greatly honored. In return, perform your duties in the most worthy way possible, for there is no more important task on earth.

Index of Subjects

Index of Persons

Index of Scripture